A One-

FAITH

Reclaiming the
central teaching of Jesus,
reengaging the miraculous

JOHN NOĒ, Ph.D.

Advance Praise for
A Once Mighty Faith

You likely have not heard of John Noē, but once you read this book you will not forget him. John has captured the central teaching of Jesus like no others have. It is provocative, eye-opening, inspiring, and deeply biblical. Even if you don't agree with him at times, you will find yourself motivated to engage yourself and your church in the great world-altering Kingdom of God! Yes, we can change the world in Jesus' name!

Dave Rodriguez, Senior Pastor, Grace Church, Noblesville, IN

This book is weighty but well-worth exploring. As an evangelistic communicator, I must continue probing the riches of the biblical message of the Kingdom of God through Jesus Christ. I have been stretched significantly from reading this book, and am still processing it!

John has provided a very unique perspective. I have never heard anyone present these concepts this way, nor connect various items as he does—such as our eschatological views impacting our actions in the Kingdom of God, and many more. This could be John's *magnum opus*.

If John's conclusions are correct and if they were then lived out by Christians, it could literally have significant consequences of epic proportions for the Christian church.

Mark Slaughter, Evangelist, InterVarsity Christian Fellowship

A Once Mighty Faith is a convicting and motivating treatise on the contemporary fullness of Christ's Kingdom. I began proofing the manuscript as an editor and finished a repentant and reanimated shepherd of my community and society. Dr. John Noē has thrown down the gauntlet. Devoted advocates of kingdom-partialism, if they dare an honest reading of this book, have a formidable task escaping Dr. Noē's admonitions and clarity about Christ's Kingdom and Kingdom life.

Dan DePriest, publisher and editorial consultant Scribe Book Company

John Noē poses a challenge to Christians worldwide with his new book, *A Once Mighty Faith,* asking us to examine ourselves to see if we really are following Jesus Christ's teachings and example in our Christian walk. Noē specifically accuses American churches of allowing humanist, non-Christians to take over our nation's government and culture. He claims the western church has abandoned the field and conceded the battle for the hearts and minds of our people by giving up the teaching and practice of Jesus' 1st century message, the Kingdom of God.

Noē poses a provocative solution: Only by reclaiming the kingdom message and acting on that message, can the American church and churches everywhere reclaim our rightful place as the spiritual head and conscience of our many nations and restore that "once mighty faith" to its rightful place. The only question he leaves unanswered is: Do we have the will to do it?

Dan L. Hassett, Assistant Pastor, The City Church, St. Robert, MO. Retired Army Master Sergeant, former newspaper editor, and former journalism instructor for the Defense Information School.

Why on earth do Christians roll over and play "dead" when Jesus brought us the fulfillment of His Kingdom? John Noe lays out the case. *A Once Mighty Faith* is an imperative and challenging read, no matter where you stand in doctrine.

A. Dru Kristenev, Political columnist, author of *Scripture Led Politics...Mutual Exclusivity Be Damned* and the Baron Series of political suspense novels.

It's a terrific read and superbly referenced! I love the subject matter! In short, Noe deals with a topic that merits high priority and his central thesis is so true! It's well worth your attention.

John S. Evans, Ph.D.

A Once Mighty Faith

By John Noē, Ph.D.

Published by:

East2West Press
Publishing arm of the Prophecy Reformation Institute

5236 East 72nd Street
Indianapolis, IN 46250 USA
(317)-842-3411

Cover: Tom Haulter

ISBN: 978-0-9834303-7-7

Library of Congress Control Number: 2016905328

Kingdom. Eschatology. Bible. Jesus. Old Testament Revelation. New Testament Revelation.

Dedication

To Dave Rodriguez, my pastor
and Senior Pastor, Grace Church, Noblesville, IN,
for proposing the title of this book
and for your support, encouragement, and other inputs
over the past twenty years or so as we've increasingly discussed
the kingdom of God.
May the Lord help us and others take this grounded, everlasting,
and ever-increasing kingdom to
Hamilton County, America, and the world.

CONTACT US:

Prophecy Reformation Institute
5236 East 72nd Street
Indianapolis, IN 46250
www.prophecyrefi.org
jnoe@prophecyrefi.org
Ph. # 317-842-3411

Contents

Introduction

The Next Great Awakening?

The kingdom of God is the most important and all-encompassing concept of Scripture. So much is contained within it! The kingdom was also *the* reason Jesus was killed. Today, sad to say, the kingdom is one of the most misunderstood, misconstrued, marginalized, confused, abstracted, abused, contested, and ignored realities of Christianity. And we are reaping mighty consequences.

Today most churches rarely mention the kingdom, let alone preach, teach, obey, and practice its established reality and intrinsic elements. For centuries, even theologians have been divided over its time of arrival and nature. All this confusion and confounding differences have led to a number of conflicting beliefs, behaviors, and avoidance practices that have no foundation in the Bible. And yet, they have long held sway over countless Christians.

The fact now is, the concept of the kingdom of God—the central teaching of Jesus Christ—has become corrupted and doctrinally written out of the faith by the traditions of men. Consequently, our "once mighty faith" termed Christianity is now characterized as having been "tamed." Ironically, this taming was not the result of outside opposing forces. Rather, it's the product of sabotage, neglect, and ignorance from within. Again, we inhabitants of planet Earth are paying a huge and dreadful price for this deficiency.

As you will discover, what we are witnessing in America, North America, and Western Europe, especially, is the decline of a civilization. Sadly, most churches therein are oblivious to this decline and/or unable, unwilling, and incapable of doing anything about it. Why so? Because we have lost the central teaching of Jesus and our kingdom orientation.

Therefore, I believe the greatest need of the Church universal today is to reclaim the central teaching of Jesus, the kingdom of God—i.e., its revelation, established reality, and available power, miraculous gifts, and ministry effectiveness. This book is dedicated and directed toward this goal, purpose, and end.

But this reclamation will not be easy. It will require another great awakening and a regal reengagement with our original faith, along with a modern-day paradigm shift. A short sermon series or a few Sunday school classes on this topic will not suffice. A solid educational foundation over time must be provided in which Christ's kingdom is systematically defined, delineated, de-traditionalized, defended, and grounded. Also, many non- and unscriptural notions added over the centuries must be confronted and dismissed. These traditions of men have devalued, diluted, diminished, and depreciated the kingdom's relevance and effectiveness down to almost nothingness. Please recall, Jesus criticized the leaders of his day for misleading the people. And so, for many Christians today, the word "kingdom" is not even in their vocabulary. Without a doubt, "something is rotten in the state of our religion."[1]

For these reasons and more, the structure of this book will be threefold. In Part I, we'll look at current problems of decline, politics, and the opportunity for restoration. All of this should awaken us to the severity and urgency of our situation. As you will see, a war is being waged for the hearts and minds of our youth and for our nation's very soul. It's a winner-take-all conflict we Christians are currently losing. Moreover, the Church seems powerless and largely uninterested in witnessing the glorious gospel of Christ and his kingdom. In Part II, we shall see that the kingdom is caught up in eschatological midair. Therefore, it must be grounded time- and nature-wise as we lay down a solid foundation for our regal reengagement and reclamation. In the two

---

[1] Brian D. McLaren, *a Generous Orthodoxy* (Grand Rapids, MI.: Zondervan, 2004), 268.

Appendices, we'll preview the dispelling of two major and technical obstructions that fly in the face of kingdom reclamation. By structuring the book in this manner, my intention is not to shame or saddle readers with a guilt trip. I write this way to increase our awareness of the seriousness of the problems we face so that my readers will better appreciate the only solution I believe is viable.

Yes, we will present a message of great hope and redemption. Nevertheless, it may be necessary to offend some if we are going to awaken us Christians out of complacency and apathy. Please be assured however, Christianity is the biggest, greatest, and best-grounded religious faith in the world. But when it is compromised, confused, and corrupted by our own people, everyone loses.

So my prayer is, you will earnestly and honestly consider and reflect on the serious and weighty content presented herein. As you will increasingly see, God did not put us on this earth merely to be saved and then sit, soak, and sour in our pews while awaiting heaven. He put us here to be saved, sent out, and to serve with his Son as He is today. He put us here to turn the world upside down, again. Most certainly, Jesus calls us upward, onward, and outward with Him. And He has given us the keys to unlock, seek, enter, and advance his fully established kingdom on this earth, during our lives, here and now. Indeed, I am calling for a full-fledged reclamation and reengagement with "New Testament Christianity." Make no mistake, this restoration will require another great awakening. But dare we settle for anything less?

As we proceed through the pages ahead to reclaim the central teaching of Jesus—i.e., kingdom of God, Jesus as King, and Christianity's historic and founding character—we must exercise great care for getting the doctrine of the kingdom *totally* right. That means, it must be based solely upon the rock of God's immutable Word and not upon the traditions of men. This level of scriptural authority and confidence must be firmly and thoroughly reclaimed. This is why I originally tested the main contents of chapters 6, 7, 8, 9, and 10 in four theological papers presented at four different meetings of the Evangelical Theological Society—the professional society of conservative, evangelical scholars. During and after these presentations I was greatly encouraged by how well each was received even though their contents contested many kingdom beliefs held by most of the scholars in attendance.

For those of you who are not scholars but are intelligent readers, seasoned laymen, and aspiring pastors, I promise that you will discover herein that our Christian faith is much more powerful, effective, and demanding than most Christians—at least here in America, North America, and in Western Europe—have been led to believe.

To my knowledge, no book ever written has approached the kingdom of God in this manner or with this degree of comprehensiveness. Why not? Because most Christian authors and leaders have been hamstrung by unscriptural traditions of men that have made the Word of God of little or no effect (Mark 7:13; Matt. 15:6). Nowhere is this tendency more evident than with the degradation, marginalization, and dismissal of the central teaching of Jesus.

Unabashedly, therefore, I maintain that the 1st-century exposition of the Christian faith is the only true version and model for how Christianity should be preached, practiced, and perceived. Sadly, most of our present-day versions pale in comparison. As a result, Gene Edwards insightfully interjects: "Jesus Christ never intended for the Christian life to be lived on so low a level as it is today."[2]

Also, one of the significant byproducts of this next awakening, reclamation, and reengagement with our "once-for-all-delivered faith" (Jude 3), if it occurs with significant breadth, may be the return of 1st-century caliber (quality and quantity) signs, wonders, miracles, and ministry effectiveness as God again confirms this authentic message with his authenticating *dunamis* powers and supernatural gifts. We will explore this exciting possibility in Chapter 7 and following.

Additionally, as I have done in my other books, I quote, reference, and interact with numerous Christian scholars, authors, and popular spokespeople—some in a supportive manner; others who oppose me. Either way, I stand on their shoulders as I employ their words to present their positions rather than rephrasing them into my own words. I do this for three reasons: 1) to honor them and their scholarship; 2) to enable you to see, first-hand, the spectrum of different beliefs and opinions on this subject; and 3) for you to realize that I am not the first to bring up some of these rather "unsettling" and "radical" ideas about Christ's kingdom.

---

[2] Gene Edwards, *Revolutionary Bible Study* (Jacksonville, FL.: SeedSowers Publishing, 2009), 110.

Some, however, may feel that I have overused this scholarly support. If you feel that way, please skip over these sections. But because of the significance of this topic and the ground-breaking approach I am dealing with in this book, if I'm going to err it's going to be on the side of overusing not under-using. That is why I've brought in these other scholars to help me bear this burden.

My Delimiting Caveat

We live in a world that's a mess. There isn't much, if any, disagreement about that. Brokenness abounds and broken places plague every nation. The suffering this universal reality produces results from our rebellion against and separation from God due to our sin and consequential alienation from Christ's kingdom.

These broken places have names, such as hunger, poverty, hatred, racism, enslavement, war, genocide, terrorism, murder, crime, corruption, lying, cheating, selfishness, envy, arrogance, immorality, wickedness, sickness, illness, disease, addictions, isolation, loneliness, anxiety, depression, confusion, suicide, lack of education, false religions, spiritual oppression, systematic injustices, pollution, tragic loss, strained relationships, death, and more. Sooner or later, these broken places affect every inhabitant of this planet. Hence, the perpetual questions raised are: Where is God in all of this brokenness? Why does He allow these bad things to happen? Why doesn't He step in and fix it all?

To my knowledge, no book ever written has approached the kingdom of God in this manner or with this degree of comprehensiveness.

Since I have dealt with these questions systematically, extensively, and theologically in another book, I will not duplicate that material herein except to summarize that the nature of this world was planned before and created at its beginning.[3] And since I am not an expert on these worldwide, multifold and complex problems (each could justify an entire book), my primary focus herein will be on America, especially our government and Church. Some may criticize this delimitation. But it is necessary. After all, I live in America and am more familiar with the situation here than elsewhere. Nevertheless, the kingdom cuts across every nation and culture. Thus, I believe readers from other nations will be readily able to draw from and apply this book's contents, illustrations, and principles. After all, the kingdom of God is universal.

So if you are weary of watered-down versions of Christianity that waver, waffle, or whiff entirely on the kingdom of God—the central teaching of Jesus—this book is for you. I also solicit your support and involvement in helping launch this reclamation message and regal reengagement call out into the broader Church and the world.

If you will join me, perhaps you, I, and others can become the stepping stones for turning the world upside down—AGAIN (Acts 17:6 KJV). Yes, we have the numbers—"70.6 percent in 2014" of Americans identify themselves as Christians,[4] along with 2-plus billion worldwide. That's one-third of the planetary population. But the crux issue is: Do we have the will?

Let's see if this book might just spark the next great awakening.

Author note:

Some of the content of this book was discussed during
28-one-hour radio programs. Podcasts are available on PRI's website at:
www.prophecyrefi.org.
Click on "Podcasts" and "Kingdom Christianity."

---

[3] John Noē, *The Creation of Evil: Casting light into the purposes of darkness* (Indianapolis, IN.: East2West Press, 2015).
[4] New statistics from the Pew Research Center's U.S. Religious Landscape Study – http://www.pewforum.org/2015/05/12/americas-changing-religious-landscape/, 5/25/15. This is down from 78.4% in 2007. More on these new statistics in Chapter 2.

Part I – Confronting Decline, Politics, and Opportunity

Two men looked through prison bars;
one saw mud, the other saw stars.

Chapter 1

Has Christianity Been Tamed?

. . . culture has transformed Christ. . . . American faith
has met American culture—and culture has triumphed.[1]

Once, a mighty faith was accused of turning the world upside
down by its opponents (Acts 17:6 KJV). But in our day and time,
that faith, now called Christianity, has been turned upside down,
but not by its opponents.

Today, various versions of this "once mighty faith"—at least in
America, North America, and Western Europe—pale in comparison with
the Christianity preached, practiced, and perceived in the 1st century, and
as depicted in the pages of the New Testament. There are exceptions, of
course. But even leaders of Pentecostal and charismatic churches agree
that they are not seeing the same caliber (quality and quantity) of signs,
wonders, and miracles, vibrancy, and effectiveness in their groups as
were manifested back in those early church times.

These lesser versions also contrast considerably with the faith that
brought our forefathers to America to establish its great institutions.
Many of them linked their coming to America with the expansion of the
kingdom of God. Thus, the kingdom of God was a prominent theme in
their faith.

---

[1] Alan Wolfe, *The Transformation of American Religion* (New York: Free Press,
2003), 2-3.

These differences prompted Dallas Willard in his thought-provoking book, *The Divine Conspiracy*, to raise three relevant questions: 1) "Why is today's church so weak?" 2) "Why are we able to claim many conversions and enroll many church members but have less and less impact on our culture?" and 3) "Why are Christians indistinguishable from the world?"[2]

Willard lamented "those who profess Christian commitment consistently show little or no behavioral and psychological difference from those who do not."[3] Others have observed "there is no significant difference between the way born-againers live at an ethical level as compared with those who are nonreligious."[4]

Even more damaging are the condescending opinions of modern critics. For instance, Jewish secular humanist Alan Wolfe in his recent book *The Transformation of American Religion: How We Actually Live Our Faith* assures his non-Christian secular humanists that they have nothing to fear from modern-day Christianity because it has been "tamed."[5]

What has happened? What has changed?

Let's begin to answer these questions by seriously contemplating six significant and historical alterations. As we shall see, we Christians have sown the seeds for our own decline. See if you agree.

Alteration #1 – Forsaken the Central Teaching of Jesus Christ

Most scholars, theologians, pastors, teachers, and well-informed Christians agree that the kingdom of God was the central teaching and all-important message of Jesus Christ. The kingdom was at the heart of his ministry and central to his worldview throughout his three-and-a-

---

[2] Dallas Willard, *The Divine Conspiracy* (San Francisco, CA.: HarperSanFrancisco, 1997), 40.

[3] Ibid., 43.

[4] David Wells, quoted in Chris Stamper, "Authors by the Dozen," *World* magazine, July/August, 2002, 53.

[5] Wolfe, *The Transformation of American Religion*, inside cover leaf.

half-year earthly ministry. It was also the very essence of New Testament Christianity.

Today, however, the kingdom is no longer the central teaching of most of his Church, at the heart of its ministry, central to its worldview, or its very essence. When was the last time you heard a sermon on the kingdom? Or attended a Sunday school class, a conference, or a seminar the topic or theme of which was the kingdom of God? There are exceptions; but mere exceptions nonetheless.

Again, what has happened? What has changed?

Willard, once again, provokes our thoughts on this glaring omission by quoting Dr. Howard Marshall of the University of Aberdeen:

> During the past sixteen years I can recollect only two occasions on which I have heard sermons specifically devoted to the theme of the Kingdom of God . . . . I find this silence rather surprising because it is universally agreed by New Testament scholars that the central theme of the teaching of Jesus was the Kingdom of God.[6]

Certainly, the kingdom of God was both the central teaching and defining theme of Jesus' entire ministry. It was so prominent that Jesus mentioned and addressed it over 120 times in the Gospels and once in the Book of Acts following his resurrection (Acts 1:3b). It is mentioned 162 times in the entire New Testament.[7] By contrast, Jesus, during his earthly ministry, only mentioned "salvation" twice (Luke 19:9; John 4:22), "born again" twice (John 3:3, 7), "redemption" once (Luke 21:28) and "church" thrice (Matt. 16:18; 18:17). But the kingdom is no longer prominent for most of his Church today.

What has happened? What has changed?

---

[6] Willard, *The Divine Conspiracy*, 59

[7] According to my count of versions of the phrase "kingdom of God," such as "kingdom of heaven," "my kingdom," "the kingdom," and "my father's kingdom."

Alteration #2 – Written Out of Biblical Worldviews

The kingdom also has been written out of most Christian- and biblical-worldview presentations.[8] Yet in 1890-1891, James Orr, a leading theologian of his day, listed, during a series of lectures in Edinburgh, Scotland entitled *The Christian View of God and the World*, nine specific areas covered by "the Christian view of the world." His eighth area was described thusly:

> (8) the founding of the Kingdom of God on earth, which includes the spiritual salvation of individuals and a new order of society ("the result of the action of the spiritual forces set in motion through Christ"); . . .[9]

In drastic contrast, one of the widely acclaimed, modern-day books on this subject, *Understanding the Times: The Religious Worldviews of Our Day and the Search for Truth*, author David A. Noebel compares his conception of a Biblical Christian worldview with those of secular humanism (the worship of man) and Marxism/Leninism. And even though our family has greatly valued and participated numerous times in his Summit Ministries, astoundingly, on page 11 Noebel lists Orr's nine specific areas—including #8 about the "Kingdom of God on earth" and its purpose of establishing "a new order of society"—but without explanation, he drops the kingdom from his worldview throughout the rest of his book.[10]

---

[8] Prominent examples of this exclusion include: David K. Naugle, *Worldview: The History of a Concept* (Grand Rapids, MI.: Eerdmans, 2002); David S. Dockery & Gregory Alan Thornbury, eds, *Shaping a Christian Worldview* (Nashville, TN.: Broadman & Holman, 2002); J.P. Moreland & William Lane Craig, *Philosophy Foundations for a Christian Worldview* (Downers Grove, IL.: InterVarsity Press, 2003); N. Allan Moseley, *Thinking against the Grain: Developing a Biblical Worldview in a Culture of Myths* (Grand Rapids, MI.: Kregel, 2003); Ronald H. Nash, *Worldviews in Conflict* (Grand Rapids, MI.: Zondervan, 1992).

[9] James Orr, *The Christian View of God and the World* (Edinburgh: Andrew Elliot, 1897), 32-34.

[10] David A. Noebel, *Understanding the Times* (Eugene OR.: Harvest House Publishers, 1991, 1995), 8-17f.

Our Founding Fathers didn't drop it. They came to this country not just to escape religious persecution, but under an optimistic, postmillennial, eschatological mandate to expand the kingdom of God. They believed that the world was to become a better and better place as it became more and more Christianized via the kingdom advancing into more and more lives and areas of society. Hence, they preached that each Christian was responsible to do his or her part to advance the kingdom. Propelled by this optimistic worldview, they founded the great institutions of our country—the government, the schools, the universities—under Judeo-Christian principles. Consequently, Christianity was established and accepted as the moral influencer in American society.

But all this began to change in America after Israel became a nation in 1948 and a pessimistic worldview was suddenly legitimized. Subsequently, the evangelical Church in America started losing its kingdom orientation, positive worldview, the culture, and our children from the Church in droves.

Let's fast forward to 2003. In a poll among Americans, Christian researcher George Barna found that "only 4% of adults have a biblical worldview as the basis of their decision making" and "only 9% of born again Christians have such a perspective on life." Even more revealing, Barna's definition of a biblical worldview contained no mention of the kingdom of God. Here is his reductionist definition:

> . . . believing that absolute moral truths exist; that such truth is defined by the Bible; and firm belief in six specific religious views. Those views are that Jesus Christ lived a sinless life; God is the all-powerful and all-knowing Creator of the universe and He still rules it today; salvation is a gift from God and cannot be earned; Satan is real; a Christian has a responsibility to share their faith in Christ with other people; and the Bible is accurate in all of its teachings.[11]

Sadly, we Christians are the ones responsible for this major deletion from our "once mighty faith."

---

[11] Barna Research Online, "A Biblical Worldview Has a Radical Effect on a Person's Life" (www.barna.org/cgi-bin/PagePressRelease.asp., 1 December 2003), 1-2.

Alteration #3 – Gospel Reductionism

"Proclaim the gospel!" "Preach the gospel!" "Share the gospel!" We are told and taught. But what is the gospel? For the vast majority of evangelicals the answer is, "the life, death, and resurrection of Jesus Christ." It answers the popular evangelism question of "How do you know you are going to heaven (and not hell) when you die?"[12]

Traditionally and succinctly, John MacArthur defines the gospel this way: "The true gospel is an offer of salvation from sin and spiritual death."[13] Dinesh D'Souza terms this "the essence of Christianity."[14] Evangelism Explosion, which has been training and equipping "millions of people . . . in more than 200 nations" for over "50 years . . . to share their faith" and claims "8,457,945 people who heard the gospel and recorded a decision to receive Jesus Christ as Savior in 2014," says "this Gospel of Jesus Christ is Good News that sets us FREE with a promise of everlasting life [in heaven]." Thus, "Step 1" of their training program instructs trainees to ask someone these two questions: "Do you know for sure that you are going to be with God in heaven?", and, "If God were to ask you 'Why should I let you into My Heaven?' what would you say?"[15]

Please be assured that I have no desire to depreciate God's gift of salvation in any way. Indeed, salvation is good news. But salvation is only part of the good news. The biblical fact is, Jesus did not come into Galilee preaching that good news. Nor did He come preaching and teaching about Himself or his death so that when we die we would go to heaven. Nor was He offering a "get-out-of-hell-free" card. McLaren has it right. "[H]is essential message: [was] *the kingdom of God*. . . . contrary to popular belief—[He] was not focused on how to escape this world and its problems by going to heaven after death, but instead was focused on how God's will could be done on earth, in history, during this life."[16]

---

[12] For more on this issue, see my book: John Noē, *Hell Yes / Hell No* (Indianapolis, IN.: East2West Press, 2011).

[13] John MacArthur, *Strange Fire* (Nashville, TN.: Nelson Books, 2013), 52.

[14] Dinesh D'Souza, *What's So Great About Christianity?* (Washington, DC.: Regnery Publishing, 2007), 286.

[15] Evangelismexplosion.org, 5/27/15.

[16] Brian D. McLaren, *Everything Must Change* (Nashville, TN.: Thomas Nelson, 2007), 21.

Thus, for the first three years of his earthly ministry Jesus preached and taught this gospel: "The time is fulfilled, and the kingdom of God is at hand: repent ye, and believe the gospel" (Mark 1:15 KJV). Please note, at that time there was no mention of the cross, salvation, resurrection, hell, or of Him dying for sins. It wasn't until the three-year point of his earthly ministry that Jesus first mentioned his death and resurrection. "From that time on Jesus began to explain to his disciples that he must go to Jerusalem and suffer many things at the hands of the elders, chief priests and teachers of the law, and that he must be killed and on the third day be raised to life" (Matt. 16:21; also Mark 8:31; Luke 18:32). Also, from that time on, Jesus kept this later-coming aspect of the gospel low profiled, only mentioning it a few times to a select few.

Today, in ironical contrast, the almost total focus of the evangelical Church is on salvation and the power of the cross. The kingdom is rarely mentioned. Billy Graham epitomizes this reductionism as he writes, "He [God] sent Jesus Christ into the world for one reason: to make our salvation possible."[17] But as we shall further see in Part II, the *two reasons* and two great works of the Messiah were that of the kingdom and that of salvation. That's the order in which Jesus brought them into human history, announced, and fulfilled them. First and foremost, Jesus came to bring a new way of life via the presence and availability of the everlasting form of the kingdom of God. Therefore, for three years that was Jesus' gospel, and his only gospel. So I ask, why shouldn't this elimination or marginalizing of the central teaching of Jesus be considered gospel reductionism if not heresy?

Concurrence of Scholars

Darrell L. Guder terms this historical transformation in kingdom orientation "reductionism of the gospel." He defines gospel reductionism as "the inadequate exposition of the kingdom of God" and as "the curious separation of salvation from the kingdom of God in the church's evangelistic proclamation."[18]

---

[17] Billy Graham, "My Answer," *The Indianapolis Star*, 3/29/16, 4E.
[18] Darrell L. Guder, *The Continuing Conversion of the Church* (Grand Rapids, MI.: Eerdmans, 2000), *xiii, ix*.

Dallas Willard calls it "the great omission"[19] and the primary reason "why . . . today's church [is] so weak."[20]

Robert Lynn laments that "the gospel we proclaim has been shrunk."[21] Rather, "it's . . . a gospel that is a new way of seeing the world and everything in it."[22]

John Eldredge confirms: "Jesus preached far more than the gospel of sin management. The good news he brought was much, much greater than forgiveness. Jesus came to announce the coming of 'the kingdom of God.'"[23]

Scot McKnight worries that "we have settled for a little gospel, a miniaturized version that cannot address the robust problems of our world"[24]

Richard Stearns affirms from his appropriately titled book, *The Hole in Our Gospel:* "The whole gospel is a vision for ushering in God's kingdom."[25]

N.T. Wright insightfully weighs in that ". . . the church is stuck on Jesus' birth, death, and resurrection, to the near exclusion of the largest chunk of gospel material—His life in between . . . . the kingdom of God. Through Jesus' work, God reigns right now on earth as in heaven . . . that truth is the best news of all."[26] In another book, Wright agonizes that "for many conservative Christians today . . . . what matters is the supernatural, world-denying salvation offered by the gospel. Any attempt

---

[19] Dallas Willard, *The Great Omission* (New York, NY.: HarperSanFrancisco, 2006), cover.

[20] Willard, *The Divine Conspiracy*, 40f.

[21] Robert Lynn, "Far as the curse is found" in Chuck Colson's *Breakpoint Worldview* magazine, Oct. '06, 14.

[22] Robert Lynn, "Worldview Church," Prison Fellowship, www.breakpoint.org., 6/24/07. 3, 4.

[23] John Eldredge, *The Journey of Desire* (Nashville, TN.: Thomas Nelson, 2000), 112.

[24] Scot McKnight, "The 8 Marks of a Robust Gospel," *Christianity Today*, March 2008, 36.

[25] Richard Stearns, *The Hole in Our Gospel* (Nashville, TN.: Thomas Nelson, 2009), 5.

[26] In a book review by Caleb Nelson, "Notable Books," *World* (1 December, 2012), 27 of N.T. Wright's book, *How God Became King: The Forgotten Story of the Gospels.*

to work for God's justice *on earth* as in heaven is condemned as the sort of thing those wicked anti-supernatural liberals try to do. . . . This convoluted distortion of the gospel is not, alas, confined to North American fundamentalism."[27] He elaborates that "the gospel is not how to escape the world; the gospel is that the crucified and risen Jesus is the Lord of the world . . . . 'If he's not Lord of all, he's not Lord at all.'"[28]

Fleming Rutledge cites "two competing ways of understanding and presenting the Christian gospel in America. They are equally valid and ideally should complement one another, but unfortunately, battle lines have been drawn on both sides. Some Christians emphasize the gospel as purely a matter of individual salvation; others see it essentially in terms of community and of social justice. This problem is partly cultural, but more significantly, it arises from insufficient knowledge of the Scriptures: 'You are in error because you do not know the Scriptures or the power of God' (Matt. 22:29)." He rightly advises that "we who are evangelicals need to widen our vision of what God does in the world."[29]

Rabbi Jonathan Cahn adamantly insists that "we must reject a watered-down gospel." He explains that "if we want to see the full power of God's Word, we must take that Word at full strength. We can't compromise to win people. Rather it is when we don't compromise that we burn with the passion of God and shine with His glory—that's when revival comes."[30]

Cindy Jacobs contributes that "we need to realize that Jesus' main emphasis was not the gospel of salvation but the gospel of the kingdom of God. . . . He was inviting people into a new kingdom, with a new government and a new King. He was inviting people to live heaven on earth."[31]

---

[27] N.T. Wright, *Surprised By Hope* (New York, NY.: HarperCollins, 2008), 220.
[28] N.T. Wright, "Mere Mission," *Christianity Today* (Jan. 2007): 41, 39.
[29] Fleming Rutledge, "When God Disturbs the Peace," *Christianity Today*, June 2008, 30, 32.
[30] Jonathan Cahn, "How America Can Avoid Calamity," *Charisma*, May 2015, 44.
[31] Cindy Jacobs, *The Reformation Manifesto* (Minneapolis, MN.: Bethany House Publishers, 2008), 63.

R. J. Rushdoony labels this misuse "reductions of Scripture. . . . The cross cannot limit the gospel"[32] and "a radical deformation of the gospel."[33] And apart from the kingdom, he claims "the gospel is perverted. . . . The ministry of the church then becomes trifling, and the life of the believer, frustrating."[34]

Steve Gregg lends this support by pointing out that "it is evident that the gospel, as preached by Jesus and His apostles, had an entirely different focus from that which has become standard evangelical fare in American evangelism. Modern presentations are commonly directed to the self-interest of the hearers ('Come to Christ so you can escape from the punishment you deserve in hell'). . . . The gospel is the good tidings of the reign of the righteous King Jesus."[35]

Allen Mitsuo Wakabayashi adds, "Christianity is not merely about isolated individuals going to heaven. It's about God transforming the entire world and making things right. . . . It's happening now through what Jesus came to establish—the kingdom of God."[36]

T.M. Moore terms "the Gospel of Christ and His kingdom the centerpiece of our every endeavor."[37]

Douglas C. Minson dualistically defines the gospel as "the cultivation of Christlikeness . . . and the transformation of culture. . . . personal holiness and social transformation."[38]

Brian D. McLaren exclaims that "the gospel is about how the world will be saved from human sin and all that goes with it . . . . I believe the gospel of Jesus is that the Kingdom of God is at hand and is open to all." He rhetorically asks, "could our preoccupation with individual salvation

[32] R.J. Rushdoony, *Law and Society,* Vol. II, (Vallecito, CA.: Ross House Books, 1986, 1982), 76-77.
[33] Rousas John Rushdoony, *The Institutes of Biblical Law* (n.l., The Presbyterian and Reformed Publishing Company, 1973), 449.
[34] Ibid., 450.
[35] Steve Gregg, *All You Want To Know About Hell* (Nashville, TN.: Thomas Nelson, 2013), 61-62.
[36] Allen Mitsuo Wakabayashi, *Kingdom Come* (Downers Grove, IL.: InterVarsity Press, 2003), back cover.
[37] T.M. Moore, "Worldview Weapons," *BreakPoint Worldview* (Oct. 2006): 9.
[38] Douglas C. Minson, "Religion & Society," Prison Fellowship, www.breakpoint.org., 6/24/07, 2, 3.

from hell after death distract us from speaking prophetically about injustice in our world today?"[39]

Myles Munroe summarizes that "the message of the Bible is primarily and obviously about a kingdom. . . . the message of the Kingdom of God is the most important news ever delivered to the human race."[40]

My Definition

The substance of the Christian gospel is not just the cross and the power of the Word of God to convict of sin and redeem us from and elevate us above our fallen nature; it's also about the kingdom of our Lord and Christ. And since most Christians have too small an understanding of the gospel, here is my working and nutshell definition of the whole or full gospel. It is: the establishment and practical relevance of the everlasting and final form of God's kingdom on earth and his salvation. Once again, these two distinct yet interrelated and eschatological realities are the two great works of the Messiah. This was also the order in which Jesus proclaimed them, brought them into human and redemptive history, fulfilled them, and made them everlastingly available. Thus, the Apostle Paul presented these two great works in this same order in Acts 28:31: "Boldly and without hindrance he preached the kingdom of God and taught about the Lord Jesus Christ" (also see Acts 19:8; 20:25, 27).

Later in this book we shall lay out the time and nature for the establishment of this everlasting form of the kingdom, as well as address how we enter and stay in it, receive its blessings, and become obedient to our responsibilities and privileges therein, and much more. Why so? It's because most Christians: 1) are kingdom illiterate; 2) haven't been raised in a kingdom-oriented tradition; 3) are not taught this in most Christian colleges and seminaries; 4) lack an effective and sound theology of the kingdom; 5) find it to be foreign territory that is intimidating. Surely, the

---

[39] Brian D. McLaren, *The Last Word and the Word After That* (Jossey-Bass, San Francisco, CA.: 2005), 69, 111, 84.

[40] Myles Munroe, *Rediscovering the Kingdom* (Shippensburg, PA.: Destiny Image Publishers, 2004), 63, 100.

kingdom was intimidating to many Jews in Jesus' day. They killed Him because of it.

Consequently, Jesus Christ did not lower Himself and come to earth merely to suffer and die for us. He did that, of course. But He also came to establish his kingdom. This is the *whole* or *full* gospel. It's a much greater gospel than is generally being preached, practiced, and perceived throughout most of his Church.

One day, while discussing this reductionist phenomenon in a Facebook group, I received these two contrasting but revealing responses:

Critical Response #1: "My pastor only cares about saving souls. That's why he's a great man."

My Response: This is another example of the partial but reductionist tradition we are facing. Remember, a partial truth parading as the whole truth is a lie and the very essence of deception.

Positive Response #2: "Yes, the teaching of the gospel of the kingdom taught by Christ, I almost totally overlooked and never saw it, although it was there right in front of me all those years . . . . So many of us read Scriptures and yet so many times, there is a veil or mist over much of what it contains. Because of this, important issues are distorted, misunderstood, and not taught to the masses of God's people, leaving the Church unprepared, not fit to lead the world, and not ready or knowing how to advance his kingdom."[41]

Alteration #4 – Abandonment Theology and the Great Retreat

Over the past 75 years or so, we Christians in America have given away almost all of the institutions our forefathers in the faith came to this country and founded—the schools, the universities, the branches of government, and being the moral influencer in society. Remarkably, we were not pushed out by a more powerful force or superior beliefs. We simply withdrew and gave it away without a fight. Into the vacuums poured the ungodly crowd, who commandeered these institutions.

---

[41] Michael Reimer in a personal email to me, 10/23/12. (Used with permission).

Consequently, we Americans are paying a huge and dreadful price for our self-inflicted abandonment and retreat.

So how do we account for our major indifference and shameful withdrawal? To answer with one word, it's eschatology. The historical fact is, during this time period the dominant, eschatological (end-time) worldview in conservative Christian circles changed from one of historical optimism to that of historical pessimism. During the mid-20th century, the optimistic postmillennial worldview of America's Founders was displaced as the majority report among evangelicals by the pessimistic dispensational premillennial worldview. This latter and relatively new end-time view in church history (originating in the 1830s by John Nelson Darby) argues that the world is supposed to get worse and worse before Christ returns. Statistically, its ascendancy into dominance perfectly coincides and correlates with the withdrawal of Christians from societal involvement (the public square), the rising of godless rule, and the rapid decline of morality and public life here in America.[42]

John W. Chalfant in his book, *America: A Call to Greatness* (formerly titled, *Abandonment Theology*) characterizes this great retreat thusly:

> . . . much of the clergy, along with their millions of victimized American Christians following their pastors' lead, have retreated from the battlefront to the social, non-confrontational, noncontroversial reservation [their church]. They say that Christians should confine their religious activities to politically noncontroversial roles and keep their Bibles out of the political process.[43]

Chalfant pinpoints dispensationalism's emphasis that "these are the 'last days'" as being the number one reason why many modern-day Christians—in stark contrast to our predecessors in the faith—now believe that "any efforts we make to restore righteousness to this nation will be in vain and need not even be undertaken."[44]

---

[42] See "Some Statistical Evidence" in John W. Chalfant, *America: A Call to Greatness* (Longwood, FL.: Xulon Press, 2003), 83-90.

[43] Ibid., 142.

[44] Ibid., 143. Unfortunately, Chalfant's book also advocates a Christian or biblical worldview without mention or inclusion of a mighty kingdom of God.

Others credit Israel's rebirth as a nation in 1948 and Hal Lindsay's mega-selling book *The Late Great Planet Earth* (1970s), which sold between 30 and 40 million copies, as the two major factors that changed American Christianity more than anything else. Subtly but surely, the societal focus switched from advancing and expanding the kingdom to a pattern of escapism that paralyzed much of the Church and resulted in this great retreat.

Another classic example of this withdrawal phenomenon, is the much-revered evangelist, Billy Graham. In a 2004 article titled "The End of the World," Graham preached that we are "heading toward a catastrophe. . . . We can't go on much longer morally. We can't go on much longer scientifically. The technology that was supposed to save us is ready to destroy us." He reported that the "Doomsday Clock" kept by "The Bulletin of the Atomic Scientists . . . . At this writing . . . stands at seven minutes to midnight – two minutes closer to potential destruction than the clock read in 1998 and seven minutes closer than it did in 1995."[45]

Popular *Left Behind* co-authors Tim LaHaye and Jerry Jenkins agree with Dr. Graham. In their 1999 book, *Are We Living in the End Times?*, they cite "twenty reasons for believing that the Rapture and Tribulation could occur during our generation." Like Graham, and to emphasize their tone of contemporary urgency, they claim that "ours is the first generation that has the technology and opportunity to uniquely fulfill many prophecies of Revelation."[46]

John MacArthur, another prominent dispensational author and a pastor, takes this gloom-and-doom specter a step further, trying to convince Christians that "'reclaiming' the culture is a pointless, futile exercise. I am convinced we are living in a post-Christian society—a civilization that exists under God's judgment."[47] From a gospel

---

In my opinion, this is equivalent to and about as effective—for rallying the troops (the Church), taking back lost territory, and producing cultural change, nowadays—as a dog barking at the moon.

[45] Billy Graham, "The End of the World," *Decision*, January 2004, on www.billygraham.org/article (1/14/04).

[46] Tim LaHaye and Jerry B. Jenkins, *Are We Living in the Last Days* (Wheaton, IL.: Tyndale House Publishers, 1999), back cover.

[47] John F. MacArthur, *The Vanishing Conscience: Drawing the Line in a No-Fault, Guilt-Free World* (Dallas, TX.: Word, 1994), 12.

reductionist position, he also argues that "people becoming saved. That is our only agenda . . . . It is the only thing that we are in the world to do."[48]

Astonishingly, fellow dispensationalists Tim LaHaye and David Noebel think MacArthur is off base. In their co-authored book *Mind Siege* they concede that "there is plenty to do in all spheres of life. The importance of Christians entering the cultural sphere . . . cannot be overlooked or underestimated . . . . Christian parents need to prepare their sons and daughters to invade the fortress of the left."[49]

Not surprisingly, in its May 2015 issue, *Charisma* magazine reported that "a recent Barna Group poll found 4 in 10 Americans—and 77 percent of evangelicals—believe the 'world is now living in the biblical end times.'" This is because of "a seeming nonstop series of crises in recent years—the Sept. 11, 2001 terrorist attacks, catastrophic natural disasters, ballooning levels of debt and growing fears of World War III." Hence, "many are asking whether the world is now in the run-up to the end time events predicted in Scripture."[50]

Savvy Voices of Sanity

Gary DeMar, a postmillennialist, is highly critical of dispensationalist calls for social activism. He writes, "Unfortunately, while LaHaye's points are well made, his call for any type of social action cannot be sustained over time because of his eschatology." DeMar further claims that LaHaye's short-term and popular eschatological worldview faces a "logical dilemma . . . . on the relationship between Bible prophecy and Christian activism." But he relents that "I would rather have LaHaye's prophetic schizophrenia than MacArthur's prophetic fatalism."[51]

---

[48] Quoted in John Zens and Cliff Bjork, "A Better Society Without the Gospel? The Unbiblical Expectations of Many Christian Leaders," *Searching Together* 27:1, 2, 3 (Spring-Fall 1999), 12.
[49] Tim LaHaye and David Noebel, *Mind Siege: The Battle for Truth in the New Millennium* (Nashville, TN.: Word, 2000), 228.
[50] Troy Anderson, "Is an 'Appeal to Heaven' America's Greatest Hope?" Charisma, May 2015, 6.
[51] Gary DeMar, "Give Up, Caught Up, or Get Up?" Biblical Worldview, November 2003, on www.americanvision.org., *Biblical Worldview* Archive.

DeMar also cites Jan Markell, president of Olive Tree Ministries, who believes and preaches that "Satan has control of this world until Jesus returns and vanquishes him," and consequently "'the church is not in the business of taking anything away from Satan but the souls of men.'" He chastises Markell as "a perfect example of someone whose unbiblical end-time views are dangerous . . . . a believer in an end-time scenario that demands the return of Christ to rescue us. Until that happens, don't look for and do not expect to be successful at any type of long-term societal transformation. In fact, to participate in this type of work, Markell tells us, is 'delusional' and will keep 'people out of heaven.'"[52]

Likewise, Steve Strang, Founder and Publisher of *Charisma* magazine, agrees that "the 'Jesus is coming' mentality . . . has kept many Bible believers from engaging more with the culture or the political process. The emphasis was always on a heavenly kingdom rather than an earthly one. Going back to World War I, most Pentecostals were pacifists . . . . That changed by the second world war but staying on the political sidelines continued for decades."[53]

Make no mistake; these ideas have consequences. And many Christians have become hoodwinked by this recent, eschatological shift of views. Most certainly, gloom-and-doom, end-time views affect how we think, how we live, what we do, and how we do it. It shows up in our character, our level of Bible knowledge, our struggles to survive or thrive, and in our engagement in or disengagement from society. But as we shall see later in this book, there is a strong societal-involvement dimension and restoration imperative to both the full gospel and the kingdom.

Massive Indifference and Ineffectiveness

Today, the internal dumbing down of our faith has not only produced masses of Christians who are indistinguishable from unbelievers in terms of thoughts, words, and deeds. They are also largely indifferent about

---

[52] Gary DeMar, "Is the World a 'Sinking Titanic?' Jan Markell Thinks So," *Biblical Worldview*, May 2007, 4.
[53] Steve Strang, "Perspective: Covering the Politics of Faith," *Charisma*, July 2015, 6.

being indistinguishable. But Jesus called all Christians to be salt and light in the world. He also warned us not to lose our saltiness or darken our light (Matt. 5:13-16; Luke 14:34-35). He further explained that "every good tree bears good fruit, but a bad tree bears bad fruit" and "by their fruit you will recognize them" (Matt. 7:17, 19). This means being weak, anemic, and casual about our faith as well as apathetic, ineffective, and impotent in being salt and light in the world results in Christians becoming "no longer good for anything, except to be thrown out and trampled by men." These are Jesus' words, not mine. And, no, He did not explain what He meant by this. But it cannot be good.

Edmund Burke, the 18th-century British statesman also once warned, "The only thing necessary for evil to triumph is for good men to do nothing." Likewise, Willard points out one of the psychological and behavioral implications of this most popular end-time view:

> If we think we are facing an irresistible cosmic force of evil, it will invariably lead to giving in and giving up—usually with very little resistance. If you can convince yourself that you are helpless, you can then stop struggling and just "let it happen." That will seem a great relief—for a while. . . . But then you will have to deal with the consequences. And for normal human beings those are very severe.[54]

For this reason, the dominant worldview in American evangelicalism today is fatalism—i.e., the world will, and is supposed to, get "worse and worse." It produces a "why fight, we're on the next flight" indifference and withdrawal mentality and "fiddling while Rome burns" behavioral reality. So how does this fatalistic worldview match up with Isaiah 9:6-7's description of the then-future messianic kingdom Jesus would bring to Planet Earth? As we shall see in Part II, it doesn't match up at all.

. . . these ideas have consequences.
And many Christians have become hoodwinked
by this recent, eschatological shift of views.

---

[54] Willard, *The Divine Conspiracy*, 343.

Instead, as Chalfant adds, "this faulty religious teaching is the only way to explain why so many well-meaning Christians are paralyzed into inaction."[55] He contends that "it comprises what is left today of the militant, power-filled, full-dimensional Christian faith of America's Founders after decades of erosion, watering down and trivializing of God's action mandates by America's Abandonment Clergy. . . . based on prophecy these are the 'last days,' and any efforts we make to restore righteousness to this nation will be in vain and need not even be undertaken."[56] He further explains:

> For this type of 'Christian,' there's no need to stand up to evil, because they're 'saved by grace, not works' (despite repeated biblical admonitions that 'faith without works is dead'). No need to obey God's commands, because they're already saved, so why bother? No need to try to help make it a better world, because they're going to be 'raptured' soon and those who remain behind can sort out the mess. Is it any wonder the church–and America–are in such trouble?[57]

Similarly, is it any wonder why the Moral Majority failed after only 20 years in existence? "At its peak it had 6-1/2 million members. . . . but that didn't always lead to action."[58] Founder, Jerry Falwell, summarized the failure and demise of this activist organization in this fatalistic and mea culpa manner:

> I see things getting worse and worse and worse. All we're doing—all we've ever been able to do—is to have the church put its thumb in the dike, but it's inevitable that [sic] it's going to come out. We are supposed to keep it plugged up as long as we can, be a restraining influence. We prevent spoilage . . . . But we're kidding ourselves if we think there's any program, any third party . . . or anything we can do to straighten things out right now . . . . these things that we have in the country are beyond repair.[59]

---

[55] John Chalfant, WorldNetDaily's *Whistleblower*, April 2005, 17.
[56] John W. Chalfant, *Abandonment Theology* (Winter Park, FL.: America – A Call to Greatness, Inc., 1996, 1999), 5 and 117-118.
[57] Chalfant, *Whistleblower*, 27.
[58] Michael Duffy and Nancy Gibbs, "Jerry's Kids," *Time*, May 28, 2007, 72.
[59] From Cal Thomas and Ed Dobson, *Blinded by Might* (Grand Rapids, MI.: Zondervan, 1999), 276.

Factually, the problem for the Moral Majority—note that it avoided using the word "Christian" in its name—was both foundational and systemic. That problem became, it was sounding "an uncertain sound"— "For if the trumpet give an uncertain sound [i.e., message], who shall prepare himself to the battle?" (1 Cor. 14:8, KJV). The leadership and membership of the Moral Majority was comprised mostly of fundamentalist, dispensational premillennialists. Therefore, this organization simply did not have a sound and solid enough theological foundation to support the level of activism to which it aspired. It was like the mythical bird with one wing shorter than the other—he just flies around in ever decreasing circles until he finally collides with himself and self-destructs. This is exactly what caused their demise.

Seriously, "why polish the brass on a sinking ship?" "Why bother trying to fix up or improve a broken world that is about to be thrown on the ash heap of history by God Himself?" It's the classic cultural downer subscribed to by many Christians who have given up without a fight while awaiting Jesus' return to take them on a flight through outer space to heaven without dying (the Rapture). Given this theology, eschatology, and worldview, it makes no sense to labor for the betterment of society and the overturning of evil and the righting of injustices. After all, things are supposed to get "worse and worse" until the end. Consequently, masses of Christians have become "less than conquerors," as Douglas W. Frank explains in his book with that condemnatory title:

> . . . the more moderate of them were sometimes willing to join civic campaigns for moral reform, risking the ire of compatriots who thought any effort to cleanse society by social or political action could only delay the Second Coming. . . . Many were building businesses or being educated for the professions—and not evangelizing. Their eschatology implied something much different from the way they spent their time and conceived of their lives. Serious Christians were being torn in two directions, and it undoubtedly added to an unconscious reservoir of guilt.[60]

---

[60] Douglas W. Frank, *Less Than Conquerors* (Grand Rapids, MI.: Eerdmans, 1986), 97, 140.

Nevertheless, some dispensationalists, like Tim and Beverly LaHaye, have done more in their lives than most Christians in attempting to restrain ungodliness in America. But the reality is, they are operating in a schizophrenic manner. According to their eschatological worldview, they should be allowing ungodliness to progress, unhampered and unimpeded, thereby "hastening the return of Christ." This conundrum of schizophrenia has existed ever since fundamentalism gained popularity in the mid-20th century. But psychologically it has undermined the social initiative of millions of Christians ever since.

Alteration #5 – Caught-Up in Eschatological Mid-Air

Positively speaking, get the kingdom of God straight and many other, vital and interrelated realities of the Christian faith fall readily into place. Miss it, even slightly, and you're liable to be way off on many other aspects. That is how pivotal the kingdom of God is.

But today the kingdom of God is caught up in eschatological mid-air. The majority of evangelicals (dispensational premillennialists) believe that God withdrew the kingdom at the cross and someday Jesus will return and reestablish it *visibly* in Israel during a future Jewish millennial era. In the meantime the Church is a parenthetical gap in God's plan for Israel and exists today without a mighty kingdom.

Others (amillennialists and postmillennialists) believe the kingdom is here, only partially "in some sense," and question in what sense. A few (cessationist full preterists) say it is here but major elements have been withdrawn by God. As we shall see in Part II of this book, however, these kingdom views stand in stark contrast to the time parameter and nature reality that Jesus and his first followers presented and which resulted in them being accused by their opponents of having "turned the world upside down" (Acts 17:6; also see 20:25, 27).

Given all this confusion and conflict, why should we today find it surprising that most Christians only give lip service to the kingdom of God and little, if any, place for it in their lives? Thus, most have totally neglected Jesus' admonition to "But seek ye first the kingdom of God and his righteousness" (Matt. 6:33 KJV).

This present-day reality is not missed by Gordon D. Fee and Douglas Stuart. They are right on target regarding the consequences of our confused understandings and ignoring of Jesus' kingdom:

> One dare not think he or she can properly interpret the Gospels without a clear understanding of the concept of the kingdom of God in the ministry of Jesus[61] . . . . the major hermeneutical difficulty . . . lies with understanding 'the kingdom of God.'[62]

Nevertheless, "the idea of the kingdom of God had indeed been the dominant idea in American Christianity"[63]—i.e., in its postmillennial version and until the middle of the 20th century. Since then, many Christians have misrepresented Jesus and his kingdom-dominating message with their unscriptural end-time agendas and shifting sands of the traditions of men, as we shall see in Part II of this book.

Alteration #6 – Tamed Indeed

The above five historical alterations are also not lost on the opponents of Christianity. Hence, Jewish secular humanist Alan Wolfe (quoted at the start of this chapter) has concluded that "faith in the United States, especially in the last half century or so, has been further transformed with dazzling speed. . . . culture has transformed Christ[64] . . . . American faith has met American culture—and culture has triumphed."[65]

Wolfe surmises that "in short, American religion has been tamed."[66] And in America, "religion" largely means Christianity. Hence, he advises secular humanists who might "worry about faith's potential fanaticism"[67]

---

[61] Gordon D. Fee and Douglas Stuart, *How to Read the Bible for All It's Worth* (Grand Rapids, MI.: Zondervan, 1981), 131.

[62] Ibid., 113.

[63] H. Richard Niebuhr, *The Kingdom of God in America* (Middletown, CT.: Wesleyan University Press, 1988, 1937), *xxii.*

[64] Wolfe, *The Transformation of American Religion*, 2.

[65] Ibid., 3.

[66] Ibid., inside cover leaf.

[67] Ibid., 4.

that they have nothing "to fear" because "believers in the United States are neither saviors nor sectarians,"[68] and because they have essentially "succumbed to the individualism and . . . narcissism, of American life."[69] In other words, the Church has lost its kingdom orientation. Consequently, at least two generations of American Christians have grown up accustomed to and comfortable with a Christianity without a mighty kingdom.

In a review of Wolfe's hard-hitting book, syndicated newspaper columnist Cal Thomas terms it "must reading" with "some sobering conclusions," and a "stinging indictment of contemporary Christianity." Thomas suggests that "people looking for reasons why the church has lost power and real influence need look no further than Wolfe's book." He credits Wolfe as having "discovered the source of the church's contemporary power failure." It is a fact that "people who call themselves evangelicals increasingly dislike sharing their faith with others for fear that doing so might 'make them seem unfriendly or invasive.'" In citing Wolfe's contention "that in the battle between faith and culture, 'American culture has triumphed,'" Thomas rightly notices that "it was supposed to happen the other way." He ends his article with this poignant and most appropriate piece of advice:

> If Christians really want to see culture transformed, Wolfe's book, especially, shows they need to begin with their own transformation. Only then do they have a prayer of seeing cultural change. To expect it to happen the other way around is futile.[70]

"in short, American religion has been tamed."
. . . they have essentially "succumbed to the individualism and . . . narcissism, of American life."

In another review of Wolfe's book, *Christianity Today* editors admit that "the cultural success of evangelicalism is its greatest weakness."

---

[68] Ibid., 5.
[69] Ibid., 4.
[70] Cal Thomas, "American culture has triumphed over religious faith," *The News-Press* (Fort Myers, FL.), 2 October 2003, 9B.

They also tend to agree with Wolfe as he "paints a picture of a privatized religion that lacks confidence and is eager to avoid offense." They term our "tamed" faith "toothless evangelicalism" since most evangelicals have grown accustomed to "'practicing the culture' rather than 'practicing the faith.'" They also recognize "that Bible study has been so personalized as to effectively block its implications for radical social transformation; the way the fear of offending others has reduced most witnesses to 'lifestyle evangelism.'" Their review closes with "a call to serious Christianity" and the conclusion that "something must be done." That something "must nurture an evangelicalism that is truer to its robust heritage" and contain a "demanding vision for both individuals and society."[71] To their concluding insights I add a hearty "Amen!" And that is exactly what we will so do in this book.

National Review magazine's review of Wolfe's book took a different stance. It focused on "those who fret about the danger of the 'Christian Right' lurking within our borders." They agreed with Wolfe "that there is 'no reason to fear that the faithful are a threat to liberal democratic values.'" They lauded that "it's great that a scholar of Wolfe's stature is willing to stand up" and put forth "the principle that a vigorous exercise of religious faith poses no threat to the constitutional separation of church and state." They cited Wolfe's three reasons for this principle: 1) "the reason people of faith should not be feared by the body politic is that religion has been watered down, robbed of both supernatural mystery and intellectual vigor." 2) "The evangelicals in their megachurches, Wolfe says, are more interested in emotion and experience than in theological disputation," and 3) "Evangelicalism" has entered "a 'Faustian pact' with the culture."[72]

Lastly, an *Associated Press* article reviewing Wolfe's book and "allegations of 'culture war'" emphasized that "Wolfe is writing for fellow secularists, whom he depicts as frightened that their devout neighbors are undermining democracy." It reported that Wolfe calms their fears by relating that "the culture has reshaped the evangelicals more than vice-versa" and that "American religion has been so

---

[71] Editors, Where We Stand: *CT's Views on Key Issues*, "Walking the Old, Old Talk," *Christianity Today* (October 2003): 34-35.
[72] Michael Potemra, "That Old Time Religion," *National Review* (15 September 2003): 46-47.

transformed that we have reached the end of religion as we have known it."[73]

James Rutz concurs as he radically recalls that:

> Two generations ago eminent Christian spokesman A.W. Tozer thundered, 'The fact is that we are not producing saints. We are making converts to an effete type of Christianity that bears little resemblance to that of the New Testament. The average so-called Bible Christian in our times is but a wretched parody of true sainthood. Yet we put millions of dollars behind movements to perpetuate this degenerative form of religion and attack the man who dares to challenge the wisdom of it.'[74]

The six historical alterations presented above have produced numerous but much lesser modern-day versions of Christianity. They can only be characterized as nominalism compared to our faith's once mighty vibrancy, power, and effectiveness as depicted in the Gospels and the Book of Acts. Consequently, as Craig S. Kenner expounds that "95 percent of the work of the kingdom never gets done today" because only "5 percent of the Christians are doing all the work."[75] If Kenner is right, that's lower than the proverbial 80/20 rule.[76]

Steve Chalke and Alan Mann claim the reason "the Church in the West – with some notable exceptions – has a tame faith [is] because it

---

[73] Richard N. Ostling, Associated Press, "Author: America is harmonious in matters of faith," *The Indianapolis Star*, 30 October 2003, E1, 8.

[74] James Rutz, *Mega Shift* (Washington, DC.: WND Books, 2011), 87.

[75] Craig S. Kenner, "Are Spiritual Gifts for Today?" in Robert W. Graves, ed., *Strangers to Fire: When Tradition Trumps Scripture* (Woodsotch, GA.: The Foundation for Pentecostal Scholarship, 2014), 153.

[76] My pastor, Dave Rodriguez, believes and preaches that 25% of Americans are non-Christians. Another 25% are cultural Christians who believe in God and maybe Jesus, that religion is a private matter, that happiness is the goal of life, lack a concept of absolute truth, and are morally ambiguous. A third 25% are congregational Christians who believe in God and Jesus, identify with a particular church or denomination, believe in order to escape hell, and equate all priorities in life as equal: happiness, success, health, family, God. A final 25% (maybe only 7 – 10 %) follow Jesus daily, are filled with the Holy Spirit, study the Bible, and prioritize Jesus and his kingdom are their top priority in life. (Sermon August 9 & 10, 2014 – listen, go to: gracechurchin.org).

has been giving a tame message for centuries. You can't breed a radical revolutionary movement on passive, middle-of-the-road rhetoric."[77]

Ed Stetzer agrees. In an article titled "Christian: It's More Than Just a Label," he contends that while "three-quarters of Americans identify as Christian . . . the vast majority don't truly follow Christ as nominalism seeps further into the church." He advises that "if the church isn't providing more of an authentic alternative, the church will lose." But sadly, "many church members see themselves as spectators today. They hold certain beliefs and often show up at church, but they don't make a connection between faith and everyday life. Faith in Christ is not widely perceived as an active lifestyle that one attempts to live out every day in all one's actions." He rightly concludes that "the issue is nominalism— when someone is a Christian in name only. They call themselves Christians but are not disciples. They are not people who follow Jesus."[78]

Likewise, Marcus Yoars broaches this subject by asking, "Why, then, do we in the 21st-century America church focus on all the elements that Jesus *didn't*? He focused on training and equipping 12 disciples; we focus on growing our crowds and spheres of influence, regardless of whether those people follow Jesus. He preached an uncompromising message of truth; we sugarcoat the gospel until we're saccharine-high on deception. He walked among His enemies in love; we ostracize our enemies by blasting them for all their sins. Indeed, most of the U.S. church is enamored with size over substance and microwave growth over true reproduction."[79]

Randy Alcorn, however, presents a slightly different take as he argues back that "the fact that there are fewer nominal Christians today is good. It's better for people to deny the Christian faith outright than to profess it in weak and shallow ways." But because of the massive amount of nominalism in the church today, Alcorn further insists that "many have become immune to Christianity by contracting a mild and unbiblical form of it. Some find . . . after getting far enough away from

---

[77] Steve Chalke and Alan Mann, *The Lost Message of Jesus* (Grand Rapids, MI.: Zondervan, 2003), 86.

[78] Ed Stetzer, "Christian: It's More Than Just a Label," *Charisma* (March 2014), 44-46.

[79] Marcus Yoars, "Will the Real Church Please Stand Up? *Charisma* (March 2014) 8.

false Christianity, [that] they can see with fresh eyes what true Christianity is—a dynamic and persuasive competitor in the marketplace of ideas."[80] To which I add another hearty "Amen!"

A Personal Challenge

Surely, this first chapter should begin to give us serious pause for cause about how different our familiar and comfortable versions of Christianity are today in comparison to our "once mighty faith" in its original version. Also, if this chapter made you angry, good; Wolfe is right. We Christians—at least here in America and Western Europe have been "tamed"—i.e., nominalized, neutralized, marginalized, and dismissed.

As we shall see in the coming chapters, this taming accounts for the massive and recent secularization of society. And the chief reason behind this travesty, in this author's opinion, is because the central teaching of Jesus is no longer the central teaching of his Church. Yes, we are paying a huge and dreadful price. For one, rapidly increasing numbers and a majority of our youth are feeling exasperated and are departing the Church in droves. We Christians need to face up to these facts and more while there is still time.

In our next chapter we'll look at more hard facts to solidify this current assessment of decline and reclamation need.

Positively speaking, get the kingdom of God straight and many other, vital, and interrelated realities of the Christian faith fall readily into place. Miss it, even slightly, and you're liable to be way off on many other aspects. That is how pivotal the kingdom of God is.

---

[80] Randy Alcorn, *If God Is Good* (Colorado Springs, CO.: Multnomah Books, 2009), 35.

Chapter 2

Are We Christians Losing America?[1]

History fails to record a single precedent in which nations subject to moral decay have not passed into political and economic decline.

There has been either a spiritual awakening to overcome the moral lapse, or a progressive deterioration leading to ultimate national disaster.[2]

General Douglas MacArthur

Make no mistake; the America you and I grew up in and have known is being fundamentally reshaped. Many voices from many corners in the body of Christ (the Church) concur and are sounding the trumpet calls of alarm and warning.

Progressively, during the past 75 years or so, America has driven God and biblical values, principles, and morals out of its schools, universities, government, courts, businesses, culture, families, and the

---

[1] Some of the material in this section was originally published as an article by yours truly in Movieguide magazine and website (Sept. 2007). It was titled: "Why Are Christians Losing America?" This question was also the front cover headline in WorldNetDaily's *Whistleblower* magazine, April 2005 (*WB*).

[2] General Douglas MacArthur, quoted in Harry R. Jackson & Tony Perkins, *Personal Faith Public Policy* (Lake Mary, FL.: FrontLine, 2008), 220.

general public square.[3] Rabbi Cahn in his bestselling book *The Harbinger* terms this reshaping "a nation's apostasy" that is a "severing of its connection to God and to the biblical foundation on which it was established."[4]

The Penultimate Question

Can one lose something one never had? In other words, was America ever a "Christian nation?" The answer depends on whom you ask and how they define this expression. But if America never was a "Christian nation," then the Christian Right's exhortation to "reclaim" or "take America back for Christ" would not make any sense.

Even evangelicals are divided on this issue. Recent surveys show that 60% of evangelicals believe that America was once a Christian Nation. Ten percent say America never was and 30% are uncertain.[5] Surveyor Christian Smith believes: "America was once what we might call a Christian nation in some important ways. [But] Much of that has eroded in the twentieth century. As a result America has lost its moral bearings, which in turn has produced a significant, harmful social breakdown."[6]

A Presbyterian pastor with whom I personally discussed this notion demanded to know "when in the world was America ever a kingdom-oriented culture, or a Christian nation?" He then exclaimed: "I find such an idea historically absurd. Would blacks have said that our government was 'kingdom-oriented' in the first two-thirds of the 20th century . . . let alone the previous 300 years? I agree with the church historians who find

---

[3] The exact start is hard to pinpoint. Jim Nelson Black feels "the 1920s is a good rough estimate. The real atrophy, however, began in the 1960s and has been gathering momentum for the past thirty years" [now over 55 years]. Jim Nelson Black, *When Nations Die* (Wheaton, IL.: Tyndale House Publishers, 1994, 208-209.

[4] Jonathan Cahn, *The Harbinger: The Ancient Mystery That Holds the Secret of America's Future* (Lake Mary, FL.: FrontLine, 2011), 189-190.

[5] Christian Smith, *Christian America? What Evangelicals Really Want* (Berkeley, CA.: University of California Press, 2000), 22-25.

[6] Ibid., 52-53.

it difficult, if not impossible, to identify a single 'Christian culture' that has emerged for longer than a few weeks in the past 2,000 years." Next, he challenged me with this question: "Where in the teaching of Jesus, in the experience of the early Church, or in a single verse in the New Testament are we commanded or even remotely encouraged to 'take back the culture?' There is no such teaching," he insisted.[7]

On the other hand, others adamantly maintain that America was not founded on Christian principles but on Enlightenment ones. Admittedly, this contention is a half-truth. *Christianity Today* takes this dualistic position and explains it thusly: "The founding was a unique combination of biblical teaching and Enlightenment rationalism" and "most of the founding fathers . . . were not orthodox Christians, but instead were primarily products of the Enlightenment." But they also issue this disclaimer: "The Enlightenment, we should recall, has never been much of a friend of biblical Christianity."[8]

Richard Land agrees and elaborates that "the genius" for forming America "as a nation was an attempt to combine Judeo-Christian values, in a very traditional sense, with Enlightenment ideas of self-government. . . . it worked only because you had both."[9]

Another factor so argued is that "there is an abundance of historical evidence that our forefathers were not all evangelical Christians and they did not set out to create a Christian nation, let alone a democracy ruled exclusively by 'righteous' men."[10] Rather, America was founded on the principle of allowing its citizens to worship freely, Christianity or otherwise, or not at all.

In this vein, Charles Haynes, a senior scholar at the First Amendment Center, states that the Constitution "clearly established a secular nation where people of all faiths or no faith are protected to practice their religion or no religion without government interference."[11]

---

[7] Comments to me over a lunch and follow-up email exchange on this topic with the senior pastor of a large and local Presbyterian church, January, 29, 2005.

[8] "Worship as Higher Politics," *Christianity Today*, July 2005, 22.

[9] Quoted in Marvin Olasky, "God & country," *World*, April 21, 2007, 31.

[10] Mel White, *Religion Gone Bad: Hidden Dangers of the Christian Right* (New York, NY.: Jeremy P. Tarcher / Penguin, 2006), 261.

[11] Quoted in Andrea Stone, "Most think Constitution is Christian," *The Indianapolis Star*, 912/07, A3.

The capstone for this never-was argument is: America has never acted or looked like Christ (taking land from the native Indians and slavery are often cited), along with the inability "to identify a point in the history of America where we can say that America was a Christian nation from a strictly spiritual perspective."[12]

But many in the Christian Right disagree. They contend that America was indeed founded on the Bible as a Christian nation to honor God and the Lord Jesus Christ. And the majority of Americans still hold this view. Furthermore, they believe that America prospered under God's blessings but is now suffering major social breakdowns and other besetting problems due to its recent and rapid removal of God from many institutions and abandonment of our founding values and principles. They insist that unless our country repents and returns to God and these values and principles, America will suffer God's judgment, if it isn't doing so already.

What is difficult to ignore, deny, or prove false, however, is America's godly heritage and numerous indications of the influence of faith-based, Christian/biblical values and principles—although, for some, these appear vague and difficult to pin down. Yet founding and later documents, such as *The Federalist Papers*, provide clear and substantial evidence that this nation was founded under God, upon his direction, by his leading, and according to Judeo-Christian standards.

To bolster this position, David Barton documents and details that "all three federal branches of government have described America as a Christian nation. . . . It means . . . we are a nation whose culture, institutions and society, were shaped by the influences of Christianity."[13] In further support Christian Overman states that this is why "Christianity was freely and openly mixed with civil affairs in this nation for 160 years—from 1787, when the Constitution was first formed, until 1947, when the Supreme Court first suggested otherwise."[14]

Below is a sample of the abundance of historical evidence cited in support of America's founding as a Christian nation:

---

[12] Jackson & Perkins, *Personal Faith Public Policy*, 15.

[13] David Barton quoted by Gary Scharrer, "Religious beliefs of founders debated," *San Antonio Express-News*, 9/27/09, 1B, 7B.

[14] Christian Overman, *Assumptions that Affect Our Lives* (Bellevue, WA.: Ablaze Publishing Co., 2006, 124.

- America's birth certificate, the Declaration of Independence (1776), clearly affirms that our rights and privileges in this country are rooted in and flow from the hand of the Creator—that we are "endowed by our Creator with certain unalienable rights." Our Founding Fathers believed that human governments could not convey rights. That's God's jurisdiction. Government's responsibility is to protect those rights.

- "Congress set aside December 18, 1777 as a day of thanksgiving so the American people 'may express the grateful feelings of their hearts and consecrate themselves to the service of their divine benefactor' and on which they might 'join the penitent confession of their manifold sins . . . that it may please God, through the merits of Jesus Christ, mercifully to forgive and blot them out of remembrance.' Congress also recommended that Americans petition God 'to prosper the means of religion for the promotion and enlargement of that kingdom which consists in righteousness, peace and joy in the Holy Ghost.'"[15]

- On numerous occasions, the U.S. Supreme Court has declared "this is a Christian nation:"

  ✓ In 1844 in *Vidal v. Girard's Executors*, the justices wrote America is "a Christian country."
  ✓ In 1892 in *Church of the Holy Trinity Decision v. the United States*, after it examined thousands of founding documents, every state constitution, and all of the compacts that led up to 1776, the Court finally concluded that "this is a religious people . . . . this is a Christian nation."[16]
  ✓ John Jay, the original chief justice of the U.S. Supreme Court and one of the men most responsible for the Constitution wrote: "Providence has given to our people the choice of their rulers,

---

[15] Gary DeMar, "Distorting the Historical Record," *Biblical Worldview*, March / April 2008, 11. From "A copy of the original document can be viewed at www.loc.gov/exhibits/religion/vc006494. jpg. The proclamation can also be seen in Gary DeMar, *America's Christian History* (Powder Springs, GA.: American Vision, 2005), 252.

[16] Church of the Holy Trinity v. the United States; 143 U.S. 457, 471 (1892).

and it is the duty—as well as the privilege and interest—of our Christian nation to select and prefer Christians for their rulers."[17]

✓ "In countless cases during the first 140 years of our nation, the judiciary reaffirmed our country's Christian foundation and encouraged government's support of the Christian faith."[18]

• Woodrow Wilson said so in a speech given on May 7, 1911 – "America was born a Christian nation."[19]

• For a lengthy documentation "affirming the rich spiritual and religious history of our Nation's founding and subsequent history . . . for the appreciation of and education on America's history of religious faith," check out "110th Congress 1st Session House Resolution 888" (December 18, 2007).[20]

<u>Scholarly Insights—Pro and Con</u>

Christian Overman – "'Christian nation' . . . . The phrase itself is a misnomer in the sense that a country can never be 'Christian.' Only individual people within nations can be Christian. . . . But what the 1892 Court did clearly say was, our laws and institutions 'must necessarily be based upon and embody the teachings of The Redeemer of mankind . . . and in this sense and to this extent our civilization and our institutions are emphatically Christian.' To say that our culture is emphatically Christian today would be blasphemy. Our revised laws are no longer based upon the teachings of Jesus, as it was once said by the Supreme Court they should be. But the point . . . is simply this: it was once thought they should be."[21]

[Author Note: a redeemed nation would have to have virtually every citizen born-again and its societal institutions, government, etc. reflecting

---

[17] John Jay, *The Correspondence and Public Papers of John Jay, 1794—1826*, Henry P. Johnson, ed., vol. 4 (Reprinted NY: Bur Franklin, 1970), 393.

[18] Robert Jeffress, *Hell? Yes!* (Colorado Springs, CO.: Waterbrook Press, 2004), 177.

[19] Woodrow Wilson, *The Papers of Woodrow Wilson*, Vol. 23, (Princeton University Press, 1977), 20.

[20] http://forbes.house.gov/uploadedfiles/hres888_final%20footnoted%20version.pdf, 6/18/15.

[21] Overman, *Assumptions That Affect Our Lives*, 130.

Christian principles and values. This was never the case at any time in America's history.]

"The very basis of law in early America was openly founded upon the Bible, as seen in the Commentaries of William Blackstone, an English jurist who greatly influenced the colonists. He wrote from the assumption that God is the source of all authority . . . . His commentaries . . . . which for many years was the standard text for lawyers trained in early America."[22]

[Author Note: All law is based upon some standard or interpretation of what is right and wrong.]

Rousas John Rushdoony – "The United States was *assumed* to be a Christian nation by courts and people up to World War I, but, since the state schools taught humanism, explicitly or implicitly, after World War II humanism began to dominate the courts and to *outlaw* Christianity. The extent to which Christianity has been outlawed is by no means as yet total, but the direction is clearly towards a total outlawing of Christianity as incompatible with democracy. . . . pure humanism and total democracy are not compatible with a faith so divisive as Christianity with its heaven and hell, the saved and the lost, and good and evil."[23]

Mel White – "It is very important for each of us to make it clear to our fundamentalist friends and neighbors that this is NOT a Christian nation. . . . There is ample evidence to support the fact that this is not nor was it intended to be a Christian nation. The only mention of God in those early documents upon which our government is based is in the Declaration of Independence, in which God is simply 'nature's God,' not defined in any way by the Bible or the Christian faith. There is no further mention of God, let alone Jesus, in the Declaration, the U.S. Constitution, or the Federalist Papers . . . . The cross, the primary sign of the Christian faith, was not included in our flag, on our coins, or in any other national symbol."[24]

[Author Note: The counter argument for the reason the federal documents aren't more religious is because the States reserved for themselves the right to mandate state churches and religious laws.]

---

[22] Ibid., 129.

[23] Rushdoony, *Law and* Society, 114.

[24] White, *Religion Gone Bad*, 260-261.

Bill O'Reilly – "The revisionist secular-progressive historians run around claiming the Founding Fathers were not at all influenced by Judeo-Christian philosophy, that their intent was to create a country where spirituality was a private matter. That is absolute nonsense, pure and simple. Just read the words of the Declaration of Independence and you'll see that the revisionists are lying."[25]

Brandon Howse – "The Founders warned us repeatedly that we could not expect God's blessings or protection—and could very well face His wrath—if we ever make a practice of violating His principles."[26] For example, Benjamin Rush, "to whom the Founders looked for wisdom regarding the passing of laws that contradict the laws of God" stated: "Upon these two foundations, the law of nature and the law of revelation [the law of nature's God], depend all human laws; that is to say, no human laws should be suffered to contradict these."[27]

Howse asserts that "the deliberate use by our forefathers of the Ten Commandments as the foundation of America's legal system and constitutional republic is further evidence that they never intended to create a secular nation or government. And they did not intend the First Amendment to be used as a tool to eradicate a religious foundation and religious expression and practices from American government."[28]

Rather, "U.S. Supreme Court Justice Joseph Story explained succinctly the actual meaning of the First Amendment: 'The whole power over the subject of religion is left exclusively to the State governments to be acted upon according to their own sense of justice and the State constitutions.' The intent of the Founders was never to restrict religion. They were clearly concerned about the government's potential to interfere with religious freedoms . . . ."[29]

David Barton – "The fact that the Founders quoted the Bible more frequently than any other source . . . in their political writings . . . is

---

[25] Bill O'Reilly, *Culture Warrior* (New York, NY.: Broadway Books, 2006), 200.

[26] Brandon Howse, *One Nation Under Man* (Nashville, TN.: Broadman & Holman Publishers, 2005), 31.

[27] Ibid., 32. From William Blackstone, *Commentaries on the Laws of England,* vol. 1 (Philadelphia: Robert Bell, 1771), 42.

[28] Ibid., 44.

[29] Ibid., 47. Quote from: Joseph Story, *Commentaries on the Constitution of the United States,* 3rd ed. (Boston, 1858), 731

indisputably a significant commentary on its importance in the foundation of our government,"[30]

Billy Graham – Offers this response to a reader's comment "I thought America was a Christian nation:"

> Since its beginning, America has been deeply influenced by the Judeo-Christian tradition and by the teachings of the Bible. . . . Our legal system was largely built on the Bible's teaching about right and wrong, and our forefathers took seriously its statement that 'Blessed is the nation whose God is the Lord' (Psalm 33:12). At the same time, not every citizen at the beginning of our nation was a committed Christian, nor are they today. In fact, some today even want to banish all mention of God from public life – something our nation's founders never intended. . . . let us pray that this will never happen . . . .[31]

Tim Ewing – Provides perhaps the best explanation of what is meant by the often-used phrase "a Christian Nation." It is "one whose laws, public policy, and form of government, are rooted in Biblical Christian principles." Yes, the evidence for this reality is abundant. Those who would deny it are demonstrating either their ignorance of the historical founding facts or their bias against them." Ewing then amplifies his position by claiming that "the notion that you 'can't legislate morality' is false; the truth is *all* laws reflect, codify, or uphold a moral code."[32]

What May We Reasonably Conclude?

This debate may never be fully resolvable. Why not? Because, as we have seen, the crux issue centers on how one defines what is or is not a "Christian nation." And yet ample historical evidence exists that America was founded upon Judeo-Christian principles and a professed faith in a Creator Who works and governs in the affairs of nations and people, Who has established absolute standards to which all are accountable, and

---

[30] David Barton, *Original Intent* (Aledo, TX.: WallBuilder Press, 1996), 225-226.

[31] Billy Graham, "My Answer," *The Indianapolis Star*, 7/4/05, E2.

[32] Tim Ewing, "Why Was America Founded as A Christian Nation? (Part 1), *Biblical Worldview*, February, 2007, 10.

Who holds that all persons are fallen creatures and cannot be their own lawgiver or judge. (See the Declaration of Independence – which also could have been subtitled "A Declaration of Dependence").

Hence, today it has become politically incorrect to claim America was founded as a Christian nation or even upon Judeo-Christian values and principles. But these following four realities are not contestable:

1. America was not founded on any other religion or on secular humanism.

2. America was more Christian a few decades ago.

3. Christianity has been and is under assault and its influence is waning rapidly as some in our nation seek to erase our country's Christian heritage and replace it with a godless one.

4. We Christians are responsible for this cultural deterioration and potential demise as our country becomes progressively more non- and anti-Christian. Most of this change has happened on our watch. Moreover, God may already be removing his blessings and protective hand from our country. Many think so. Thus, America's moral tailspin and rapidly accelerating decline are becoming more and more evident. Bigger upheavals, hardships, persecutions, and judgments from God may be ahead if this trend is not stopped and reversed.

A 20-Year Compilation of Decay and Decline

Much has changed in America over the past 20 years. Below is a selected compilation of events, warnings, predicaments, predictions, and testimonies that graphically exemplify and characterize this accelerating deterioration (1997 – 2016).

Caution: This 20-year compilation includes points of view from people representing a wide range in the theological/ideological spectrum. If you do not value someone included herein, please skip his/her opinion and move on to the next one. But all are voicing a rather unanimous observation. Therefore, see if you think we are progressing or regressing as a nation, are better or worse off, and if we Christians are or are not in the process of losing America. Or, is all of this a naively enmeshed conspiracy theory that is much to do about nothing? I shall let you decide.

In 1997—Tony Evans captures America's current situation:

Let me put the problem to you in the form of a question. How can we have all these churches on all these street corners, filled with all these members, led by all these preachers, elders, and deacons . . . and yet still have all this mess in America? Something is wrong somewhere!

But when we turn the education of our children over to the state, and the state removes biblical ethics from its curriculum, what you get is the mess we have now."[33]

This is what is happening in America today. The glory of the Lord is on its way out . . . ."[34]

In 2000—This comparative speech by Rev. Laurence White airs twice on James Dobson's Focus on the Family radio program. It was titled, *For Such a Time as This*.[35] Dobson introduced it by calling it "a powerful message . . . it moved me very deeply." In dramatic fashion, White pondered if we Americans are repeating the mistakes of the Church in Nazi Germany. Below is an excerpt (bold emphasis mine):

The Christians in Germany learned only too late that the people of God in Christ cannot disengage from the culture in which they live. We cannot withdraw to the comfortable security of our beautiful sanctuaries and sit in our padded pews while the world all around us goes to hell. For to do so is a betrayal of the Lord whose name we bear and is a denial of the power and efficacy of his Word, the Word that He has given us to proclaim.

In Germany, as here in the United States, one of the most clever tools in the enemy's arsenal used to silence and intimidate Christians, to drive them out of the public square was the lie of the separation of Church and State. . . .

So Hitler called together the most important preachers in the land . . . . to reassure them, and intimidate them, if he could, to silence their criticism so he could go on with his plans for the country . . . . He told

---

[33] Tony Evans, *What a Way to Live!* (Nashville, TN.: Word Publishing, 1997), 294, 76.

[34] Ibid., 251.

[35] Laurence White, *For Such a Time as This*, (Colorado Springs, CO.: Focus on the Family, BR292/22119, 1998, 1999), audio cassette, side 1 (an excerpted transcription).

them their state subsidies would continue, their tax exemptions were secure, that the church had nothing to fear from a Nazi government.

And finally, one brash young preacher who was there . . . had had enough. He was going to tell the truth even if that truth was not popular. And he pushed his way to the front of the room until he stood eye to eye with the German dictator. And he said, "Herr Hitler, our concern is not for the Church. Jesus Christ will take care of his Church. Our concern is for the soul of our nation." It was immediately evident that the brash young preacher spoke only for himself, as a chagrined silence fell over that room and his colleagues hustled him away from the front.

Hitler with a natural politician's instinct saw that reaction and he understood exactly what it meant. And he smiled as he said to himself almost reflectively: **"The soul of Germany, you can leave that to me." And they did.**

In 2002—R.C. Sproul on the heels of 9/11 reflects:

Since the September 11 attacks on the United States, there has been much public discussion about the role of God in our lives, and we have seen an unprecedented response of the American people in prayer and public worship. Suddenly, the God who had been exiled from the public square, who had been banished to the other side of the wall that separates church and state, was called upon to get back into the game. It became fashionable for the nation to stage religious rallies featuring film stars, politicians, and clerics. Televised worship services called upon the nation to put aside theological differences and come together in a show of religious unity. . . . Instantly we saw all spheres of American culture rushing to call upon God."[36]

But "after 9/11 there was no genuine repentance or turning back to God and His ways. And before long churches were back to pre 9/11 levels and most everyone was back to business as usual."[37]

---

[36] R.C. Sproul, *When Worlds Collide* (Wheaton, IL.: Crossway Books, 2002), 12.
[37] Darrel & Cindy DeVille, *God's Answer for America* (Lake Mary, FL.: Creation House, 2015), 73.

In 2003—U.S. Supreme Court lays down the legal groundwork for gay marriage. In a sodomy case the court follows up its 1996 decision, which provided the legal foundation for gay marriage by striking down a Texas law making sodomy a crime, with a similar decision.

In 2003—Chuck Colson warns that in "several children's books . . . . our children are consuming a dumbed-down version of Christian history. They're taught that the Pilgrims risked their lives traversing the ocean for economic gains, not religious freedom. And that first Thanksgiving feast? It's described as nothing more than a three-day binge with the Indians. . . . And when it comes to Thanksgiving itself . . . . [one] author states flat-out, 'This was not a day of Pilgrim thanksgiving' – thanksgiving to God . . . . 'This was pure celebration.' Odd. That's not the way the Pilgrims themselves remembered it." Colson then cites this "account by William Bradford, who was actually there: 'The Lord sent them such seasonable showers,' that 'through His blessings [there was] a fruitful and liberal harvest. . . . For which mercy . . . they set apart a day of thanksgiving.'" Colson poignantly asks: "Why aren't we hearing this side of the Thanksgiving story?" He answers because "it has become a fun game for secularists to deride Christians as poor, ignorant, and easily led."[38]

In 2004—Fox News' controversial talk-show host Bill O'Reilly asks:

> What kind of a country do you want? Denmark—where pretty much any conduct is acceptable? Do you want gay marriage? Do you want legalized drugs? Do you want vile entertainment mainstreamed by powerful media companies? Do you want your kids taught about all kinds of sexual activity in the 2nd grade? Well, those things may well happen in America and soon, because the forces that want them are well-financed, well-organized, and extremely aggressive. All the things the traditionalists are not. . . .[39]

---

[38] Chuck Colson, "Putting the Thanks Back into Thanksgiving," originally published November 27, 2003, cited on: www.colsoncenter.org/the center/columns/colson-files/13407-putting-the-thanks-bac. . ., 11/9/2009.

[39] A transcription of Bill O'Reilly's memo on Fox News' "The O'Reilly Factor" (aired March 4, 2004).

In 2004—*Fox News'* Bill O'Reilly hits hard on this topic: "War on Christianity."

> The harsh truth is that many American Christians don't care about what is happening . . . . we are rapidly losing freedom in America. Judges are overruling the will of the people and fascist organizations like the ACLU are imposing their secular will. And, when was the last time you heard a priest, minister, or rabbi talk about this? For me, the answer is simple. . . . Never![40]

In 2004—Robert Jeffress sounds this alarm: "Our society suddenly seems totally out of control. . . . And the church seems to be standing by powerlessly. It's time again for Christians to act in righteousness, truth, and compassion. . . . before it's too late. . . . no society can afford to condone what God has condemned . . . ."[41]

In 2004—"THE SUPREME COURT, in declaring all sodomy laws unconstitutional, has in effect DECLARED THE NATION PAGAN."[42]

In 2005—Gene Edward Veith reports:

> A Federal Court has ruled that the Indiana House of Representatives may not open with any kind of prayer that mentions "Christ's name or title." This ruling is far more significant than banning the Ten Commandments in courthouses or taking "under God" out of the Pledge of Allegiance. What the Indiana decision does is to outlaw Christian prayer in the civic arena. And, if it stands, it will mean that no Christian clergyman or layperson can in good conscience pray at public events. . . . That is not religious tolerance; it is religious intolerance. It does not promote religious diversity; it eliminates religious diversity. And when a federal court tells people who they can and cannot pray to and how they are allowed to pray, what we have is state-sponsored religion."[43]

---

[40] Bill O'Reilly, "War on Christianity" on "Talking Points," June 2, 2004.
[41] Jeffress, *Hell? Yes!*, inside front leaf, 2.
[42] "The Christian Future of America: Two Views," *Christianity Today*, August 2004, 41.
[43] Gene Edward Veith, "Rock of offense," *World*, December 17, 2005, 28.

In 2005—*Whistleblower* magazine's April front-cover headline ponders: "Why Are Christians Losing America?" Inside it informs its readers that (**bold emphasis mine**):

- "Four out of five Americans describe themselves as Christians.
- "45% of us attend worship services on any given weekend.
- "The popularity of Mel Gibson's *The Passion of the Christ* and Rick Warren's book, *The Purpose-Driven Life.*
- "America appears to be bursting its seams with vibrant Christianity."

And yet . . . "America's popular culture, its laws, public education system, news media, entertainment industry, and other major institutions have become progressively *un*-Christian – even *anti*-Christian. . . ."

"On the 4th of July we sang 'God Bless America,' while much of America is doing everything it can to sabotage that."

The reason Christians are losing America is . . . . "Christians have been seduced . . . hoodwinked . . . sold a bill of goods . . . are operating under a misguided and simplistic interpretation of scripture . . . . Christianity – the deepest, most meaningful and awe-inspiring religion ever – has been ***dumbed down*** . . . . The churches remain the last, best hope Americans have for bringing about a rebirth of Western Judeo-Christian culture."[44]

In 2007—Brandon Vallorani writes: "The enemies of Christ are relentless in their mission to remove everything that's Christian from this nation. Government schools are brainwashing our children to become secular humanists. Of the small percentage of children that survive public education, many see their faith shipwrecked on the shores of liberal college campuses. Worse, yet, churches are either paralyzed by an obsession with the 'end times' or just too busy with 'programs' to do anything about it."[45]

---

[44] All quotations above are from several articles in WorldNetDaily's *Whistleblower* magazine, April 2005 (*WB*).
[45] Brandon Vallorani, "American Visions Opens New Distribution Facility," *Biblical Worldview*, October/November 2007, 12.

In 2007—Gary DeMar announces: "The New Atheists are the new radical warriors. They want to use the force of law to impose their atheistic worldview on the rest of us. Our children and our nation are in jeopardy. . . . If children are to be taught anything about God, these atheists contend, it's that He's a myth. Their proposal is that children should not be schooled in any faith, except, of course, the faith that claims there is no god."[46]

In 2008—Indiana State Representative, Cindy Noe (my wife) declares: "We are in the 'last days' of the golden age of America, because our institutions and our culture have taken on a secular-humanist, post-modern worldview. We cannot sustain our form of government and society and are on our way to anarchy unless our churches and Christians rise up and do something significant."

In 2009—Newt Gingrich relays these deterioration tidbits: "In 1934 a group of veterans erected a cross in the Mojave desert of California to honor their fellow veterans who had died in combat. Now, in 2009, the extreme liberal ACLU says the Mojave Cross must be torn down because it is 'too offensive.' . . . The ACLU has proven that they'll stop at nothing to try to ban all public religious expressions in our country:

     ** The ACLU has sued to prevent school children from reciting the Pledge of Allegiance.
     ** The ACLU has sued to remove our national motto, 'In God We Trust' from our currency.
     ** The ACLU has targeted the Boy Scouts for destruction because they're offended by the Scout's embrace of traditional values."[47]

In 2009—Ken Ham, in his hauntingly titled book, *Already Gone*, dramatically illustrates the reality of the tragic exodus of young people from the Church: "I dare you to try it this Sunday. Look to the right, and look to the left. . . . Look at the children and look at the teens

---

[46] Gary DeMar, "Atheism's Annual Revival Meeting," *Biblical Worldview*, December 2007, 3.
[47] Newt Gingrich, "Pledge of Support," letter, received 10/13/09, pp. 1-2. Also, reported by Edward Lee Pitts, "Rugged Cross," *World*, 24 October, 2009, 9.

around you. Many of them will be familiar faces. . . . imagine that two-thirds of them have just disappeared from your church. . . . Why? Because they are *already gone.* . . . The numbers are in . . . . A *mass exodus is underway. Most youth of today will not be coming to church tomorrow.* Nationwide polls and denominational reports are showing that the next generation is calling it quits on the traditional church."[48]

- If we don't change this exodus trend "we are less than one generation away from being a nation of hollow, empty, churches"—like post-Christian England and much of Western Europe.
- "The church is sick and it needs to be told the truth."
- Churches are "driven by denominational and congregational expectations rather than Scripture."
- He calls for a "vibrant new vision for unleashing God's Word."[49]

In 2009—R. J. Rushdoony emphasizes this point: "because they call such evil as abortion, homosexuality, and euthanasia, good, and good evil . . . . As a result, we are in a cultural revolution. . . . [But] the culture of humanism is thus a doomed one. . . . Humanism all around us is consuming the Christian capital of the Western world and is descending rapidly into disaster and death. . . . Rome fell because it was dead within . . . . This should not surprise us: In a world at war with our Lord."[50]

In 2009—Billy Graham in answer to a reader's question: "Why do you think there is so much violence in our communities today . . . . in our schools . . . . [Is it] because of all the violence that kids see on TV? [Or is it] something deeper? Dr. Graham responds: "our children are assaulted by images of violence that would have shocked previous generations. . . . this is a recipe for disaster. [But] there is a larger problem today . . . . We have lost sight of the meaning of right and wrong. . . . we have forgotten God. When we ignore him and his will for our lives, we end up in chaos and destruction."[51]

---

[48] Ken Ham & Britt Beemer, *Already Gone* (Green Forest, AR.: Master Books, 2009), 21-22.
[49] Ibid., 79, 109-110, 155, 157, 158.
[50] R.J. Rushdoony, *In His Service* (Vallecito, CA.: Ross House Books, 2009), 10-12.
[51] Bill Graham, "My Answer," *The Indianapolis Star,* 10/32/09, C-11.

In 2009—Darrell Scott, the father of Rachel Scott, a victim of the Columbine High School shootings in Littleton, Colorado, on April 20, 1999, addresses the House Judiciary Committee's subcommittee. Here is an excerpt of what he said to our national leaders:

> I am here today to declare that Columbine was not just a tragedy -- it was a spiritual event that should be forcing us to look at where the real blame lies! Much of the blame lies here in this room. . . . I wrote a poem just four nights ago that expresses my feelings best.

> Your laws ignore our deepest needs,
> Your words are empty air.
> You've stripped away our heritage,
> You've outlawed simple prayer.
> Now gunshots fill our classrooms,
> And precious children die.
> You seek for answers everywhere,
> And ask the question "Why?"
> You regulate restrictive laws,
> Through legislative creed.
> And yet you fail to understand,
> That God is what we need![52]

In 2010—Leslie Leyland Fields highlights this daunting statistic:

> The exodus of young adults from evangelical churches in the U.S. is well reported . . . . The Barna Group reported in 2006 that 61 percent of young adults who had attended church as teenagers were now spiritually disengaged, not participating in worship or spiritual disciplines. A year later, LifeWay Research released similar findings, that seven in ten Protestants ages 18 – 30 who had worshiped regularly in high school stopped attending church by age 23.[53]

---

[52] In a forwarded email, subject: "Columbine High School, 5/1/09.
[53] Leslie Leyland Fields, "The Myth of the Perfect Parent," *Christianity Today*, January 2010, 24.

In 2010—This statement was purportedly read over the PA system at the football game at Roane County High School, Kingston, Tennessee, by school Principal Jody McLeod:

It has always been the custom at . . . High School football games, to say a prayer and play the National Anthem, to honor God and Country.

Due to a recent ruling by the Supreme Court . . . saying a prayer is a violation of Federal Case Law. As I understand the law at this time, I can use this public facility to approve of sexual perversion and call it "an alternative life style," and if someone is offended, that's OK.

I can use it to condone sexual promiscuity, by dispensing condoms and calling it, "safe sex." If someone is offended, that's OK.

I can even use this public facility to present the merits of killing an unborn baby as a "viable means of birth control." If someone is offended, no problem . . .

I can designate a school day as "Earth Day" and involve students in activities to worship religiously and praise the goddess "Mother Earth" and call it "ecology . . ."

I can use literature, videos and presentations in the classroom that depict people with strong, traditional Christian convictions as "simple minded" and "ignorant" and call it "enlightenment . . . ."

However, if anyone uses this facility to honor GOD and to ask HIM to bless this event with safety and good sportsmanship, then Federal Case Law is violated. . . .

Nevertheless, as a school principal, I frequently ask staff and students to abide by rules with which they do not necessarily agree. For me to do otherwise would be inconsistent at best. For this reason, I shall "Render unto Caesar that which is Caesar's," and refrain from praying at this time. However, if you feel inspired to honor, praise, and thank GOD and ask HIM, in the name of JESUS, to bless this event, please feel free . . . . As far as I know, that's not against the law—yet.

One by one, the people in the stands bowed their heads, held hands with one another and began to pray. They prayed in the stands. . . .the team huddles. . . .the concession stands . . . in the Announcer's Box.[54]

In 2011—*The Harbinger* by Rabbi Jonathan Cahn lands on the *New York Times* best-seller list. It reveals "a prophetic warning to the American masses about God's impending judgment on the nation. . . . He is convinced that God is warning the nation to turn back to Him and

---

[54] Author not known. Emailed to me 9/11/2010.

uses nine harbingers, or prophetic signs, to shake us up and wake us up."[55]

In 2012—Steve Strang, publisher of *Charisma* magazine, writes and warns: "As the culture has become more hostile and most of the church has become more lukewarm . . . . a war is raging . . . and the other side believes 'anything goes.' The only thing holding back every form of sin from becoming culturally accepted are those who still believe in biblical values. . . . But as we've seen with changing opinions on drinking, gambling, easy divorce, abortion-on-demand and now so-called same-sex marriage, the laws are being changed as the culture slides toward decadence. We must act before it's too late. . . . It's war! . . So wake up. Things are bad in America. . . . It's time to stand up."[56]

In 2012—"Dear Billy Graham: If most of the people in our country are Christians, then why do we have so many problems? Aren't Christians supposed to make the world a better place? . . . Dear Reader: You are right about one thing: Christians are supposed to make a difference. They aren't supposed to withdraw and let evil advance unopposed."[57]

In 2013—Marcus Yoars comparatively notes how "God used America to spread the gospel to the world. Now we see many of its citizens shaking their fists in the face of Almighty God. Indeed, the spiritual and moral decline of this nation has reached an unprecedented low, as each month seems to usher in new evidence of our defiance against God. . . . 'No question, we're in a spiritual crisis,' says Franklin Graham . . . . 'We see it at the very top of our country, from the White House to Congress. We have turned our back on God as a nation. [We think] God's laws don't apply, and our government doesn't want God's standards.' . . . The

---

[55] Jennifer LeClaire, "Is the Next Move of God Beginning?" *Charisma* (May 2015): 33.
[56] Steve Strang, "The Pentecostal Change Our Nation Needs," *Charisma*, November 2013, 8.
[57] Billy Graham, "My Answer," *The Indianapolis Star*, IN., 1/17/12, E-4.

problem . . . is that most American Christians are as apathetic as unbelievers in actually doing something to change the nation's course."[58]

In 2013—R.R. Reno provides this scholarly perspective:

> Religious liberty is being redefined in America . . . . Our secular establishment wants to reduce the autonomy of religious institutions and limit the influence of faith in the public square. . . . today our secular culture views orthodox Christian churches as troublesome, retrograde, and reactionary forces. They're seen as anti-science, anti-gay, and anti-woman—which is to say anti-progress as the Left defines progress. . . . And there won't just be arguments; there will be laws as well. We're in the midst of climate change—one that's getting colder and colder toward religion."[59]

In 2013—Samuel Rodriguez, head of the National Hispanic Christian Leadership Conference exclaims: "As born-again Christians, we're always talking about the great ills that affect our society, but the number one problem is a lukewarm church . . . . That lukewarmness stems out of a lack of biblical engagement."[60]

In 2013—U.S. Supreme Court overturns DOMA. In a landmark 5-4 decision the court rendered null and void the Defense of Marriage Act (DOMA) signed by President Bill Clinton in 1996, which restricted the federal interpretation of marriage to being between a man and a woman. This new ruling guarantees that gay couples married in states where gay marriage is legal must receive the same federal health, tax, Social Security, and other benefits that heterosexual couples receive. This decision paves the way for state legislatures to pass laws legalizing gay marriage and soon for it to become the law across America.

In 2014—Rabbi Jonathan Cahn, author of *The Harbinger*, prophetically speaks out to members of Congress in the Capitol

---

[58] Marcus Yoars, "America Shall Be Saved!" *Charisma* (September 2013), 28-33.

[59] R.R. Reno, "Religion and Public Life," *Imprints: A Publication of Hillsdale College* (April 2013, Vol. 42, Number 4), 1-5.

[60] Reported by: Karla Dial, "Passion Play," *Citizen*, March 2013, 19.

Building re: George Washington's prophetic message to our nation at this first-ever presidential address on the day of his inauguration in New York City. Cahn asks this series of poignant questions:

> Can a nation drive out the name of God from its public squares and the word of God from its schools, and the ways of God from its culture and still expect the smiles of God to shine upon it?
>
> Can the blood of 50 million unborn children cry out to heaven from this land and the smiles of heaven still remain?
>
> Members of Congress, can a government call good evil and evil good and forge laws that war against the laws of the Almighty and the smiles of heaven still remain?
>
> Supreme Court justices, can you strike down the statutes of the Almighty and overturn the judgments of the Most High and still expect the smiles of heaven to remain?
>
> And Mr. President, can you place your left hand on the Word of God to assume your office and then with your right hand sign laws that break the very Word upon which you swore and still expect the smiles of heaven to remain?
>
> The voice of our first president cries out to us tonight and answers, "no, you cannot do so and still expect the smiles of heaven to remain upon this land." Kingdoms rise and kingdoms fall. America has risen by the hand of God. And without that hand it cannot endure. The voice of God cries out: "Return America and I will have mercy on you."[61]

In 2014—*Fox News'* Bill O'Reilly pontificates on: "Why America Is Changing So Drastically:"

> Everywhere I go folks ask me what has happened to their country. We have gone from a traditional country to a secular society where politically correct thought dominates, especially in the mass media. It is quite clear that the Founders based our justice system on Judeo-Christian tenets, which is why a sculpture of Moses holding the Ten Commandments adorns the Supreme Court building. But today you could never put Moses and the Commandments on a public wall anywhere; the secular progressives would scream. Enter Jesus, the most famous human being who has ever lived. If you're a child attending a

---

[61] Transcribed from a two-minute clip posted on video on YouTube, "The Mystery of the Shemitah with the author Rabbi Jonathan Cahn at Joshua Springs," 10/20/14; 1:11:00.

public school and living in a secular home, chances are you know little or nothing about Jesus because the schools are frightened to mention his name. . . . Here's the bigger picture: When you have a secular progressive society, behavior changes. Fewer judgments are made; more lenient criminal sentences are handed out; abortion and drug use become more acceptable. With a progressive president and a very left-leaning Democratic Party, you have an acceleration of secularism. The outcome is likely to be a much weaker nation with less discipline, less motivation, and less generosity because the secular position preaches that it's all about "me." So the next time you ask me where your country went, I'll tell you to read this Talking Points.[62]

In 2014—A Gallup poll shows that twice as many Americans in 2014 believe same-sex marriage should be legal than did in 1996. In 1996, 27 percent said same-sex marriage should be valid, and 68 percent said it shouldn't. In 2014, 55 percent said it should be valid, and 42 percent said it shouldn't.[63] And this shift is projected to continue going higher as America's demographics keep changing—the older, more conservative generations die off and the younger more liberal generations take their place. According to this poll nearly eight out of 10 people under age 30 affirm gay marriage. These trends are also being manifested in Republican and Democrat parties—61 percent of 18-29 age Republicans favor gay marriage; 77 percent of 18-29 age Democrats favor gay marriage.[64]

In 2015—David Barton and George Barna sound this alarm:

We live in a "New America" where the masses believe in unscriptural values and the church no longer has a voice in the culture. . . . Survey data makes it clear that the Church in America is being influenced by society more than it is influencing that society. This data also reveals that the moral and spiritual condition of America is in serious decline.

Seventy-seven percent of Americans say religion is losing its influence on American life.

---

[62] Bill O'Reilly, on "Talking Points," "The O'Reilly Factor," April 4, 2014.
[63] Justin McCarthy, "Same Sex Marriage Support Reaches New High at 55%: Nearly 8 in 10 young adults favor gay marriage," *Gallup Politics*, May 21, 2014.
[64] Jocelyn Kiley, "Most Young Republicans Favor Same-Sex Marriage," *Pew Research Center*, March 10, 2014.

Seventy-four percent of Americans argue that the state of moral values in the nation is getting worse.

Fifty-six percent of Americans believe that the Bible does not have enough influence on American society these days. . . .

The United States is now entering its own version of the Dark Ages. Other once-great nations walked the same path we are traversing today, only to discover it led to their demise. Of course, we have convinced ourselves that we are different . . . .[65]

In 2015—World Magazine Reports: "The Congressional Budget Office projects in 2030 Medicaid, Medicare, Social Security, and interest payments on the national debt will consume all federal revenue. . . . we can't simply put more people into a broken system that doesn't work."[66]

In 2015—Troy Anderson, Executive Editor of *Charisma* magazine terms our time as a "critical hour when many believe America is under God's progressive judgment" and "more people are awakening to the realization that the country must return to its biblical roots or face calamity." Next, he quotes these words from Rabbi Cahn to a recent crowd of 1,000:

America's apostasy from God has quickened. It's as if there is an unraveling in the world . . . . (The harbingers) have progressed and the sequence is that the nation is being warned that if it doesn't turn back to God . . . then the shakings will continue until the nation either comes back to God in revival or in total judgment.[67]

In 2015—*Charisma* Magazine recaps and reflects: "There's been an increasingly rapid decline in America's morality since prayer was removed from schools in 1962. Abortion was legalized in 1973. Massachusetts became the first state to legalize gay marriage in 2004. . . . God has lifted a measure of His hedge of protection around America. Christians are meeting with persecution in the marketplace, and anti-Christian agendas are working overtime to send America into a downward spiral of darkness. . . . No politician can fix the problems our

[65] David Barton & George Barna, "U-Turn: How the Church Can Save America," *Charisma* (February 2015), 29.
[66] J.C. Derrick, "Coverage vs. Care," *World* (May 16, 2015): 40.
[67] Troy Anderson, "Is an 'Appeal to Heaven' . . ." *Charisma*, May 2015, 6.

nation is facing. We need another Great Awakening. . . . He's [God] just waiting for us to get in line with His Spirit like our Founding Fathers did when they fought to establish one nation under God. . . . so many voices from so many camps in the body of Christ . . . . are essentially saying the same thing. America is a nation in crisis—and God wants to wake us up, bring us in line with His heart and heal our land."[68]

In 2015—Evangelist Rodney Howard-Browne: "Without divine intervention, what we call America will be gone within the next couple of years. It's that critical. . . . This is not a game. If we don't see a turn in the next two or three years, America as we know it will sink into the abyss and will be gone forever."[69]

In 2015—Rabbi Cahn laments:

> I take no joy in being the bearer of bad news. . . . While individual believers, churches and ministries may see success in ministry and many brought to salvation, the state of the church as a whole with regard to the culture that surrounds it is another matter altogether. . . . there has been a great apostasy. And that apostasy has deepened in its intensity, widened in its scope and accelerated in its speed. . . . And in the midst of the greatest moral and spiritual decay in modern times, the pulpits have largely grown silent . . . . And we wonder why the culture around us is going to hell. If the American church had been the salt and light it was called to be, there is no way that the culture could have grown so dark and rotting.[70]

In 2015—Signs of shaking are evident per Hubert Synn:

> America was founded as "one nation under God." God was morally and spiritually intertwined with our society with evidence of sincere faith woven into the Constitution, Pledge of Allegiance, and the national anthem. Scriptural mottos were displayed in government buildings and inscribed onto our currency. Sadly, our culture has steadily removed God as the anchor of this nation and the Bible as our standard for living. Christians are increasingly persecuted. The depth of moral and

---

[68] Jennifer LeClaire, "An Appeal to Heaven," *Charisma* (May 2015): 24, 30.
[69] ibid., in quotation of evangelist Rodney Howard-Browne.
[70] Cahn, "How America Can Avoid Calamity," 41.

spiritual division and decline in this country grieves my spirit. Today, America is a country, but no longer one, indivisible nation under God. . . . The signs of shaking [God's] are evident in both national and global current events. . . . America is almost at the breaking point where it cannot halt the slide of what is going to come. . . . the blessing of His hand over this nation enabled its rapid ascent to greatness, but the removal of His hand will result in a rapid decline into weakness. . . . Let's pray for a spiritual awakening, accompanied by repentance and humility.[71]

In 2015—Moody Bible Institute President announces:

Much like a person waking from a decades-long coma . . . evangelicals are just awakening to the reality that they have lost the culture war in this country. We are seeing the rapid deterioration and dismantling of a Judeo-Christian culture . . . and believers are finding themselves in unfamiliar positions. Values once held sacred are being discarded. Freedoms once offered are being withheld. Biblical absolutes once embraced are being replaced by relativism. Trend lines, unless altered, point to accelerated cultural change and even greater drift from the historic roots of this country. As a result, there is a growing intolerance towards believers and their message. Increasingly, followers of Jesus are being viewed as narrow, bigoted, and hateful. . . .[72]

In 2015—Christianity in Decline in America:

New statistics from the Pew Research Center's U.S. Religious Landscape Study show that "the percentage of adults (ages 18 and older) who describe themselves as Christians has dropped by nearly eight percentage points in just seven years, from 78.4% in . . . in 2007 to 70.6% in 2014. Over the same period, the percentage of Americans who are religiously unaffiliated – describing themselves as atheist,

---

[71] Hubert Synn, "The Signs of Shaking Are Evident" in "The Word of the Prophets," *Charisma* (May 2015): 54.

[72] Amazon.com description of Moody Bible Institute President J. Paul Nyquist's book tellingly titled: *Prepare: Living Your Faith in an Increasingly Hostile Culture*, (2015), 6/27/15.

agnostic or 'nothing in particular' – has jumped more than six points, from 16.1% to 22.8%.[73]

In 2015—62% in Ireland vote to legalize same-sex marriage:

Sadly, the tried and true tactics of bullying, intimidation, media bombardment, aggressive activism, and massive U.S. funding won another victory in Ireland for the gay revolution. . . . as this predominantly Catholic nation voted decisively to redefine marriage . . . . What can we learn . . .?
> 1) Traditional "Christian" religion cannot stop the juggernaut of gay activism. Only a living, vibrant faith will have the energy and commitment and depth to stand firm.
> 2) Sex-scandals in the Catholic Church in the 1990s robbed the Church of its moral authority. . . .
> 3) Ireland was not ready for the massive influx of gay activist funding from America. Sadly, from President Obama down, America has been an aggressive force for normalizing homosexuality, and without American funding and vision, it is doubtful that Ireland would have voted so strongly for such radical change. What happened in Ireland should be a wake-up call for the Church worldwide.[74]

In 2015—"Other countries poised to follow suit: Australia . . . . Germany . . . . Italy . . . . U.S. The Supreme Court will decide if gay-marriage bans are unconstitutional by July, following its 2013 decision to overturn the Defense of Marriage Act."[75]

In 2015—Same-Sex Marriage legalized throughout America. On June 26, five unelected, liberal, activist, and Harvard- and Yale-educated lawyers on the U.S Supreme Court in a landmark decision defy God and the Bible by finding a 14th Amendment right to redefine marriage and make same-sex marriage the law of the land, thus imposing it on all 50

---

[73] http://www.pewforum.org/2015/05/12/americas-changing-religious-landscape/, 5/25/15.

[74] Dr. Michael L. Brown, "What really happened in Ireland? You need to know," "One News Now," OneNewsNow.com, 5/27/15.

[75] "The Explainer," "Where Gay Marriage Might Become Legal Next," *Time,* June 8, 2015, 11.

states. This controversial ruling overturns bans in 14 states and the votes of over 50 million Americans.

But now that the battle against gay marriage has been lost in the courts, the fight is far from over. More is coming, claim LGBT equality and civil rights supporters. Consequently, Christians and conservatives now fear the loss of more religious freedom and freedom of speech, along with accompanying anti-discrimination persecutions and lawsuits and "hate crime" charges.

In 2015—Tony Perkins issues a foreboding warning:

In the last seven years we've witnessed our federal government's view of religious freedom go from indifference to outright hostility. This indifference is seen not only in the policies advanced by the Obama administration but even in the president's word choice. The president has largely avoided using the term religious freedom, choosing to instead use the phrase "freedom of worship," which falls woefully short of the recognized liberty in the First Amendment. The term 'freedom of worship' represents a narrow view of religious liberty that suggests that orthodox faith can be quarantined within the walls of a church or synagogue. . . . In fact, Democratic presidential candidate, Hillary Clinton, recently spoke of how religion is an impediment to abortion rights at the Women in the World Summit. "Laws have to be backed up with resources and political will," she asserted. "And deep-seated cultural codes, religious beliefs and structural biases have to be changed." . . . By whom, Mrs. Clinton? The federal government? It is this open hostility toward religious freedom from our own government that must change.[76]

In 2015—Planned Parenthood exposed: (July) In a shocking two-hour, 42-minute, undercover video, Dr. Deborah Nucatola, senior director of Medical Services for the Planned Parenthood Federation of America, sips wine and lunches on a salad as she discusses the marketplace's demand for intact livers, lungs, and brains harvested from aborted babies, describes her organization's illegal sales of these baby body parts, and explains in graphic detail how she fulfills these orders.

---

[76] Tony Perkins, "Why America's First Freedom Is in Jeopardy," *Charisma,* July 2015, 48, 50.

Convictions to the Contrary

Not everyone agrees with the above assessments, warnings, and predictions.

Perry Stone – "America is only one out of hundreds of nations or regions, and at times more positive spiritual results are happening outside the United States than within our boundaries. . . . So is there any hope left for America? . . . it would be easy to conclude that our nation has fallen so far from God that we've passed the point of no return. And yet in America God has always had a faithful remnant who would pray in soul-winning revivals and times of refreshing—yes, even during times when mainstream culture reveled in its defiance toward God."[77]

Restoring all Things: God's Audacious Plan to Change the World through Everyday People – "For all those convinced 'all is lost' for Christianity, I say, 'Read this book!' Stonestreet and Smith aim to restore some balance to the doom and gloom narrative by pointing us to the stories that prove that God is still at work today, through people who are addressing the brokenness and taking the opportunities right in front of their noses. Inspiring!"[78]

No matter how you slice it, a significant reversal away from our founding values and principles has happened in this country over the past 20, 60, or 75 years. So has secular humanism now surpassed Christianity as the consensus in America, as it has in Western Europe? What do you think the next two, six, 10, or 20 years will bring?

To Pledge or To Not Pledge?—That Is the Question

If it is true that America is fast becoming a nation that no longer desires to be "one nation under God" but rather "one nation under secular humanism" or "one nation divided by God" (take your pick) . . .

If it is true that rapidly growing numbers of Americans either want to forget God or are shaking their fists at Him . . .

---

[77] Perry Stone, "A Prophetic Code To America's Future," *Charisma* (February 2015), 36, 35.

[78] Eric Metaxes, endorsement of: Warren Cole Smith and John Stonestreet, *Restoring All Things* (Grand Rapids, Ml.: Baker Books, 2015), *i*.

If it is true that God has been expelled from most areas of public society, except for allowing Him to be cloistered in our churches . . .

If it is true that the secular humanists control the courts, schools, media, entertainment, etc. and are planning to remove every vestige of God from this great land and hijack our country. . .

Then, with all these God-expelling changes in America that we have witnessed over the past 20 years or so, can we committed Christians still make this pledge? Or are its words and meaning no longer valid or viable and needing to be changed, again?[79]

> I pledge allegiance to the Flag of the United States of America,
> and to the Republic for which it stands,
> one Nation under God, indivisible, with liberty and justice for all.

This question and issue was brought home to me in stark fashion in May 2014 when my wife, son, daughter, and I attended the graduation of one of our adopted grandchildren from a public high school in a small rural town in southeastern Indiana. After the Processional, everyone stood and recited the Pledge of Allegiance with its phrase "one nation under God." Immediately thereafter, we were asked to observe a "Moment of Silence" for no announced reason. It lasted about eight or ten seconds. During the rest of the graduation, there was no prayer and no mention of God at any time in the four student speeches or in comments made by the Principal and Superintendent of Schools. How telling, I thought. And if you think God doesn't notice these omissions, think again (see Heb. 4:13).

Perhaps we have already reached the point President Ronald Reagan once warned about: "If we ever forget that we are one nation under God, then we will be a nation gone under"[80]—notwithstanding our silent tribute to "In God We Trust" that still appears on our nation's currency and coins.

Likewise warned John Winthrop, first governor of Massachusetts:

---

[79] Originally composed in 1892. Adopted by Congress in 1942. The official name of *The Pledge of Allegiance* was adopted in 1945. The words "under God" were added in 1954.

[80] Michael Reagan, quoting his father, President Ronald Reagan, in Foreword for, Howse, *One Nation Under Man?*), *xiii*.

But if our hearts shall turn away so that we will not obey, but shall be seduced and worship other gods, our pleasures, and profits, and serve them . . . we shall surely perish out of the good Land whether we pass over this vast Sea to possess it. Therefore let us choose life, that we and our seed may live, by obeying His voice and cleaving to Him, for He is our life and our prosperity.[81]

Similarly warned Daniel Webster (1782-1852), a famous attorney and a leading political figure of the United States House and Senate, who served as Secretary of State for three presidents:

If we abide by the principles taught in the Bible, our country will go on prospering and to prosper . . . If we, and our [future generations], shall be true to the Christian religion, if we and they shall live always in the fear of God, and shall respect His Commandments. . . . we may have the highest hopes of the future fortunes of our country. . . . But if we and our [future generations] reject religious instruction and authority; violate the rules of eternal justice, trifle with the injunctions of morality, and recklessly destroy the political constitution which holds us together, no man can tell how sudden a catastrophe may overwhelm us and bury all our glory in profound obscurity.[82]

Seriously, if our increasingly secular country is no longer "one nation under God"—as many voices are increasingly pointing out—then why should we committed Christians continue pledging our allegiance? Please understand, it's painful for most of us to be experiencing these changes. And I'm not questioning our love for this country, paying taxes, or being a law-abiding citizen. But doesn't pledging allegiance to a God-defying, God-expelling, God-ignoring nation or entity of any type constitute what the Bible calls idolatry?

Of course, attempts have been made to remove the words "under God" from the Pledge of Allegiance. So far they have been unsuccessful.

---

[81] John Winthrop, "A Model of Christian Charity by Governor John Winthrop, 1630," *The Winthrop Society,*
http://www.winthropsociety.com/doc_chrarity.php (accessed February 3, 2015 – quoted in DeVille, *God's Answer for America*, 25.
[82] Daniel Webster, *The Writings and Speeches of Daniel Webster* (Boston, MA.: Little, Brown, & Company, 1903), quoted in DeVille, *God's Answer for America*, 23.

But for the secularists, this phrase is a theocratic-sounding slogan that, sooner or later, they will want removed. The reality of this phrase, however, may already have been stripped away.

Similarly, if you are a committed Christian and a citizen of another country—such as France, England, South Africa, Mexico, Canada, Israel, or Sweden, etc.—would you pledge your allegiance to it? Why shouldn't we committed Christians in whatever country we live honor the lordship of Jesus Christ over any national, social, cultural, or political loyalties and only pledge our ultimate devotion of allegiance to our Creator and his kingdom? Where am I wrong on this? In the Conclusion of this book, as I did in its Dedication, I shall propose a new pledge of allegiance for committed Christians in every nation.

. . . with all these God-expelling changes in America that we have witnessed over the past 20 years or so, can we committed Christians still make this pledge?

So, are we Christians losing America? Is God's judgment already upon us? Are we, perhaps, ensnared in our Second American Revolution and dancing "the dance of history" into decline and demise? Or am I naively enmeshed in a conspiracy theory regarding much ado about nothing? Let's explore this situation more fully in our next chapter.

Chapter 3

Welcome to the Second American Revolution

"Civilizations come and go (don't you know)
Dancing onto oblivion (oblivion)
The birth and death of nations is of civilizations
Can be viewed down the barrel of a gun!

Nobody knows who calls the tune (calls the tune)
It's been on the hit parade so many years (can't you hear)
You and I must join the chorus like ancestors before us
And like them we're going to disappear!

Chorus
You're all invited to The Empire Soiree
We'll see each other there just wait and see (wait and see)
Attendance is required at The Empire Soiree
We'll all dance the dance of history!" [1]

---

[1] Lyrics from the song "The Empire Soiree" from the hit musical, "Billy Bishop Goes to War." Music, lyrics, and script by John Gary, 1979. Produced by Tapestry Records and Tapes Ltd., 60 Yonge Street, Suite 200, Toronto, Ontario, Canada M5E 1H5. Distributed by / Distribué par: RCA Inc. (One of my favorite stage plays.)

The Dance of History

Four hundred years ago, our forefathers sailed to this country not only to escape religious persecution and establish a new civilization in the new world, but also to expand the Christian faith, advance the kingdom of God, and bring glory to God. In their own words, here are three of many examples . . . (**bold** emphasis mine):[2]

> **In the name of God**, Amen. We, whose names are underwritten, the loyal subjects of our dread Sovereign Lord King James, **by the Grace of God**, of Great Britain, France, and Ireland, King, defender of the Faith, etc. **Having undertaken, for the Glory of God, and advancements of the Christian faith . . . .** (Mayflower Compact of 1620, modern version)
>
> We all came to these parts of America, with one and the same end and aim, namely **to advance the Kingdom of our Lord Jesus Christ**. (New England Confederation of 1643)
>
> . . . for ye propagating & **advancing ye gospel of ye kingdom** of Christ in those remote parts of ye world (William Bradford, 1656).[3]

Please note that these founding pilgrims did not limit God's Word and Christ's work to personal salvation. Rather, they saw personal salvation as a gift from God and the starting point for advancing the kingdom, then and there, in their lives, in their society, and throughout the world. They also believed it was every Christian's duty and responsibility to positively impact their world and society according to kingdom values and principles. Consequently, blessings in this life and the next would accrue to them through their obedience or be lost through their disobedience. As we shall see later in this book, their optimistic and powerful version of Christianity was totally biblical.

A little over 100 years later, our forefathers danced the dance of history when they were forced to throw off the chains of British tyranny,

---

[2] For many more similar pronouncements, see David Barton, *The Myth of Separation* (Aledo, TX.: WallBuilder Press, 1992), 84-90.

[3] William Bradford, *History of Plymouth Plantation* (Boston, MA.: Little Brown, and Company, 1856), 24.

fight the armed troops sent over by the king of England to enforce his excessive demands, unlawful policies, and increasing injustices. They won their freedom in the American Revolutionary War (1775-1783).

During the midst of this war on November 1, 1777 and upon the occasion of several unexpected victories, Congress approved a proclamation for a national day of prayer and thanksgiving, which declared (**bold** mine):

> Forasmuch as it is the indispensable duty of all men to adore the superintending providence of **Almighty God**; to acknowledge with gratitude their obligation to **Him** for benefits received and to implore such farther blessings as they stand in need of . . . [to offer] humble and earnest supplication that it may please **God**, through the merits of **Jesus Christ**, mercifully to forgive and blot [our sins] out of promotion and **enlargement of that kingdom** which consisteth 'in righteousness, peace, and joy in the **Holy Ghost**.'[4]

In 1780, Samuel Adams sent this reminder to the American troops:

> May every citizen in the army and in the country have **a proper sense of the Deity** upon his mind and an impression of **the declaration recorded in the Bible**, 'Him that honoreth me I will honor, but he that despiseth me shall be lightly esteemed' [I Samuel 2:30].[5]

On September 12, 1782, one year after the British laid down their arms at Yorktown and more than a year before the formal peace treaty, Congress approved and paid for the printing of the first English-language Bible produced in America. In the front of that Bible was printed this endorsement: "Whereupon, *Resolved*, That the United States in Congress assembled . . . recommend this edition of the Bible to the inhabitants of the United States."[6]

The above examples are merely a few of the numerous government documents written by our country's Founders and leaders during this

---

[4] *Journals of . . . Congress* (1907), Vol. IX, 1777, pp.854-855, November 1, 1777.

[5] Samuel Adams, *Writings*, Vol. IV, p. 189, Samuel Adams article signed "Vindex" in *Boston Gazette* on June 12, 1780.

[6] *Journals of . . . Congress* (1914), Vol. XXIII, p. 574, September 12, 1782.

period of separation from Great Britain. They openly acknowledged God and reliance on God and were boldly and openly Christian.[7]

Sadly, a little over 200 years later and right before our eyes, everything our nation's Founders fought, died for, and won in our first revolution is under attack and rapidly being undone. This time, however, we are not under siege from a foreign nation. We are at war within our own nation. Nor does this second revolution involve cannons, guns, or bullets—yet. The weapons of choice are the courts, the media, entertainment, and special interest groups. The major battlegrounds are the public schools, college classrooms, statehouses, halls of Congress, courtrooms, communities, and the homes of every American.

Some think this second revolution does not exist. They believe it's a hoax, an over-exaggeration, or perhaps a joke with *"clowns to the left of me, jokers to the right, here I am, stuck in the middle with you."*[8]

Admittedly, America has always been a reflection of its citizens. And it still is. That's why the rallying cry of America's first revolution was: "No king but King Jesus." But today, it's: "Separation of Church and State." Quite a difference!

In 2005, Chuck Colson termed this conflict "the new civil war" between "two cultures existing within one nation. . . . as with the first Civil War, fundamental issues divide us." He next appropriately asked, "How did we get into this mess?" He insightfully answered: "The death of moral truth has fractured America into two warring camps, with each side's preferences hardening into an ideology. . . . This is why politics has become so ugly today."[9]

Colson also insisted that these two ideologies are "irreconcilable. Along with lower taxes, religious conservatives argue for moral order, respect for tradition, protection of life and religious expressions. Many secularists, by contrast, dismiss the idea that the government should enforce any moral good. Indeed, they want government to protect individuals from having any such standards imposed on them . . . . This is at the heart of the culture war. . . . It's a struggle for ultimate power."[10]

---

[7] For more, see Barton, *Original Intent*.
[8] Song by Stealer's Wheel, *Stuck in the Middle With You*.
[9] Charles Colson, "The New Civil War," *Christianity Today*, February 2005, 128.
[10] ibid.

One of the undeniable casualties of this national conflict are the 55 million unborn babies who have been killed since 1973 when the United States Supreme Court legalized the pregnancy terminating procedures of abortion in its *Roe v. Wade* decision. These never-born babies will never become or enjoy being contributing citizens of our country. Surely, this evil must also be seen as the supreme loss of rights and privilege.

Make no mistake, once again, the effects of this second revolution are just as radical and overthrowing as our first revolution, perhaps more so. This revolution has already taken place in Western Europe and is well underway in Canada. It's a godless, secular humanist (the worship of man), hostile, and aggressive assault on the God of all Creation and his followers, past, present, and future. Enormous sums of money and effort are being poured into this conflict. It's a battle for the heart and soul of our nation, for power and privilege, and for the right to define the way things will be. It will be won by the stronger and more persistent side.

So where is the Church and what is its attitude regarding this systematic and rapid secularization of American culture? As we've seen, it's mostly missing in action, apathetic, ambivalent, and rather cavalier.

Question: Is America, once again, dancing the dance of history?

The Decline and Fall of Nations—What Can We Learn?

Throughout world history, major and minor civilizations, nations, and political regimes have come and gone. Most were overthrown through revolutions, some violent, some not. Others met their demise due to destabilizing forces from within. Other regimes took their place.

The list surely includes the decline and fall of ancient Israel (twice), the Roman Empire, the Aztecs, and possibly the fall of Communism in 1989. Revolutions include the bloody French Revolution, the Russian Revolution, and our own first American Revolution.

Over the past three centuries, numerous books have been written attempting to dissect the reasons, trends, and parallels for why so many great nations and civilizations have risen and fallen. Their purpose is to see what we might learn from these examples. Howse's singular perspective is, "there is one common theme . . . . Each one rejected its

core principles: the values and worldview that once made them great."[11]
Their end was either a collapse into chaos and anarchy or being
conquered by another nation.

In a similar vein, D. James Kennedy reports that "historians tell us
that virtually every great civilization down through history has gone
through two phases. First, there is the phase of its ascendancy until it
reaches the pinnacle of its power, where it will last for a little while."[12]
He especially emphasizes that in "the ancient pre-Christian world" life
"was rife with sexual immorality and perversion."[13] He warns, therefore,
that "as many in the West continue to reject Him [God/Jesus] and His
standards of right and wrong, we seem to be regressing to the vile and
unspeakable sins that besmirched the ancient pagan world."[14]

In another sobering and forebodingly titled book, *When Nations Die*
(1994), author Jim Nelson Black saw ominous parallels from the decline
and demise of many other nations to what was occurring in America,
back then and there. He assessed: "As I have looked back across the
ruins and landmarks of antiquity, I have been stunned by the parallels
between those societies and our own." He characterized most of these
collapses as a "slow withering decline" and listed these three aspects:
social decay, cultural decay, and moral decay. His trends of social decay
were: "the crises of lawlessness," "loss of economic discipline," and
"rising bureaucracy."[15] Black then drew this parallel from the disastrous
consequences of the collapse of law and order:

> In ancient Greece, the first symptoms of disorder were a general loss of
> respect for tradition and the degradation of the young. Among the early
> symptoms were the decline of art and entertainment. The medium of
> communication was distorted by the philosophers and pundits. Rhetoric
> became combative and intolerant; intellectuals began to deride and
> attack all the traditional institutions of Hellenic society.[16] [Sound
> familiar today?]

---

[11] Howse, *One Nation Under Man?*, 103.
[12] D. James Kennedy, *What If Jesus Had Never Been Born* (Nashville, TN.:
ThomasNelson, 2001), 126.
[13] Ibid., 127.
[14] Ibid., 171.
[15] Black, *When Nations Die, ix.*
[16] Ibid., 35-36.

Black's four main trends demonstrating "cultural decay" were: "decline of education," "weakening of cultural foundations," "loss of respect for tradition," and "increase in materialism." His three main trends demonstrating "moral decay" were: "rise in immorality," "decay of religious belief," and "devaluing of human life."[17]

Kerby Anderson breaks down this demising process into 10 stages from birth through decline to death of a nation:

> Stage 1 – bondage → spiritual faith
> Stage 2 – spiritual faith → great courage
> Stage 3 – great courage → liberty
> Stage 4 – liberty → abundance
> Stage 5 – abundance → selfishness
> Stage 6 – selfishness → complacency
> Stage 7 – complacency → apathy
> Stage 8 – apathy → moral decay
> Stage 9 – moral decay → dependence
> Stage 10 – dependence → [back to] bondage

He contends that "this is the direction this and every other country is headed. . . . And this country will do the same unless revival and reformation break out and reverse the inexorable decline of this nation." He terms the final stage as the falling of "God's judgment."[18]

"As I have looked back across the ruins and landmarks of antiquity, I have been stunned by the parallels between those societies and our own."

So where do you think America stands in this regard? Some believe it is somewhere between complacency and apathy with a sizeable minority of us already in the dependence stage.

Lastly and monumentally is the English historian Edward Gibbon's classic work, *The Decline and Fall of the Roman Empire* (published in

---

[17] Ibid., *ix*.

[18] Kerby Anderson, "The Decline of a Nation," Probe Ministries, www.leaderu.com/orgs/probe/docs/decline.html, 12/11/05.

the same year of America's independence, 1776, and termed "the grand chronicle of empires and civilizations").[19]

According to Black (above), Gibbon "observed that the leaders of the empire gave into the vices of strangers, morals collapsed, laws became oppressive, and the abuse of power made the nation vulnerable to the barbarian hordes." Black next rhetorically but appropriately, asked (again, back in 1994), "But how are we any different today?"[20]

Interestingly, Gibbon cited Constantine and his embracing of Christianity for being partly to blame:

> Yet the salutary event approved in some measure the judgment of Constantine. . . . we may hear without surprise or scandal that the introduction, or at least the abuse, of Christianity had some influence on the decline and fall of the Roman empire. The clergy successfully preached the doctrines of patience and pusillanimity; the active virtues of society were discouraged, and the last remains of military spirit were buried in the cloister; a large portion of public and private wealth was consecrated to the specious demands of charity and devotion; and the soldiers' pay was lavished on the useless multitudes . . . . the church and even the state, were distracted by religious factions whose conflicts were sometimes bloody and always implacable; the attention of the emperors was diverted from camps to synods; The Roman world was oppressed by a new species of tyranny; and the persecuted sects became the secret enemies of their country."[21]

A.D. 476 is the date usually assigned for the fall of the Roman Empire. But Rome was not overrun by foreign armies; rather it was invaded by illegal immigrants: Visigoths, Franks, Anglos, Saxons, Ostrogoths, Burgundians, Lombards, Jutes, and Vandals. At first they were assimilated and worked as servants. But they came so fast that they did not learn the Latin language or the Roman form of government. Does this scenario sound familiar?

Consequently, not all nations in history came to their demise from foreign invasions. Some gradually faded away as they were brought

---

[19] Daniel F. Boorstin, Introduction in Edward Gibbon, *The Decline and Fall of the Roman Empire* (New York, NY.: The Modern Library, Mass Mkt edition, 2005), *xviii.*

[20] Black, *When Nations Die,* 187.

[21] Gibbon, *The Decline and Fall of the Roman Empire,* 803-804.

down from within. Either way, if and when the fall of the American Empire happens and is dated, historians might likely lament its passing as a once-great and mighty nation and a civilization that brought peace and prosperity to much of the world and tried to make the world more compatible for freedom. Likewise, if the glory that has been America's does someday lie in ruins, it most likely will be said that it was not from an invasion of a foreign army or terrorists, but by its own hand, via its own debauchery, irresponsibility, complacency, etc.

All in all, one thing should be obvious. The similarities, trends, and parallels between the rise and fall of many nations and present-day America are striking and sobering. Do they apply to America today? Many think so; some say, "No, America is different." Others contend that it's already happening and reference this quote attributed to the Scottish advocate, judge, writer, and historian, Alexander Fraser Tytler (or Tyler) 1747 - 1813; also attributed to Alexis de Tocqueville:

> A democracy is always temporary in nature; . . . [it] will continue to exist up until the time that voters discover that they can vote themselves generous gifts from the public treasury. From that moment on, the majority always vote for candidates who promise the most benefits from the public treasury, with the result that every democracy will finally collapse over loose fiscal policy, (which is) always followed by a dictatorship.[22]

Does this scenario also sound familiar? Over the past 15 years, America's leadership has grossly and notoriously employed this exploitation technique to appease the voters and to put or keep themselves in power, have they not?

Finally, historians maintain that the average age of the great civilizations is around 200 years. Great Britain exceeded that. The United States is now just above it. But history has proven, time and again, that the disregard of authority and disobedience is culturally devastating and ushers in the stages of decline and collapse. And so, I must ask, is American doomed to repeat this dance of history? If not, why not? If so, at what stage are we? Some historians believe that once a nation gets to the apathy stage the cycle cannot be stopped or reversed.

---

[22] There is no reliable record in any writings.

Obviously, these stages of decline are not just an American problem. Other nations have, are, and may be going this way as well. Western Europe, which was the birthplace of the Protestant Reformation 500 years ago, is now essentially a spiritual wasteland consumed with agnosticism, humanism, reflecting ignorance of God and his Word, and many other problems. For one, they are being invaded by foreign immigrants, as are we. So are we Americans committing national suicide by allowing this decline and demise to happen without much of a fight? Let's take a closer look at where we in America stand and may be headed.

Dancing onto Oblivion?

For more than 200 years following the first American Revolution, America was a blessed nation. But starting in the 1950s or 1960s, that began to change when the courts were infiltrated by appointed secular-humanist, activist judges. They then began their onslaught by removing prayer and Bible reading from the public schools. Next, they removed references to God, Jesus, and the Bible (including the Ten Commandments) from public institutions and the halls and offices of government. Then it was on to the public square—the removal of nativity scenes, crosses, monuments, and prayers to Christ, the renaming of Christian holidays, abortions of unborn babies, and legalizing of other sins. All this was done in the name of tolerance, neutrality, non-discrimination, and not offending people of other faiths or no faith. All of which was judged to fall under the legal banner of "unconstitutionality."

As a result, a growing consensus among Christians has become: we're in a "culture war." Others describe these assaults as "the new civil war"[23] or the "secular revolution."[24] I simply call it the Second American Revolution. And it affects "every part of American culture."[25]

---

[23] Colson, "The New Civil War," 128.
[24] Nancy Pearcey *Total Truth* (Wheaton, IL.: Crossway, 2008), 98 and Christian Smith, *The Secular Revolution* (Berkeley, CA.: University of California Press, 2003), title.
[25] Pearcey, *Total Truth*, 98.

In 2005, D. James Kennedy framed it like this:

In less than forty years our culture has gone from the strong family values of a society with a Christian consensus to a society that glorifies violence, illicit sex, and rebellion. We have severed ourselves from the roots of what made us great in the first place. . . . Today, we are engaged in another type of civil war . . . .[26]

For more than a century, men and women who are not aliens have being [sic] working feverishly to deconstruct American society from the inside out, to eradicate our belief in the Creator God, and to turn America into a nation that is neither free nor democratic. . . . but too many Americans seem to be wearing blinders these days.[27]

Paradoxically, this Second American Revolution, like our first, is being waged under the mantra of freedom. During our first, we fought for a dual Declaration of Independence *from Britain* and dependence *on God*. Accordingly, our Constitution was truly unique with its coupling of self-government principles with dependency on God and Judeo-Christian values. This uniqueness among current nations is why the founding of America was termed the "American experiment."

But today, an elite minority (estimated at 2% of the population)[28] within America seek freedom *from God and religion* and dependency *on the State* as the new ultimate authority. They are driving this second revolution and have been extremely successful. Day-by-day, America has, and is becoming, a nation more and more divided by views about God and from God instead of "one nation under God" and "In God We Trust."

Obviously, these stages of decline are not just an American problem. Other nations have, are, and may be going this way as well.

---

[26] D. James Kennedy, *What If America Were A Christian Nation Again?*, (Nashville, TN.: Thomas Nelson, 2005), 3-4.
[27] D. James Kennedy in Jim Nelson Black, *America Adrift* (Fort Lauderdale, FL.: Coral Ridge Ministries, 2002), 7-8.
[28] Rush Limbaugh, radio program, 6/26/15.

Astonishingly, within two generations, this elite minority has largely taken over our major institutions—the courts, schools, universities, seminaries, media, Hollywood, government—and gained control over many law-making institutions. Every day, these powerful institutions are churning out advocates who will advance their secular humanist agenda to "remake America" in an anti-God, anti-Christian direction.

Rushdoony perceptively summarizes that "when a culture denies its faith . . . . Unless it adopts another and a viable faith, it commits suicide. The humanism adopted by modern culture has had the capital of Christian civilization, but this capital is rapidly disappearing."[29]

The Goal of the Second American Revolution

This elite minority of secular humanists wants nothing to do with God or to be accountable to his standards, principles, or moral values. They want total and unbridled freedom. Therefore, their goal is to purge every vestige of religion, especially Christianity, from the public square, reduce our influence down to little or nothing, and silence our voice.

But, as the president of Moody Bible Institute warns: "If this can be accomplished through threats, there's no need to turn up the heat. But if the 'squeeze' on believers fails to achieve its desired end, beware. The pressure will escalate into ugly physical attacks attempting to close our mouths."[30] As a result, everything won in America's first revolution is being undone and replaced with a godless dependency on the State.

Their primary strategy has been to take away our children, educationally, and eventually our country. Since the 1960s over 90% of America's children have been educated in godless public schools. This revolutionary campaign was spearheaded by the U.S. Supreme Court and lower courts and their appointed activist judges who do not consider themselves bound by the Bible or the Constitution. For them, the former is an ancient and irrelevant tome; the latter is a living and evolving document that means whatever they say it means. That means they must ignore the fact that, under the Constitution, the government is not to

---

[29] Rushdoony, *Law and Society*, 151.
[30] Paul Nyquist, *Prepare: Living Your Faith In an Increasingly Hostile Culture* (Chicago, IL.: Moody Publishers, 2015), 17.

create rights (only God does that), but to protect the rights God has given humankind. Big difference. Hence, via judiciary fiat (i.e., legislating policy and writing law from the bench rather than by the will of the people), they have taken America away from being a nation that affirms our dependence role on God and Judeo-Christian values and principles to one that is now openly hostile to those foundations.

These second revolutionaries dominate the government, the courts, the media, academia, the law, etc. They are largely unelected and motivated by a deep-seated hatred of America, its history, founding, and past exceptionalism among the nations. They are the elite minority that is driving the secularization of America by force of judicial fiat and sanitizing this insurgency with euphemisms or code words, such as: "choice," "tolerance," "human rights," and "nondiscrimination." Fervently, they assume their godless, secularized, and "enlightened" minds will lead us into a man-made utopia of peace and prosperity. And with each passing day, they are growing more arrogant and confident that they will achieve their goal(s)—despite the total lack of evidence that a secular utopia ever results.

Not surprisingly, they resent Christians and want us to shut up, get out of way, and stay sequestered in our churches, at least for now. Sadly, most American Christians have been compliant with their wishes.

Moreover, these new revolutionaries are not alone. They, along with their allies like the ACLU, are no longer just chipping away at our culture. They are taking out huge chunks at a time. Make no mistake; it's a real battle of worldviews for America's heart, mind, and soul, and reminiscent of what happened in Nazi Germany (see again pp. 45-46). Abortion, marriage, homosexual rights, or public education are only skirmishes. But everything that made this country great and incentivized multiple millions to flock here from other countries is under attack.

Also, let's recall, America and Western Europe were great because of Christianity. Christianity was and is not great because of them.

Their primary strategy has been to take away our children, educationally, and eventually our country. Since the 1960s over 90% of America's children have been educated in godless public schools.

Tyranny of Judiciary Fiat—the Primary Weapon

Without a doubt, the Founders intended the Judiciary branch of the federal government to be the weakest of the three branches (Legislative, Executive, Judicial). David Barton explains (**bold** mine):

> . . . not only their writings but also their actions confirmed this fact. . . . [therefore] **no** building was planned for the Judiciary. In fact, the Supreme Court was housed in the basement below the Senate chambers for almost fifty years and did not have its own separate building until 1935. The Legislature, not the Judiciary, was the true guardian of the people's liberties. . . . in today's society the Judiciary has become the ruling branch. . . . The result has been that over a period of decades, the Court has succeeded in completely redefining both the Constitution and its own role. It has usurped Executive, Legislative, and State powers, centralizing them in the hands of the federal courts. Jefferson had warned that this centralization of power would result in the loss of local controls."[31]

Unfortunately, "Jefferson's fears have become a reality through the unchecked power of the Judiciary."[32] As a result of this overreach and abuse of judiciary power "current national policies in a number of moral, social, educational, and religious arenas do not reflect the will of the people but rather the will of philosophical minorities decreed through the courts." And We the People have "been absolutely powerless to overturn the will of the minority in these areas."[33]

Thus, social structures we have known for centuries are being changed and the Constitution corrupted with a stroke of a judiciary pen. This tactic to win by imposing their agenda on the nation and to diminish and degrade Christianity through the courts via activist judges and secularist litigation was necessitated because they could not and cannot win through legislative majorities, at the polls, or through the electoral process—although this specter may also be changing. This tactic and primary weapon are at the core of this second revolution and the so-called culture war. Seriously, then, what good is the Constitution when

---

[31] Barton, *Original Intent*, 258, 262-263.
[32] Ibid., 264.
[33] Ibid., 266.

its clear wording can be overruled and reinterpreted by judicial fiat, executive orders, or compromising legislators?

O'Reilly sets this sorrowful stage this way. He estimates that "90 percent of Americans have no idea this is going on. They hear snatches . . . but they don't put it all together. And they certainly don't know the powerful, powerful people behind the secular progressive movement who dominate the media now."[34]

Consequently, Barton concludes that "the Founders would be stunned by both the position and the power of today's Court. The separation and division of powers between the branches which they so carefully crafted and established have now been obliterated." He adamantly admonishes that "America must reclaim its right to be a republic, returning the judicial branch to its proper position."[35]

In sum, the tyranny of judicial fiat is revolutionizing the sovereignty in our nation from God to the State, which is now our new god.

What good is the Constitution when its clear wording can be overruled and reinterpreted by judicial fiat, executive orders, or compromising legislators?

Therefore, we are reaping the domino effects of this second revolution, its sinful misuse of power and politics, and the great retreat of Christians en masse from the public square. If this Second American Revolution continues its advance, be prepared for the increase of oppression and persecution of Christianity and Christians. These realities are common consequences that accompany and follow revolutions.

Emphatically, Kennedy warns "if the secularists and atheists succeed in replacing our nation's Christian foundation with a godless one . . . . the religious liberty that made this nation great will become a thing of the past. We've seen repeatedly that when atheists take over a country, not only does religious liberty go but so do other basic freedoms."[36]

---

[34] Bill O'Reilly, Interview, "O'Reilly's Fight to Save the Culture," *NewsMax*, October 2006, 60.

[35] Barton, *Original Intent*, 268.

[36] D. James Kennedy, *The Gates of Hell Shall Not Prevail* (Nashville, TN.: Thomas Nelson, 1996), 134.

Mounting Problems and Costs

The "American Experiment" has already been showing significant signs of social breakdown and other mounting problems and costs as a byproduct of the failures of secular humanist policies in education, welfare, public safety, federal and state debt, and so on. The evidence is not hidden;—22 years ago:

> William Bennett, in *The Index of Leading Cultural indicators* (1994), pointed out that in the thirty years since 1960, violent crime in America increased more than 500 percent, illegitimate births increased by more than 400 percent, the percent of children living with single parents tripled, as did the teenage suicide rate, while the divorce rate doubled. . . . Over the past three decades we have experienced substantial social regression. Today the forces of social decomposition are challenging . . . . And when the decomposition takes hold, it extracts an enormous human cost. *Unless these exploding social pathologies are reversed, they will lead to the decline and perhaps even to the fall of the American republic.*[37]

These damaging statistics certainly have not improved over the past 22 years. Add to these breakdowns the massive invasion of illegal immigrants, soaring debt, terrorist attacks, fighting worldwide conflicts in vain, trade deficits, runaway welfare, rampant drug problems, violent and sexually explicit entertainment, big and corrupt government and bureaucracies, moral degradation, godless and ineffective education, and on and on—all things that will conquer a nation.

The Only Way Self-Government Works

As hostility to Christianity grows throughout the popular culture and the holy is profaned and swept away, it's pertinent for us to draw attention to the only way self-government can work in a free society. At numerous times and in various ways, America's Founders and

---

[37] Overman, *Assumptions That Affect Our Lives*, 152; from William J. Bennett, *The Index of Leading Cultural Indicators* (New York, NY.: Simon & Schuster, 1994), 8.

subsequent leaders have made this way plain and clear. Our self-governing nation is only workable when its people are self-governed by adherence to moral and religious principles. In their own words:

> We have no government armed with power capable of contending with human passions unbridled by morality and religion. . . . Our Constitution was made for a moral and religious people. It is wholly inadequate to the government of any other.[38] (**John Adams**, the second president of the United States, in 1798)

> The highest glory of the American Revolution was this: it connected in one indissoluble bond, the principles of civil government with the principles of Christianity.[39] (**John Quincy Adams**, the sixth president of the United States – 1825-1829)

Assuredly, these presidential statements are a far cry from the so-called "separation of church and state" battle cry of the secular humanists. But there is more:

Benjamin Franklin (1706-1790) echoed this truism in this nutshell: "Only a virtuous people are capable of freedom. As nations become corrupt and vicious, they have more need of masters."[40]

Edmund Burke (1729-1797) wisely affirmed: "There must be some restraining influence upon the wills and passions of men, and the less there is from within, the more there must be from without."[41]

---

[38] John Adams, *The Works of John Adams, Second President of the United States*, Charles Frances Adams, ed. (Boston, MA.: Little, Brown and Company, 1854), Vol. IX, 229, to the Officers of the First Brigade of the Third Division of the Militia of Massachusetts on October 11, 1798.

[39] Quoted in Kennedy, *What If Jesus Had Never Been Born*, 82. From Verna M. Hall, *The Christian History of Constitution of the United States* (San Francisco, CA.: Foundation for American Christian Education, 1966), 372. From J. Wingate Thornton, "The Pulpit of the American Revolution" (Gould & Lincoln, 1860).

[40] Benjamin Franklin, *The Works of Benjamin Franklin*, John Bigelow, ed. (New York, NY.: G.P. Putnam's Sons), 1904, Vol. XI, April 17, 1787, 318.

[41] Quoted in Kennedy, *What If Jesus Had Never Been Born*, 89. From Russell Kirk, *The Conservative Mind* (Washington, DC.: Henry Regnery Company, 1953), 37.

Robert Winthrop concurred and frankly proclaimed in 1852: "Men, in a word, must necessarily be controlled either by a power within them, or by a power without them; either by the Word of God, or by the strong arm of man; either by the Bible, or by the bayonet."[42]

Barton expounds:

The transcendent values of Biblical natural law were the foundation of the American republic. . . . The Founders understood that Biblical values formed the basis of the republic and that the republic would be destroyed if the people's knowledge of those values should ever be lost . . . . a republic is the highest form of government devised by man, but it also requires the greatest amount of human care and maintenance. If neglected, it can deteriorate into a variety of lesser forms, including a democracy (a government conducted by popular feeling); anarchy (a system in which each person determines his own rules and standards); an oligarchy (a government run by a small council or a group of elite individuals); or dictatorship (a government run by a single individual).[43]

Hence, Tony Evans is alarmed and fully aware that . . .

. . . what you and I are witnessing today in the rapid deterioration of our culture is the reality that God is removing more and more of His restraint. . . . But once God is removed from or marginalized in a culture, then the standard for a society is gone and God becomes one's worst enemy and worst nightmare. That's what had happened in Israel. When the rule of God's law is missing, chaos replaces community. You cannot have order and structure in society without God, and men becoming enslaved by the very freedom they seek. . . . As long as God is front and center in a culture, there's hope. But when He is removed . . . the net result . . . is . . . the 'devolution' of mankind. The more we marginalize God, the worse things get.[44]

For Evans, the fact of the matter is this: "Any attempt to be autonomous from God will produce divine intervention and

[42] Robert C. Winthrop, *Addresses and Speeches on Various Occasions,* (Boston, MA.: Little Brown and Co., 1852), 172.

[43] Barton, *Original Intent*, 326-327.

[44] Evans, *What a Way to Live!,* 10-12.

decentralization so that men will once again seek God (see Acts 17:24-28). God . . . judges the nations that forget Him (see Rom. 1:18-32)."[45] He concludes, in agreement with our Founding Fathers, that "when people govern themselves under God, you have peace and blessing. When people look to everything and everyone else to govern them except God, you have anarchy." [46] Hence nowadays, "America . . . is a classic example of what happens in a society that rejects God's rules and tries to live by man's rules. The result is moral and spiritual chaos."[47]

Similarly, Kennedy lamented back in 1994 that "we are approaching in this country today a situation somewhat similar to France of the 1780s—where sin becomes flagrant and the morals debased. Many people today are beginning to look at Christianity as an impediment to the continuation of their 'freedom'—to sin. . . . to fulfill all of their lusts."[48]

Consequently, "that's why our public education system is in trouble."[49] And as D. Eric Schansberg makes note, "Every time we pass another law or regulation . . . we are admitting that failure of individuals to govern themselves."[50]

A Comparative Summary

If the Roman Empire could not survive, perhaps America will not survive either. After all, as historians often say and the old adage goes: "those who do not learn from history are condemned to repeat its mistakes."

Allan Bloom in his book *The Closing of the American Mind* puts America's dilemma quite simply: "This is the American moment in

---

[45] Ibid., 73.

[46] Ibid., 85.

[47] Ibid., 103.

[48] Kennedy, *What If Jesus Had Never Been Born*, 89.

[49] Evans, *What A Way To Live!*, 100-101.

[50] D. Eric Schansberg, *Turn Neither to the Right Nor to the Left* (Greenville, SC.: Alertness Ltd, 2003), 35.

world history, the one for which we shall forever be judged."[51] The only question that remains is: Will we rise to the occasion or will we succumb and suffer a similar fate? The task is not easy; but the stakes are high. Will we be pulled back from the brink or be pushed over the edge? Will we tread a path of reclamation and restoration or will we "dance the dance of history . . . . onto oblivion." The choice is ours.

ISSUE	1ST REVOLUTION	2ND REVOLUTION
Purpose	Religious and civil liberty	Secular-humanist liberty
Freedom	*Of* religion	*From* religion
Goal	Independence from Britain	Independence from God
Purpose	Advance God's kingdom	Remove God
Dependence on	God and the Bible	Man and government
Truth Source	God and the Bible	Man and reason alone
Chief weapons	Canons and guns	Courts and schools
Mantra	"No king but King Jesus"	"Separation of Church and State"
Worldview	Kingdom of God	Utopia of man
Hope	Heaven, rewards, loss	A man-made utopia, then nothing

Will God Be Mocked?

Practically speaking, we Bible-reading, believing, and committed Christians know "who calls the tune." We simply cannot escape or ignore the biblical reality of God's sovereignty and his ruling of our world, the universe, the nations, and everything. He has told us so in many scriptures. He has demonstrated it in many historical instances.

The New Testament also tells us that God cannot be mocked without consequences. This is termed the "law of sowing and reaping." It's applicable for individuals, groups, and nations: "Do not be deceived: God cannot be mocked. A man reaps what he sows. The one who sows to please his sinful nature, from that nature will reap destruction; the one

---

[51] Allan Bloom, *The Closing of the American Mind* (New York, NY.: Simon & Schuster, 1987), 382.

who sows to please the Spirit, from the Spirit will reap eternal life" (Gal. 6:7-8). This revealed law is true and applicable, whether we choose to believe it or not.

Some, today, think this God of all Creation is just giving us Americans enough rope to hang ourselves. For 1st-century Israel, that length of rope and time was around 40 years (based on Jesus' "this generation" time warning for the coming judgment of Jerusalem and the Temple—A.D. 30 – 70 (see Matt. 24:34)). America may also be that close or closer. Perhaps, we are already experiencing divine judgment on many fronts. Romans 1:26-27 also states that there comes a time when God abandons a rebellious people and turns them over to their own sins. This abandonment is part of the revealed judgment and wrath of God. He simply withdraws his blessings and protection. It's a frightening possibility and one Dr. Billy Graham readily recognizes:

> . . . when we repeatedly scorn God's ways and continually follow paths that are destructive and immoral, we will eventually pay a terrible price. We will pay it as a nation, leading to conflict and social disruption and widespread evil. And we will pay it as individuals, leading to addictions and broken relationships and unhappiness and death. The Bible warns, "Do not be deceived: God cannot be mocked . . . . Whoever sows to please their flesh, from the flesh will reap destruction" (Galatians 6:7-8).[52]

Why Bother? Who Cares? Does It Matter?

Regrettably, many evangelical Christians think and act this way. In essence, they have traded the victorious and positive Christian worldview of our country's forefathers for a Johnny-come-lately pessimistic, and defeatist scheme (1830s origin).[53] In the process, they have also jettisoned Jesus' kingdom. What's left is a worldview that produces a fatalistic philosophy of life and cultural surrender. They reason, "If these bad things must happen before Christ can return and fix everything, then

---

[52] Billy Graham, "My Answer," *The Indianapolis Star*, 2/20/16, 4E.
[53] See John Noē, *Off Target* (Indianapolis, IN.: East2West Press, 2012), 103-105.

let's do nothing to diminish or slow them down." Hence, when bad things happen, they secretly celebrate, thinking, "We're one step closer!"

Ironically, almost every generation throughout church history has thought that they were living in the "last days" and that their generation was Jesus' "this generation" (Matt. 24:34). This still-futuristic, deferment brand of eschatology dominates the worldview and outlook of many on the Christian Right. Culturally, they expect to lose before winning by escaping (alive) from this world via a rapture.

During these same times, other Christians have clung to another of Jesus' statements: "No one knows about that day or hour, not even the angels in heaven, nor the Son, but only the Father" (Matt. 24:36, also 24:44; 25:13). But only one generation during church history has had the advantage of inspired Scripture to back up its claim to being Jesus' "this generation." Back in the 1st century, the Apostle John knew the hour. Twice, he proclaimed it. "Dear children, this is the last hour . . . . This is how we know it is the last hour" (1 John 2:18). How could John have known this? After all, even Jesus said He did not know the day or hour.

The reason John knew, back then and there, was because something extremely significant occurred between Jesus' not-knowing statement in A.D. 30 and John's knowing in A.D. 67. That "something" was the pouring out of the prophesied Holy Spirit at Pentecost in those "last days" (see Acts 2:1-21). And one of the purposes of the Holy Spirit, as Jesus revealed, was to "guide you into all truth" and "tell you what is yet to come" (John 16:13). That's how John could and did know it was the "last hour" (1 John 2:18). That's also how Peter knew it was the "last days" (Acts 2:16-17), back then and there.

. . . they have also jettisoned Jesus' kingdom. What's left is a worldview that produces a fatalistic philosophy of life and cultural surrender.

Likewise, 35 years or so following Pentecost the writer of Hebrews (likely Paul), emphatically declared, "but in these last days he [God] has spoken to us by his Son [Jesus] . . ." (Heb. 1:2a). Once again by inspiration, the writer of Hebrews affixed two specific historical events to the biblical expression "these last days:" 1) the earthly ministry of

Jesus Christ; and 2) the time in which he was writing this epistle (A.D. 65-67).

In spite of this biblical documentation (and much more), millions of Christians today continue to misplace their hope into a futuristic, "last days" scenario. Consequently, they have left the social battlefields in droves awaiting Jesus' arrival. Like the revered Dr. Billy Graham, they believe we today are "living in the last days of which Jesus spoke."[54] Hence, "the standard response" of those who so misbelieve is, "the world cannot improve ethically until Jesus comes to rule with a rod of iron."[55]

Can you begin to see something severely wrong with this deferment view? And there is much more at odds with that eschatology. But since I have extensively dealt with this issue in other books, and will address it later in this book, at this point I'll simply refer you to those books and move on to three pertinent reasons we committed Christians should be bothered and care and why all this matters a great deal.[56]

Reason #1 – Seriously, do you think the decline of Christian influence in America, North America, and Western Europe during the past century is the scenario Jesus had in mind when He instructed his followers to be "the salt of the earth" and "the light of the world" (Matt. 5:13-14)? Similarly, do you think we culture-abandoning, retreating, present-day Christians will ever hear the words someday, "Well done, good and faithful servant" from our Lord if we leave this world with this kind of secular humanist legacy—and it has happened on our watch?

It's hard to imagine what kind of world this will be like for our children, grandchildren, and future generations if strong Christians and church leaders don't stand up with courage, and appropriate ammunition and say "enough" . . . and organize, mobilize, and activate to change all this. Again, we've got the numbers. What we have lacked is the will.

---

[54] Billy Graham, "My Answer," *The Indianapolis Star*, Indianapolis, IN., 5/1/03, n.p.

[55] Kenneth L. Gentry, *He Shall Have Dominion* (Tyler, TX.: Institute for Christian Economics, 1992), *xxxiv*.

[56] See especially: John Noē, *The Perfect Ending for the World* (Indianapolis, IN.: East2West Press, 2011) and *Unraveling the End* (Indianapolis, IN.: East2West Press, 2014).

Reason #2 – Only two nations in history were ever conceived, dedicated, and consecrated to God—ancient Israel (see 2 Chron. 6 & 7) and America.[57] As Rabbi Jonathan Cahn presents, both are "unique among nations . . . conceived and dedicated to the will of God from . . . conception."[58] Over and over, our historical documents show that our Founding Fathers and subsequent generations of leaders up through the middle of the 20th century honored this consecration and America was blessed and prospered. But this uniqueness comes with a responsibility for honoring this consecration and we risk major negative consequences if we cease to honor it. (see 2 Chron. 7:19-22).

In his Inaugural Day speech, America's first president, George Washington acknowledged our nation's dependence upon and gratitude toward God and then warned future generations with these words:

> It would be peculiarly improper to omit in this first official Act, my fervent supplications to that Almighty Being who rules over the Universe, who presides in the Council of Nations, . . . No People can be bound to acknowledge and adore the invisible hand, which conducts the Affairs of men more than the People of the United States. . . . The propitious smiles of Heaven, can never be expected on a nation that disregards the eternal rules of order and right, which Heaven itself has ordained . . . ."[59]

Sadly, however, during the middle of the 20th century and accelerating rapidly during the past 20 years, "all that had once defined America was being blurred or erased, one principle at a time. Bible reading and prayer were banned from public schools by the courts. And with a single ruling, America was changed overnight from a pro-life nation to a country that condoned the killing of innocent, unborn children." And all this "ugly and extreme transformation" was being done "at the hands of radical secularists. . . . in attempting to dismantle and rebuild America in its own godless image."[60]

---

[57] Of course, God made a covenant with Israel; He has not made a covenant with America, nor any other nation.

[58] Cahn, *The Harbinger*, 19.

[59] Quoted in Perkins, "Why America's First Freedom Is in Jeopardy,"46. Also, see again Rabbi's Cahn's comments in Chapter 2, pp. 53, 56, 59.

[60] Jackson & Perkins, *Personal Faith Public Policy*, 2.

So what do you think the God of the Bible to Whom America was consecrated and Who tells us that He does not change (Mal. 3:6a) and beckons us today to "return to me, and I will return to you" (Mal. 3:7) thinks about all this change?

We don't have to wonder or speculate. He provides a list of detestable acts in Leviticus 18—among them are incest, adultery, bestiality, and homosexuality—and He warns: "Do not defile yourselves in any of these ways, because this is how the nations [note the plural] that I am going to drive out before you became defiled. Even the land was defiled; so I punished it for its sin, and the land vomited out its inhabitants" (Lev. 18:24-25). What does this divine warning mean for America or any nation? Jacobs answers, "just what it says: . . . Nothing or no one who tries to live there will prosper. The land will 'vomit' them out. There are numbers of other passages that relate to this issue of land being defiled through sin."[61]

Another powerful passage is Hosea 4:1-3,6: "Hear the word of the LORD, you Israelites, [and you Americans and all other nations], because the LORD has a charge to bring against you who live in the land: There is no faithfulness, no love, no acknowledgment of God in the land. There is only cursing, lying and murder, stealing, and adultery; they break all bounds, and bloodshed follows bloodshed. Because of this the land mourns, and all who live in it waste away. . . . my people are destroyed from a lack of knowledge. Because you have rejected knowledge, I also reject you as my priests; because you have ignored the law of your God, I also will ignore your children."

Comparatively, the great sin of most 1st-century Jews was their rejection of Christ, his kingdom, and his followers. Does this sound familiar? Forty years later, their nation was destroyed. Regarding all nations and peoples who have forgotten God or thumbed their noses at Him, they have not gotten away with it forever either. For the God of the Bible has revealed that He controls the nations and peoples, lifting up, carrying forward, and bringing down. He warns that He will have the last word. Indeed, these are hard revelations. But they are the inspired teachings of Scripture and ones we need to know, learn from, deal with, and heed. Here are a few examples from the Old Testament (see Psa. 2:1-2, 10-12; 9:15-17; 50:22-23; Job 8:12-13; Ezek. 14:13-21; Ezek. 15:7-8).

---

[61] Jacobs, *The Reformation Manifesto*, 89.

God has also revealed that He is "a jealous God" (Exod. 20:5; 34:14; Deut. 4:24; 5:9; 6:15; 32:16, 21; Josh. 24:19) and that the universe is a theocracy (see Psa. 24:1; 33:12; 47:8; 103:19; Deut. 8:18; 28:1-3).

From these prophetic and revelatory utterances (and many more), we have been put on notice that the fortunes of nations rise and fall, not by the plans and ambitions of their leaders, but by the will, reign, and rule of the Lord. And let us not forget that He does not change (Mal. 3:6). Life and death, blessings and curses hang in the balance (Deut. 30:19-20).

Today in America many are saying, asking, singing, desiring, and praying for God to bless America. But we must remember that this blessing is a two-way street. We must also bless, acknowledge, honor, and obey Him. According to the Bible, that's how it works. Let us dare not forget it.

Reason #3 – Your and my involvement in this life, or lack thereof, will determine how we spend our eternal life in heaven. It's called the doctrine of eternal rewards, loss, and punishment for believers. Rarely, however, is this biblical doctrine and teaching ever mentioned, taught, or preached in most churches. Therefore, there are countless Christians who believe they have a ticket to heaven and nothing else matters.

The neglect and ignorance of this doctrine of eternal rewards, loss, and punishment for believers was vividly brought home to me one Sunday morning. The senior pastor's sermon (in an evangelical mega-church I formerly attended) was on the topic of "Universal Judgment." Confidently, this pastor assured the large congregation that "if they are believers in Jesus Christ, they have nothing to fear, nothing to worry about, concerning judgment because Christ has taken care of it for us."

In a follow-up conversation, I asked if he was familiar with the doctrine of eternal rewards, loss, and punishment for believers. He said he wasn't interested. I mentioned that there are over one hundred verses that speak of this and I'd be happy to send them to him. He replied that "there are many more verses that speak of God's grace and love and of setting people free. He would focus on those, thank you." End of conversation.

Of course, this pastor is both a victim and a perpetrator of a dumbed-down and ignorant version of Christianity. Clearly and emphatically, Scripture teaches:

- Everyone is "destined to die once, and after that to face judgment" (Heb. 9:27).
- Every believer's "work will be shown for what it is . . . . It will be revealed with fire, and the fire will test the quality of each man's [and woman's] work. If what he has built survives, he will receive his reward. If it is burned up, he will suffer loss; he himself will be saved, but only as one escaping through the flames" (1 Cor. 3:13-15).
- "So then, each of us will give an account of himself to God" (Rom. 14:12).
- Since I have written extensively on this biblical doctrine in another book and laid out over a hundred other verses in a systematic manner, I'll refer you there.[62]

In closing this chapter, McLaren speaks frankly and directly to our inevitable moment when each of us will stand before God and be called to account for things we did and did not do during our time on this earth:

> What could be more serious than standing in front of your Creator—the Creator of the universe—and finding out that you had wasted your life, squandered your inheritance, caused others pain and sorrow, worked against the good plans and desires of God? What could be more serious than that? To have to face the real, eternal, unavoidable, absolute, naked truth about yourself, what you've done, what you've become? . . . Nothing could be more serious than that . . . . We cannot select out comfortable passages and ignore those that make us uneasy.[63]

McLaren also explains that he is "not denying salvation by grace . . . . I'm just advocating judgment by works," and that "being judged isn't the same as being condemned and that being saved means a lot more than not being judged."[64]

---

[62] For more on the biblical doctrine of eternal rewards, loss, and punishment for believers, see Noē, *Hell Yes / Hell No*, 230-231, 317, 357-360, 371-374.
[63] McLaren, *The Last Word and the Word After That*, 79, 80, 96.
[64] Ibid., 138.

Likewise, Dietrich Bonhoeffer cut to the chase: "Silence in the face of evil is itself evil. God will not hold us guiltless. Not to speak is to speak. Not to act is to act."[65]

And so I ask you, would you like to know about this biblical doctrine of eternal rewards, loss, and punishment for believers now while you can still do something about it, or later when it's too late?

In our next chapter we shall explore these three questions: What now can you and I do? Is there any viable hope? What are our options as Christians to save this country, other countries, our children, our grandchildren and future generations from further decline and demise?

So what do you think the God of the Bible to Whom America was consecrated and Who tells us that He does not change (Mal. 3:6a) and beckons us today to "return to me, and I will return to you" (Mal. 3:7) thinks about all this change?

---

[65] Quoted in Eric Metaxas, *Bonhoeffer: Pastor, Martyr, Prophet, Spy—A Righteous Gentile vs. the Third Reich* (Nashville, TN.: Thomas Nelson, 2010), back cover flap.

Chapter 4

What Now Can We Do?

For whom the bell tolls; it tolls for thee.[1]

~

Oh dear, what can I do?
Baby's in black and I'm feeling blue
Tell me, oh what can I do?[2]

For the sake of our children, grandchildren, and future generations (not to mention our own, personal, and eternal rewards, losses, or punishments in heaven) . . . whose vision for the world will now win? Is America headed for the abyss of secular humanism, decline, decay, and demise, or onto the bliss of a revival of genuine Christianity? Or, is all of this angst much-to-do-about-nothing?

---

[1] John Donne, *The Works of John Donne,* Vol. III., Henry Alford, ed., London: John W. Parker, 1839, 574-5. Also, *For Whom the Bell Tolls* is the title of a novel by Ernest Hemingway published in 1940 and regarded as one of his best.
[2] Opening stanza, John Lennon / Paul McCartney, The Beatles, "Baby's In Black," Sony/ATV Tunes LLC.

Welcome to the 'Givens'

Let's see how many of these assessments you would now agree or disagree with. <u>Warning</u>: Some of these "givens" carry politicized overtones. But, and arguably so, that is how we Christians have lost and are losing our influence in America and elsewhere—i.e., politically:

<u>For Our World:</u>

Given that we live in a world in which brokenness abounds . . .

<u>For America:</u>

Given that we Christians are losing America—whatever that may or may not mean . . .

Given that the Second American Revolution is attacking and undoing all that our Founding Fathers and their generation founded, fought, and died for . . .

Given that "our Founding Fathers warned us that if America were to abandon God and His biblical truths and principles that our nation was founded upon then everything would fall apart."[3] . . .

Given that America, as a nation, was originally consecrated to and publicly acknowledged as dependent upon God but now, as a nation, has turned away from Him . . .

Given "the alarming reality" that "America, like ancient Rome, is experiencing all the historical warning signs of an empire on the verge of implosion. . . .[and] as a nation it seems we are in the midst of the greatest moral and spiritual crisis we have ever witnessed, both inside and outside the church."[4] . . .

Given that our nation's problems grow more complex and volatile with each day . . .

Given that all efforts up to this point to stop and reverse this decline into demise have been in vain . . .

---

[3] Darrel and Cindy Deville, "Swing Vote," *Charisma*, July 2015, 27.
[4] ibid.

Given that we have driven God out of our schools, out of our universities, out of our government, out of our judiciary, out of our media, out of our culture, and out of our public square . . .

Given that the consensus in America is drifting further and further away from God and the way He instructs and commands us to live . . .

Given the anti-God and anti-biblical laws and rulings being forced upon us . . .

Given the fact that current trends show no sign of abating—only of accelerating and intensifying . . .

Given that God may already have begun withdrawing his blessings and protective hand from America and other nations and we sit in imminent danger of a greater judgment . . .

Against Christianity and the Church:

Given the rapid rise of hostility that seeks to silence the Christian voice and eliminate its influence in society at large . . .

Given the prospect of growing threats to religious freedom in the years ahead . . .

Given that we Christians are more known for what we are against than what we are for. . .

Given the startling possibility that Christianity could someday be outlawed . . .

Within the Church:

Given that Christianity has been "tamed," at least here in America, North America, and Western Europe . . .

Given the despair many are feeling over the fate of our nation and the fear that there is nothing we can do . . .

Given that the only reason we Christians are losing is because we are allowing all this to happen . . .

Given that we Christians need to wake up the "sleeping giant" of the Church . . .

Given that we are getting the kind of government and nation we deserve . . .

Given that the other side wants to define our nation more than we Christians do . . .

Given that Christianity will not prevail if it is watered down . . .

Given the large number of young people abandoning the organized church when they are no longer under their parents' tutelage . . .

Given that we Christians are about "to hand the nation our forefathers fought and died for over to the forces of darkness simply because we're too busy to be bothered with voting and politics."[5] . . .

Given that "the primary measure of 'success' used by churches is the weekly attendance figure."[6] . . .

Given that most of God's people are not engaged in this cultural battle but are sitting on the sidelines . . .

Given that most churches appear disinterested in awakening themselves to the impending decline and disaster . . .

Given that the church has never been more perceived as irrelevant and impotent in our country's history than it is now . . .

Given that the majority of Americans, as well as American Christians, place their children into a godless educational training system for 12 years or more without hesitation or concern . . .

Given that many, if not most, American Christians huddle together in their churches, Christian schools, and fellowship groups and insulate themselves from any significant contact with unbelievers . . .

Given that the humanistic world revels in the ease of advancement of its agenda provided by a Church that has basically abandoned its role as salt and light . . .

Given that there is little dissimilarity in the public behaviors between most Christians and non-Christians . . .

Given that the Church keeps looking for better programs and methods to attract and keep people . . .

Basis for Hope:

Given that America is still the most religious nation on earth . . .

Given that "there are more than 335,000 Christian churches in this country."[7] . . .

---

[5] ibid.

[6] Foreword by George Barna in Jim Henderson & Matt Casper, *Jim and Casper Go To Church* (Carol Stream, IL.: Tyndale Momentum, 2012), x.

[7] Barna in Henderson & Casper, *Jim and Casper Go To Church*, x.

Given that in America worship attendance exceeds that of any other nation . . .

Given that there may still be time to change our nation's self-destructive course toward chaos and calamity . . .

Given that the Church needs to find a way to take a more credible, effective, and right stand in response to this tidal wave of sweeping change . . .

Given that the American church needs to attain a much higher level of unity than we have ever seen before . . .

Given that "the Founding Fathers never meant for people of religious convictions to be drummed out of public discourse or fearful of operating in the public square."[8]

Therefore, here is what we are left with . . .

A Growing Suspicion

If we Christians are to be God's stewards and ambassadors on this earth to set things right, and if each of us will be held accountable by our Creator for how we do or do not respond to that calling and responsibility, a growing suspicion is emerging that we have not done well. As a result, we have spawned multitudes of professing Christians who are willing to die as Christians but aren't willing to live as Christians.

Willard summarizes these daunting realizations thusly: "There is a great deal of disappointment expressed today about the character and the effects of Christian people, about Christian institutions, and—at least by implication—about the Christian faith and understanding of reality. Most of the disappointment comes from Christians themselves, who find that what they profess 'just isn't working.'"[9]

McLaren adds that "Jesus Himself said that this would occur. He anticipated that his followers would cool in their passion and drift from his message. He warned them not to hide their light under a bucket or

---

[8] Ben Carson, "Religious Freedom: Why the Church Cannot Remain Silent Any Longer," *Charisma*, July 2015, 20.

[9] Willard, *The Great Omission*, ix.

lose their saltiness; if they did, they would be 'trampled under foot' (Matthew 5:13 NRSV)."[10]

Gregory A. Boyd totally agrees and suggests that "the church has been co-opted by the world. To a large degree, we've lost our distinct kingdom-of-God vision and abandoned our mission. We've allowed the world to define us, set our agenda, and define the terms of our engagement with it."[11] Later, he clarifies that "my goal . . . is not to critique America. . . . my critique is rather toward *the American church*."[12]

Indeed, Christianity here in America has been largely co-opted. We have turned away from and abandoned our "once mighty faith." For this reason, our nation is now being built on the shifting sands of secular humanism where the government is supreme and obedience to God and his kingdom is largely a thing of the past.

For example, when "a woman who had worked for many years with prostitutes on the streets of Chicago. . . . was asked . . . . What do you think of the Church? . . . Her reply: 'I see the Church as a very, very old grandmother who does not see well anymore, does not hear well anymore, and does not get out much anymore. She is clinging too tightly to life. Though we love her dearly, we should let her die."[13]

Rushdoony concurs that "churches have produced impotent and humanistic Christians and the world around them has steadily collapsed into humanism."[14] Accordingly, James Rutz makes this note: "The #1 gripe of most pastors I know is, 'What on earth do I have to do to get these people off their fannies?' It seldom dawns on them that they might be their own worst enemies, giving their flock an hour or two of practice every week in *sitting and doing nothing*. The Sunday morning drill in suspended animation is perfect for zombies-in-training."[15]

---

[10] Brian D. McLaren, *The Secret Message of Jesus* (Nashville, TN.: W Publishing Group, 2006), 79.

[11] Gregory A. Boyd, *The Myth of a Christian Nation* (Grand Rapids, MI.: Zondervan, 2005), 64.

[12] Ibid., 89.

[13] Matthew Fox, *The Coming of the Cosmic Christ* (San Francisco, CA.: Harper & Row, 1988), 27.

[14] Rushdoony, *The Institutes of Biblical Law*, 767.

[15] Rutz, *Mega Shift*, 126.

On the other hand, Black admonishes that "we do not have to accept that destiny. . . . Once we understand who we are and whom we serve, we will have the means to find our moral compass and bring the ship of state back onto its true course."[16] To which I offer a hearty, "Amen!"

So what are our options?

Seven Options

God's Word rhetorically but appropriately asks, "If the foundations are destroyed, what can the righteous do?" (Psa. 11:3). In other words, is there anything that we committed Christians can now do to stop and reverse this godless trend and deterioration of American culture and country, and in other countries? Is there any viable hope? Are there any realistic options? Is there any feasible chance to turn things around?

I believe we have seven options. They range from the ridiculous to the sublime. The first six may strike a familiar chord, but are hardly capable of producing or sustaining a forceful effort of the magnitude needed to transcend the opposition.

. . . "churches have produced impotent and humanistic Christians and the world around them has steadily collapsed into humanism."

Be assured, however, there is hope. If people can change, a nation can alter its course. But something significant has to occur to spark and sustain that change. Nevertheless, the traditional idea that "the only solution is to return to God"[17] is far too general and vague to have value. It's like simply trying to tell people to love one another. Here are our seven options, as I see them.

---

[16] Black, *America Adrift*, 73.
[17] Cahn, *The Harbinger*, 134.

Option# 1 – Business as Usual, Maintain the Status Quo

It's been termed "the most overused cliché of all time." It's a quote usually attributed to Albert Einstein. But is it applicable for the situation we are discussing? Here it is: "The definition of insanity is doing the same thing over and over and expecting a different result."

Many, perhaps most Christians and churches, are not sure what to make of the massive culture shift. Moreover, they are uncomfortable with any kind of social activism, even as meager as handing out voter guides a week before election day. Consequently, they would rather ignore this problem, maintain church business as usual, and continue the status quo. Thus, by default, they are capitulating to the secularists.

If we elect this option, there is little hope of halting our nation's slide down the slippery slope of secular humanism. And the consequences are predictable. The secularization of America will continue unabated and increasingly so. Thus, DeMar aptly notes and asks: "America's moral and cultural crisis is the result of Christians not applying the Christian worldview to every area of life. . . . there is no such thing as 'neutrality.' While Christians stand by and do nothing, the other side is working feverishly to implement their godless, humanistic, destructive worldview. Which worldview will ultimately prevail and how will it affect your family, the Church, and America?"[18]

Unfortunately, the reality for many pastors, elders, and leaders in the church today is that they are so consumed with church activities, meetings, and increasing membership that they are unaware and/or unconcerned about the culture changing outside their church. Oh, sure, they want more people to come into their church and become tithe-giving members. They also want them to stay put and not cause any problems.

Intriguingly, Chalke and Mann posit this blunt and relevant question from a friend: "If Jesus was half the revolutionary you claim, how come he is now represented by one of the most conservative, status quo institutions on the planet?" They respond that "in many parts of the world the Church is dynamic, bold, engaged and prophetic." To which the friend smiled and insightfully replied, "Well, then there must be two kinds of Christianity, and somehow we've got stuck with the tame

[18] "The Worldview War," advertisement in *World*, August 26, 2006, 1.

version."[19] Indeed, we have. But there are more than two kinds of Christianities.

The tamed-down versions of our "once mighty faith" have produced the Church's "hands-off" policy for shaping the thinking and behavior of our culture. It's the social and spiritual malaise of our time in much of the Church—fretting and wringing of hands about how bad our nation and the world have become, along with the apathy, indifference, and a keen sense of the impotence for how to deal with it. Largely, it's the byproduct of gospel reductionism. The Church to a large extent, whether liberal, conservative, evangelical, mainstream, or whatever, is essentially "at ease in Zion"—a position condemned in Scripture—"Woe to them that are at ease (are complacent) in Zion" (Amos 6:1, KJV/NIV). Emotionally, psychologically, and theologically, far too many of us have been programmed into this "at ease" status quo. But now is no time to rest on our laurels or pull up lame.

Appropriately, Anthony D. Baker asks, "Can we afford to engage in business as usual if business as usual—doing the same thing Sunday after Sunday—is sinking the church?" He, too, cites the statistics and concludes that "the Christian faith is broken."[20] If he's right, how do we fix it?

But many churches, pastors, and Christians are not interested in a fix. They like their version of Christianity just the way it is, thank you. Why so? Here are two reasons: 1) They've been indoctrinated for so long with the eschatological view/belief that it's God's will for things to get worse and worse before Jesus comes back and fixes everything. 2) They are afraid, afraid of the flak, the controversy, of losing people if they would begin speaking out on the issues of our day, and of losing their 501(c)(3) tax-exempt status from the government.[21] Therefore, according to Kennedy, some "300,000 pulpits are silent" on these external matters, while focusing on internal matters: "the church-wide supper," "raising money to put a new floor cover on the kitchen," last Sunday's sermon on

---

[19] Chalke & Mann, *The Lost Message of Jesus*, 85.

[20] Anthony D. Baker, "Learning to Read the Gospel Again: How to address our anxiety about losing the next generation," *Christianity Today* (December 2011): 30 and in quoting Stanley Hauerwas.

[21] For more on this, see John Noē, *The Greater Jesus* (Indianapolis, IN.: East2West Press, 2012), 257-262.

"How to Have a Positive Attitude," "organizing a softball team," "a program . . . to recruit new members. . . . because we are losing membership."[22]

In a similar vein, Jacobs senses that "while most evangelicals still keep the light of Jesus Christ bright in the area of preaching salvation, many no longer see it as their Christian duty to extend that saving grace beyond the four walls of their church."[23]

The bottom line is this. No amount of business as usual will stem the rising tide against us or stop this Second American Revolution. Under this first option, we are in danger of losing our country in a way reminiscent of how the church in Nazi Germany lost their country. They left the "soul of Germany" to Hitler and the Nazis. Similarly, we are leaving the "soul of America" to the secular humanists (see again Chapter 2, pp. 45-46). Why so? Once again, it's because "we like our Christianity just like it is, thank you."

On the positive side, however, a secular humanist culture run by an authoritarian elite would probably tolerate a watered-down and weakened version of Christianity, in which faith is considered a private matter, while they enforce non-Christian absolutes on society. After all, that's what they've been doing and more of the same lies ahead if our opponents continue winning victory after victory. Again, a similar Christian acquiescence paved the way for Hitler and the Nazis. They got and we are getting the kind of government and nation we deserve. And the only reason this Second American Revolution is succeeding is because Christians in this country and en masse have checked out.

Consequently, the other side owns the schools, universities, law schools, judiciary, government bureaucrats, and many/most elected officials, the media, and more. They are entrenched and smelling complete victory within their reach. They have also targeted the influence of we Christians for complete elimination. We have got to understand this. We cannot just "get along" or hope to "find common ground." This ideological battle will either be won or lost by us.

DeMar well recognizes what is at stake in this conflict:

---

[22] Kennedy, *The Gates of Hell Shall Not Prevail*, 218.
[23] Jacobs, *The Reformation Manifesto*, 203.

The philosophy of the classroom in this generation will be the philosophy in the next generation. Our earliest founding fathers understood this. . . . education has been used as a vehicle for social change from Karl Marx and Adolf Hitler to secular humanism and radical Islam. Our worldview opponents understand that education is where the war of ideas is fought. If Christians are serious about securing the future for their children, they must understand the nature of the war they are fighting.[24]

Lessons learned from history have shown that when a nation removes God from public life, immorality and lawlessness abound. Inevitably the State will be forced to pass more laws to prevent the breakdown of society. Will we learn from these lessons?[25]

So why are these lessons so difficult to learn and apply? Perhaps, it's because, as John Eldredge explains, "We live in a world at war. We are supposed to fight back. It is apparently a difficult reality to embrace, as witnessed by the passivity that marks much of modern Christianity. We just want the Christian life to be all about the sweet love of Jesus. But that is not what's going on here."[26]

So to where will we flee when America is finally lost? This question brings us to our second option.

Option #2 – 'The Benedict Option'

Termed the "The Benedict Option," it's a planned and all-out withdrawal from politics and society in general in order to "develop a flourishing Christian sub-culture as a testimony to the world and a haven." This option is being considered by growing numbers of conservative Christians who are convinced "they are living at the turning point in Western civilization, and it will not turn back." It's "the new

[24] Gary DeMar, "Whoever Controls the Schools Rules the World," book advertisement, *Biblical Worldview*, February 2007, 16.
[25] "Will you choose Liberty or Tyranny? " book advertisement, *Biblical Worldview*, February 2007, 25.
[26] John Eldredge, *The Way of the Wild Heart* (Nashville, TN.: Nelson Books, 2006), 144.

world . . . and it is unfriendly to their faith."[27] These Christians have given up any hope or desire for "reclaiming America for Christ."

Damon Linker provides these details:

> It's the name of a deeply pessimistic cultural project that's capturing the imaginations of social conservatives as they come to terms with the realization that the hopes and assumptions that animated the religious right over the past 35-odd years have been dashed by the sweeping triumph of the movement for same-sex marriage. . . . it's because they have been co-opted by a secular liberal minority that has placed itself in control of such elite institutions as the media, Hollywood, the universities, the judiciary, and the federal bureaucracy.

These Christians have also given up "play[ing] by the rules of the democratic game . . . primarily elections" as well as any hope that they "will eventually triumph." They see no hope because the opposition has co-opted "the judiciary to thwart the will of the people." They see that social conservatives are no longer the American majority and "same-sex marriage has come to be accepted by more than half of the country and Democrats have begun to embrace it without apology." They now fear "the unthinkable. Is it possible that we're now in the minority, with our freedoms subject to the whims of a hostile majority that will use the power of the modern liberal state (especially anti-discrimination laws) to enforce public conformity to secular, anti-Christian norms. That's where the Benedict Option comes in."

St. Benedict, for whom this option is named, was "the founder of Western monasticism during the waning days of the decadent and declining Roman Empire." He and his followers constructed "local forms of community within which civility and the intellectual and moral life can be sustained . . . ." This precedent serves as the model some in the Christian right are now considering in their withdrawal from "the new dark ages" and since they have "lost any reasonable hope of gaining and wielding political power." Hence, "cultivating and preserving the faith" is becoming "a pressing priority – perhaps the most pressing one of all" as "potentially . . . many millions of conservative Christians across numerous denominations" prepare "to

---

[27] D.C. Innes, "The call of a 'Benedict Option,'"
www.worldmag.com/2015/06/the_call_for_a_benedict-option, 6/5/15.

band together in communities aimed at cultural self-preservation and political self-defense."

Linker summarizes that today "for those who embrace the Benedict Option, the time of national political crusades and playing a decisive role in presidential politics is probably over," as well as "the good old days of the religious right" and "the culture war." In other words, they now feel that they have been "profoundly disenfranchised by the rise of the modern secular state" in which they "have been forced by events to accept without doubt that they are a minority in a majority secular nation. We have entered uncharted territory."[28]

The problem here, however, is there can be no peace in retreat and isolation if the country is ruled and controlled by those opposed to one's beliefs. Isolation is an illusion that will collapse. Furthermore, God's Word does not call for retreat and isolation. Rather, it calls for radical "salt-and-light" action and genuine change. But there is a third passive option.

Option #3 – Surrender and Prepare for Persecution

Instead of taking back our nation or conquering our world for Christ and kingdom by aggressive action, why not have tea parties with our opponents where we sing *Kumbaya* while they ravage our country and world? As John Bright points out, many desire to "give up all hope and responsibility for this world, retire from it, and let it go its own suicidal way to perdition." They find comfort in this position as they sit back and cry out, *"Marana tha"*—"Come, Lord Jesus." To support their passive resignation, they claim the Bible offers "no strategy for world conquest . . . no program of political or social action is even suggested; no ecumenical organization . . . is pushed . . . . except to *be the Church*."[29] Obviously, this third option provides a ready excuse for their inactivity

---

[28] Damon Linker, "The Benedict Option: Why the religious right is considering an all-out withdrawal from politics," *The Week*, http://theweek.com/articles/555734/benedict-option-why-religious-right-considering-allout-withdrawal-from-politics, 6/5/15.

[29] John Bright, *The Kingdom of God* (Nashville, TN.: Abingdon, 1978, 1953, 253.

and indifference to seriously engage people and society at large with their faith.

The sad reality is, as Bright further explains, "they have no power to redeem society and to make it the Kingdom of God, because they are themselves attached to society, involved in society, and participants in its sin. [Hence] they cannot win the victory for Christ . . . . [Therefore, these] visible churches are condemned to lie ever at the mercy of Caesar . . . . But that is not the Church."[30]

Along this same surrendering vein, J. Paul Nyquist, the current president of Moody Bible Institute, offers up what is being termed "a theology of persecution"[31] in his book, *Prepare: Living Your Faith in an Increasingly Hostile Culture.* In the book's foreword, David Jeremiah announces that "for all our efforts to preserve the soul of our nation, we are failing. We are losing the spiritual war and we have already lost the cultural war." He cites leaders such as Erwin Lutzer, Billy Graham, and Dr. Nyquist who are declaring that "we have crossed an invisible line, the die is cast, the tipping point has been reached, and apart from a gracious intervention from God [the ultimate Christian caveat], this nation is not going back to the culture and values it held in the past." He pessimistically prognosticates that "in other words, *Roe v. Wade* will never be overturned. The sanctity of marriage is a relic of the past, and God will never again be welcome in our schools."[32]

Additionally, Nyquist portends that "for two centuries, American followers of Christ have been protected from persecution, but those days are over. As we move forward into the next decade, suffering will become the new normal for believers! . . . While our ultimate hope is the return of Christ to take His people Home, our immediate hope is the return of Christ to bring revival to His church."[33]

But barring the occurrence of this long-anticipated event, he advises: "Get ready. An exciting, yet terrifying era is beginning for American believers. . . . we're witnessing an epic change in our culture—a spiritual climate shift threatening to reshape life as we know it. Hostility and intolerance are replacing toleration. Rejection and even hatred are

---

[30] Ibid., 256.
[31] Albert Mohler in endorsement of Nyquist, *Prepare*, 1.
[32] David Jeremiah in Forward, Ibid., 9.
[33] Ibid., 10.

pushing aside acceptance." Next, he quotes John S. Dickerson from his book *The Great Evangelical Recession* (2013), who writes: "In the coming decades United States evangelicals will be tested as never before, by the ripping and tearing of external cultural change—a force more violent than many of us expect. . . . Remember, the goal is to silence our voice and eliminate our influence."[34] He, too, characterizes this scenario as the "new normal" and as being "uncomfortable and unfamiliar territory. . . . [because] we have not been forced to live our faith in a hostile environment."[35]

Of course, Nyquist and the scholars he cites all believe we are now living in the biblical "last days" and, therefore, these adverse and hostile conditions are exactly what the Bible long ago prophesied would come. This popular eschatology drives their assessment that "the culture war is over—and we lost."[36]

So what does Nyquist recommend we American Christians now start doing? First, is to be "forewarned." Then, per the one-word title of his book, we must *"Prepare"* because "the day of the casual Christian is over. . . . There will be no place to hide, and there will be no way to remain silent. . . . The question is whether evangelicals will remain true to the teachings of Scripture and the unbroken teaching of the Christian church for over two thousand years on the morality of same-sex acts and the institution of marriage."[37]

Next to come "will be death of religious freedom by a thousand little cuts here and there; cancelled speeches of religious figures at state universities, lost HHS grants, the refusal of city governments to recognize churches that don't permit gay marriages, 'hate crime' legislation that extends to opposition to gay marriage, and so on."[38]

He summarizes accordingly:

> . . . with an increasingly shrinking minority status, Christians are being ordered to leave the room and take their Bible talk with them. . . . Examples abound . . . . It's painful for me to admit that the country I

---

[34] Ibid., 14, 17.
[35] Ibid., 18.
[36] Ibid., 26.
[37] Ibid., 32 – the latter portion is in quotation of Erwin Lutzer and Albert Mohler, respectively.
[38] Ibid., 35 – in quotation of George Neumayr.

love has radically changed, and the pace of change is accelerating. Followers of Jesus who awakened from a cultural sleep are facing hostility, rejection, and marginalization. The trend lines point to increased opposition—including genuine persecution.[39]

The die has been cast. The tipping point has been reached. We have lost the war. What now? . . . we must be realists. . . . with the current, accelerating trends in America, we can expect our voices to be silenced. We can expect to be persecuted for our views. We can expect to be rejected and punished in the land of the free—for standing on scriptural truth. Since this is a new experience for nearly all of us, we need to understand what the Bible says about persecution. The verses that didn't apply to us before will take on new meaning.[40]

Bill Bennett, who was Secretary of Education under President Ronald Reagan, agrees with Nyquist's dire prognostications in predicting that "everything we've seen points that way." Look for his new book on this perspective, appropriately titled *Tired by Fire* to come out shortly.[41]

"for two centuries, American followers of Christ have been protected from persecution, but those days are over. As we move forward into the next decade, suffering will become the new normal for believers!"

Blatantly missing, however, from Nyquist's treatise was any mention of the kingdom of God, the central teaching of Jesus Christ. That's because, as we shall see in Chapters 6 and 8, in his view the kingdom Jesus was presenting during his earthly ministry is no longer here.

Overman, on the other hand, summarizes our present dilemma, differently:

---

[39] Ibid., 37-40.
[40] Ibid., 56.
[41] Joel Belz, "Stormy forecast: What some prominent Christians say about predictions of persecution," *World*, 31 October, 2015, 3.

The similarities between decadent Greece and our current situation are sobering, and the fruit of present day Humanism is not looking very good at all. . . . For reasons such as these, we believe the consequences of failing to integrate the unchanging and enduring biblical worldview into the minds of the next generation are enormously serious, for both individuals as well as the entire culture. Furthermore, if there ever was a time to articulate the basics of the biblical worldview to the next generation, and to demonstrate how this worldview connects with all of reality, it is now. This is our hour of opportunity.[42]

With this brighter perspective, let's look at the first of four aggressive, take-action options.

Option #4 – Armed Rebellion

"I'm as mad as Hell and I'm not going to take this anymore!"[43] It's another option that is clearly ridiculous when some people take it too far. That is, when persecution breaks out, to defend ourselves and fight it. This aggressive action can vary from legal defense in a court of law (Paul defended himself as a Roman citizen) to the extreme of physical combat and armed rebellion. Yes, this option appeals to some Christians. But it also contradicts Jesus' principle of turning the other cheek (Matt. 5:39), Paul's command not to seek vengeance (Rom. 12:19), and Christ's example against retaliation cited in 1 Peter 2:23. But let's also not forget Jesus' aggressive action of twice entering the Temple and turning over the tables of the moneychangers (Matt. 21:12-13; John 2:13-16). And after all, aren't we Christians supposed to emulate Jesus?

Nonetheless, the more government becomes hostile to Christianity and ungodly in its moral, legal, social, and political policies and laws in America, or any country of the world, conflicts among churches, individual Christians, and the government and its agencies will multiply and intensify.

DeMar relents that "these conflicts may make it necessary for Christians to say no to statist laws that will force them to violate the laws of God. . . . Because of a desire to see the current corruption in our own

---

[42] Overman, *Assumptions That Affect Our Lives*, 152, 160.

[43] Howard Beale, played by Peter Finch in the movie *Network*, 1976.

nation reversed, some Christians may take it upon themselves to bring about change by revolutionary means."

But DeMar correctly concludes and advises that "there is no warrant in Scripture for a revolutionary spirit. In fact, there is no need for an armed revolt. If Christians would involve themselves in the political process, at least in the United States, the realm of civil government could be changed at the ballot box."[44]

Nyquist, of course, condemns even the thought of this aggressive option as he points out that "both Romans 13 and 1 Peter 2 call us to submit ourselves to our governing authorities, for in doing so we show submission to God. No exceptions are listed. It is clear that the believer's general obligation is to obey government." But then he vacillates. "Is it ever permissible to disobey our governing authorities? Yes, but only when obeying man's law requires you to disobey God's law. . . . Clearly the Bible allows for civil disobedience in limited situations. But it's limited. We're to obey our governing authorities even if we passionately disagree with the law."[45]

With responses under this option ranging from noncompliance to civil disobedience to morally justified revolution, this one fact remains: The Crusades—military campaigns sanctioned by the Catholic Church in the Middle Ages—were a sad example of exercising an extreme of this option.

Option #5 – Calling for Massive, Extreme, Continuous, and Sustained Prayer – á la 2 Chronicles 7:14

Extreme times call for extreme measures. And the calling of an entire congregation of any church by its leadership to massive praying, day and night, passionate, persistent, and not just one day every now and then, but not ceasing until things change dramatically (which could take many years), would certainly qualify as "extreme" in most Christians' vernacular.

Nevertheless, the DeVilles suggest: "imagine God's people nationwide praying day and night. We would see such an outpouring and

---

[44] Gary DeMar, *Myths, Lies & Half Truths* (Powder Springs, GA.: American Vision, 2004), 278.
[45] Nyquist, *Prepare*, 98-99.

change in our nation it would defy description!" They then ask these two challenging questions and passionately urge: "Will you answer His call? Begin today? . . . it is imperative that all churches give the highest importance to the ministry of prayer. . . . Pastor . . . it is critical your people understand the power and benefits of prayer that will stir and motivate them to pray. . . . So we must ask ourselves: 'What are we willing to do?' The price for complacency would be devastating to this nation. There is so much at stake and God is counting on all of us (His leaders and people) to follow through. . . . don't wait! We believe now is the time for every pastor and church in America to begin implementing God's Answer . . . . Help set the example and lead the way today."[46]

And so I ask you, how do you think this approach would be received in your church? How long do you think this level of intensity, if achieved, could be sustained? Let's be honest. We Christians stink at prayer—at least prayer beyond ourselves and immediate family—almost as much as we stink at evangelism. Of course, prayer is important and can make a difference. But practically speaking, calls to prayer meetings or prayer-and-fasting conferences fall mostly on deaf ears in most of today's churches. Or, like revivals, these efforts come and go as the few participants soon grow weary and drift away.

The fact is, prayer alone will not get the job done. Please note that the often-cited verse 2 Chronicles 7:14 requires more than prayer: "if my people, who are called by my name will humble themselves and pray and seek my face and turn from their wicked ways, then will I hear from heaven and will forgive their sin and will heal their land."

This verse also requires that God's people "humble themselves," "seek my face," and "turn from their wicked ways." What "wicked ways?" For starters, how about gospel reductionism, kingdom reductionism, stinking at evangelism, and withdrawing from being salt and light in society, not to mention many other sins of omission and commission? Hence, it takes more than prayer to meet God's requirements for national forgiveness and healing here!

. . . how do you think this approach would be received in your church?

---

[46] DeVilles, *God's Answer for America*, 152, 154, 183, 186.

And fervent prayer is hard work. So are the other requirements. But prayer along with the other three requirements, along with active involvement and dynamic engagement with the issues and problems, can make a huge difference.

Also, given the high level of societal apathy and indifference and the major foci on personal salvation, going to heaven, and self-improvement principles and practices, especially in American churches over the past half century, the prospects for employing 2 Chronicles 7:14, by itself, to initiate and sustain anything of significance are probably dim.

Option #6 – Moral Exhortation (aka – Browbeating)

Most assuredly, and once again, we Christians in America have the numbers to effect major change in the direction of our nation's culture. But the two critical questions are, do we have the will and will enough of us wake up in time?

No, it's not enough just to get people saved. We must become motivated, activated, and mobilized to apply God's Word to every area and facet of life. Anything less is less than our faith commands us to be and do as salt and light.

So what will it take to stir Christians to such a high and unified level of societal action within a pluralistic society? Some fear this won't happen until America slides into total anarchy or Islam takes over and people are faced with a "convert-or-die-by-the-sword" alternative. Yes, Christianity is foreordained in God's Word to triumph. But that does not mean that Western Europe and America will achieve a spiritual revival and be part of that triumph. Perhaps Christians in other nations will simply take over and surpass us.

Much is at stake. The testimony of decline and ruin is everywhere. The problems we have today we hardly knew a few decades ago. And yet the Church is growing like never before, mostly abroad, but also here in America. Naturally, it would be great to heal our nation's and the world's ills with a wave of a magic wand. But that's not an option.

This next option for motivating, activating, and mobilizing the troops is moral exhortation—in other words, shaming, guilt-riding, brow-beating Christians out of our comfortable pews, nice houses, luxurious offices, and enjoyable vacations and into the "dirty" arenas of societal action and confrontation.

In this regard, I once asked a senior pastor friend of a mega-evangelical church what would happen if he would start morally exhorting his congregation to go out and get more engaged and involved on a regular basis in social-activism—i.e., taking on social injustice issues, eliminating poverty and racism, battling the culture war, and advancing the kingdom, etc. "Oh, I could probably get away with it for one or two sermons," he quickly replied. "But any more than that, the elders would come speak with me and remind me they hired me to preach salvation, and if I didn't they'd fire me."

The hard reality in most churches and denominations today is, a "fired" pastor's likelihood of finding a similar position with another church in his denomination is very limited—especially when word gets out that he/she was "fired." And finding another position in another denomination is almost impossible. Therefore, the unmistakable message is: "toe the line, pastor, with normative, acceptable Christianity, and leave that culture-changing kingdom stuff alone." After all, we don't want to offend anyone. And then we wonder why there is not more zeal for following Christ and engaging the world? Thus, many churches offer plenty of entertainment but ask for little commitment. But perpetuating seeker-friendly, user-friendly, growth-oriented, faith-compromising, and culture-losing churches is not going to accomplish any more than business as usual.

Think of it this way. . . Moral exhortation is like trying to push a string across the top of a wooden table. Try it sometime. Lay a two-foot length of string straight out in front of you. Next, place your fingers on the front portion of the string closest to you and start pushing. What happens? The string goes sideways and every which way except the direction you are pushing it. That's a perfect illustration for why this moral exhortation option won't work, or won't work for long.

So what will it take to stir Christians to such a high and unified level of societal action within a pluralistic society?

Remember, Jesus warned the generation of his day that "even the elect" would be deceived "if that were possible" (Matt. 24:24b). Is this deception of the elect still possible today?

Indeed, the anti-God forces are emboldened by the lack of Christian response and effectiveness. They are happy to have us sitting in our churches—the more often we sit there each week the better. Consequently, the secular revolutionaries seem to be getting everything they want. Certainly, the church needs to reclaim her proper place in our society as the head and not the tail (see Deut 28:13). But how do we awaken this "sleeping giant" and shake off its "hands-off" policy of cultural disengagement, and reshape the thinking and behavior of our attendees?

Moving onto Our Seventh Option

Like it or not, if we are to overcome this secular assault against our faith and values, then a significant majority of the Church will need to be prepared and willing to engage in the battle. Let's also never forget that each of us will be held accountable. And since we face an opposition that is well-organized, well-financed, and highly motivated, how could we ever compete? Does this seem like an unattainable pipe-dream?

Tony Evans believes the problem is, "we have so many Christians who aren't proclaiming anything." And "proclamation has to become a priority if the church is to fulfill its kingdom agenda. We need to become bold about our message as everybody else has become about his or her message. . . . everybody else is coming out. We might as well come out too!"[47]

But scared and timid, comfortable and incompetent people will never stand up against opposition or go out and engage and influence the culture. Hence many, if not most, Christians (here in America, at least) are not "good soil" (see Jesus' parables in Matt. 13:3-9, 18-23; Luke 8:4-15) for moral exhortation. They've been contaminated and blinded by their reductionist traditions. We have to change that. But how, when so many Christians have been sequestered in their churches for so long waiting for heaven, the rapture, and Jesus?

It's quite a problem, as Russell D. Moore recognizes: "A unified, widespread conservative Christian campaign to 'reclaim the nation for

---

[47] Evans, *What A Way To Live!*, 307.

Christ,' . . . is simply not in evangelicalism's organizational 'cards' or its cultural 'DNA.'"[48]

Kennedy elaborates on this problem by noting that "most Christians give lip-service to the command to spread the gospel. . . . the Church in the last seventy-five to a hundred years has often ignored the cultural mandate, and we wonder why we have so little impact on the world. . . . recent surveys show that most people feel the Church is irrelevant to modern society. . . . [But] we have allowed ourselves to be irrelevant, and we're reaping the consequences."[49]

Once again, it seems "we like our Christianity just like it is, thank you." Ron Sider terms this inertia mentality *"The Scandal of the Evangelical Mind* [name of his book] . . . . that evangelicals live just like the world." He challenges his readers to: "contrast that with what the New Testament says about what happens when people come to a living faith in Christ" and adds that: "There's supposed to be radical transformation in the power of the Holy Spirit. The disconnect between our biblical beliefs and our practice is just, I think, heart-rending. . . . the stats just break my heart. They make me weep. And somehow we must face the reality and change it."[50]

When asked, "How do we turn the ship around?" Sider responds: "We need to rethink our theology. We need to ask, 'Are we really biblical?' . . . Cheap grace results when we limit salvation to personal fire insurance against hell . . . . I would think that evangelicals would want to get biblical and define the gospel the way Jesus did—which is that it's the Good News of the *kingdom.*"[51]

Unfortunately, as Wright poignantly pinpoints: "One more exhortation to love, to patience, to forgiveness, may remind us of our duty. But as long as we think of it as a duty we aren't very likely to do

---

[48] Quoting Christian Smith in Russell D. Moore, *The Kingdom of Christ* (Wheaton, IL.: Crossway Books, 2004), 166.

[49] Kennedy, *What If Jesus Had Never Been Born?*, 240.

[50] Interview by Stan Guthrie, "The Evangelical Scandal: Ron Sider says the movement is riddled with hypocrisy, and that it's time for serious change," *Christianity Today*, April 2005, 70. Ron Sider, *The Scandal of the Evangelical Mind* (Grand Rapids, MI.: Baker Books, 2005).

[51] Ibid., 72.

it."[52] Rather, we are inclined to believe that God is in control and be content to just sit back and watch.

Once again, as I have previously quoted, Chalke and Mann put it well and like this: "The Church in the West – with some notable exceptions – has a tame faith because it has been giving a tame message for centuries. You can't breed a radical revolutionary movement on passive, middle-of-the-road rhetoric."[53] They further illuminate that our "way of 'doing evangelism' . . . is not only ineffective, but hard (if not impossible) to find in the Gospels. We have developed a 'them' and 'us' culture – saints and sinners, ins and outs, saved and unsaved. . . . And on that basis we have convinced ourselves that we need two messages – the first for the outs to get them in, and the other for the ins to make sure they stay there."[54]

For all these reasons and more, motivating, activating, and mobilizing the body of Christ will not likely be accomplished via any of the six options presented in this chapter. So, seriously, how would you recommend we overcome the massive resistance, inertia, apathy, and complacency against engaging and confronting the major issues of our country and world that exist in much of the church today?

Most certainly, this realization presents us with a daunting challenge. It therefore brings us to our final, aggressive, and scriptural option. It's our seventh option and well worth careful consideration. We'll devote our whole next chapter to exploring its credibility, authority, and potential.

And since we face an opposition that is well-organized, well-financed, and highly motivated, how could we ever compete? Does this seem like an unattainable pipe-dream?

---

[52] Wright, *Surprised By Hope*. 287-288.
[53] Chalke & Mann, *The Lost Message of Jesus*, 86.
[54] Ibid., 140.

Chapter 5

Big Problems Call for a Big Solution

*We Christians cannot continue to avoid knowing
what we already know:
that something is rotten in the state of our religion.*[1]

L ike it or not, we can't turn back the calendar to the 1950s and a re-
50ized "Leave-It-to-Beaver" family, "The Life of Riley," or
"Father Knows Best." Nor can we go back to a re-Christianized
America at just any time in America's history. Likewise, none of the six
options in our last chapter is capable of making this happen or stopping
and reversing American's plunge into being a secular-humanist,
dominated society.

Part of the problem, as Shane Claiborne bluntly lays out in his book
Irresistible Revolution is, "Our research shows that local churches have
virtually no influence in our culture." He cites "seven dominant spheres
of influence . . . movies, music, television, books, the Internet, law, and
family. His second tier of influencers comprises entities such as schools,
peers, newspapers, radio, and businesses. The local church appears
among the entities that have little or no influence on society."[2]

---

[1] McLaren, a *Generous Orthodoxy*, 268.
[2] Shane Claiborne, *Irresistible Revolution* (Grand Rapids, MI.: Zondervan,
2006), 118.

Recently, a cynic emailed me his analogous perspective of Christianity: "Where's the excitement? Where's the vibrancy? Where's the enthusiasm? Most Christians I've met are so paranoid, it's almost like they have a sixth sense that their faith is flawed but won't admit it. So they come across as just a bunch of timid, trepid Christians walking around. And these are the people who can turn the world upside down, again? Excuse me."

For many, modern-day Christianity, or Christendom, to be more exact, has become a reformulated "brand" that's market-driven to appeal to the seeker-friendly, user-friendly, growth-oriented tastes and preferences of masses of consumers seeking religious goods and services. As a result, those who subscribe to these "rebranded" versions of our "once mighty faith" have largely lost sight of the central teaching of Jesus and retreated from being salt, light, and of service for humanity. They have little, if any, desire to engage or influence society. They are quite comfortable being sequestered in their enclaves (churches and schools), even while inviting the less fortunate into the soup kitchen. This book, of course, aims to change this status quo.

As we shall see in the pages ahead, the prime reason the Church has lost its power and influence is because it has strayed far from its original faith that Jesus Christ "once for all" established and delivered during the 1st century (see Jude 3). That form of Christianity still has the same power and potential in our 21st century to turn the world upside down, AGAIN.

So what do you think future generations will think of us today if we fail to impact and change our culture? Perhaps, they will say that we "fiddled while Rome/America burned," ignored the warning signs, and were preoccupied with other things for our own comfort and convenience. But the further truth is, and unlike our ancestors in the faith, we became "cultural eunuchs,"[3] discredited our faith, and are leaving future generations with a mess. Make no mistake; *big problems call for a big solution*.

Pearcey accurately appreciates the largeness of this problem when she writes: "This internalization or privatization of religion is one of the

---

[3] John Barber, *America Restored* (Fort Lauderdale, FL.: Coral Ridge Ministries, 2002), 36.

most monumental changes that has ever taken place in Christendom."[4] She adds that "not only do we fail to be salt and light to a lost culture, but we ourselves may end up being shaped by that culture."[5] Rightly, she also recognizes that "if we privatize our faith, however, we will play right into the hands of the philosophical naturalists" and "unless Christians tackle this attitude head on, our message will continue to pass through a grid that reduces it to an expression of merely psychological need."[6] Hence, "unable to answer the great intellectual questions of the day, many conservative Christians turned their back on mainstream culture and developed a fortress mentality."[7]

"Where's the excitement? Where's the vibrancy? Where's the enthusiasm?
Most Christians I've met are so paranoid, it's almost like they have a sixth sense that their faith is flawed but won't admit it."

So where does this Christian reductionism leave us today? Kennedy claims, "the Church has withdrawn to a large extent into a pietistic ghetto . . . . We have turned our educational system, which was founded by Christians, over to unbelievers. We have turned science, which was founded by Christians . . . over to unbelievers in many cases. We have turned much of the media over to the rankest of unbelievers, so that we are continuously bombarded by their godless thoughts and ideas. We have handed over the reins of government, to a large extent, to unbelievers who have been busily engaged in legislating the devil's agenda for the world. We have been in retreat and have not sought to fulfill the Cultural Mandate."[8]

---

[4] Quotation of "the great historian of religion Marty Martin" in Pearcey, *Total Truth*, 35.
[5] Ibid., 44
[6] Ibid., 202.
[7] Ibid., 291.
[8] Kennedy, *What If Jesus Had Never Been Born?*, 241.

Most assuredly, much of the Church today is not the Church Jesus had in mind. If He was to walk into most churches in America next week, He'd probably be turning the tables over again. Tenaciously, we Christians hold on to our comfortable reductionist traditions, while ignoring much of God's Word. But if we are truly concerned about reaching the world for Christ, we have to change from being weak and timid into being "strong and courageous" (Joshua 1:6a). If we don't so change, however, "God can rule without Washington's permission and will continue to do so long after the American empire has joined the Babylonian, Assyrian, Persian, Greek, Roman, British, and Soviet ones on the scrap heap of history,"[9] if indeed that ends up being the case.

Nonetheless, most current brands (versions) of Christianity being preached, practiced, and perceived today, as Smith concludes, "hardly represent(s) an ideology capable of sustaining a forceful reclaiming America for Christ. . . . in fact few ordinary evangelicals actually subscribe to James Kennedy's program of 'reclaiming America for Christ' . . . . In the end while 'Christian America' does strike a certain warm chord for some evangelicals, it simply will not serve as a deep cultural wellspring sustaining a major Christian political movement that will somehow 're-Christianize' America."[10] Incidentally, Kennedy's Center for Reclaiming America for Christ is "now-defunct."[11]

Rather, and once again, *big problems call for a big solution.* And I'm not willing to surrender our great nation, our "once mighty faith," and our children and grandchildren to the dance of history. I hope you are not either. I agree with Brandon Vallorani, I "cannot bear to see apathetic Christians in America lose the religious freedom that our forefathers fought, lived, and died for."[12] It's time for the Church to get its proverbial head out of the sand of reductionist traditions. But how do we do that?

---

[9] Craig A. Carter, *Rethinking Christ and Culture* (Grand Rapids, MI.: Brazos Press, 2006), 24.
[10] Smith, *Christian America?*, 53, 60.
[11] Stan Guthrie, "A Hole in Our Holism," *Christianity Today*, January 2008, 56.
[12] Brandon Vallorani, "America, Return to God," *Biblical Worldview*, March 2006, 12.

First, we need a sound, potent, and effective theology for turning the world upside down again. As McKnight astutely observes: "The less influential Christianity becomes in a given country, as one sees at the turn of the twentieth century in many countries, the greater the temptation for Christianity to become a spiritual religion that has nothing or little to do with social realities. This clearly happened in the United States. Fundamentalism tossed fire and brimstone at culture and state, withdrew in some ways into sacred enclaves, and focused on personal holiness and going to heaven."[13]

He further and astutely observes that the Moral Majority "'Despite all the media tumult . . . the high public visibility of its leader [Jerry Falwell], its extensive solicitation of funds during a six-year political crusade—claiming to speak for six million households—*has not achieved passage of a single major piece of legislation cherished by the conservative right.*'" Perhaps, he suggests, "evangelicals do not have sufficient political power to achieve their aims and maybe ought to rethink their entire approach . . . ."[14] To which I add a hearty, "Amen."

We must now seriously ponder what it will take to stir, shake, or even frighten us Christians out of our complacency and into action. Or shall we simply sit idly by while our country and civilization are lost to the ungodly crowd? Indeed, the stakes are tremendous, and so far we have been opting out.

Some feel that the only way to awaken "the sleeping giant" of the modern-day church from its normative nominalism is for it to be shaken by persecution. They may be right. But there is another way. I maintain that it can also be stirred into action by a more appealing, authoritative, and comprehensive Christian message. But not just any message will do. Assuredly, another spiritual revival won't get the job done. Revivals, historically, come and go.

Predominantly, most people desire to be involved with something bigger than themselves in the here and now. Neither your church or mine, or a denomination, is big enough. That something must be large enough to open, penetrate, and change the hearts and minds of both

---

[13] Scot McKnight, *Kingdom Conspiracy* (Grand Rapids, MI.: Brazo Press, 2014, 217.

[14] Ibid., 214-215 in quotation of Carl F.H. Henry, *Confessions of a Theologian* (Waco, TX.: Word, 1986), 394.

Christians at various levels of belief and dedication and non-Christians, alike.

That something is precisely what we present throughout the rest of this book. It's a drawing and compelling theology for initiating, engaging, supporting, and sustaining Christian activism in today's culture as the salt and light we are called to be. It's a powerful and thought-provoking theology for confronting a culture that proudly and without fear of reprisal ridicules and dismisses biblical truth, rejects the Word of God, and despises Christians. We must put an end to merely decrying secular decadence and decay, roll up our sleeves, and offer a positive and fully relevant alternative. The good news is we have that alternative. The bad news is we aren't using it.

Secondly, we need to acknowledge that we are under attack and in a cultural war. We Christians did not start this war. The secular humanists did. They declared war on Christianity and the Church and began their systematic attacks some time ago. Since then, they have made great strides toward total victory. But battles are still raging and being lost by us. We're losing battles over issues that were unthinkable just a few decades or years ago. It is the great battle for the right to redefine and reshape America and much of the world, and for religious freedom in contrast to a secular humanist "theocracy."

Thirdly, we people of God must repent of our apathetic, lethargic, ineffective, and reductionist versions of Christianity as well as being seduced by the popular "last days" craze and waiting for Jesus to come and provide an easy way out. Make no mistake; we watered-down, neutralized, and ridiculed Christians are largely responsible for America's societal breakdown.

David Barton minces no words when nailing this responsibility squarely on the head of today's churches and Christians: "The current condition of our government and our country is simply a reflection of the action—or lack thereof—by the God-fearing community." He cites Jesus' parable describing "a man who had a good field, growing good fruit. He awakened one morning to find that field filled with tares, weeds, and bad fruit. How did it change from good to bad? In Matthew 13:25, Jesus identified the problem: while the good men slept, the enemy came in and planted the tares. Jesus never faulted the enemy for doing what he did; the problem was that the good men went to sleep." Striking, isn't it, "the neglect of civic stewardship by God-fearing citizens?"[15] It's time to wake up "the sleeping giant" called the Church, get out of our pews, and back into the field.

Fourthly, this cultural battle is not *necessarily* between conservatives and liberals or Republicans and Democrats. Neither group nor political party is capable of addressing or resolving the numerous problems, issues, and broken places. They've proven that. Christ's Church is the only institution capable of addressing the big problems of this world and offering a big solution—provided they reclaim and fully embrace the central teaching of Jesus. Then, and only then, can these problems be effectively addressed.

. . . offer a positive and fully relevant alternative. The good news is, we have that alternative. The bad news is, we aren't using it.

Fifthly, the battle is not over; maybe it's far from over. So many today feel overwhelmed by the problems of this world, the ground we have lost, and the challenges yet to be faced. But these situations are not hopeless. Here in America, I believe we have not reached the tipping point, but we may be close. A window of opportunity still may be open. Therefore, we must awaken apathetic pastors, apathetic believers, and the apathetic Church to become the salt and light we are called to be in society. Otherwise, God will have the right to judge us and this country even more severely. But when asked, "Do you know of any culture that has made the turn" in history at this stage of decay and decline, Overman was forced to admit, "No, I don't." Except for "the Hebrew model itself. The history of ancient Israel is one of drifting away from God, and turning back again. . . . But it is also a sober reminder that while turning back to God is always possible, keeping it that way is never guaranteed by one generation for the next."[16]

Similarly, Dr. Martin Luther King, Jr., in his last book addressing segregation and racism issues indicated that "we may now be in only the initial period of an era of change as far-reaching in its consequences as

---

[15] Barton, *Original Intent*, 357.
[16] Overman, *Assumptions That Affect Our Lives*, 163-164.

the American Revolution . . . . If we do not act, we shall surely be dragged down the long, dark, and shameful corridor of time reserved for those who possess power without compassion, might without morality, and strength without sight."[17] One thing, however, is for sure. Our times are critical times! America is at a crossroads in its history.

Sixthly, all the problems of the world are rooted, fundamentally and ultimately, in moral and spiritual problems within human hearts. The outworking of these inner problems results in what Pope John Paul II labeled "the culture of death." Solving these problems, therefore, requires both inner/internal and outer/external transformation. But transformations cannot be forced. They must come through voluntary conversions.

Cal Thomas knows this well: "Too many Christians think if they shout loud enough and gain political strength the world will be improved. That is a false doctrine. I have never seen anyone 'converted' to a Christian's point of view (and those views are not uniform) through political power. I have frequently seen someone's views changed after they have experienced true conversion and then live by different standards and live for goals beyond which political party controls the government."[18]

Unfortunately, many, if not most, of our modern-day versions of Christianity have been hamstrung by the traditions of men that "nullify the word of God for the sake of your traditions" (Matt. 15:6; Mark 7:13). Consequently, they are deficient. This is why Christianity today is very different and far less attractive and effective than it once was. Our diluted and reductionist versions have produced masses of "lukewarm" Christians, whom Jesus says He will "spit (literally vomit) you out of my mouth" (Rev. 3:16). To the church of Ephesus in the Book of Revelation, Jesus also threatened to "come to you and remove your lampstand from its place" (Rev. 2:5b). Much of the Church in America may currently be at or close to this same point of jeopardy.

Armed with the knowledge of the destructive forces and trends operating in America and throughout the world, and given the assaults upon the Christian faith and its people that we have presented, we must

---

[17] Dr. Martin Luther King in his last book, *The Trumpet of Conscience,* quoted in McLaren, *Everything Must Change,* 254.
[18] Cal Thomas, "Stop sending money," *The Indianapolis Star,* 8/31/05, A16.

shake off our compromised and reductionist versions of our "once mighty faith." But how and with what?

   Seventhly, there is only one practical, effective, and proven way out of this cultural, moral, and spiritual morass. No, it's not just praying 2 Chronicles 7:14 or invoking moral exhortation, although that's part of it. What is needed is a drawing, compelling, authoritative, articulate, well-reasoned, passionate, and credible vision for the future, along with a counterrevolutionary approach that encompasses the full range of individual and social problems, is capable of awakening and activating the Church. Moore spells out this great need in a nutshell: "Until evangelicals fortify 'a deep biblical sense of the corporate identity of the new people of God, we will not be able to present the gospel of peace on the front lines of our 'cultural wars.'"[19]

   So, does such a vision and counterrevolutionary approach exist for America and for others worldwide?

- One that could rejuvenate the culturally and politically disengaged Church and override the traditional objection that such "engagement would turn evangelicals aside from their primary task: the personal regeneration of individuals."[20]
- One that could erase the remembrances of "the failures of evangelical activism in the 1970s and beyond, [and their] unrealistic expectations about the possibilities of political action . . . ."[21]
- One that could reform the entrenched pessimistic eschatology that "the only hope for the world is the return of Christ—nothing else."[22]
- One that could take back a theology that "has been hijacked by an eschatology that ignores sociopolitical issues in an apocalyptic flight from the world."[23]

---

[19] In quotation of Edmund Clowney in Moore, *The Kingdom of Christ*, 167.
[20] Moore, *The Kingdom of Christ*, 82.
[21] Ibid., 77.
[22] Ibid., 68.
[23] Ibid., 69.

- One that could boldly and courageously recognize that "the failure of evangelical politics is often, at root, the failure of an evangelical theology . . . ."[24]
- One that could strike directly at the heart, mind, and present-day fact that "Christians are not motivated to save the future for their children and grandchildren because they are waiting on an imminent heavenly rescue from an ever-darkening world. We must issue a wake-up call nationwide."[25]

The answer is, such a vision and approach not only exists; it also is readily available. But we have to be willing to do some things differently if we're to change the course on which America, and much of the world, is currently going down and down.

The greater good news is, we may have now reached the point of frustration and shame to realize that something of major significance must change. And yet admonishments to repent and turn or return to God are far too vague and nebulous to be effective for this pertinent reason: "Right now, if across America on prime-time TV there was a great message calling for our nation to turn back to God, it would probably be scoffed at and mocked by most, including national leaders [and many Christians, as well]. Why? Because the soil and soul(s) of the nation must be first prepared, for so many hearts are hardened and deceived because of sin. . . . [and] most of the people's hearts grew [have grown] hardened towards the warnings and cry of God . . . . [because] they had heard it all before so many times."[26]

**The answer is, such a vision and approach not only exists; it also is readily available.
But we're going to have to be willing to do some things differently . . .**

---

[24] Ibid., 15.
[25] Brandon Vallorani, *"The Gary DeMar Show* Goes Daily," *Biblical Worldview*, April 2007, 12.
[26] DeVilles, *God's Answer for America*, 178, 219-220.

Thus, a great vision and empowered approach must be recast for preparing, penetrating, and transforming hearts and minds, exposing false notions, and uniting us modern-day Christians into action. Grasping this vision and approach will necessitate a return to our roots. Of course, some will dismiss it saying this isn't possible. But "with God all things are possible" (Matt. 19:26). This will only happen if we align ourselves with his heart, mind, will, and plan for this world. Dare we settle for less?

Option #7 – Transformational Imagination (T.I.)

Great ideas, well-imagined, move people and nations and shape world history for good or evil, positively or negatively. In his book, *To Change the World*, James Davison Hunter elaborates:

> . . . it is ideas that move history. . . . Mind. Imagination. Heart. Though driven by ideas, worldviews exist primarily in the hearts and minds and imaginations of individuals and take form in choices made by individuals. . . . 'Our choices are shaped by what we believe is real and true, right and wrong, good and beautiful. Our choices are shaped by our worldview. . . . history is little more than the recording of the rise and fall of *the great ideas—the worldviews—that form our values and move us to act.* If we're going to succeed in restoring a moral influence in American culture . . . we need to cultivat[e] a Christian mind' and 'live out a biblical worldview.'[27]

Jesus knew all this and much more. Arguably, He is the greatest genius of communication and most intelligent person who ever lived on earth—"in whom are hidden all the treasures of wisdom and knowledge" (Col. 2:3). That's why He employed the communication technique of transformational imagination (T.I.) to implement his central teaching amongst his followers and all who would come after them.

Today, and as I have previously written, "educators, psychologists, and communication experts tell us the world runs on ideas. And ideas are crucial to all of life. They are the foundation upon which our lives are

---

[27] James Davison Hunter, *To Change the World* (New York, NY.: Oxford University Press, 2010), 25, 7 and in quotation of Chuck Colson.

shaped, our dreams are generated, and our nations are built. Conversely, ideas can ruin lives, devastate dreams, and crumble kingdoms."

"Perceptions shape our ideas. And perceptions are fragile; they are formed by both the words we hear and the pictures we see. This is how we humans process information. Of course, words are important. But if a picture is worth a thousand words, then pictures (and word pictures) have a greater effect on us than words (alone). The advertising industry is built on this principle."

"Let's face it, we are susceptible to what we both hear and see. But more and more we moderns have become a people governed by pictures. The experts tell us that we think in terms of pictures, so our ideas are most often shaped by the pictures we see."[28]

Indeed, imagination is a powerful motivator. It's part of the nature of all human beings who are made in the image and likeness of God (Gen. 1:26a). We desire what we positively imagine. If you can't imagine something—or if you imagine it as something negative, drab, or unappealing—you cannot get excited about it, you will not internalize it, and you will not seek it. Hence, T.I.'s drawing power and compelling appeal is without equal for capturing hearts, opening minds, and attracting us humans toward its vision. And we become certain kinds of people based on the imaginations we choose.

J. Richard Middleton and Brian J. Walsh encapsulate the transformational power of imagination quite well in their book *Truth Is Stranger Than It Used to Be*:

> It is only when we can imagine the world to be different than the way it is that we can be empowered to embody this alternative reality, which is God's kingdom and resist this present nightmare of brokenness, disorientation and confusion. . . . A liberated imagination is a prerequisite for facing the future. . . . If we cannot have such a liberating imagination and cannot countenance such radical dreams, then the story remains closed for us and we have no hope.[29]

Dr. Martin Luther King, Jr. is fondly remembered for his utilization of imagination in his "I have a dream" speech that was focused on racial

---

[28] Noē, *The Perfect Ending for the World*, 50.
[29] J. Richard Middleton and Brian J. Walsh, *Truth Is Stranger Than It Used to Be* (Downers Grove, IL.: InterVarsity, 1995), 192.

reconciliation in the United States and the world. This is also why slogans, rallying cries, and mottoes that cast a vision are so effective—such as the American Revolution's "No king but King Jesus" and President Ronald Reagan's "Mr. Gorbachev, tear down this wall."

Likewise, Jesus knew exactly what He was doing when He cast a transformational vision far different from the kingdoms of this world. The historical fact is, prior to the coming of Jesus, human life on this earth was cheap and expendable. But Jesus gave us humans a new and imaginative perspective on the value of human life, our role in making it even better, and the transformed reality achievable. If He had not come, we might *never* have known or seen this transformational change. But, sad to say, human life is becoming cheap once again.

Comparatively, however, seeing the kingdom is like putting on a new set of eyeglasses; everything looks different from that day on. And Jesus not only invites us to see but also enter and live in this new reality in our contemporary world. He also invites us to participate in changing our world from its hates, broken places, disharmonies, and injustices into God's desired plan and kingdom of love, joy, peace, power, mercy, justice, and more.

Sadly, the hard truth is, most Christians have never seen or entered his kingdom; or if they entered, they soon exited. One reason is because of the reductionist gospel they are taught. Another is that they are essentially kingdom-illiterate, having heard little, if anything, about the kingdom of God in their churches. And there are other reasons as we shall see in our next chapter and in Part II.

Also, as we shall see, Jesus' kingdom penetrates into and helps us recognize our deepest longings, hopes, and everything that matters—things that all human beings desperately desire and yet deep down know we can't produce or attain through our own natural efforts. Nor can the state provide or achieve them through laws, policies, and politics, nor can organized religion through programs. Yet everyone yearns for such a life and a society, whether they realize it or not.

For these reasons and more, I believe we moderns would be well-advised to follow Jesus' lead and open our hearts, minds, and souls anew to his primary methodology and approach of presenting the kingdom of God in this T.I. manner. Only when we can imagine the world to be different in the way Jesus presents the kingdom can we be motivated and empowered to be part of making it happen. Again, Jesus knew all this and desires your and my participation. That's why He employed the powerful and drawing communication technique of transformation imagination.

How Jesus Employed T.I.

Everything Jesus touched during his earthly ministry He utterly transformed. Similarly, everything Jesus taught during his central teaching on the kingdom of God was utterly transformational. Through this creative communication technique (often used in poetry, song, and story) Jesus presented to his listeners back then and to us moderns today, the world as God intends it to be. He further inspired and enticed his listeners and us today to see it, seek it, enter it, and live within it. Thus, Jesus offered to them, and us, the reality (not merely the hope) of a radically transformed life on this earth for individual lives and societies.

Only when we can imagine the world to be different in the way Jesus presents the kingdom can we be motivated and empowered to be part of making it happen.

Of course, Jesus used other communication techniques, such as asking questions. But when reading the Gospels, one is struck by his creative use of this T.I. technique and the enthusiastic responses of many of his listeners. Here's one way Matthew recorded their response. "When Jesus had finished saying these things, the crowds were amazed at his teaching, because he taught as one who had authority, and not as their teachers of the law" (Matt. 7:28-29).

Mark Earley emphasizes how "*Jesus made careful and appealing use of words* to entice His followers to desire the life of beauty they saw in Him . . . . to communicate the values . . . and the truths of the kingdom of God. He never simply assumed that people would 'get it' . . . . He knew He would have to use words to teach them well, and teach them well He did."[30]

---

[30] Mark Earley, "A Life of Beauty," *BreakPoint Worldview* (May 2007), 4, 5.

Jesus presented the kingdom in numerous parables and metaphors—"the kingdom of heaven is like . . ." He pictured the kingdom as a party, a feast, a banquet, and leaven to impact the whole of life and the world. In many beatitudes—"blessed are the . . . " [those who are / you if]. In many teachings—"you have heard that it was said . . . . But I tell you . . ." In many direct statements—:

- "You are the salt of the earth . . . . You are the light of the world."
- "Do not store up for yourselves treasures on earth . . . . But store up for yourselves treasures in heaven . . . . For where your treasure is, there your heart will be also."
- "But seek first his kingdom and his righteousness (justice), and all these things will be given to you as well."
- "Ask and it will be given to you; seek and you will find; knock and the door will be opened to you."
- "Knowledge of the secrets of the kingdom of heaven has been given to you . . . ."
- For more examples of the nature of the kingdom, true human life as intended by our Creator, and a positive program for kingdom living, see Matthew, chapters 5-7, 13, 18, 20, 22, 25.[31]

Truly, truly, this is the kingdom of God that Jesus came to establish and empower. That kingdom is about more than just saving sinners, although it includes that. It also stands in stark contrast to a judgmental approach of evangelizing that utilizes guilt and condemnation of sin and separation from God as its primary overture, and pushes many people away. Jesus never used that approach. To the contrary, Jesus created word pictures that illustrate the nature and principles of the kingdom and drew people toward what He was offering. His ability to articulate a divine vision of the kingdom enabled them to re-imagine their lives and the world as it could be. Many were drawn to and rallied around that offered and new reality.

---

[31] Some question whether Jesus' Sermon on the Mount and his parables were truly attainable and fully applicable, or merely an ideal or wishful notion. Others defer these realities to a yet-future millennial period, which we'll address in Appendix B.

In this author's opinion, Jesus' model of presenting the kingdom in this manner is still the best way for we Christians today to educate, energize, and mobilize ourselves to impact our world's cultures for Christ and his kingdom. It bears repeating, that this methodology of drawing, encouraging, and persuading the people at their deepest levels and about their greatest needs and desires is far superior to any of the six options presented in our last chapter. Hence, McLaren notes, "once we get a glimpse of the kingdom of God [from Jesus' perspective], nothing else will ever fully satisfy us. . . . [it] raises the level of discourse to a higher plane entirely. . . . [introducing] new ways of responding to injustice . . . ."[32]

Jesus created word pictures that illustrate the nature and principles of the kingdom and drew people toward what He was offering.

Now it's our turn. Jesus is still calling everyone to this higher and greater way of life, here and now on this earth. What will we moderns do with Jesus' kingdom? What will it take to stir us into action? Once again, please make no mistake; we are talking about a sea change in the way Christianity is currently being preached, practiced, and perceived. And it is vital that multiple thousands of churches and millions of Christians be re-educated, re-motivated, re-trained, re-equipped, and divinely empowered to reclaim and take this kingdom of God out into America and the world for the dual purpose of personal and societal transformations. Undeniably, as Rutz concludes, this will be "a complete paradigm shift, taking us back to the time of Christ"[33] in order to stir hearts and penetrate minds into massive cultural action.

No question about it, we need to go beyond political solutions to this divine solution for our world's problems. If this reclamation would happen, it could produce a reformation much larger and more significant than the Protestant Reformation of the 16th century and result in turning the world upside down, AGAIN.

---

[32] McLaren, *The Secret Message of Jesus*, 199, 125.
[33] Rutz, *Mega Shift*, 230.

Transformational Imaginative Insights of Others

Myles Munroe: "Everybody is looking for the Kingdom; many people just don't realize it yet. They know they are looking for something, but don't know what it is. People all over the world are desperate for something to believe in, somewhere to put their trust, something that will bring peace, stability, balance, order, and meaning to their lives. Only the Kingdom of God can fill this need. . . . People everywhere have been worn down by the world. Beaten up, broken down, battered by disease and disaster, torn apart by grief and loss, many of the world's people pass their days in lives that seem utterly hopeless. They long to believe in something that works, something that will enable them to overcome the world."[34] . . . "Humanity's quest for power is what makes the message of the Kingdom so appealing. The Kingdom of God represents power."[35]

James K.A. Smith: "This is just to say that to be human is to desire 'the kingdom.' . . . Every one of us is on a kind of Arthurian quest for 'the Holy Grail,' that hoped-for, longed-for, dreamed-of picture of the good life—that realm of human flourishing—that we pursue without ceasing. . . . it is such visions of the kingdom that pull us to get up in the morning and suit up for the quest."[36]

Steve Chalke & Alan Mann: "It is about a calling *to* something rather than *away from* something; about putting God's agenda at the centre of your life, and in doing so being good to yourself and bringing goodness into the world."[37]

Tony Evans: "Now, if God's kingdom is comprehensive, so is His kingdom agenda. That has some serious implications for us. The reason so many of us believers are struggling is that we want God to bless our agenda rather than our fulfilling of His agenda. . . . We want God to bring us glory rather than our bringing Him glory"[38]

---

[34] Myles Munroe, *Rediscovering Faith* (Shippensburg, PA.: Destiny Image Publishers, 2009), 182.

[35] Munroe, *Rediscovering the Kingdom*, 112.

[36] James K.A. Smith, *Desiring the Kingdom* (Grand Rapids, MI.: Baker Academic, 2009), 54.

[37] Chalke & Mann, *The Lost Message of Jesus*, 119.

[38] Evans, *What A Way To Live!*, 15.

Brian D. McLaren: "The goal of Jesus is the kingdom of God, which is the dream of God, the wish and hope and desire of God for creation—like a parent's hopes and dreams for a beloved child."[39]

"It's about changing this world, not just escaping it and retreating into our churches. If Jesus' message of the kingdom of God is true, then everything must change."[40]

The kingdom offers a "new kind of community or society . . . . [It] represents a counterforce, a countermovement, a counterkingdom that will confront all corrupt human regimes, exposing them, naming them, and showing them for what they really are. . . . unlike its evil counterparts—doesn't force itself where it is not wanted and welcome. For all its power and reality, it comes subtly, gently, and secretly."[41]

"The eschatology of abandonment is being succeeded by an engaging gospel of the kingdom."[42]

Brian Sanders: "Jesus . . . . brought the alternative of heaven into the realities of earth. He was the consummate idealist; . . ."[43]

Dallas Willard: "Motivation comes from vision, and vision should come from the preaching of the kingdom of God. . . . the fulfillment of the highest human possibilities and as life on the highest plane."[44]

John Eldredge: "Christianity begins with an invitation to *desire*. Look again at the way Jesus relates to people. . . . he is continually taking them into their hearts, to their deepest desires. . . . since the life you've chosen obviously isn't working. . . . really and truly spoke to our [their] dilemma."[45]

C.S. Lewis: "While reason is the natural organ of truth, imagination is the organ of meaning."[46]

---

[39] McLaren, *a Generous Orthodoxy*, 267.

[40] McLaren, *Everything Must Change*, 23.

[41] McLaren, *The Secret Message of Jesus*, 66.

[42] McLaren, *a Generous Orthodoxy*, 237.

[43] Brian Sanders, *Life After Church* (Downers Grove, IL.: IVP Books, 2007), 151.

[44] Willard, *The Great Omission*, 174, 12..

[45] Eldredge, *The Journey of Desire*, 35, 36, 44.

[46] C.S. Lewis, "Bluspels and Flananspheres: A Semantic Nightmare," quoted in Randy Alcorn, *Heaven* (Wheaton, IL.: Tyndale House Publishers, 2004), 22.

Francis Schaeffer: "The Christian is the one whose imagination should fly beyond the stars."[47]

Randy Alcorn: "*Let that truth fuel our imagination.* Imagination should not fly *away* from the truth but *fly* upon the truth."[48]

James Davison Hunter: "The dominant ways of thinking about culture and cultural change are flawed, for they are based on both specious social science and problematic theology. In brief, the model on which various strategies are based not only does not work, but it cannot work. . . . Christians just aren't Christian enough. Christians don't think with an adequate enough Christian worldview."[49]

Gene Edward Veith: "The problem of secularism is not just with the outside culture thinking it can do without God. The deeper problem is that the church itself has become secularized. A smaller but purer church may well have more impact than the diffuse cultural Christianity that has lost its saltiness and its savor."[50]

Shane Claiborne: "Another world is possible. . . . This thing Jesus called the kingdom of God is emerging across the globe in the most unexpected places, a gentle whisper amid the chaos."[51]

Danita Estrella: "My struggle stems from the fact that the gospel I read in my Bible is dramatically different from the gospel that is preached in many American churches today."[52]

Robert Lynn: "Only a great Gospel opens our eyes to great purposes and only a great Gospel strengthens us to pursue great ends. The only Gospel great enough, grand enough, and big enough to do that is the biblical Gospel, a worldview Gospel, a Gospel so vast in its scope that it encompasses a vision for a new creation. Armed with that good news, we become a people who bless with beauty those places scarred by ugliness and bring freedom where there is oppression; we bring joy

---

[47] Francis Schaeffer, *Art and the Bible* (Downers Grove, IL.: InterVarsity, 1973), 61

[48] Randy Alcorn, *Heaven* (Carol Stream, IL.: Tyndale House Publishers, 2004), 22.

[49] Hunter, *To Change the World*, 5, 24.

[50] Gene Edward Veith, "Papal pruning?: A smaller but purer church many actually have more influence," *World*, May 14, 2005, 32.

[51] Claiborne, *Irresistible Revolution*, 22, 25.

[52] Danita Estrella, "An Easy Gospel?" *Charisma*, June 2007, 20.

where there is suffering and healing where there is pain; wholeness where there is brokenness and life where there is death."[53]

Lack of Imagination in the Church

Not everyone in the 1st-century Church, or in today's churches, has ears to hear or eyes to see, as Jesus revealed numerous times (Matt. 13:13-15; Luke 8:8b; Rev. 2:7, 11, 17, 29; 3:6, 13, 22). That is one reason why much of the Church today suffers from a lack of imagination, or the wrong imagination. And most of the flock is simply content to "go along with the flow" of their particular church.

Brian Sanders, in his book *Life After Church*, spells out this deficiency:

> By and large, our ecclesia structures have become bomb shelters, places to hide from the world we believe is doomed for destruction, places stocked with Christian canned goods for the coming disaster. We think that being church means providing an alternative to the world. It's as if we believe that God has jammed a stick of dynamite into the earth and is just waiting to light it. Since the world will soon be incinerated, we turn our heads, plug our ears and hold on until that day comes.[54]

Indeed, our world and many of our churches today are mired in a state of brokenness and desperation. People from all nations are searching for meaning and relevance, here and now, in this life. And since the vast majority of our planet's inhabitants believe in God (90 percent of Americans say they do), beginning our presentations of our "once mighty faith" with the announcement of the "good news" that "the kingdom of God is at hand," and centering our discussions on the transformational imagination approach of Jesus would seem to make a lot of sense and be a most refreshing change, don't you think?

---

[53] Robert Lynn, "Far As The Curse Is Found," *BreakPoint WorldView*, October 2006, 19.
[54] Sanders, *Life After Church*, 111.

A Church / Kingdom-Centered Comparative

Issue	Church-Centered	Kingdom-Centered
Focus	Our church	Christ's kingdom
Motivation	Build our church	Advance the kingdom
Direction	Bring people in	Send people out
Philosophy	Seeker/User friendly	Transformation of lives and society
Evangelism	Judgmental / hell-avoidance based	Visionary / kingdom-based

Tony Evans again hits the biblical nail on the head: "The church is supposed to be the leading university of the culture . . . . The church should be leading the way in educating the culture because it is the one entity that will interject a kingdom agenda into all the affairs of the culture. . . . What God wants from His people is not revolution but transformation."[55]

This is why I am proposing that Christ's kingdom be reclaimed and re-prioritized as the Church's No. #1 agenda item—after all the kingdom was No. #1 for Jesus (see Mark 1:15; Matt. 6:33). To advance that kingdom and salvation, in that order, is why the Church and we Christians have been placed on this planet for a temporary stay. As we shall continue to see, that's the order in which Jesus announced them; that's the order in which Jesus accomplished them.

This means that Jesus' central teaching of the kingdom of God will need to be moved from the periphery to center stage. That further means we must rededicate ourselves to promoting the kingdom agenda by educating, equipping, empowering, and sending out kingdom ambassadors to impact lives, families, relationships, laws, institutions, nations, and our whole world. Hence, our rallying cry also needs to be changed from such slogans as "Take back America for Christ" and "Re-Christianize America," to simply "Reclaim God's Kingdom," "For Christ and Kingdom," and from the American Revolution, "No king but King Jesus!"

Without a doubt, this re-prioritization is urgently needed for stopping and reversing the secular-humanist revolution that is rapidly reshaping

---

[55] Evans, *What A Way To Live!*, 465, 458.

America and much of the world. Unquestionably, this change will require courage, commitment, and discipline, especially because of the amount of Christian indifference and marginalization we have been experiencing over the past 75 years or so. But reclaiming the central teaching of Jesus, the kingdom of God, is our only viable option for reclaiming the soul of this country and bettering our world. In so doing, we must also follow the dualistic example of the Apostle Paul, as he "boldly and without hindrance preached the kingdom of God and taught about the Lord Jesus Christ" (Acts 28:31).

. . . we must rededicate ourselves to promoting the kingdom agenda by educating, equipping, empowering, and sending out kingdom ambassadors to impact lives, families, relationships, laws, institutions, nations, and our whole world.

No question about it, as Munroe emphasizes: "The most effective way to reach people is to first whet their appetites with the good news of God's kingdom. After they know about the Kingdom and desire it for themselves, then explain to them how to get into it by trusting Jesus Christ to cleanse and save them from their sins and by yielding their lives to His control."[56] This is the full gospel message, in that order. Anything less is less.

Brothers and sisters, the hard reality is, we are facing a battle of two faiths, two worldviews. "Christianity teaches that God is sovereign over all of His creation. Secularism teaches that man is sovereign over all that has evolved up to this moment in time. The winning faith will determine the future of America [and many other countries] and whether or not your grandchildren will live in a society that is free or oppressive."[57]

Once again, make no mistake, our "young children are plainly being targeted for conversion to Secularism, whether in schools or otherwise

---

[56] Munroe, *Rediscovering the Kingdom*, 150.
[57] "Will you choose Liberty or Tyranny?" advertisement, *Biblical Worldview*, February 2007, 25.

. . . . [and] for conversion to the Secular teaching on homosexuality."[58] Consequently, drawing them out of that veritable moral wilderness that's being promulgated in the public schools, colleges, and universities is absolutely essential.

However, if we want to transform our declining culture, we first must transform ourselves and our churches, and plenty of us and them. And if unity on this issue of the kingdom was impossible, Jesus would never have prayed for his followers to be as one (see John 17:20-23). Won't you agree?

. . . the hard reality is, we are facing a battle of two faiths, two worldviews.

Obviously, not all will be attracted. Some will hate Christ's kingdom and you and me for proclaiming it, just as they did in Jesus' day and time (see John 15:18). But many will be drawn by its vision and compelled by its transformational offers of love, joy, peace, power, mercy, justice, and more. It's a winning proposition and faith for persuasively drawing people of all nations to desire the beauty of life in the kingdom of God, to better themselves, and to see and enter this universally available reality, here and now.

The kingdom of God—it's the world's brightest hope. It's the doorway to seeing yourself differently and realizing the fullness of God. It's the avenue to everything the Christian agenda should be about today. It's the river of life that transcends human politics, secular social movements, and stodgy/reductionist Christian traditions. Most certainly, Jesus' kingdom-centered redemption goes through and beyond personal salvation into the ultimate salvation of the entire world—lives, families, relationships, laws, institutions, nations, and our whole world. As we shall continue seeing, this realization is the complete mission of Christ to bring the kingdom of God and salvation into our world, and in that order.

---

[58] David Klinghoffer, "That Other Church," *Christianity Today*, January 2005, 62.

Unfortunately

When we come to the subject of the kingdom in today's Church we run smack into a bewildering maze of conflict and confusion. I call this maze the kingdom conundrum. It seems many Christians understand the kingdom of God quite differently from the way Jesus presented it. This significant deficiency demands our next chapter.

Chapter 6

The Kingdom Conundrum—A Maze of Conflict and Confusion[1]

For God is not the author of confusion . . . (1 Cor. 14:55a)

In view of the significance the kingdom of God has in the Bible, the central emphasis Jesus placed on it, and it's primacy in the worldview of our forefathers in the faith who founded this country, I propose we again place it front and center and proclaim and teach it "boldly and without hindrance," as did the Apostle Paul (Acts 28:31; 19:8; 2 Tim. 4:17). Hence, many erroneous notions and unsound concepts must be corrected and unlearned. And unlearning is the hardest form of learning.

Sad to say, most Christians today are kingdom-illiterate—especially in regard to the time and nature for the arrival of the everlasting kingdom. Consequently, we are paying a tremendous price by settling for a kingdom-deficient faith, gospel, and worldview. No question, we are reaping what we have sown as many different, competing, and conflicting views have long held a sway over the people of God. Most of

---

[1]Some of this chapter was presented as a theological paper at the 49th Annual Meeting of the Midwest Region of the Evangelical Theological Society at Lincoln Christian College and Seminary in Lincoln, Illinois, March 19-20, 2004.

these views will not stand up to an honest and sincere test of Scripture. But such is the danger of exalting human speculations, theories, and beliefs above the Word of God.

As you proceed through the maze of confusing and conflicting kingdom beliefs below, ask yourself these three questions wisely raised by McLaren: 1) "What if the core message of Jesus has been unintentionally misunderstood or intentionally distorted? 2) What if many have sincerely valued some aspects of Jesus' message while missing or even suppressing other, more important dimensions? 3) What if many have carried on a religion that faithfully celebrates Jesus in ritual and art, teaches about Jesus in sermons and books, sings about Jesus in songs and hymns, and theorizes about Jesus in seminaries and classroom . . . but somewhere along the way missed rich and radical treasures hidden in the essential message of Jesus?"[2]

Indeed, we have seriously misunderstood and substantially undervalued the essential message and central teaching of our Lord Jesus Christ, to our detriment.

Welcome to the Maze of Misconceptions and Conceptions

- It's <u>here</u>. It's <u>not</u> here. It's <u>not fully</u> here. It's kind of here "<u>in some sense.</u>"
- It's <u>partially</u> here but will be completed in the future— <u>already/not yet.</u>
- Jesus has <u>not</u> yet <u>set up/established</u> his kingdom.
- Jesus <u>failed</u> to deliver/bring in the promised kingdom.
- It's <u>in mystery</u> form now and only <u>spiritually</u> discerned. But <u>someday</u> it will be established <u>in glory</u> for all to see.
- Today, all we have is a <u>foretaste</u> of the kingdom.
- It's a <u>political</u> administration.
- It's a <u>social</u> order.
- It's a religious <u>experience</u> and exists only in <u>human hearts</u>.

---

[2] McLaren, *The Secret Message of Jesus*, 3-4.

- Now, it's the <u>invisible</u> kingdom of grace. But the <u>visible</u> kingdom of glory is yet to come at Christ's second coming.
- The <u>world</u> is his kingdom and we are his <u>subjects</u>.
- The kingdom is the <u>Church.</u>
- The kingdom is <u>Christianity.</u>
- The kingdom is a <u>blanket term</u> for the <u>salvation</u> believers have and are awaiting.
- It's the <u>Holy</u> <u>Spirit</u> empowerment <u>within</u> Christians.
- It's <u>everywhere</u> Christians <u>live</u> and <u>work</u>—i.e., in all of society.
- It's God's <u>future</u> <u>program</u> for the world.
- It's God's <u>future</u> <u>program</u> for Israel.
- The kingdom of <u>God</u> and the kingdom of <u>heaven</u> are two different kingdoms.
- They are <u>synonymous</u>.
- The kingdom is <u>within</u> you.
- The kingdom is <u>the people</u> who are <u>redeemed</u> and <u>ruled</u> by Jesus.
- It's the <u>perfected community</u> of God's people (Israel, kingdom citizens, church).
- It's <u>good deeds</u> done by <u>good people</u> in the public sector for the <u>common good</u>.
- The kingdom is a <u>transformed earthly society</u>.
- When it comes, everyone will <u>know</u> it and <u>see</u> it.
- It's a <u>spiritual</u> kingdom <u>in heaven</u>.
- It's <u>hidden</u> and <u>obscured</u> today by sin.
- It's a <u>progressive</u> <u>Christianization</u> of the world.
- It's achieved on earth through a <u>natural</u> process of <u>social</u> actions.
- It's <u>not</u> <u>present</u> today at all but was <u>postponed</u> and <u>withdrawn</u> by God due to the <u>Jews'</u> rejection and crucifixion of Jesus.
- When Jesus comes back (second coming), He'll set up his visible kingdom for <u>1,000 years</u> in Israel.
- When Jesus comes back, He'll set up his kingdom, <u>forever</u>.
- The <u>Church</u> is a<u> temporary</u> <u>substitute</u> for the kingdom, a <u>parenthesis</u> in God's plan for Israel.
- It's a <u>general</u> symbol.
- It's a <u>concrete</u> reality.
- It's <u>not of this world</u> but of the next.

- It's an apocalyptic symbol standing for realities the human mind cannot apprehend—a transcendent order beyond time and space.
- It won't come until the world (as we know it) ends.
- It's here fully, as a spiritual kingdom, but with its miraculous signs, wonders, and miracles manifested by Jesus et al. withdrawn by God.
- We are currently living in a pre-kingdom time. When Jesus returns, He'll set up his theocratic, millennial kingdom in Jerusalem (a restored nationalistic Israel) to be followed by the eternal and final kingdom.
- When Jesus' kingdom comes, He will transform our present world, comfort every sorrow, and heal every imperfection. It will put everything right that has been wrong, and bring perfect harmony in place of discord. There will be no more sin, evil, wars, injustice, strife, sickness, disease, pain, dying, crying, or pollution. There will be abundance of food, animals and man living in perfect harmony, people living to be a thousand years old, a perfect world, a restored garden of Eden with everything provided, perfect joy, perfect fellowship with God and Christ as Christians reign and rule over this entire world.

Quite a maze of conflict and confusion, don't you think? It meets us at every turn in the church whenever the topic of the kingdom of God is brought up, which is not that often. Many Christians just accept some of these beliefs, uncritically. They never bother to investigate to see if they are true or to check out alternative interpretations and explanations.

Therefore, as Gene Mims points out, "to many Christians the kingdom of God is about as clear as mud. We are taught little about it, so as a result our understanding of and excitement about kingdom things is simply absent from our lives."[3]

And yet, Jesus proclaimed to his disciples, as well as for us today, that "the knowledge of the secrets of the kingdom of God has been given to you . . ." [past-tense] (Matt. 13:11; Luke 8:10). So how many of these "secrets" can you or people in your church name? Most certainly, ideas have consequences.

---

[3] Gene Mims, *The Kingdom-Focused Church* (Nashville, TN.: Broadman & Holman Publishers, 2003), 42.

Attitudes and Behavioral Comparatives

Depending on how one envisions the kingdom, he or she will be motivated differently in regard to what believers should or should not be doing, here and now, in this world. Below is a comparative of conflicting attitudes and behaviors produced by different views of the kingdom:

Wait until the kingdom comes.	Advance the kingdom that's here.
The world is destined to get worse and worse until Christ comes back.	The world must get better and better so Christ can come back.
There's nothing we can or should do to bring in the kingdom.	God has commanded His people to seek and advance the kingdom.
We win by leaving and forsaking this world.	We win by staying and taking dominion over this world.
Let's save as many people as we can before it's too late.	Let's take over this world for Christ before it gets away.
Set your mind on things above not on things of this earth as God and Christ have commanded.	Take authority over all things in heaven and on earth as God and Christ have commanded.
Pessimistic for the future of humankind.	Optimistic for the future of humankind.
Resigned to the failure of the Church in today's world.	Upset with the failure of the Church in today's world.
Social-political indifference/ impotency.	Social-political activism/potency.
Separate yourselves from the evil of this world – world negating, pietism.	Bring all society and institutions of this world under the rule of Christ – world transforming dominionism.

So, who's right? No question about it, these are real differences and they create real problems for Christians and the Church. So which view represents true Christianity and determines how we should live the Christian life? Unfortunately, many of these views have blinded us to our responsibilities on earth. That's because, as Munroe explains, we "do not understand the nature or significance of the Kingdom. . . . many in the Church have discovered the King but they have no clue about the Kingdom that He came to bring to mankind."[4] And the Church's response has been grossly inadequate. Is it any wonder, therefore, why we Christians are so divided and ineffective compared to what we could and should be?

Absence of a Scriptural Definition

Another issue contributing to the conflict and confusion surrounding God's kingdom is the absence of a scriptural definition. So what did Jesus mean, and not mean, by the "kingdom of God?" Basically, the word "kingdom" refers to a people governed by a king, with the king in dominion over them—thus, "king – dom." But from here definitions vary widely.

George Eldon Ladd acknowledges that while "New Testament scholars generally agree that the burden of Jesus' message was the Kingdom of God . . . . The critical problem arises from the fact that Jesus nowhere defined what he meant by the phrase."[5] As perplexing and ironic as this omission may seem, a definition by at least one biblical writer would surely have alleviated much of our modern-day conflict and confusion.

Ladd also notes, yet erroneously deduces, that "it is not recorded that anyone asked him [Jesus] what 'the Kingdom of God' meant. He assumed that this was a concept so familiar that it did not require definition."[6] But to the contrary, Jesus' presentations of the kingdom

---

[4] Munroe, *Rediscovering the Kingdom*, 147, 125.
[5] George Eldon Ladd, *The Presence of the Future*, (Grand Rapids, MI.: Eerdmans, 1974), 122. Jesus' kingdom-is-like parables are perspectives, and not definitions.
[6] Ibid., 45.

departed radically from the Jewish expectations. In that 1st century, many Jews (and many Christians still today) were looking for their Messiah to bring a visible and political kingdom which would overthrow the Roman authorities and elevate Israel to supremacy over all the nations (Acts 1:6). Thus, a major difficulty for them was, Jesus never taught, promised, or delivered that kind of a kingdom.

. . . these are real differences . . . . So which view represents true Christianity and determines how we should live the Christian life?

Kaylor, while agreeing "that the meaning of the kingdom is 'undefined,'" still assumes it must have "involved the destiny of Israel as a nation."[7] But he also maintains Jesus and his kingdom "sought the transformation of society" and that "Jesus was apparently a revolutionary, but not a violent political revolutionary."[8] Then, he addresses this compromising factor: "In the context of its evangelical preaching, the church tended to use kingdom as a metaphor for eschatological salvation (=eternal life or life after death). Thus the church transformed . . . . It removed the implications for social and political change the term had for Jesus, just as it transformed Jesus into a more spiritual savior."[9] After all his waffling, Kaylor ends up leaving his readers hanging empty-handed when he concludes: "We cannot be sure . . . what he [Jesus] meant by kingdom of God."[10]

Donald B. Kraybill takes a different but even weaker stance. He asserts that the kingdom of God "defies exact definition."[11] He terms it "a general symbol [that] offers us many referents with multiple meanings."[12] Vaguely, he adds that it is "a new order of things that

---

[7] R. David Kaylor, *Jesus the Prophet* (Louisville, KY.: Westminster/John Knox Press, 1994), 88.

[8] Ibid., 90.

[9] Ibid., 75.

[10] Ibid., 87.

[11] Donald B. Kraybill, *The Upside-Down Kingdom* (Scottsdale, PA.: Herald Press, 1978, 1990), 20.

[12] Ibid., 27-28.

appeared upside-down in the midst of Palestinian culture in the first century . . . . its contemporary expression has upside-down features today as it breaks into diverse cultures."[13] Later, he rambles on that "the *kingdom* refers to the rule of God in our hearts and relationships."[14]

Ladd, like so many others, subscribes to the commonly accepted, short definition of the kingdom as simply "the rule of God."[15] He ends up, however, saying more about what the kingdom is *not* than what it is: "The Kingdom of God cannot be reduced to the reign of God within the individual soul or modernized in terms of personal existential confrontation or dissipated to an extraworldly dream of blessed immortality."[16]

Willard defines God's "kingdom" or "rule" as: "the range of his effective will, where what he wants done is done. The person of God himself and the action of his will are the organizing principles of his kingdom, but everything that obeys those principles, whether by nature or by choice, is *within* his kingdom."[17] Evans simply defines it as "His comprehensive governance in all creation."[18]

Further confounding this definitional issue, McKnight offers this perspective, that "an array of shifts will occur when Jesus becomes King over a people, but the word 'kingdom' cannot be reduced either to justice or salvation without doing serious damage to the story that animates the word 'kingdom.'"[19] Others contend that Romans 14:17 is a definition. "For the kingdom of God is not a matter of eating and drinking, but of righteousness, peace and joy in the Holy Spirit." And surely the kingdom is that; but it's also much more. I believe the closest to a possible definition we can find in the Bible is this sentence in the Lord's prayer: "Thy will be done in earth, as it is in heaven" (Matt. 6:10b KJV).

---

[13] Ibid., 12.

[14] Ibid., 172.

[15] Ladd, *The Presence of the Future*, 171. Another example of a simple definition is: "the realm in which God's rule is to be exercised . . . here in our world and in our history."— Arthur F. Glasser, *Announcing the Kingdom* (Grand Rapids, MI.: Baker Academic, 2003), 188.

[16] Ladd, *The Presence of the Future*, 331.

[17] Willard, *The Divine Conspiracy*, 26.

[18] Tony Evans, *Kingdom Man* (Carol Stream, IL.: Tyndale House Publishers, 2012), 27.

[19] McKnight, *Kingdom Conspiracy*, 74.

But because of this absence of a definition in Scripture, Munroe summarizes that "most of us do not really understand what Jesus meant when He spoke of the Kingdom."[20] That is why, in this author's opinion, we need to carefully seek and craft a clear, concise, and cogent definition while avoiding the vagueness and ambiguities that have plagued the writings of so many scholars and theologians. Admittedly, this task may be fraught with difficulties as Stephen J. Nichols rightly points out and cautions. "There is a long and winding train of defining the kingdom of God from the purview of where one stands and of what one prefers. We must guard against seeking the kingdom as we define it, as we construct it, and as we prefer it. The temptation to do so is all too strong."[21]

Nevertheless, we shall next proceed in that direction.

My Working Definition

To help us begin resolving this absence of a definition, here is my working definition for what is meant by the phrase *kingdom of God* or *kingdom of heaven*.[22] First, it is not a political administration, a geographic territory, an abstract notion, or heaven *per se*. However, the Greek word translated as kingdom is *basileia*, which means "royalty, rule, realm, reign"[23] or "sovereignty, royal power, dominion."[24] Therefore, it is a rule and reign by royalty, has a realm or territory, and is a pragmatic and dynamic reality. Simply defined, the kingdom of God is:

---

[20] Munroe, *Rediscovering the Kingdom,* 123.

[21] Stephen J. Nichols, "The Kingdoms of God," in Christopher W. Morgan and Robert A. Peterson, eds., *The Kingdom of God* (Wheaton, IL.: Crossway, 2012), 48.

[22] Most scholars recognize no difference between the "kingdom of heaven" (used in Matthew) and the "kingdom of God" (used in the other gospels). They are synonymous and used interchangeably. This can be verified by comparing the following verses: Matt. 11:12; Luke 16:16; Matt. 4:17; Mark 1:14, 15; Matt. 5:3; Luke 6:20; Matt. 10:7; Luke 9:2; Matt. 13:31; Mark 4:30, 31; 10:14; Matt. 19:23; Luke 18:24.

[23] *Strong's Exhaustive Concordance of the Bible*, #932.

[24] *W.E. Vine: An Expository Dictionary of Biblical Words*, 624.

The sphere of God's will, reign and rule.
It is located throughout heaven and the cosmos, and wherever on earth the dynamic manifestations of his sovereignty, holiness, power, and kingly authority are acknowledged and obeyed, or denied, ignored, and disobeyed. That means it is realized both internally and externally, within and among, to draw human hearts to Him, to bless and discipline his people, to defeat his enemies, to bring his shalom (peace and justice), and to bring Him glory. It is to be unlocked, entered, exercised, and advanced by every Christian who follows Jesus Christ and experienced in every aspect of life and society. However, it is not universally recognized; it is contested, opposed, persecuted, and greatly under-realized.

I welcome your input. That's why I've termed it "my working definition." But let's also keep in mind the old evangelical saying that perfectly harmonizes with my working definition: "If he's not Lord of all, he's not Lord at all." To which N.T. Wright insightfully notes and adds: "That was always applied personally and pietistically. I want to say exactly the same thing but apply it to the world. We're talking about Jesus as the Lord of the world—not the Lord of people's private spiritual interiority only, but of what they do with their money, with their homes, with the wealth of nations, and with the planet."[25]

The Great Eschatological Divisions

God's kingly will, reign, and rule over the entire creation and everything in it existed from the beginning. As long as there has been a King, there has been a kingdom. That's why the kingdom theme is traceable from Genesis to Revelation. It is derived from the fact that God is sovereign and has the right to exercise ruling authority.

Most succinctly, Ladd identifies the two key problems in a study of Jesus' ministry and his central teaching on the kingdom of God as being those of "time" and "nature."[26] Hence, in Chapter 1, we began to see that

---

[25] Interview with N.T. Wright by Jim Stafford, "Mere Mission," *Christianity Today*, January 2007, 39.
[26] Ladd, *The Presence of the Future*, 125.

the Church today has the kingdom caught-up in eschatological mid-air in both of these categories.

Consequently, much that has been written and is currently being taught and believed about the kingdom of God is *wrong—scripturally wrong!* It will not stand up to an honest and sincere test of Scripture (1 Thess. 5:21). Why not? Because the people who write commentaries, teach in seminaries, stand in pulpits, teach Sunday School classes, serve in elderships, and evangelize on TV and radio have refused to accept what the Bible actually says and does not say. They claim, "We must interpret it for you." As one scholar once admonished me during a meeting of the Evangelical Theological Society, "Our duty is to find out what the Bible teaches, regardless of the terminology used." As a result, we have another mess and maze of conflict and confusion in scholarly circles.

. . . the two key problems in a study of Jesus' ministry and his central teaching on the kingdom of God as being those of "time" and "nature."

As you are about to see, scholars and theologians also have had a hard time getting the kingdom of God straight and thus, getting Christianity right. Why should it surprise us, therefore, when very few churches today preach and teach the gospel of the kingdom. They preach and teach a lot of other stuff, good stuff, but not the central teaching of Jesus. But who can blame them for being confused and silent if even the academicians cannot agree? Munroe laments this sad situation that while "the message of the Bible is primarily and obviously about a kingdom . . . . over the past 2,000 years the true concept of kingdom has been lost." Therefore, "for the most part, people in the Western world know very little about kingdom and the concept of royalty and monarchy."[27]

This is why most Christians are ignorant and unconcerned about the kingdom of God—the central teaching of Jesus Christ. Below are some specific and prime examples of these scholarly divisions from respected spokespersons in each of the four major, evangelical and eschatological views. Let's hear these conflicting divisions in their own words.

---

[27] Munroe, *Rediscovering the Kingdom*, 63.

Dispensational Premillennialists[28] **(the most popular view)** – The kingdom of God is not here anymore. Then whatever happened to the kingdom Jesus was announcing, manifesting, and conferring back in the 1st century?

- The "kingdom was postponed when the Jews rejected Jesus as their Messiah, but it will be established when Christ returns."[29]
- In the interim, "Jesus established the church as the 'mystery' form of his coming kingdom." It is a "spiritual reality" with the "physical messianic kingdom, promised in the Old Testament . . . yet to come"[30]
- "When He comes, the kingdom that we experience in our hearts will be seen in a way that no one can imagine right now."[31]
- "When Jesus returns to this earth, He will come physically to set up His long-promised kingdom"[32]—in Israel, for 1,000 years, with a rebuilt Old Covenant Temple in Jerusalem and a resumption of animal sacrifices officiated over by Jesus Himself.
- After the millennial kingdom comes and goes, "the eternal kingdom" will be "established."[33]

---

[28] I will not break out historic/classic premillennialism or progressive dispensationalism views in this book since these positions along with the amillennial position basically cover the same territory.

[29] John H. Sailhamer, *Biblical Prophecy* (Grand Rapids, MI.: Zondervan, 1998), 80. Some in this view maintain that the kingdom is still here but only in "mystery" form. The idea of a mystery form arises from two sources: 1) Matthew 13:11 – "to know the mysteries of the kingdom of heaven" in the KJV version (Charles C. Ryrie, *The Basis of the Premillennial Faith* (Neptune, NJ.: Loizeaux Bros., 1953), 94, 95); 2) "The conclusion is easily reached. Since the fundamental characteristics of the Church are called mysteries, the Church itself is a mystery, that is, it was unforeseen in the Old Testament but revealed only in the New Testament" (Ibid., 134, 132). "The real form is still expected in the future" (Ibid., 101).

[30] Ibid., 68.

[31] Mims, *The Kingdom-Focused Church*, 44.

[32] Tim LaHaye and Thomas Ice, gen. eds., *The End Times Controversy* (Eugene, OR.: Harvest House Publishers, 2003), 9.

[33] Sailhamer, *Biblical Prophecy*, 33.

This position is the most prominent view in evangelicalism. It's the view you most often see on TV, hear on radio, find in bookstores (Christian and secular), and hear preached in evangelical churches. However, this postponement view is not without its problems and consequences, which are vehemently criticized. For instance, postmillennialist DeMar charges, "What we believe about God's kingdom will impact how we live. If the kingdom has been postponed, then God is a bystander with His hands tied and our efforts hopeless."[34]

But inspired Scripture, written some 20 or more years after this supposed postponement-and-withdrawal event of the kingdom by God Himself (at the cross), still speaks of the kingdom as present and operative on earth, then and there (see for example Acts 1:3; 19:8; 20:25; 28:31; Col. 4:11; Heb. 12:28). Additionally, "the Sovereign Lord does nothing without revealing his plan to his servants the prophets" (Amos 3:7). And no Old Testament prophet, nor Jesus, nor any New Testament writer ever spoke of something as significant as a postponement and withdrawal of the kingdom of God. Those scriptural facts should speak loudly and clearly, don't you think?

My friend pastor Dan Carroll thinks so. In his sermons he frequently mentions what he terms "my pet peeve." In it, he characterizes those who subscribe to this most popular view as being: "New Covenant Christians living with an Old Covenant mentality."

Amillennialists (the second most popular view) – The kingdom of God has arrived; it has not been postponed or withdrawn. It is here, "in some sense," but as a foretaste, in an eschatological tension between the "already" and the "not yet" of partial fulfillment and partial establishment:

- "The *already – not yet* concept is closely tied to Jesus' teachings about the kingdom of God and to New Testament eschatology in general. . . . God has started his kingdom project, but he has not completely finished it. The kingdom of God has *already* arrived, but it has *not yet* come in all its fullness."[35]

---

[34] DeMar, *Myths, Lies & Half Truths*, 236.
[35] J. Daniel Hays, J. Scott Duvall, C Marvin Pate, *Dictionary of Biblical Prophecy and End Times* (Grand Rapids, MI.: Zondervan, 2007), 22-22.

- "Many scholars maintain that the life, death, and resurrection of Jesus inaugurated the kingdom of God, . . . The kingdom has 'already' dawned but is 'not yet' complete."[36]
- "*Inaugurated eschatology* . . . . views the first coming of Christ as the beginning of the kingdom that will be consummated at his second coming. As a result, believers live between the overlap of the 'already' and the 'not yet.'" This view claims (as does each view) that their eschatological position "most adequately represents the evangelistic understanding of the biblical material"[37]
- Others say "the interim messianic kingdom begun at the resurrection of Christ will one day give way to the eternal kingdom of God." In the meantime, it's "a temporary kingdom."[38]
- "the kingdom of God is now hidden . . . . to all except those who have faith in Christ . . . . but some day it shall be totally revealed . . . . when the final phase of the kingdom is ushered in by the Second Coming of Jesus Christ."[39]
- "This is the mystery of the kingdom of God."[40]
- "the here and now *anticipates* the final kingdom."[41]
- We await the kingdom's "final establishment . . . at the time of Christ's Second Coming,"[42] as well as the "final judgment" and "final stage"[43] "at the end of history"[44] or "at the end of this present age . . . . at the time of Christ's Second Coming."[45]

---

[36] Ibid., 88.

[37] Ibid., 140.

[38] Ibid., 245.

[39] Anthony A. Hoekema, *The Bible and the Future*, (Grand Rapids, MI.: Eerdmans, 1979, 1991), 52.

[40] Ibid., 296.

[41] McKnight, *Kingdom Conspiracy*, 96, 201.

[42] Ibid., *ix*.

[43] Ibid., 1.

[44] Ibid., 253.

[45] Ibid., 255.

- Today we are "living between the times" of the "'already of the coming of the kingdom" and "the 'not yet' of its consummation."[46]
- This interim time is the time of the "semirealized kingdom."[47]
- "God's great plan . . . . includes not only the salvation of individuals and the redemption of the church but also the reestablishment of God's kingdom of righteousness, peace, and justice in a new heaven and a new earth."[48]
- Hence, this view "sees good and evil growing together during this age. . . . no definitive triumph of the kingdom of Christ in history. . . . [and is] relatively pessimistic concerning the progress of history prior to his glorious return."[49]

At best, this view's partial concept is ambiguous. At worst, it's unscriptural. Its stipulation that all we have today is a "foretaste" or a tension between an "already" and the "not yet" is not supported by Scripture. Hence, as Russell D. Moore unscripturally stipulates: "From the apostolic age to the digital era, the 'already – not yet' tension has proven difficult to understand. . . . The kingdom comes in two stages, because King Jesus himself does. . . . but Jesus doesn't rule over the whole universe yet. . . . I long for the arrival of the kingdom that has long bubbled around us, invisible as yeast."[50]

This massive misconception was awkwardly brought home to me and seventy-some other participants during a theological seminar where the amillennial presenter proclaimed, matter-of-factly, that "the kingdom of God was the central teaching of Jesus, at the heart of his ministry, and

---

[46] Guenther Haas, "The Significance of Eschatology for Christian Ethics," in David W. Baker, ed., *Looking into the Future: Evangelical Studies in Eschatology* (Grand Rapids, MI.: Baker Academic, 2001), 326.

[47] Vern S. Poythress, *Understanding Dispensationalists*, (Phillipsburg, NJ.: P& R Publishing, 1987, 1994), 36.

[48] Paul G. Hiebert, in Forward to, Arthur F. Glasser, *Announcing the Kingdom*, 8.

[49] Kenneth L. Gentry, ed., *Thine Is the Kingdom* (Vallecito, CA.: Chalcedon, 2003), 24.

[50] Russell D. Moore, "A Purpose Driven Cosmos," *Christianity Today*, February 2012, 32-33 .

the very essence of 1st-century Christianity and its worldview [so far so good]. But, of course, all we have today is a foretaste of the kingdom."

I immediately raised my hand and asked, "Where did Jesus or any of the New Testament writers ever say or write that all they had, back then and there, was a 'foretaste of the kingdom?'" You could have heard pins drop as we patiently awaited his thoughtful response. After a few awkward seconds of silence, he quipped: "Okay, that was George Eldon Ladd," and quickly moved to his next point to prevent any follow-up questions from me. Whether or not you know who the late theologian George Eldon Ladd was, one thing should be evident. He was not Jesus or any of the inspired New Testament writers. None of them ever qualified, disclaimed, or delimited the kingdom with the expressions "foretaste," or "already / not yet"—and for a good reason, as we shall see in Chapter 8.

McKnight frankly admits that this partial-fulfillment position means God's plan of redemption [salvation] is "incomplete until the final kingdom. We gladly announce that the kingdom has drawn near; we also gladly announce that someday the kingdom will be fully established." In the meantime, "we live between two times" and "redemption and holiness and love and peace are only partly realized in the now . . . . *to the same degree that the kingdom has been inaugurated in Jesus, the kingdom can be realized among us. . . . to the degree that the kingdom has not yet been realized, it cannot be lived out in the present. . . .* Someday the inaugurated kingdom will be a consummated kingdom."[51]

Once again, as was true with the previous view, this view is highly problematic. The biblical facts are, neither Jesus nor any Old or New Testament writer ever used any of these words or expressions or taught these concepts: "already," "not yet," "inaugurated," "first coming," "second coming," "interim messianic kingdom," "eternal kingdom," "temporary kingdom," "the mystery of the kingdom," "partly realized," "final kingdom," "final establishment," "final judgment," "final stage," "end of history," "between the times," "semi-realized kingdom," or "foretaste"—for a good reason. They are completely inappropriate as we shall see in Chapters 8, 9, and 10.

Likewise, this view's ambiguity and incompleteness undermines the willingness of God's people to be "fellow workers for the kingdom of

---

[51] Ibid., 39, 179 – italics his.

God" (Col. 4:11), as well as, to be the "kingdom and priests" God "has made us to be"—to serve Him and reign with Him, here and now, on this earth (Rev. 1:6; 5:9-10). We simply must reclaim a more robust and scripturally sound kingdom theology, which brings us to our next view.

Postmillennialists (the third most popular view, formerly the most popular view) – The kingdom of God is mostly here and will continue to grow, fill, and subdue the earth. But much more is yet to be fulfilled and established when Jesus physically returns:

- "The *postmil* looks for a . . . glorious age of the church upon earth through the preaching of the gospel under the power of the Holy Spirit. He looks forward to all nations becoming Christian and living in peace one with another."[52]
- "A brighter era is destined to arrive; a golden age is to dawn upon us, when the predictions of prophets, and the descriptions of apostles, are all to be fulfilled."[53]
- There is "a clear distinction between the Messianic kingdom and the consummated kingdom in eschatology." The former "begins in time and ends in time." The latter comes at "the last judgment"[54] . . . . when "the Lord will terminate history. . . . [at] the second coming"[55] . . . . "at the end of time."[56]
- When Christ returns He will take his Church to be with Him, bring an end to all earthly existence and to the earth itself, execute "the final judgment,"[57] and institute "the eternal state."[58]

---

[52] J. Marcellus Kik, *An Eschatology of Victory* (Phillipsburg, NJ.: Presbyterian and Reformed Publishing Co., 1971), 4.

[53] Ibid., 9-10.

[54] Ibid., 17.

[55] Ibid., 166.

[56] Ibid., 258.

[57] Keith A. Mathison, *Dispensationalism*, (Phillipsburg, NJ.: P&R Publishing, 1999), 126.

[58] Loraine Boettner, *The Millennium* (Philadelphia, PA.: Presbyterian and Reformed, 1987), 18.

But once again, what does Scripture say about a "glorious / golden age," "last judgment," "terminate history," "end of time," "second coming," "the eternal state," a "return" of Christ, "the final judgment," or a distinction between the "Messianic kingdom" and the "consummated kingdom?" The answer is: absolutely nothing. You will find none of these expressions used in the Bible and for a good reason. They are completely inappropriate.

Preterists (the least-known view) – The kingdom of God is fully here, but parts of it were repossessed by God after the destruction of Jerusalem and the Temple in A.D. 70. Not all preterists adhere to this cessationist reductionism. But many of its major leaders do.

- "the charismata . . . . the charismatic gifts which the Paraclete poured out upon the first century church for revelatory, confirmatory and consummatory purposes [ceased] . . . . once the plan [of redemption] was completely revealed and consummated."[59]
- "The last days of the Jewish nation ended then. A new age had begun. The charismata associated with the last days ceased."[60]
- "Christ's advent at the time of the destruction of Jerusalem to receive the Kingdom, the church of the firstborn, terminated an altogether exceptional state of things which had prevailed since the day of Pentecost, and caused these abnormal miraculous gifts of the Holy Spirit to cease."[61]

We shall address the issue of cessation theology from both the futurist and preterist view in Appendix A.

But this one thing should be obvious by now. With all these different and conflicting views floating around, is it any wonder why most Christians are confused about the kingdom? Likewise, is it any wonder

---

[59] Edward E. Stevens, *What Happened in A.D. 70?* (Bradford, PA.: Kingdom Publications, 1997), 23.
[60] Ibid., 29.
[61] Max R. King, *The Cross and the Parousia of Christ* (Warren, OH.: Writing and Research Ministry sponsored by the Parkman Road Church of Christ, 1987), 370.

why they have basically ignored Jesus' admonition to "But seek ye first the kingdom of God and his righteousness" (Matt. 6:33 KJV)? After all, how can you seek something that either is not here anymore or is only partially, "in some sense," already/not yet, kind of, sort of, somehow here? After all, how would you know when you found it?

Fortunately, understanding the time and nature of the eschatological and everlasting kingdom is not as complicated and confusing as these above views have made it. It is quite straightforward. In the chapters 8, 9, and 10 we shall address this task for reclaiming and restoring the kingdom-of-God worldview to the Church and the world as we ground its establishment time-wise and nature-wise.

Four Kingdom Killers

The four most popular misconceptions, if not outright heresies, in the Church today that utterly cut the knees right out from under Christ's kingdom and kill a proper understanding are: 1) Jesus is not yet King. 2) The kingdom belongs to Israel. 3) The kingdom won't arrive again until Christ's future 1,000-year reign (Rev. 20:1-10). 4) The kingdom and the Church are synonymous. As you might expect, each misconception is based on flawed interpretations and errant misunderstandings of Scripture. In the balance of this chapter, we shall expose, dispel, and dismiss each one of these four kingdom killers before continuing.

Kingdom Killer #1 – Jesus Is Not Yet King

So-called prophecy "expert" and "Left Behind" co-author, Tim LaHaye, emphatically declares "When Jesus comes, He is going to be 'King of kings and Lord of lords . . . to say Christ is ruler now is a statement that reaches almost blasphemous proportions."[62] As in Old Testament times when Israel rejected God as their king (see 1 Sam. 8:7), many today, like LaHaye, have currently rejected Jesus as King.

But Scripture emphatically refutes LaHaye's contention. In the most uncontested portion of the Book of Revelation, John writes that Jesus Christ "*is* [not someday will be] the faithful witness, the firstborn from

---

[62] LaHaye, *The End Times Controversy*, 11.

the dead, and the *ruler of the kings of the earth*" (Rev. 1:5; also 1 Tim. 6:15).

Regrettably, the much-revered Dr. Billy Graham also holds to LaHaye's deferment view. He writes in two of his newspaper columns: "Someday all God's enemies will be defeated and Jesus Christ will rule forever as King of kings and Lord of lords. . . . Someday God will defeat all evil, and Jesus Christ will rule forever."[63] . . . "Someday Jesus Christ will return to rule the world in perfect peace and justice."[64]

But what will Jesus rule over, "someday," if all evil, sin, and bad people have been removed, as their view also holds? Moreover, if Jesus is *not* now ruler and King, as LaHaye and Dr. Graham believe, what is the meaning of:

- Jesus sitting at the right hand of God (Rom. 8:34; Eph. 1:20; Col. 3:1; Heb. 1:13; 8:1; 12:2l; Acts 2:33-36; Psa. 110), Who is seated on his heavenly throne (Psa. 2:4; 11:4; 22:28; 47:2, 8; 103:19; Prov. 8:13; Isa. 66:1)? Is Jesus "now crowned with glory and honor" (Heb. 2:9)? Or, is Jesus merely sitting passively waiting to reign someday? Not according to Peter who declares that Jesus is sitting there "at God's right hand – with angels, authorities and powers in submission to him" (1 Pet. 3:22).

- Jesus' Great Commission and past-tense statement that "all authority in heaven and on earth has been given to me" (Matt. 28:18)?

- Jesus telling Pilate, straight up, "You are right in saying I am a king. . . ." (John 18:37a)?

- Paul's present-tense statement that "he must reign until he has put all his enemies under his feet" (1 Cor. 15:25; Heb. 10:13)?

- Jesus "sustaining all things by his powerful word" (Heb. 1:3)?

Perhaps it is LaHaye's contention that is "almost blasphemous," if not outright blasphemy. In contradistinction, A.A. Hodge offers this scripturally sound conclusion on this matter: "In the strictest sense we must date the actual and formal assumption of [Christ's] kingly office, in the full and visible exercise thereof, from the moment of His ascension

---

[63] Billy Graham, "My Answer," *The Indianapolis Star*, 5/7/13, E-4.
[64] Billy Graham, "My Answer," *The Indianapolis Star*, 5/2/13, E-4

into heaven from this earth and His session at the right hand of the Father."[65]

Glasser concurs that Jesus, after Jesus completing his atoning work, ascended and was seated at the right hand of the Father, "the reign of the risen Christ had now begun."[66] But as we shall contend in Chapter 8, Christ's reign actually started much before his ascension.

Rushdoony rightly terms LaHaye's and Graham's dispensational premillennial view "an abandonment of Christianity not to see Jesus Christ as now and forever 'the blessed and only Potentate, the King of kings, and Lord of lords' (1 Tim. 6:15)."[67] And yet this deferment view is held by "40-50 or more million Americans . . . [and is] a very major roadblock to any Christian action which will further 'justice, peace or righteousness.'" He further cites Gary North's article on this issue fittingly titled "Backward, Christian Soldiers" and blasts dispensationalists for paying "no attention to all the Scriptures which declare Jesus to be *Lord* (or God-King) and Savior." Therefore, "if He is not our King, then we will obey another king and enthrone Satan as god of this world"[68]—which is exactly what has been done by many, if not most, of these 40-50 million American dispensationalists.

Perhaps it is LaHaye's contention that is "almost blasphemous," if not outright blasphemy.

But I believe Lynn Hiles, not LaHaye, is biblically right as he summarizes: "I don't believe Jesus is *going* to be King. I believe Jesus is King *right now!* He's not going to be the Lord at some future date; He's already been made Lord by the Father. God declared Him to be Lord and King of Heaven and earth by resurrecting Him from the dead. This occurred some two millennia ago, and He is presently reigning."[69]

---

[65] A.A. Hodge, *Evangelical Theology* (Edinburgh: Banner of Truth, [1980] 1976), 227.
[66] Glasser, *Announcing the Kingdom*, 253.
[67] Rushdoony, *In His Service*, 151.
[68] Rushdoony, *Law and Society*, 303-304, 306.
[69] Lynn Hiles, *The Revelation of Jesus Christ* (Shippensburg, PA.: Destiny Image Publishers, 2007), 159.

Kingdom Killer #2 – The Kingdom Belongs to Israel

"Lord, are you at this time going to restore the kingdom to Israel?" (Acts 1:6). Back then, this was a major misconception of many Jews. It was based on their false expectation of the time and nature of the kingdom the Messiah would bring to them. Today, this is still a major misconception and expectation of both orthodox Jews and most evangelical Christians.

In short, if this expectation were true, it would make the kingdom of God synonymous with the nation of Israel. But notably, Jesus did not even dignify this question with a direct answer. Instead, He dismissed it with this side-stepping response: "It's not for you to know the times or dates the Father has set by his own authority" (Acts 1:7). Why did He not answer it directly? It's because Jesus had previously told them before his crucifixion: "Therefore, I tell you that the kingdom of God will be taken away from you and given to another people who will produce its fruit" (Matt. 21:43). And "they knew he was talking about them" (Matt. 21:45b). No previous or subsequent scripture hints at, prophesies, or promises that the kingdom will be given back to Israel and the Jews, exclusively, ever again. That "another people" or "nation" is the Gentiles and/or the "Church." And this removal of the kingdom from Israel and giving of it to another people is part of Christianity's "once for all delivered" faith (Jude 3).

Perhaps a simple syllogism will help clarify the ramifications of this misconception:

> Premise #1 – The kingdom given by God to Israel and the Jews was to be taken away at a coming of Jesus.
>
> Premise #2 – But this coming hasn't happened, according to the dispensationalists.
>
> Inescapable Conclusion – The kingdom still belongs to Israel and the Jews, and we Christians are left without a mighty kingdom. As David Jeremiah prominently believes, "Jerusalem, of course, we know as the historical capital of God's chosen nation, Israel, and the future capital of His eternal kingdom."[70]

---

[70] David Jeremiah, "Why Babylon?", *Charisma*, September 2015, 1.

But as we shall see in Chapter 9, this coming of Jesus happened; the kingdom was taken away from them and given to another people; and there is no promise in Scripture that it will ever be given back. Hence, Bright rightly maintains that "the hope of the fruition of God's kingdom is thus completely divorced from the Israelite state . . . . a total rejection of the state as the vehicle of the Kingdom of God."[71]

Assuredly, the complete destruction of Jerusalem and its Temple was also their loss of the kingdom. This scenario was exactly what the Jewish prophets foretold would happen to Israel in its last days (see Deut. 31:29; 32:1-42; Isa. 5:1-7 compare with Matt. 21:33-46; Isa. 61:1-2 compare with Luke 4:16-21 and Luke 21:22; Heb. 1:1-2). The fall of that nation and desolation of its Old Covenant Temple and system (Matt. 23:36, 38; 1 Pet. 4:7, 17), which had previously been made "obsolete" (Heb. 8:13), occurred during a cloud coming of Jesus in a day-of-the-Lord, age-ending judgment, circa A.D. 70 (see John 5:22).[72]

So where am I wrong on this? If I'm wrong, however, then the kingdom still belongs to Israel and the Jews, and we Christians are without a mighty kingdom. It's that simple; it's that straightforward.

Kingdom Killer #3 – The kingdom won't arrive again until Christ's future 1,000-Year Reign (Rev. 20:1-10)

In support of this misconception, premillennial dispensationalist Thomas Ice writes: Due to "the rejection of Jesus as Messiah by Israel and consequently, the postponement of the kingdom. God is prolonging the time of Israel's kingdom. However, this time God promises that when the current age of grace comes to an end, the next period of time will include the restoration of the kingdom to Israel (Acts 1:6, 11; 3:19-21). Yet the length of our current church age is a mystery—part of the secret, unrevealed plan of God (Ephesians 3:2-13)."[73]

---

[71] Bright, *The Kingdom of God*, 75.
[72] For major expositions on this, see my books: Noē, *Unraveling the End* and *The Perfect Ending for the World*.
[73] Thomas Ice in LaHaye and Ice, *The End Times Controversy*, 107.

What many modern-day Christians do not understand about this prominent view is it also proclaims that during this time, the Old Covenant Temple will be rebuilt and animal sacrifices resumed. Arguably, this resumption is the greatest heresy (i.e., "false doctrine") in evangelical Christianity and the rankest and vilest of idolatries. (For scriptures on Christ's "once for all" sacrifice, see Heb. 9:12, 26-28; 10:10; 1 Pet. 3:18.) God destroyed that Temple in A.D. 70 for this very reason. Why would He want to bring back that old, inferior, animal-sacrificing system compared to what we have now (see Heb. 8:6; 9:9-10; 10:3-4, 9, 11, 18)?

But to LaHaye's credit, he rightly states that "studying God's Word" is "hard work. . . . That requires a pastor with strong self-discipline in studying the Bible so he can impart a well-thought-out biblically based message in the fire of the Holy Spirit."[74] So let's test LaHaye's criterion for how "well-thought-out" his dispensational premillennial understanding and explanation of this Revelation 20:1-10 passage truly is. See what you think.

As we do, please bear in mind that this passage is the only place in the Bible where a 1,000-year reign is ever mentioned. Furthermore, Morris terms these 10 verses "one of the most difficult parts of the entire book"[75] of Revelation. Nonetheless, this idea of a so-called "thousand-year reign of Christ" has been the subject of vast eschatological speculation and investigation throughout church history. Today, it is a highly volatile subject that is "hotly debated"[76] and a large part of the "war zone"[77] of eschatology. So please read this passage, carefully. Then we're going to ask some pertinent and testing questions.

---

[74] Tim LaHaye, "Silent Pulpits," *Charisma*, September 2015, 49, 52.

[75] Leon Morris, *Revelation* (Leicester, England & Grand Rapids, MI.: InterVarsity & Eerdmans , 1987, reprinted 2000), 227.

[76] G.K. Beale, *The Book of Revelation* (Grand Rapids, MI: Eerdmans, 1999), 972.

[77] Gordon J. Spykman, *Reformational Theology: A New Paradigm for Doing Dogmatics* (Grand Rapids, MI.: Eerdmans, 1992), 531.

The 1,000-Year Reign Passage In Revelation

20:1 And I saw an angel coming down out of heaven, having the key to the Abyss and holding in his hand a great chain. ² He seized the dragon, that ancient serpent, who is the devil, or Satan, and bound him for a thousand years. ³ He threw him into the Abyss, and locked and sealed it over him, to keep him from deceiving the nations anymore until the thousand years were ended. After that, he must be set free for a short time.

⁴ I saw thrones on which were seated those who had been given authority to judge. And I saw the souls of those who had been beheaded because of their testimony about Jesus and because of the word of God. They had not worshiped the beast or its image and had not received its mark on their foreheads or their hands. They came to life and reigned with Christ a thousand years. ⁵ (The rest of the dead did not come to life until the thousand years were ended.) This is the first resurrection. ⁶ Blessed and holy are those who share in the first resurrection. The second death has no power over them, but they will be priests of God and of Christ and will reign with him for a thousand years.

⁷ When the thousand years are over, Satan will be released from his prison ⁸ and will go out to deceive the nations in the four corners of the earth—Gog and Magog—and to gather them for battle. In number they are like the sand on the seashore.⁹ They marched across the breadth of the earth and surrounded the camp of God's people, the city he loves. But fire came down from heaven and devoured them. ¹⁰ And the devil, who deceived them, was thrown into the lake of burning sulfur, where the beast and the false prophet had been thrown. They will be tormented day and night for ever and ever.

So let's test LaHaye's criterion for how "well-thought-out" his dispensational premillennial understanding and explanation of this Revelation 20:1-10 passage truly is.

My Seven Pertinent and Testing Questions
(1) Where in this passage is any mention of a second coming, a temple, a re-built temple, re-institution of animal sacrifices, or Jesus sitting on an earthly throne? (2) Where does this passage speak of Israel, an earthly Jerusalem, a gathering of the Jews back to Palestine, a revived Jewish kingdom, an earthly utopian paradise, or material prosperity on the earth? (3) Where does this passage even speak of a "1,000-year reign of Christ?" (4) Doesn't it speak only of the saints reigning *with* Him a thousand years? (5) Does it anywhere limit Christ's reign to only a thousand years? (6) Where does this passage speak of a "millennial kingdom"? (7) Lastly, these conjoined questions are my favorites to ask a dispensational premillennialist. "Are you planning on literally reigning and ruling with Christ during his future and literal 1,000-year reign here on earth?" "Oh, yes," he or she will confidently answer. "Then when are you planning on literally getting beheaded?"

Conspicuously, with the lone exception of the beheading, all of these other popular elements are totally missing from this passage. They are also totally absent from the entire New Testament and the whole Bible. And yet they are vital elements of this most popular millennial view. How has this happened? Simply and sadly, they have been fabricated and imported into the text. It seems LaHaye and his view have succumbed to an all-to-common human tendency of adding things that are not there—a practice specifically warned against in the Book of Revelation, along with severe consequences for those violating this warning (see Rev. 22:18-19). Today, Israel's Old Covenant system is an "old wineskin" (Matt. 9:17; Mark 2:22; Luke 5:37) that God will never reuse. Yet this practice of adding is commonly and casually done and has become accepted—much to our detriment (more on this in Appendix B).

Kingdom Killer #4 -- The Kingdom and the Church Are Synonymous

When the Church became institutionalized in the 4th century, it started seeing itself as the kingdom. This interpretation was made popular by Augustine in his book, *The City of God*, and is found in different versions of Christianity throughout its history.

Rushdoony recaps this historical coupling, thusly: "Augustine, because of his amillennialism, saw no hope in world redemption. Rather, the church itself was the kingdom of God, called to save souls out of a perishing world, not to make the kingdom of this world the kingdom of Christ."[78] (But, to the contrary, check out the message of the seventh trumpet in Revelation 11:15.)

He continues "in the medieval era, the great conflict in Christendom was between those who saw Christ's Kingdom in terms of the state, i.e., the Holy Roman Empire, and those who saw it in terms of the church, i.e., the Holy Catholic Church. Their vision of the Kingdom was institutional, and, in either camp, their efforts were directed towards building up their particular institution. The same division prevails today. Modernism sees the Kingdom in terms of the state, and its gospel is social, or, more accurately, statist. . . . Conservative Catholics and evangelical and Reformed Protestants tend to the other error, to see the Kingdom of God as the church, and the building of the church as the key to triumph."[79]

But as Bright admonishes, "It [is] all too easy to identify our churches with the Kingdom of Christ, to understand the progress of that Kingdom in terms of their numerical growth, and to assume that any program that fortifies our organization automatically extends the Kingdom."[80] He scripturally points out that "there is no tendency in the New Testament to identify the visible church with the Kingdom of God. The church that makes such an identification will soon begin to invite God to endorse its own very human policies and practices . . . . Such an identification is a great snare . . . ."[81]

When the Church became institutionalized in the 4th century, it started seeing itself as the kingdom.

I. Howard Marshall adds these three insights regarding "the disastrous effect of the medieval equation of the KG with the Church:" 1) "the increasingly secular and unchristian expression of authority claimed by church leaders . . ." 2) "the refusal to recognize the saving rule of God

---

[78] Rousa John Rushdoony, *The Institutes of Biblical Law*, Vol. 3 (Vallecito, CA.: Ross House Books, 1999), 199.
[79] Rushdoony, *Law and Society*, 62-63.
[80] Bright, *The Kingdom of God*, 261.
[81] Ibid., 236.

outside the Catholic Church;" and 3) "there has been a strong reaction against the identification of the KG as the Church."[82]

But if the Church and the kingdom are synonymous, then one should be able to interchange these nouns—i.e., take statements made about the kingdom and apply them to the Church, and vice versa. Here are a few examples. See for yourself if this works or not:

- "But seek ye first the kingdom [church] of God and his righteousness" (Matt. 6:33a).
- "We must go through many hardships to enter the kingdom [church] of God" (Acts 14:22b).
- "Boldly and without hindrance he preached the kingdom [church] of God and taught about the Lord Jesus Christ" (Acts 28:31).
- ". . . and the time came when they [the saints of the Most High] possessed the kingdom [church]" (Dan. 7:22b).
- "And I tell you that you are Peter, and on this rock I will build my church [kingdom]" (Matt. 16:18a).
- "If he refuses to listen to them, tell it to the church [kingdom]; and if he refuses to listen even to the church [kingdom], treat him as you would a pagan or a tax collector" (Matt. 18:17).

Many scholars agree that this swapping of terms does not work and there are no places in Scripture where the kingdom is identified with the Church. As we shall see in Part II, the kingdom encompasses much more than the Church.

In summary, let us state these five postulates regarding the kingdom and the Church: 1) Neither the Church or its people are the kingdom; 2) The kingdom is bigger than the Church; 3) The Church is subordinate to the kingdom; 4) Christians are to be the people of the kingdom; 5) Both the Church and its people are to be instruments of the kingdom as they proclaim, advance, and manifest its redemptive truths, principles, works, and powers in the Church and in society; 6) Thus the kingdom extends beyond doing "church work;" 7) By no means does this subordination devalue the institution or role of the Church. And if the Church would

---

[82] I. Howard Marshall, *Jesus the Savior* (Downers Grove, IL.: InterVarsity Press, 1990), 230

begin doing the works of the kingdom, more scripturally and abundantly, more properly and correctly, we wouldn't have as many problems in America and throughout the world.

A Call for Serious Kingdom Christianity

Given that there is so much conflict, confusion, and errant thinking with how we Christians understand and present, or ignore and avoid, the kingdom of God . . .

Given that we have raised at least two generations of Christians here in America who are kingdom illiterate and have been conditioned to lesser versions of Christianity without a mighty kingdom . . .

Given that Christianity has been "tamed" and "culture has triumphed"[83] . . .

Given that "the compartmentalization and trivialization of Christianity . . . has ushered in a generation of shallow, ineffectual, and invisible Christians . . . . America's churches have been subverted"[84] . . .

Given that "as a result, Christian faith [has] become increasingly personalized, privatized, and marginalized"[85] . . .

Given that Jesus warned us to "watch out that no one deceives you" (Matt. 24:4) . . .

Given that a firm grasp of the kingdom is indispensable for a proper understanding of the Person of Christ and the fullness of the redemption He has accomplished and made everlastingly available in this world . . .

And given that God's people must become better motivated, re-educated, and enabled to proclaim the kingdom "boldly and without hindrance" (Acts 28:31a) . . .

In the pages ahead, we shall solidly ground the everlasting form of the kingdom of God, time- and nature-wise, in five steps (comprised in five chapters, followed by two critical Appendices) and in a scriptural, clear, and undeniable manner. But first, we have one more challenging issue and great opportunity to explore.

---

[83] Wolfe, *The Transformation of American Religion*, inside flap, 3.

[84] WorldNetDaily, *Whistleblower*, 29.

[85] McLaren, *The Last Word and the Word After That*, 169.

... and if the Church would begin doing the works of the kingdom, more scripturally and abundantly, more properly and correctly, we wouldn't have as many problems in America and throughout the world.

Chapter 7

Return of the Miraculous[1]

And in the church God has appointed first of all apostles, second
prophets, third teachers, then workers of miracles, also those having
gifts of healing, those able to help others, those with gifts of
administration, and those speaking in different kinds of tongues
(1 Cor. 12:28).

W ould the Apostle Paul, or even Jesus, recognize the Church in
America, North America, or Western Europe today if they
were to walk into a typical service some Sunday morning? Or
would they bring out the whip and turn over the tables? After all, isn't
the Church mentioned in the above scripture still here?

Then why aren't we seeing and experiencing these same supernatural
powers and gifts in operation—i.e., the same caliber of signs, wonders,
miracles, gifts of the Holy Spirit (the *charismata*), and ministry
effectiveness as depicted as normative Christianity in the four gospels
and the Book of Acts? By caliber, we mean: *the same quality and*
quantity thereof.

In this chapter we shall explore the reasons why we are not seeing
them and what we might do differently in order to see their return of

---

[1] Some of this chapter was originally presented and read as a theological paper
at the 48th Annual Meeting of the Evangelical Theological Society, November
1996, in Jackson, Mississippi.

these mighty manifestations of God once again operative and normative in our midst.

Ironically, Christians in some third world countries are frequently reporting the operation of these powers and manifestations. J.P. Moreland affirms: "a major factor in the current revival in the Third World—by some estimates, up to 70 percent of it—is connected to signs and wonders as expressions of the love of the Christian Father-God, the lordship of his Son, and the power of his Spirit and his Kingdom. A manifestation of the supernatural power of God through healings, demonic deliverances, and the prophetic are central to what is going on today."[2] Philip Jenkins concurs that "worldwide, Christianity is actually moving toward supernaturalism . . . and in many ways toward the ancient world view expressed in the New Testament."[3]

But to the contrary, are the comments of many charismatic and Pentecostal leaders (the fastest growing segment of Christianity, worldwide, and its influence is incalculable) who readily admit they are *not seeing or experiencing* this caliber of signs, wonders, miracles, and gifts of the Holy Spirit in their gatherings or ministries. A few scholarly examples should suffice.

Craig S. Keener: ". . . few of us currently witness them with the same magnitude and regularity as in Acts. Yet many of us who acknowledge that miracles of a biblical scale can happen today (including some Pentecostals) would be scared out of our wits if one actually happened to us. So pervasively has Enlightenment culture's anti-supernaturalism affected the Western church . . . that most of us are suspicious of anything supernatural. . . . Although I have heard of miracles such as those in Acts happening regularly in some places, I frankly confess that I have not witnessed many miracles on that scale."[4]

Andrew T. Floris: ". . . in the Post-Apostolic Era down to this very day. It cannot be denied, however, that these manifestations of the Spirit became less frequent in that period. And the reason for this was not because God had a different plan for that age, nor because there was not

---

[2] J.P. Moreland, "Restoration of the Kingdom's Miraculous Power," in Robert W. Graves, ed., *Strangers to Fire*, 283-284.
[3] Philip Jenkins, "The Next Christianity," *Atlantic Monthly*, October 2002, 54.
[4] Craig S. Keener, "Are Spiritual Gifts for Today?" in Robert W. Graves, ed., *Strangers to Fire*, 137, 160.

need of them anymore, but because the church had lost her first zeal and love. Little by little a more fixed and ceremonial type of worship was developing. Both Protestant and non-Protestant church historians are in accord on this point. . . . that the church does not have the same power and does not demonstrate the same signs as the apostles did because the lives of most Christians were not conformable to the evangelical precepts of purity and holiness."[5]

Jack Deere: ". . . admits the prophecies of charismatic seers are full of error, and he acknowledges it is well-nigh impossible to interpret extrabiblical messages with any degree of confidence. Deere even concedes, 'We may mistake our own thoughts for God's revelation.'"[6]

Marcus Yoars: "Though there have been seasons of Holy Spirit revival in our nation, even charismatic churches today are de-emphasizing such things as praying for the sick, demonic deliverance or the prophetic." But he argues back that "Making room for the Spirit's supernatural movement isn't an option; it's the mark of those who truly follow Christ."[7]

Sid Roth: "When I attend meetings of top healing evangelists, I see a few people in wheelchairs get healed. But hundreds wheel off into the night, confused, hurt and not healed. Why the disconnect? Why haven't we received what God has already provided for us?"[8]

Kevin Turner: "A Chinese Christian recently visited the United States and toured churches here. At the end of the trip he was asked what he thought about American spirituality. He answered, 'I am amazed at how much the church in America can accomplish without the Holy Spirit.' We have large buildings and many programs but still no move of God. We have more trained ministers and more Bible colleges than any

---

[5] Andrew T. Floris, "The Charismata in the Post-Apostolic Church," in Ibid., 370, 379, 381.

[6] MacArthur, *Strange Fire*, 69 – Deere quoted from: Jack Deere, *The Gift of Prophecy* (Ventura, CA.: Gospel Light, 2008), 141.

[7] Marcus Yoars, "Will the Real Church Please Stand Up?" *Charisma*, March 2014, 8.

[8] Sid Roth, "Why Is There a Disconnect With Healing?" *Charisma*, May 2014, 20.

other nation but no revival. We have seminars on revivals and huge campaigns to promote our meetings. But where is the revival?"[9]

John MacArthur: "'There is almost uniform testimony from all sectors of the charismatic movement *that prophecy is imperfect and impure*, and will contain elements which are not to be obeyed or trusted.' In light of such an admission, one wonders, how can Christians differentiate a revelatory word of divine origin from one concocted in their own imaginations? . . . Put simply, modern prophecy is no more reliable in discerning truth than a Magic Eight Ball, tarot cards, or a Ouija board."[10] And, "no modern healing ministry comes anywhere close to this [the] biblical standard."[11]

J. Lee Grady: ". . . today in churches that claim to be Spirit-filled. We say we believe the Bible, but when it comes to the Holy Spirit, we've become cowards. In trying to be trendy and relevant, we've replaced spiritual anointing with cool music, graphics, sermons and programs that look and sound great but lack a spiritual punch. If we are full of the Spirit, the nine *charismata*, or spiritual gifts mentioned in 1 Corinthians 12:8-10 should be manifested regularly. But few Christians today have even heard of these gifts; fewer have seen them in operation. We need these nine gifts in our churches today."[12]

Jim Cymbala: "Too many churches have 'programmed out' the power and presence of the Holy Spirit. . . . Even God would have a difficult time breaking into that tight schedule. Sure enough, the service went off without a hitch. The run sheet was followed exactly. And though we had a meeting, I doubt whether many had a meeting with God. . . . Isn't that why strong prayer for His presence is rare? . . . I haven't met many leaders who tell me that's what they want to see happen at their church, too."[13]

---

[9] Kevin Turner, "Why Isn't the American Church Great," *Charisma,* January 2005, 52.
[10] In quotation of Wayne Grudem in MacArthur, *Strange Fire*, 114-115.
[11] MacArthur, *Strange Fire*, 168.
[12] J. Lee. Grady, "Why We Can't Ignore the Gifts of the Spirit," *Charisma*, January 2015, 74.
[13] Jim Cymbala, "Why Many Churches Exclude the Holy Spirit on Sunday," *Charisma*, February, 2015, 50, 54.

R.T. Kendall: "Those on the Spirit side stress getting back to the Book of Acts, signs, wonders, and miracles, gifts of the Holy Spirit . . . . Until we recover the power of the Spirit, the honor of God's name will not be restored. . . . In my half century of ministry I have seen the worst excesses of the charismatic movement—spurious prophecies, fake healings, fleshly speaking in tongues. . . . I can't always take the party line, and yet I believe in the gifts of the Holy Spirit as much as anybody I know. . . . There is admittedly a lot of strange fire around these days. I regret this. And there is not nearly enough holy fire in my own life and ministry in the places where I go. . . . for some reason the miraculous healings diminished in the 1950s, although some of the evangelists did their best to keep praying for people as they had previously done—but with fewer results."[14]

A.W. Tozer: "If the Holy Spirit was withdrawn from the church today, 95 percent of what we do would go on and no one would know the difference."[15]

These findings prompt travelling evangelist Lynn Hiles "to wonder when I travel outside of the country, 'Why does the miraculous seem to work in other places outside of America more so than it does in this country?' What I began to discover is that they have not been taught all of the unbelief and the rules and the regulations of man-made religion that deteriorates the faith of many . . . ."[16]

But I believe Munroe succinctly hits the proverbial nail on the head as he assures us the answer to this lack of seeing and experiencing is part of "the lost message of Jesus that needs to be resurrected in our times."[17] So fasten your seatbelts as we explore some significant reasons behind these well-documented facts and the fascinating possibility of a return of the miraculous in our day and time.

---

[14] R.T. Kendall, *Holyfire: A Balanced, Biblical Look at the Holy Spirit's Work in Our Lives* (Lake Mary, FL.: Charisma House, 2014), *xxxi, xxxv*. 73-74, 113.

[15] A.W. Tozer, quoted in Kendall, *Holyfire*, 9.

[16] Lynn Hiles, *Unforced Rhythms of Grace* (Great Cacapon, WV.: Lynn Hiles Ministries, 2011), 102.

[17] Munroe, *Rediscovering the Kingdom*, 149.

Launching Premise and Diagnosis

If, as Martin Luther penned and many Christians believe, "the Spirit and the gifts are ours,"[18] then why aren't we seeing 1st-century caliber signs, wonders, miracles, gifts of the Holy Spirit, and ministry effectiveness today? After all, these mighty manifestations were "the basic dynamic of New Testament Christianity." So doesn't "the Gospel" still have to be "boldly proposed and radically embodied if the church is to grow and the wounds of a culture of self-absorption are going to be healed?"[19]

As the often contentious and heated debate over the modern-day presence or absence of miraculous (*charismata*) powers continues on unabated, neither side really wants to hear what the other side has to say, nor likes the other side. Each side only wants its entrenched view validated and becomes rabidly defensive whenever it is threatened. Hence, cynical, cutting, smug, self-righteous, and/or mocking challenges and remarks are frequently raised by cessationists who claim the empowering gifts of the Holy Spirit are no longer available—having ceased sometime in the 1st century. A few examples should suffice:

- "Why don't you Apostles start visiting hospitals, find patients with verifiable major problems (like missing limbs, spinal deformities, massive tumors, etc.) and then heal them on the spot with video verifications?"
- "Why are you wasting time hanging out in a building? Why don't those who advertise miracle services get out in the streets and heal people; or walk down the corridors of the hospitals and empty the beds of patients?"
- "Take me some place, any place, and show me someone who measures up to the apostles' use of spiritual gifts."
- "Better yet, if major types of miracles happened visibly, they would be enough to cause people to believe in the not-so-visible ones, which anyone can claim is the power of God or whatever!"

---

[18] *A Mighty Fortress Is Our God,* verse 4, line 2.
[19] Jon Meacham, "Preach Like Your Faith Depends on It," *Time*, 25 March 2013, 46.

- "There's a good reason this stuff doesn't happen. When it supposedly happens it's always in some foreign country, or in some hidden place only a few people know about, or some rural countryside where there aren't any medical records or ways to validate the claims made after the fact."

Even worse, as J. Lee Grady reports, in John MacArthur's "new book *Strange Fire*, he [MacArthur] declares in no uncertain terms that anyone who embraces any form of charismatic or Pentecostal theology does not worship the true God." Grady then laments: "My brother in Christ has written me off" and "unfortunately, some charismatics have given MacArthur plenty of new ammunition to support his case that we are all a bunch of sleazy con artists and spiritual bimbos. Our movement is fraught with problems. . . . But instead of offering fatherly correction, he [MacArthur] pulls out his sword and hacks away."[20]

It's termed "cessationist theology." It's the idea that some or all of the miraculous powers and gift manifestations of God *ceased* sometime after the last apostle died, or when the canon of Scripture was complete, or circa A.D. 70 when Jerusalem and the Temple were destroyed. And it's variously contended and contested. As Grady further reports, MacArthur believes: "God's miracle-working power stopped around A.D. 100. He says healing, tongues, prophecy, visions and other supernatural manifestations described in the New Testament don't work today. MacArthur is particularly irked that charismatics emphasize speaking in tongues (which he calls 'gibberish'); he also complains that we have a 'perverse obsession with physical health' (in other words, if you get sick, just accept it because God doesn't heal anymore). But the New Testament doesn't tell us that heaven flipped a switch and turned off the Spirit's power. That is MacArthur's opinion, not a biblical doctrine. . . . *Strange Fire* was not written out of a heart of love."[21]

Charisma publisher Steve Strang adds: "what MacArthur said isn't new: that the gifts of the Spirit ended with the death of the apostles and that the manifestations of the Holy Spirit, including charismatics' worship style, are 'strange fire.' Yet when MacArthur characterized the entire Pentecostal-charismatic movement and all its elements as works of

---

[20] J. Lee Grady, "Grace to John MacArthur," *Charisma*, January 2014, 74.
[21] ibid.

the devil, it couldn't help but sound like blasphemy of the Holy Spirit to me." He concludes by noting: "people such as MacArthur are comfortable with dogma; they aren't comfortable with the experience of the power of God when it hits a believer's life."[22]

Practically speaking, it's probably unfair, unwise, and imprudent to broad-brush paint the entire Pentecostal/charismatic movement with one negative stoke as being "strange fire" (a la MacArthur's book). Nevertheless, nothing silences a critic or skeptic like personally observing or receiving a bona fide miracle or supernatural manifestation from God. But manifestations of the supernatural also attract extremists, pretenders, counterfeiters, and those who think these encounters are end-all experiences. Sadly, as Yoars concedes, this situation "still runs rampant within Spirit-filled churches and charismatic conferences as we elevate supernatural experiences over everything else."[23]

In my opinion, the criticisms of Christian cessationists deserve more thoughtful and honest answers than have been offered to date. Therefore, in this chapter we shall address three explanations, three critical areas of discrepancy, and propose a working great hypothesis for how and why we 21st-century Christians could see the return of 1st-century caliber of signs, wonders, miracles, gifts of the Holy Spirit, and ministry effectiveness. But as you will see, this exposition has absolutely nothing to do with a so-called "last days" revival. Rather, we'll go straight to the root of the problem for why the supernatural gifts of the Spirit are not being manifested today in the same quality and quantity that we see as normative in the New Testament gospels and the Book of Acts.

Explanation #1 – The Sovereignty and Will of God

First and foremost, God is sovereign over all things including how and when what we call the "miraculous" does or does not occur. Always, He is in complete control even when we might have hoped for a different result. Moreover, we shall never fully understand the mystery of his interventions and non-interventions (see Deut. 29:29; Rom. 11:33). After all, even Jesus didn't heal everyone all the time. He revealed that

---

[22] Steve Strang, "Responding with 'Holy Fire,'" *Charisma*, January 2014, 10.
[23] Marcus Yoars, "6 Things a Supernatural Lifestyle Doesn't Do," *Charisma*, May 2014, 8.

He could only do what He "saw" the Father doing (John 5:19-20). He also only healed when the power was present (Luke 5:17; John 3:2). And Jesus was and still is the only Person to Whom God gave "the Spirit fully" and "power over everything" (John 3:34-35).

Contrary to some beliefs within our faith, the intervention of miraculous powers and the witness of supernatural signs, wonders, and spiritual gifts are never exclusively subject to our bidding, regardless of who we are, our spiritual gifting, our calling in the church, our spiritual maturity, our prayer life, or anything. Nor can we manufacture them or demand their occurrence. No human being has that power to invoke or work the miraculous on his or her own accord or at any time he or she pleases. God's sovereignty always takes precedence. In this regard, we have no absolute control or ultimate responsibility. But in our next two explanations, we do have some control and responsibility.

Explanation #2 – Unbelief

Jesus "could not do any miracles there" (in his home town) and only "a few sick people" were healed because of unbelief (Mark 6:5; also Matt. 13:57-58; 17:20). "And He [Jesus] was amazed at their lack of faith" (Mark 6:6). Not only do these verses describe an infertile atmosphere Jesus encountered, it also describes a similar quenching atmosphere toward God's miraculous in much of the modern-day church. Yes, there are different types of unbelief. But today, both doctrinally and functionally, quite a disparity of beliefs and practices exist compared to the mighty and normative faith depicted in much of the New Testament.

Thus, Billy Graham sagely advises: "No, he [Jesus] didn't heal everyone he met; those who disbelieved and turned their backs on him had no part in the blessings he offered. This should be a warning to us of the dangers of disbelief."[24]

Consequently for many Christians today, their church has become a familiar and comfortable place. It makes few demands on them and arouses little opposition. Most likely, the introduction or even allowance of 1st-century miraculous activity would dramatically change that status quo and be quite upsetting for some, many, most, or perhaps all.

---

[24] Billy Graham, "My Answer," *The Indianapolis Star*, 2/15/14, E4.

As appealing and comfortable as our or any church might be, we would be well advised to reread the harsh words Jesus used in condemning the atmosphere of "lukewarmness" in the Laodicean church in the Book of Revelation (see Rev. 3:14-16). Whether our Lord's admonishment here applies, you can decide. But the inertia factor at work is this: Most Christian denominations and churches have spent centuries, or decades, in developing their particular traditions. These traditions guide how they do and do not practice their particular version of the Christian faith, how they conduct worship services, and what is and is not acceptable in their midst. This modern-day reality leads us directly into our most poignant explanation for the lack of the miraculous today in most churches and other Christian gatherings.

Explanation #3 – To Authenticate the Message

The "main purpose behind the many miracles Jesus performed throughout his three-year public ministry . . . was to signify and demonstrate the arrival of the kingdom of God."[25] These manifestations also identified Jesus as the Messiah (see Luke 7:22-23). Another purpose, however, for providing these 1st-century signs, wonders, miracles, and gifts of the Holy Spirit was to authenticate the validity of the message about the kingdom, the Lord Jesus Christ, his teachings, their philosophy of ministry, and the Holy Spirit-guided expectations of soon-coming, eschatological events (see John 16:13). This was how people in those times could distinguish between what was true from what was false (see Deut. 18:21-22; Matt. 9:4-7; 11:2-6; John 9:1-7).

On the other hand, these authenticating manifestations, were not, as some think, to authenticate the messenger, *per se*. Not one scripture states that the miraculous manifestations authenticated the Twelve Apostles or the writers of the New Testament. Rather, these miraculous manifestations authenticated the message by anyone (including Jesus) who presented a correct message (for a dramatic illustration of this truth, see Mark 9:38-40).[26] Nor were they to confirm any "slightly off"

---

[25] Clinton E. Arnold, "The Kingdom, Miracles, Satan, and Demons," in Morgan and Peterson, *The Kingdom of God*, 157.

[26] Also see Jack Deere, *Surprised by the Power of the Spirit* (Grand Rapids, MI.: Zondervan, 1993), 103-107. I highly recommended this book as a resource for

message. It is doubtful if the new faith Jesus and the early Church presented could have survived and attracted the multitudes without these mighty acts. Today, however, many of our modern-day messages about Christianity are far removed from the messages being delivered back in the 1st-century. Hence, God is not obligated to authenticate them in that same manner, and mostly has not.

For instance, the biblical fact is that during that 1st-century the central message being proclaimed was "the time is fulfilled," the long-promised and everlasting form of the kingdom of God was "at hand," there and then (Mark 1:15 KJV).[27] Later on, Jesus sent his disciples out to proclaim that same message and to manifest his kingdom works: "As you go, preach this message: 'The kingdom of heaven is at hand. Heal the sick, raise the dead, cleanse those who have leprosy, drive out demons. Freely you have received, freely give" (Matt. 10:7-8; also see Luke 10:1-20). These were the same kingdom works He had been doing (Matt. 4:23-25).

After his resurrection, and during one of his many comings and appearings, Jesus commanded his followers of all generations to do likewise. In the most overlooked portion of his Great Commission, Jesus specified that they and those who would follow them (including us today) should "go and make disciples of all nations, baptizing them in the name of the Father and of the Son and of the Holy Spirit, *and teaching them to obey everything I have commanded you*" (Matt. 28:19-20; italics mine, also see John 14:12). But that's not all.

This *correct* message also included the Holy Spirit-guided expectations of the Lord's soon coming in age-ending, on-the-clouds, day-of-the-Lord judgment (John 16:13; Matt. 10:23; 16:27-28; 24:3-34; 26:64; and more) as well as the fulfillment of every Old Testament eschatological promise and prophecy within the time-restricted frame of that 1st-century generation of Jesus' hearers (see Luke 21:20-22, 28).

---

additionally refuting other cessationist arguments and deductive reasoning. Dr. Deere is an ex-Dallas Theological Seminary professor and ex-cessationist who came to realize the errors and destructiveness of cessation theology. His change of belief on this matter, not surprisingly, resulted in his dismissal. That's how sensitive is God's miraculous.

[27] "Near" is a weak translation. "At hand" is a more graphic translation. It means "graspable, reachable, there to be seized."

No question about it. Those were the messages and the nearness (imminent or imminence) expectations God was authenticating with signs, wonders, miracles, and gifts of the Holy Spirit following. Thus, the Apostle Paul wrote to the Thessalonians, "Our gospel came to you not simply with words, but also with power, with the Holy Spirit and with deep conviction" (1 Thess. 1:5; also see Rom. 15:18-19; Heb. 2:4; Mark 16:17-20). Arnold affirms "that God enabled them to do these signs and wonders as an authenticating testimony to the gospel that they proclaimed."[28]

Nowadays, most evangelical Christians are doing fairly well with their message about Christ's birth, death, resurrection, ascension, and the provision of salvation.[29] But after that, our messages and versions of Christianity drop off rather sharply. In those other major areas, we are in open conflict with and contradiction of the messages God was authenticating back then and there.

Three Critical Areas of Departure

Frankly put, the messages being presented and ministries being performed in most churches today pale in comparison with that of our 1st-century brethren. Our modern-day versions simply are not close enough to them to warrant authentication by God with the same caliber (quality and quantity) of authenticating signs, wonders, miracles, and gifts of the Holy Spirit following. Certainly, in his sovereignty, God can override our errant theologies and practices. But mostly He is not doing so. Let's look at three critical areas of departure:

1) A Different Philosophy of Ministry

The pervasive influence of cessation theology, liberalism, and secularism in the Church today has significantly obscured what exactly is or is not the genuine philosophy of ministry of our Christian faith. On the

---

[28] Arnold, "The Kingdom, Miracles, Satan, and Demons," in Morgan and Peterson, *The Kingdom of God*, 174.

[29] However we are mostly presenting a message of an incomplete salvation that still awaits Jesus' so-called return to finish the job.

one hand, some Christians doctrinally believe the power to operate in the supernatural spiritual gifts of the New Testament Church (1 Cor. 12:4-11, 28; Rom. 12:6-8; Eph. 4:11-13) does not exist today because it was withdrawn by God in the 1st century and is no longer needed. Again, this position is termed cessation theology.

Others believe God has not withdrawn these blessings and powers from his Church. They contend that they are part of his on-going kingdom and are available to every Christian, subject always to God's sovereignty. This position is termed "continuance theology." The monumental problem for this group is, however, it has a hard time proving these miraculous gifts are still operative. But then, there is a large middle ground of Christians who don't subscribe doctrinally to a cessationist view but do subscribe functionally. In their assemblies, they simply do not practice, expect, seek, or perhaps even want these gifts to be manifested. In other words, they like their lesser version of Christianity just the way it is, thank you. So which view is correct?

Regardless of how the cessationist, continuance, or middle-ground position is theologically justified or contested, the bottom line is: a cessationist view—doctrinally or functionally—posits a different-natured kingdom and version of Christianity from what was presented, taught, modeled, and practiced in the 1st century by Jesus and the early Church. Such a changed nature must be considered a significant departure from that which God was authenticating, wouldn't you agree?

The Scriptures, however, are quite clear that the Christian faith was and always is to be "built on the foundation of the apostles, the prophets, with Christ Jesus Himself as the chief cornerstone" (Eph. 2:20; also Rev. 21:14). This is the *only* foundation on which we are to build and upon which we must be "careful" how we build and lay no other foundation (see 1 Cor. 3:10-11 for the consequences of not doing this). But cessationism does not build on this same foundational philosophy of ministry or nature of the kingdom. Instead, it removes foundational and intrinsic elements and dismisses their purposes for today.

In this author's opinion, the theological and exegetical arguments for the continuity of this 1st-century-modeled philosophy of ministry, as well as nature of the *only* everlasting kingdom (see Dan. 2:44; 7:14, 21-22, 27) that Jesus came to usher in, are far stronger than those for a discontinuity—1 Corinthians 13 notwithstanding (the major cessationist text). We shall begin a discussion of this passage and issue of continuity or discontinuity, continuance or cessation in Appendix A. In the meantime, below are a few tidbits to whet your appetite.

Jesus' growth parables strongly contend for a continuance nature and against any discontinuity of his and ever-increasing kingdom (see Matt. 13:1-33; Mark 4:30-33; Isa. 9:6-7). Nowhere does Jesus hint at a cessation of any of the kingdom's distinctives. Moreover, the kingdom's *dunamis,* "powers of the age to come" (Heb. 6:5), belong to and are possessive of the in-breaking age of the New Covenant, not the "last days" of the Old Covenant. Scripture further equates "the age to come" and the eternal life of Jesus' "at hand" kingdom as synonymous (Mark 10:30; Luke 18:30). That in-breaking age superseded the Old Covenant "this present age" (see Matt. 12:32; Mark 10:30; Luke 18:30; 20:34-35; Gal. 1:4; also 1 Cor. 7:31; Heb. 8:13; 12:26-28). And Christ's kingdom, along with its intrinsic elements, have "no end" (Isa. 9:7; Luke 1:33). Thus, what is true of the whole is true of its constituent parts. They were not to pass away or ever to be destroyed (see Dan. 7:14; also 2:44).

As we shall see in our next chapter, Jesus' 1st-century kingdom is *the only everlasting kingdom.* No other kingdom was promised, and no other is yet to come. Cessation theology, however, discontinues (i.e., destroys or causes to pass away) a significant portion of Jesus' "just as" kingdom that He was "conferring" back in the 1st century (Luke 22:29). Thus, cessationism alters and diminishes the kingdom's integrity and basic nature. Yet Paul adamantly confirmed: "the kingdom of God is not a matter of talk but of power" (1 Cor. 4:20). Paul's "power" is, again, the Greek word *dunamis*. It means "miraculous power!"

With all due respect, many cessationists are sincere people who love God, but, in a word, they've been "had." Again, and as we shall begin to discuss in Appendix A, cessation theology must be judged for what it truly is—not just a mistake in interpretation, but rather a bankrupt scholarship and a dispiriting philosophy of ministry. It has cut itself off from a significant portion of the foundation of the faith, perverted the witness of God's kingdom and, by its subtraction methodology, lost its right to "the tree of life" [Jesus] (see Rev. 22:19). And, of course, no one can exercise gifts that one thinks have ceased.

But as the heated debate over the presence or absence of the kingdom's miraculous powers continues, it must be based solely on Scripture, and not on our positive or negative experiences or lack thereof. Scripture is the absolute standard in this matter. And the fact is, not one text of Scripture teaches that the miraculous or the spiritual gifts were confined to a 1st-century time period. Notably, much Christian literature of the 2nd century confirms their continuance.[30] Likewise, no verse ever states that the Bible replaces the need for the miraculous in God's kingdom or the world.

Let's stop and think for a moment. How are we moderns supposed to "do the works of Jesus" (John 14:12) and obey his Great Commission to teach "them to obey everything I have commanded you" (Matt 28:20) without the same gifting and empowerment our 1st-century ancestors enjoyed and employed? Or, why is Jesus considered the model for Christian piety, but not the model for the operation of supernatural gifts? Then how "Christ-like" is the Christ-like we are called to be?

Disappointingly, cessationism's unbelief deprives God's people and other people of the benefit of these God-given gifts and powers. It's not merely that God *will not,* but even Jesus *could not* do his mighty works among them because of their unbelief. Rushdoony nails this cessationism issue directly on the head, thusly: "There is no 'problem' with God and His power. The problem is with us."[31]

Interestingly, Albert Mohler, president of the Southern Baptist Convention's flagship seminary (largely a cessationist institution), predicts, "The evangelical movement in America in the 21st century is going to be forced back into the Book of Acts."[32]

2) A Different Gospel

Several times in four verses, the apostle Paul cautioned about "turning to a different gospel – which is really no gospel at all" and "some people . . . are trying to pervert the gospel of Christ. . . . If anyone is preaching to you a gospel other than that what you accepted [in the 1st century], let him be eternally condemned" (Gal. 1:6-9).

---

[30] See theological paper, *When Did Prophecy Cease? The Testimony of the Second Century,* presented at the 47th Annual Meeting of the Evangelical Theological Society in November 1995 in Philadelphia by Gary Steven Shogren, Biblical Theological Seminary, 200 N. Main Street, Hatfield, PA 19440.

[31] Rushdoony, *In His Service*, 60.

[32] Meacham, "Preach Like Your Faith Depends on It," *Time*, 25 March, 2013, 46.

Please note that for any gospel to be "different," it does not have to be totally different. Slightly different is different. Therefore, why shouldn't the modern-day gospel reductionism, which we discussed in Chapter 1 (pp. 14-20), be construed as "a different gospel?" Several times, Jesus even termed his gospel "the gospel of the kingdom" (Matt. 24:14; also 4:23; 9:35; Mark 1:14). But today, as we have seen, the kingdom has been removed from gospel presentations. Surely, any honest biblical scholar would be strained to contend that our gospel reductionism is not "a different gospel" and does not go forth with Paul's eternal condemnation. Hence, if we are proclaiming, preaching, and teaching "a different gospel" in this regard, why should we expect God to place his authenticating stamp of 1st-century miraculous manifestations upon it?

Similarly, cessationism's diminished version of the kingdom today is fundamentally different enough that it, too, has to be considered "a different gospel" compared to the one being preached and practiced in New Testament times. Without a doubt, these depreciations of our faith have sapped the very life-affirming powers out of much of the body of Christ (the Church), depersonalized God for many believers, and hamstrung God's will being done on earth as it is in heaven. Wouldn't you agree?

3) Different Eschatological Expectations

Most churches and Christians today are decreeing that the imminent (nearness), Holy Spirit-guided, eschatological expectations of the New Testament writers and early Church *proved false*. Almost all biblical scholars agree that Jesus' first followers were given the Holy Spirit to "guide" them "into all truth" and "tell" or "show" them "what is to come" (John 16:13). Without exception, they expected the Lord's eschatological coming and the fulfillment of all things promised to occur within their lifetime. Evidently, what the Holy Spirit showed and told them formed their imminent expectations.

Let's also understand that eschatology (the study of last things) is not a stand-alone doctrine or an appendix to Christianity. It's the completion of God's plan of redemption. That's central to our faith and not fringe. But today many are told, taught, and think they are seeing prophecy unfold right before their very eyes inside a godless and unbelieving

Israel. Remember, "Hope deferred makes the heart sick." And surely this deferment has made the Church sick for more than 1,900 years. "But a longing fulfilled is a tree of life" (Prov. 13:12). Please, let's keep foremost in mind that the Holy Spirit-guided imminent expectations of fulfillment within their generation were a large part of the message God was authenticating back and there in that 1st century.

Today, however, the popular postponement views of eschatology (pre-mil, post-mil, a-mil, even historicism) deny that those 1st-century expectations were correct. In their attempts to explain away this disparity, biblical scholars have ignored the key hermeneutic of audience relevancy and invented what they call "delay theory."[33] The huge problem with delay theory is: it directly contradicts Scripture (see Hab. 2:3; Ezek. 12:21-28; Heb. 10:37). This invented device then forces these scholars to inject arbitrary time gaps, employ numerous sidestepping exegetical gimmicks, and devise other clever manipulations in order to justify their various futuristic, yet-to-be-fulfilled scenarios. Not surprisingly, all of their subsequent fulfillment expectations and various predictions, as voiced by some of their leading spokespeople over the centuries and still today, have been proven wrong.

But since I have written systematically and extensively on this matter of Holy Spirit-guided expectations, audience relevancy, and precise past fulfillment, I'll only list some significant topics and portions below for your future reference:

- "The Great End-Time Fiasco—Things that were supposed to happen didn't happen as New Testament expectations proved false" and forced the Church to invent "'delay theory' in direct contradiction of Scripture."[34]
- "Divine Perfection in Two Creations—The God of the Bible is the God of order and design. Everything He created He did so with a plan, purpose, timeframe, and mathematical precision." This perfection encompasses both the physical creation and the covenantal creation. The latter is what we call God's plan of redemption. Its completion was expected by the New Testament

---

[33] Hays, Duvall, Pate, *Dictionary of Biblical Prophecy and End Times*, 114-115, 410.
[34] Noē, *Unraveling the End*, 124-127.

writers and the early Church to occur within their lifetime. It did, precisely.[35]

- "Harmony in the New Testament" and the "Intensification of Nearness Language. . . . as Jesus' literal, forty-year, 'this-generation' time period wound down, from A.D. 30 to A.D. 70, the sense of nearness language in the New Testament dramatically picked up."[36] This intensifying dynamic further verifies that their Holy Spirit-guided expectations were for a soon-coming fulfillment.

- "Reframing Jesus' Most Dramatic Prophecy . . . . Four Sidestepping Devices . . . . Why Can't We Take Jesus at His Word? . . . 13 Crucial and Contested Elements."[37]

- "The End that Was, the Last Days that Were . . . . Eight Confirmatory Insights."[38]

- "Seven Demanding Evidences of Jesus' Timely Coming on the Clouds . . . . Eight Challenging Objections."[39]

- In sum, not only did Jesus die for us "at just the right time" (Rom. 5:6), but everything else also occurred "at just the right time"—exactly *as* and *when* specified and expected—no delay, no gaps, no exegetical gimmicks. Again, this is what I call "divine perfection." Anything less is less.

- In support, Klein, Blomberg, and Hubbard, Jr. emphasize in their hermeneutical textbook *Introduction to Biblical Interpretation*: "*The historical defensible interpretation has greatest authority.* That is, interpreters can have maximum confidence in their understanding of a text when they base that understanding on historically defensible arguments."[40] That authority is exactly what you will find in the above referenced and detailed materials.

---

[35] Ibid., 128-140, 213-236.

[36] Ibid., 237-248.

[37] Ibid., 285-330.

[38] Noē, *The Perfect Ending for the World*, 171-202.

[39] Ibid., 219-276.

[40] William W. Klein, Craig L. Blomberg, and Robert L. Hubbard, Jr., *Introduction to Biblical Interpretation* (Dallas, TX.: Word Publishing, 1993), 149.

Unfortunately, the arbitrary devices and unscriptural schemes concocted by the traditions of men over the centuries have made a mockery of the plain meaning of many scriptures and led to a multitude of misunderstandings. These misunderstandings permeate much of contemporary Christian thinking and beliefs. They have also undermined the credibility and perspicuity of Scripture. As a result, we moderns are severely hamstrung in our proper understanding and presentation of our "once for all delivered" faith (Jude 3).

And since most of our modern-day eschatological messages contradict the imminency expectations of the New Testament writers and the early Church, it should not be too difficult to fathom why God may not be willing to put his authenticating stamp of 1st-century caliber signs, wonders, miracles, and gifts of the Holy Spirit upon our some 1,900-years-delayed expectations. These man-made traditions must be purged if we truly desire to see the return of the 1st-century caliber miraculous and ministry effectiveness.

But if they were not timely and precisely fulfilled, the quintessential question next becomes: "Who messed up? Were our 1st-century founders in the faith misled, mistaken, or deceived by the Holy Spirit on such an important aspect of our faith as eschatological expectations? Or, did the Holy Spirit do an inadequate job? If any of these scenarios is true, how can we trust them to have conveyed other aspects of our faith along to us accurately—such as the requirements for salvation?

Let's face it. In our attempts to promote a yet future, non-scriptural, and so-called "return" and "second coming" of the Lord and fulfillment of other eschatological promises, we've decreed that 1st-century believers waited and watched in vain. Even worse, if possible, we are verifying that history has proven the 1st-century scoffers were right, after all (see 2 Pet. 3:3-4; Jude 16-19).

To top it off, our deferment views of a better kingdom yet to come someday out in the future cut the knees right out from under the kingdom Jesus announced, modeled, and conferred upon his followers, back then and for us today (more on this in Chapters 8, 9, and 10). These postponement traditions make Christ's kingdom of little or no effect (Matt. 15:6), degrade the very words and credibility of Christ, and impugn the inspiration, inerrancy and trustworthiness of Scripture. Far better we let God be God, let the Scriptures be the Scriptures, and let the eschatological Holy Spirit-guided-expectation chips fall where they may, and should. If we truly want to see the return of the 1st-century miraculous, we must be willing to correct all the above deficiencies.

My Working Great Hypothesis

As a direct result of what we have covered so far in this book, most of our modern-day versions of Christianity must be seen for what they truly are—depreciated and lesser versions of the authentic Christian faith. Not only do our modern-day discrepancies undermine our faith and reduce the gospel, they are fundamental reasons why many of us are not living up to our founding tradition and why the Church today is so much less effective than it could and should be.

For instance, survey after survey in recent times show virtually no difference in the lifestyles of "born-again American Christians" from the rest of the population. This certainly wasn't the case in the 1st century, when our faith was so powerful and so effective that it was accused, by its adversaries, of having turned the world of that day and time "upside down" (Acts 17:6). Nowadays, however, the conversion process has gone the other way.

Yet many Christians have grown up being quite comfortable with their lesser versions and have developed a calloused sense of what genuine Christianity is all about. Even though we still call it Christianity, it doesn't look much like the original. Of course, some pockets of authentic Christianity are evident on occasion. But, unfortunately, they are exceptions, not the rule. Hence, we in the Church have been, and are, paying an awful price for our self-inflicted flaws and different practices of our faith (see Matt. 22:29).

So is there a solution to this discrepancy dilemma? The answer is, there is *only one* solution. It is not another "end-times" revival gambit, as some futurist prognosticators are anticipating, "where miracles are the norm and not the exception."[41] It's something far more relevant. Assuming my above diagnosis, three explanations, and three critical areas of departure are accurate, here is my working great hypothesis:

---

[41] Larry Sparks and Troy Anderson, "The Healing Miracles Preacher," *Charisma*, March 2015, 22-23.

To the degree we modern-day Christians get our faith straightened out so that it harmonizes with the faith depicted in the four gospels and the Book of Acts—the faith God authenticated with signs, wonders, miracles, and gifts of the Holy Spirit following—we may again move the hand of God and begin witnessing the return of these miraculous manifestations at a level approaching 1st-century caliber. Indeed, I believe God is prepared and desires to revive his mighty authenticating powers and blessings to the degree we so move in this direction. Anything less is less.

My caveat must be, however: I'm not saying this will happen. I'm saying this *could* happen. For it to happen, many Christians may need to be shocked or even shamed into reclaiming our "once mighty faith." That's because "we like our Christianity just like it is, thank you." We like our comfort zones. But if we truly desire to see a return of a great movement of the Holy Spirit, I do believe these changes must be made, enthusiastically embraced, and widely implemented.

A Mighty Corrective

If my above hypothesis is correct and God is only waiting for us moderns to get in line with the right messages and ministry, which He authenticated in New Testament times, then we must see quite a change in how our faith is preached, practiced, and perceived:

Our philosophy of ministry must match the 1st-century church's philosophy of ministry; our gospel message must match their gospel message; our eschatological message must also conform to and confirm that the Holy Spirit-guided imminency expectations of the New Testament writers and the early Church were the correct ones. Anything less is less.

Since this corrective will require a mighty realigning of our messages and ministry with the New Testament standards and expectations, I will elaborate a little further:

1. Returning to the philosophy of ministry Jesus and his disciples taught, practiced and modeled. It makes no sense for Christ to command believers of all ages to do these same kingdom works He and his disciples did (see John 14:12; Matt. 28:20) without providing the same level of empowerment. Our part is to obey by taking the initiative. His part is to empower. The supernatural gifts of the Holy Spirit, signs, wonders, and miracles are intrinsic elements of his kingdom and still function to authenticate the Word of God, its right preaching, and the full and correct gospel message. Again, and as we shall further see in Appendix A, God never withdrew these miraculous elements. If we don't understand this relevant reality or agree with it, we'll never properly understand our "once for all delivered" faith (Jude 3).

Moreover, all of God's miraculous provisions are still needed today by needy and hurting people throughout our broken world. Make no mistake; God still desires to heal, deliver, redeem, and provide for the inhabitants of this planet, and for us to experience Him in this manner. He also still desires his faithful followers to show forth his truths and demonstrate his power—not to avoid, ignore, deny, or fake it.

2. Recovering the full gospel message to encompass the good news of both the kingdom and salvation. As we shall see in Part II, that's the order in which Jesus announced them; that's the order in which He accomplished these two great works of the Messiah. I also agree with Hiles, who defines the full gospel as being both "the preaching of the person and work of Jesus Christ."[42] All of this in its completion was the true and full eschatological mission of Christ.

3. Conforming to and confirming that the 1st-century eschatological expectations were the correct ones, as they pinpointed the imminent fulfillment and establishment of "all things" in their lifetime. The eschatological expectations of our 1st-century founders in the faith were not mistaken, misguided, nor misled by the Holy Spirit into

---

[42] Hiles, *Unforced Rhythms of Grace*, 15.

falsehood. They were guided by the Holy Spirit "into all truth" and told exactly when and "what is to come" (John 16:13-14).

If we sincerely desire for God to authenticate our eschatological message today, it must be in total harmony, agreement, and alignment with their Holy Spirit-guided expectations, back then and there. That means we must recognize and affirm that their expectations were the correct ones, and not our 1,900-years-and-counting extrapolations of those expectations. Simply put, our postponed extrapolations are at variance with those 1st-century imminency expectations.

To be in harmony, we must acknowledge that what they looked forward to, we look back on as fulfilled. What was near-future for them is far-past for us. All occurred exactly as and when it was literally expected and precisely fulfilled. That is the only "correct" eschatological message for us today versus our perpetually delayed one. If we can grasp this precision and nature of fulfillment, then we can come into harmony with their eschatological expectations and the message that God was authenticating back then and there.

In stark contrast to our postponement eschatologyies, Hiles rightly testifies: "the word that flows from the [this] finished work of Christ and the rest of God is the word that can liberate, set free, and change the nations of the world."[43] He further affirms: "one of the great shocks coming for the Church will be felt as we fully awaken to the reality of what has been available to us all these years, eternal vitality we have not accessed. We've lived like strangers in the Land of Promise. The dismay of God's people will be great as we realize that we could have walked in much more divine dimension and Kingdom power [as] we see what God has already done in the finished work. . . ."[44]

For sure, we moderns need to be liberated from our "one-of-these-days," delayed, and futuristic mentality in order to realize our present inheritance in Christ's kingdom. Then, and only then, can we walk in the fullness of our faith and embrace our "once mighty faith." No doubt some pastors and elders will be afraid they will lose people and "their" ministry if they go this route. Hiles terms such churches and leaders, "the harlot system."[45] In another book, I've termed it "the Great Prostitute"

---

[43] Hiles, *The Revelation of Jesus Christ*, 147.
[44] Ibid., 154-155.
[45] Ibid., 239.

and provided 14 textual clues from Revelation chapters 17 and 18 for identifying who she is today.[46] Here is an example of her musings.

Critical Objection: "We're teaching the same eschatology the early Church taught. They were expecting an imminent return of the Lord and consummation of all things. We are expecting the same today."

My Response: While this bit of logic might sound the same, it's not the same. Rather, it's an extrapolation of imminency expectations that actually teaches that 1st-century, Holy Spirit-guided expectations proved false. Again, it bears repeating, in order for us today to be in eschatological harmony with the New Testament expectations, we must honor—not conflict with or contradict—by affirming that their expectations were the correct ones and were fulfilled exactly *as* and *when* expected.

If, however, we choose to persist in our denial of consummated eschatological reality, it only betrays our bondage to the flawed eschatological traditions of men. No person, for example, can honestly and sincerely contend that our faith has been only "partially delivered" when the Bible emphatically declares that it was "once for all delivered" (Jude 3). Nor can anyone legitimately extrapolate out Peter's statement that "the end of all things is at hand" 1,900 years and counting to our day and time (1 Pet. 4:7). If Peter's end is yet to be fulfilled, then he was mistaken and uninspired, and the recipients of his letter were literally deceived. For the nature of that precise fulfillment see 1 Peter 4:17.

Onto a Serious Kingdom Christianity

It's time for God's miraculous manifestations to again become the norm. For this regal reengagement to happen—assuming my great hypothesis is correct—means the Church must reclaim the central teaching of Jesus and a 1st-century philosophy of ministry, reform our gospel, and teach and accept a fulfilled view of eschatology and the ongoing reality of our once mighty faith.[47] It's that simple; it's that profound.

---

[46] Noē, *The Greater Jesus*, in chapter titled, "He Plagues the Great Prostitute," 251-289.

[47] For more on this, see Noē, *Unraveling the End*, 113-140f.

Furthermore, if we are truly sincere about representing Christ as his ambassadors (2 Cor. 5:20), glorifying Him, and expanding his kingdom, we must have the goods to show for it. That means we must have the evidence in our lives that makes a difference and be so full of confidence in God's Word and power that we can offer the world something demonstrably better than anything else out there.

So let us stop standing idly by, complaining about how bad things seem to be, and succumbing to any attitude or theology that claims we can't have full access, dumbs down, or defines away anything from Christ's everlasting and present kingdom. Certainly, while God's name is to be "hallowed" (Matt. 6:9), his kingdom is not to be "hollowed," gutted out, or dismembered in any manner. That only produces deviant and depreciated versions of Christianity incapable of "turning the world upside down" again.

But if the contents of this chapter are correct and we implement them, then, and only then, might we see and experience our God once again authenticating our "corrected" messages and ministry with extraordinary signs, wonders, miracles, and gifts of the Holy Spirit following (Acts 19:8-11), and for the same reasons He did before (see John 7:17). Therefore, and as my pastor has publicly preached, these miraculous manifestations "should become (once again), the ordinary, fully expected, waited upon, and experienced dynamic of corporate worship everywhere and always."[48]

Now it is time to shift into a higher gear as we continue un-shrouding the truths of the central teaching of Jesus. No question, we have been lulled to sleep by our leaders and mired in a muddle of ignorance and mediocrity. Those who might otherwise have been strong believers and kingdom servants of Christ have been held down and captive long enough. Munroe dramatically and factually captures our current dilemma thusly:

> The problem for so many of us is that we don't know who we are. We have become a kingdom of ignorant kings: ignorant of our identity, ability, power, and authority. . . . Deposed, defeated, and dejected, like the prodigal son we sit in the mud and stench of the pigsty, nibbling on

---

[48] Dave Rodriguez, Senior Pastor, Grace Church, Noblesville, IN, sermon, 8/24/13.

dry corn husks, never lifting the eyes of our spirit to behold the riches of our Father's estate that are ours if we will only reach out and claim them. Our greatest enemy today is neither satan nor sin, because Jesus defeated both at the cross. Power is not the problem, either. . . . Our greatest enemy today is ignorance. What we don't know is killing us; or at least depriving us of a full and abundant life. The antidote for ignorance is knowledge. . . . Christ came to remove our ignorance about God and His Kingdom and to teach us of our heritage and kinship as children of the Father.[49]

If you find Munroe's above assessment offensive, maybe that is because you need to hear it. But I believe many today want to experience the return of the real deal and not more avoidance, ignorance, hype, or faking it.

Therefore, starting in Part II and throughout the rest of this book, we shall address this ignorance factor, lay out the foundational concepts for the time and nature of establishment of the everlasting kingdom of God, reclaim the central teaching of Jesus, reestablish a sure foundation for our "once mighty faith," and encourage development of *kingdom-centered and kingdom-focused churches and Christians.* Admittedly, this is a first step. But it's absolutely essential that we better understand and become solidly grounded in the present realities of the everlasting kingdom of God.

Anything less is less.

So if you are ready to soar into serious kingdom Christianity, let's go into Part II!

If we truly want to see the return of the 1st-century miraculous, we must be willing to do all the above.

---

[49] Munroe, *Rediscovering the Kingdom*, 206.

Part II – Grounding the Everlasting Kingdom —Time and Nature

. . . we in the body of Christ, have too frequently ignored the teachings on God's kingdom. As a result, we have failed to understand kingdom theology and kingdom rule.[1]

In Part II, we shall take the kingdom of God seriously. Unfortunately and currently the kingdom is caught up in eschatological mid-air. But without the proper grounding of the kingdom (eschatologically, exegetically, theologically, and historically—as so many have failed to do) we will only be building a proverbial second story on a vacant lot. Or, as Jesus warned, we'd only be foolishly building a house on sand. Without a rock-solid foundation, whatever we profess is sure to crumble, fall to the ground with a great crash, and accomplish little (see Matt. 7:24-27).

A prime example is James Davison Hunter's insightful but critically flawed book, *To Change the World: The Irony, Tragedy, & Possibility of Christianity in the Late Modern World.* Since Hunter believes that "the establishment of his kingdom . . . will only be set in place at the final

---

[1] Evans, *Kingdom Man*, 26.

consummation at the end of time" and that all we have now is "a foretaste of the coming kingdom,"[2] he gives the kingdom of God little attention and is forced to conclude his book with this last sentence: "Christians, at their best, . . . they will help to make the world a little bit better."[3]

But as you will see, we can do much better than Hunter's hamstrung approach and lackluster conclusion. This is why Part II is so necessary and significant. It is the core of this book.

Caveat alert: What you are about to read and experience in these five chapters of Part II, to my knowledge and awareness, has never been presented in church history. Naturally, I have not read every book or article ever written on the kingdom, but I have read a lot of them. None refers or alludes to such an approach and scope as you will find herein.

In this Part II, we shall lay down a rock-solid, biblical foundation for the time and nature of the arrival and ever-increasing reality of the everlasting form of the kingdom of God. This firm foundation will provide us Christians with the credibility and ability to reeducate and better motivate ourselves for entering and living in the kingdom and for transforming our lives and world. I'm going to further suggest this reclaimed and reformed foundation should also be the prime focus and driving direction of Christian evangelism, as it was for Jesus. Perhaps with this solidly grounded kingdom focus and direction, we Christians may become capable of turning the world upside down—AGAIN (Acts 17:6 KJV)! Let's see.

---

[2] Hunter, *To Change the World*, 233-234.
[3] Ibid., 286.

Chapter 8

Step #1 – The Appointed Time and Established Nature of Arrival[1]

If the axe is dull and he does not sharpen its edge,
then he must exert more strength.
Wisdom has the advantage of giving success (Eccl. 10:10 NAS).

In the Swiss Alps a story is often told about two woodchoppers—an old woodchopper and a young woodchopper. The old woodchopper was a hard worker. He chopped wood from sun up to sun down every day without stopping. At the end of the day he had assembled his customary pile of wood. This went on for years.[2]

---

[1] Some of this chapter was presented as a theological paper at the 49th Annual Meeting of the Midwest Region of the Evangelical Theological Society at Lincoln Christian College and Seminary in Lincoln, Illinois, March 19-20, 2004.
[2] I first heard this folklore story while climbing mountains in the Swiss Alps. I've often shared it with audiences to illustrate a principle of peak performance (see John Noē, *Peak Performance Principles for High Achievers*, Revised Edition (Hollywood, FL.: Frederick Fell Publishers, 2006, 1984).

Then one day a young woodchopper arrived. He, too, was a hard worker. He chopped wood next to the old woodchopper from sun up to sun down. But every hour on the hour he would stop, sit down, and take a 10-minute break. At the end of the day, the old woodchopper had assembled his customary pile of wood. But the young woodchopper's pile was twice as high!

The next day the same thing happened. Perplexed and befuddled, the old woodchopper decided to speak to the young woodchopper.

"Young man," he began, "I notice that you are a hard worker. But every hour on the hour you stop chopping, sit down, and take a break. I never stop. Yet at the end of the day your pile of wood is twice as high as mine." So he inquired, "How can this be?"

The young woodchopper sighed and replied, "Did you not notice that while I was sitting down taking my breaks I was also sharpening my ax?"

Many Christians today are strong believers and hard workers for their faith. Unfortunately, most are not. They have become accustomed to and content with lesser versions of Christianity, especially one without a mighty kingdom. I submit, therefore, that since the kingdom of God was the central teaching of our Lord Jesus Christ, was at the heart of his earthly ministry, and was the very essence of the New Testament faith, this loss from our authentic faith is akin to chopping wood with a dull ax. Even the hard workers, need to stop now and then, sit down, and sharpen their axes. How do we do that? By reclaiming and restoring the preaching, teaching, practices, and ministry of the kingdom of God to the Church and the world. This chapter begins that ax-sharpening process.

Always Been a Kingdom

The biblical reality is, as long as there has been a King, there has been a kingdom. God is King and his kingdom (will, reign, and rule) is eternal. In Old Testament times, God acted in kingly power to create the world, and to deliver and judge his people. Consequently, and by inspiration, King Nebuchadnezzar proclaimed, "How great are his signs, how mighty his wonders! His kingdom is an eternal kingdom; his dominion endures from generation to generation" (Dan. 4:3). Hence, both the King and his kingdom are eternal (also see Dan. 4:34; 5:21;

6:26; Psa. 45:6; 47:2, 6-8; 103:19; 145:1, 13; 1 Chron. 29:11; Zech. 14:9). But over the course of redemptive history both the King and his kingdom have varied in their earthly manifestations and in relationship with humankind. This occurred through a series of covenants.

In this chapter, we will address the appointed time for the arrival of the final form of the everlasting kingdom of God, predicted and anticipated throughout most of the Bible. It is an eschatological reality, as is salvation. Both are the work of the Messiah (see Acts 28:31; Rev. 12:1). Most evangelicals agree that the kingdom's final and everlasting form was to be established on earth by the promised Messiah (Dan. 7:14-28). And with the birth-coming of Jesus into human history, God's everlasting form of his kingdom began to manifest itself in new and clearly different ways from anything before.

Restoring the centrality of the kingdom of God, and what Jesus meant by it, however, is no small topic or task. That's because almost everything in this arena is contested. And even though "the knowledge of the secrets of the kingdom of God has been given" [past-tense] (Matt. 13:11; Luke 8:10; Mark 4:11), this knowledge and these secrets have been covered up by subsequent traditions of men. These traditions include the positions taken by all of the major eschatological views in the Church. They are based on many falsehoods, partial versions, impotent worldviews, as well as a reductionist gospel. As we shall see, Scripture does not support them. As a result, an amazing number of Christians, and others, are essentially ignorant about what the kingdom and, therefore, Christianity are all about. Not surprisingly, modern-day Christianity's myopic gospel focuses "almost exclusively on the afterlife [and] reduces the importance of what God expects of us in this life."[3]

Yet what we believe about the kingdom largely determines our concept of the whole Christian faith and its reality in this life, on this earth, here and now, as well as in the future. Sadly, most false notions of Christianity can be traced to false notions of the kingdom. And as we have seen in Chapter 6, there is much conflict and confusion as to what Christianity really is and what the Christian life really should be. These differences erode unity and produce flawed and lesser versions of our "once mighty faith." Consequently, most churches today rarely mention the kingdom, let alone teach, practice, and model its established and

---

[3] Stearns, *The Hole in the Gospel*, 17.

present-day realities and powers. All this foolishness just signals "irrelevance" to an increasingly skeptical and indifferent secular society.

For these reasons and more, a proper understanding of what Jesus meant by the kingdom of God is crucial. Not to properly understand and practice its available components and realities is to be mired in mediocrity. Sad to say, this compromised condition is fairly typical of far too many modern-day Christians and most western churches.

But when we get the kingdom of God straight—time- and nature-wise—all things fall into place. Miss it even slightly, and we're liable to be way off on many other interrelated and vital aspects of our "once for all delivered" faith (Jude 3). That's how pivotal the kingdom is.

Please be assured, this book is dedicated to the reclamation and restoration of the "gospel of the kingdom." (Matt. 24:14). When properly introduced and taught, this gospel and this kingdom will effectively build up, motivate, and empower the Church as God's will, reign, and rule transform human lives and ultimately society. Therefore, I make no apologies. This book will present a victorious eschatology and ecclesiology that are solidly grounded in Scripture. As you will see, there is plenty of Scripture to back my optimism and none to refute it.

Unfortunately today, many Christians have given up on being salt and light in their spheres of influence. For them, the rest of this book will provide a much needed corrective. For others of you it will provide a solid foundation for educating, equipping, and motivating the saints of God to follow Jesus as He is today, to rule and reign with Him, here and now, and to advance his kingdom. Anything less is less.

But when we get the kingdom of God straight —time- and nature-wise—all things fall into place.

Most certainly, God's plan for his Church must be solidly grounded on the foundation of the Messiah's two great works—that of the kingdom and that of salvation—in that order. That said, let's dive into the Scriptures. But I caution you. What you are about to experience will be a paradigm shift in your understanding of the central teaching of Jesus—the gospel of the kingdom. That's because most American denominations see the kingdom as largely, or totally, a future, not-yet-fully available reality. But what does Scripture say?

'In the Days of Those Kings'

Everything concerning the time and nature for the arrival of the everlasting form of the kingdom of God has been clearly revealed through the prophets and grounded within human and redemptive history. "Surely the Sovereign LORD does nothing without revealing his plan to his servants the prophets" (Amos 3:7). And He did exactly that in foretelling the coming of the everlasting kingdom. We do not need to deductively interpret anything in this regard. Rather, we can rest assured that God gave his Word to common and ordinary people (not just to highly educated linguists and theologians). And He expects us to understand, obey, and apply it. Regrettably, the various traditions of men have confounded a clear and straightforward understanding and mis-programmed multiple billions of Christians over the centuries (see Titus 1:15, for instance).

In order to begin reversing these reductionist traditions that have produced our kingdom-deficient gospel, the kingdom-deficient practice of our faith, and kingdom-deficient results, we must start with, as Guder puts it, "rigorous biblical learning . . . . into fuller and fuller apprehension of the truth."[4] And "through rigorous engagement with the Bible . . . to discover and repent of these reductions of the gospel so that it [the Church] can become more faithful as [an] incarnational witness."[5]

By God's grace and guidance, I believe He has shown us how this debilitating dilemma and associated difficulties can be resolved. So throughout the rest of this book, we shall lay down the biblical foundation for a theological reclamation, restoration, and reformation of our conflicting and confusing beliefs and views of the central teaching of Jesus, the kingdom of God. As you will see, we should not be satisfied with how our traditions have handled the kingdom of God. Let's get to it.

We do not need to deductively interpret anything in this regard.

---

[4] Guder, *The Continuing Conversion of the Church*, 160.
[5] Ibid., 202.

The Time of Arrival

At the start of his earthly ministry, "Jesus went into Galilee proclaiming the good news of God. The time is fulfilled . . . the kingdom of God is at hand . . . ." (Mark 1:15 KJV). What "time" (Greek word *kairos* meaning "set," "proper time," or "season") was Jesus talking about that He claimed was "fulfilled?" Astoundingly, many scholars maintain with Ladd: "it is impossible to know the time."[6] Hence, they end up wrestling with the tension of the kingdom still being both present and future, and insist that the "time of apocalyptic consummation remains in the future."[7] Or does it?

Six centuries before Christ, and in two parallel dream-visions and general time prophecies, God revealed the appointed time parameter *within human history* for the establishment of the eschatological and everlasting form of the kingdom of God on this earth. Please be assured, time is important to God and should be for us as well (for example, see Rom. 5:6; Gal. 4:4; 1 Tim. 2:6; 1 Pet. 1:11; also Psa. 18:30):

- **In Daniel 2:** Daniel both declared and interpreted the king's dream of a *statue* with *four sections* of different metals (head of

---

[6] Ladd, *The Presence of the Future*, 328. Some cite Jesus' answer to his apostles' question in Acts 1:6-7 to support their contention that neither they nor we can know the time. But here Jesus is answering a flawed question based upon a false understanding of the kingdom with basically a non-answer. Moreover, his answer that "It is not for you to know the times and dates" [note the plural] cannot be extrapolated to meaning that they and we cannot know the general time. Similarly, another popular assumption is attached to Jesus' statements that "No one knows that day or hour" (Matt. 24:36, 42, 44; 25:13). Here, Jesus' only restriction against knowing was "day or hour." Literally, this does not preclude knowing the week, month, year, or the generation. Nor can this specific restriction be extrapolated to not knowing at all. Jesus certainly knew the generation. And, his first followers were to know, too. But not knowing "that day or hour" is why Jesus gave specific signs for them to watch for and instructed them to flee when they saw them occur. Also, later both Paul and John knew the "hour" (see Rom. 13:11; 1 John 2:18). How could they have known this? For more see Noe, *The Perfect Ending for the World* and *Unraveling the End*.

[7] Ladd, *The Presence of the Future*, 120.

gold, chest and arms of silver, belly and thighs of bronze, and legs and feet of iron and clay). He said these symbolize four earthly and successive kingdoms or world empires (Dan. 2:31-43). Daniel isolated and described this time, thusly:

> *"In the days (time) of those kings*, the God of heaven will set up a kingdom that will never be destroyed, nor will it be left to another people. It will crush all those kingdoms and bring them to an end, but it will itself endure forever" (Dan. 2:44, *italics mine*).

- **In Daniel 7:** Daniel's prophetic dream of *four beasts* (a lion, a bear, a leopard, and a ten-horned beast) symbolizes the same four earthly kingdoms or world empires (see Dan. 7:1-7, 27).

I agree with the majority of evangelical scholars that these two dream-visions and time prophecies portray the same thing. *Four*—not five—Gentile kingdoms or world empires that would transpire in a continuous succession during this divinely predetermined course of history—no gaps, no hiatus, no fifth or "revived" empire. They began in Daniel's day and were successively set up and displaced (see Dan. 2:21). They were: Babylon (606 – 538 B.C.), Medo-Persia (538 – 331 B.C.), Greece (331 – 168 B.C.), and the old Roman Empire (168 – 476 A.D.), respectively.[8]

---

[8] The prevailing view attempts to make five world kingdoms out of the four described in Daniel 2 and 7. It's done by spinning off some of the descriptive attributes of the fourth kingdom, inserting a time gap of indeterminable length and making them into a futuristic, fifth earthly kingdom, which is then called the revived (or revised) Roman Empire. No scriptural basis or sound reason exists for taking such latitude. It's totally arbitrary and is only asserted and inserted to support a particular futuristic doctrine. Not only does it not fit the picture given by Daniel, but Daniel emphatically stated that these visions represented four—not five—earthly kingdoms (Dan. 2:40; 7:17). Their attributes were portrayed by *four* sections of a statue and *four* beasts, and not five. Furthermore, each of the two parallel descriptions of the fourth kingdom fully applied to the old Roman Empire and was historically and precisely fulfilled. Several scholars have historically documented the symbolically portrayed attributes of each kingdom, and I will not duplicate their work here. But Daniel assured both the

But because Daniel had prophesied the rise and fall of these Gentile kingdoms so accurately, some scholars insist that these sections in Daniel must have been written after-the-fact in the 2nd century B.C. If that were true, this would still leave a two-hundred-year-plus foretelling factor, which they cannot explain. Rather, and to the contrary, this divine placement in world history also perfectly harmonizes with the precise, literal, sequential, and chronological fulfillment (no gaps, no delays, no exegetical gimmicks) of Daniel's two specific time prophecies—Daniel's 70 weeks of years (Dan. 9:24-27) and "time of the end" prophecy (Dan. 12:4-13). Therein, Daniel unerringly foretold the specific time when the Messiah would come and God's appointed end would be carried out by the power of Rome.[9] Thus, everything Daniel prophesied happened in that 1st century A.D. exactly *as* and *when* it was supposed to happen, and precisely *as* and *when* expected (John 16:13).

Please recall from Chapter 7 that the 1st-century fulfillment expectations (of being in their lifetime) were the ones God was affirming with signs, wonders, miracles, and gifts of the Holy Spirit. Also, as we saw in Chapter 6, the prime reason most Christians have not accepted the plain, natural, and straightforward understanding of Daniel 2:44 is because our four traditional, evangelical, and eschatological views will not allow it. Each is at variance with some aspect of the everlasting kingdom having been established "in the days of those kings." They are classic examples of the unscriptural traditions of men making the Word of God of little or no effect (Mark 7:13; Matt. 15:6). But since the arrival and establishment of this everlasting kingdom is a major component in the whole eschatological scenario, its past-fulfillment within this time-restricted period should be a real eye-opener.

---

king and us that his interpretation was "trustworthy" (Dan. 2:45). All Daniel's prophesied events happened and were fulfilled within this time frame in history. There is no credible reason to repeat these events or to revive the political, social, and religious conventions of those times.

[9] For this exposition, see Noē, *Unraveling the End*, 213-236. Or, Noē, *The Perfect Ending for the World*, 109-133

Four Key Questions

Daniel's time-restrictive words in Daniel 2:44 seem clear and straightforward. *The Wycliffe Bible Commentary* agrees about Daniel 2:42-47 that "the grammatical meaning of the verses is not obscure." But most Christians have great difficulty accepting a plain and natural meaning. *Wycliffe* acknowledges this difficulty and explains: "disagreement about interpretation is rooted in the varying points of view [eschatological] with which readers approach the passage." In other words, they are forced by their deferment and diminishing views not to accept a plain and straightforward meaning.

To be *sure* we are understanding Daniel 2:44 correctly, let's present the variety of answers, along with the correct answer, to the following four, simple and clarifying questions:

Question #1 – How many coming kingdoms of God (or forms thereof) are prophesied here? THE CORRECT ANSWER IS, "one." But, as we have seen in Chapter 6:

Dispensational premillennialists' answer is "four" – 1) Jesus' 1st-century kingdom, 2) the withdrawn or present mystery kingdom, 3) the millennial kingdom, 4) the eternal kingdom (when God's will, reign, and rule will be superimposed on all humanity beyond the realm of history (whatever that means). Note: the latter three kingdoms are different-natured from the first.

Amillennialists' answer is "two" – 1) the present kingdom Jesus brought, which is a foretaste, 2) the eternal-state kingdom in its fullness. Note: the latter kingdom is different-natured from the first.

Postmillennialists' answer is "two or three" – 1) the present kingdom Jesus brought, 2) a future golden age, 3) the eternal-state kingdom. Note: the latter two kingdoms are different-natured from the first.

Cessationist Preterists' answer is "two" – 1) the pre-A.D. 70 version of the kingdom brought by Jesus, 2) the post-A.D. 70 spiritual version with major intrinsic elements removed (depending upon whose version one reads, this can include the charismatic gifts, all ministries of the Holy Spirit, the miraculous, even angels). However, not all preterists subscribe to a cessation theology. Note: the latter kingdom is different-natured from the first.

But once again, according to Daniel, there is no other, further, or final manifestation of the kingdom still to come.

Question #2 – When would this kingdom be set up? THE CORRECT ANSWER IS, "In the days of those kings."

Matthew Henry's Commentary confirms this natural and plain understanding of Daniel 2:31-45:

> It was to be set up in the days of these kings, the kings of the fourth monarchy, of which particular notice is taken (Luke 2:1). That Christ was born when, by the decree of the emperor of Rome, all the world was taxed, which was a plain indication that that empire had become as universal as any earthly empire ever was.

Again, the problem is, most commentators and most Christians cannot accept this natural, plain, and straightforward meaning of Daniel's inspired prophetic words. Why not? It's because "the days of those kings" *ended in A.D. 476*—when the Roman Empire was toppled by Germanic tribes!

To alleviate this time problem, the essence of most scholarship has been to find ways to re-explain Daniel 2:44. To do so, one must either reinterpret (i.e., redefine) the "time" or the "nature" of fulfillment of this verse. In other words, one must concede that the Bible does not mean what it clearly says. As Charles L. Holman admits, "the prophetic hope of a culminating act of God in history has continued to be reinterpreted."[10]

A classic case in point is the *Jamieson, Fausset, and Brown Commentary*, which emphatically states: "'these kings' cannot mean the four successional monarchies." Instead, these commentators look for a

---

[10] Charles L. Holman, *Till Jesus Comes* (Peabody, MA.: Hendrickson, 1996), 133.

future "final state of the Roman empire." They further and confusingly comment:

> Moreover, the visible "setting up of the KINGDOM" of glory on earth by the God of heaven is plainly here meant, not the unobserved setting up of the kingdom of grace. That kingdom of glory is only to come [at] Christ's second advent (Acts 1:6). We pray, "Thy kingdom come." The kingdom was and is still preached as "at hand" (Matt 4:17), but not yet come in manifestation (Luke 19:11-27). We live under the divisions of the Roman empire, which began 1,400 years ago . . . .

Well-known dispensational premillennialist John Walvoord concurs that the kingdom was not established back in the time of Jesus or in the times of those four world empires. Yet his popular eschatological view does recognize that it was supposed to have been set up and established back then. So he and other dispensationalists have been forced to conceive of the idea of "a revival of the Roman Empire"[11] to accommodate a yet-future fulfillment of Daniel's prophecy, "in the days of those kings."

The *Baptist Faith and Message* (IX) asserts: "the full consummation of the kingdom awaits the return [coming again] of Jesus Christ and the end of the age."

Likewise, amillennialists disregard a plain, straightforward meaning of Daniel's words. They, too, advocate a yet-future (to us today) fulfillment. Thus, Willem A. VanGemeren writes: "Even the coming of Jesus Christ did not fully establish the kingdom of God, though he did inaugurate it more fully."[12] Guder adds that Jesus only "announced and inaugurated" the kingdom and "the formation of the church" provided its "foretaste, firstfruits, and agent."[13]

D.S. Russell, in his commentary of Daniel, contributes to the confusion by disclaiming: "in a literal sense the hopes of the writer [Daniel] fell short of realization, and the kingdom did not come in the way that he and others had hoped and prayed it might." Yet he

---

[11] John F. Walvoord, *Major Bible Prophecies* (Grand Rapids, MI.: Zondervan, 1991), 162-164.

[12] Willem A. VanGemeren, *Interpreting the Prophetic Word* (Grand Rapids, MI.: Zondervan, 1990), 347.

[13] Guder, *Missional Church*, 76.

acknowledges: "the coming kingdom is 'eternal' in retrospect as well as in prospect. . . . There will come a day . . . when the kingdom will come 'in power' . . . That coming will mark the end of history and indeed the consummation of all things."[14] But Daniel clearly prophesied the kingdom would be set up *within* human history and not at its supposed end.

Historic premillennialist Ladd tries to circumvent Daniel's apparent time-restriction this way: "The great image of gold, silver, brass, and iron represents four successive nations in history *before* the coming of God's kingdom (Dan. 2), as do the four beasts in Daniel 7."[15] But Daniel said the everlasting eschatological kingdom would be "set up" *in* those days—i.e., "during" and not after those days.

Apparently, these commentators only want the Bible to mean and say what they want it to mean and say, so compromises are made and abusive liberties taken. In other words, man says what God meant. At best, this is a slippery slope theologically and highly problematic. In reality, these are factual denials of the simple, clear meaning of Scripture. But what standard for understanding should we use?

I submit that these two parallel and general time prophecies of Daniel must be literally honored (most have not). They solidly ground in human history the time for the establishment of the everlasting kingdom of God—no delays, no postponement, no gaps, no exegetical gimmicks. Therefore, the modern-day nation of Israel cannot be still waiting for its kingdom and king. In this regard, Klein, Blomberg, and Hubbard, Jr., further elaborate in their textbook on hermeneutics, by asking and then answering these most relevant questions:

> What do we do when interpreters disagree? How do we proceed when well-intentioned Christians come to different interpretations about the meaning of a text or passage? First, we should set out precisely the nature of the difference . . . . Second, . . . did either interpreter misconstrue some evidence or engage in shoddy reasoning, or were there other flaws in the process that indicate one of the positions must be relinquished? Third . . . . Where one view more readily emerges from the historical sense of the text, it must stand. *The historically*

---

[14] D.S. Russell, *Daniel* – The Daily Study Bible Series (Edinburgh: The Saint Andrews Press / Philadelphia: The Westminster Press, 1981), 54-55.
[15] Ladd, *The Presence of the Future,* 86.

defensible interpretation has greatest authority. That is, interpreters can have maximum confidence in their understanding of a text when they base that understanding on historically defensible arguments.[16]

That is precisely the methodology you find employed throughout *A Once Mighty Faith*. Everything we present herein is scripturally and historically defensible. This assurance stands in stark contrast to the popular postponing notion that "Jesus came once to die for sin, conquer death, and win our salvation [partially]. He will come again to establish the kingdom in all its perfection. This final kingdom . . . . will usher in a new kind of embodiment, one that is perfect, complete, and eternal, fit for the new age of the kingdom."[17]

Question #3 – What do the words 'set up' really mean? THE CORRECT ANSWER IS, "Established."

If we follow basic hermeneutical principles, it is not difficult to determine what the Hebrew word *quwm* (pronounced "koom" and translated as "set up" in Daniel 2:44) literally means:

1) *Quwm* in *Strong's* means to "appoint, establish, make, raise up, stand, set (up)."[18] According to *Vines*, its primary meaning is "to arise, stand up, come about . . . . It may denote any movement to an erect position."[19] The only qualification *Vine* mentions is: "when used with another verb, *qum* [sic] may suggest simply the beginning of an action."[20] But *quwm* is not used with another verb in Daniel 2:44.

2) Daniel uses this same word eight times in his very next chapter (Dan. 3:1, 2, 3, 5, 7, 12, 14, 18). This singularly employed verb describes King Nebuchadnezzar's erection of a 90-foot-high image of gold on the plain of Dura—i.e., he "set up" this image.

---

[16] Klein, Blomberg, Hubbard, Jr., *Introduction to Biblical Interpretation*, 149.

[17] Jerry Sittser, *A Grace Revealed* (Grand Rapids, MI.: Zondervan, 2012), 243-244.

[18] *Strong's Exhaustive Concordance of the Bible*, #6966.

[19] W.E. Vine: *An Expository Dictionary of Biblical Words*, 1984), 10.

[20] Ibid., 11.

This hermeneutical usage and grounding is profound! Why so? It's because "the days of those kings"—that last world empire—ended in A.D. 476, over 15 centuries ago.

3) Furthermore, Nebuchadnezzar did not just begin to or only *partially* "set up" this 90-foot-high image. Nor did he merely *announce* that he was going to do it, or only *initiate* or *inaugurate* it. He finished the job. He established the image. He completed and fulfilled his plan. Nor did he come back later and remove an arm and a leg, or any other intrinsic parts. It stood established, completed, and erect. This comparative usage and illustration is in such close scriptural proximity that, contextually, it must not be ignored or diminished.

Likewise, the *one*, "never [to] be destroyed," and to "endure forever" kingdom in Daniel 2:44 was "set up"—i.e., established, completed, and fulfilled—"in the days of those kings." I suggest that this literal meaning and realization is absolutely demanded by the text. And, its eschatological and worldview implications are profound!

Further validating this understanding, and surprisingly so, is the popular dispensational-premillennial eschatological view. Its proponents recognize this same literal meaning for the Hebrew word translated as "set up." But then they are forced to conceive and impose the false ideas of "a revival of the Roman Empire" and a rebuilt Jewish temple to accommodate their yet-future fulfillment of Daniel's prophecy.[21] As an appropriate aside, however, and as the 'ole' saying goes: "If we don't understand history, we are doomed to repeat it." That's essentially what dispensationalists are doing. They don't understand fulfilled prophetic history, so they must repeat history by reviving these historical, political, and religious circumstances, institutions, and conventions so fulfillment can happen, again!

Thus, J. Dwight Pentecost insists that the kingdom "was withdrawn and its establishment postponed until some future time when the nation

---

[21] Walvoord, *Major Bible Prophecies*, 162-164.

[of Israel] would repent and place faith in Jesus Christ."[22] But there is no such withdrawal or postponed condition expressed in Scripture as these dispensationalists continue to insist. Nor is there any promise to restore the kingdom to Israel, as we shall see in our next chapter.

<u>Question #4 – How long would it last? THE CORRECT ANSWER IS, "Forever."</u>

God similarly prophesied of this same, coming, and messianic kingdom to David with these words, "I will raise up your offspring to succeed you, who will come from your own body, and I will establish his kingdom. He is the one who will build a house for my Name, and I will establish his kingdom forever. I will be his father, and he will be my son. . . . Your house and your kingdom will endure forever before me; your throne will be established forever" (2 Sam. 7:12-14a, 16).

Notably, neither dispensational premillennialism's mystery kingdom nor its millennial kingdom in a so-called "revived Roman Empire," "endure[s] forever."

Likewise, amillennialism's current kingdom, which was only inaugurated "in the days of those kings," does not "endure forever."

Neither does postmillennialism's current kingdom, which was inaugurated "in the days of those kings," nor does its anticipated golden age millennial kingdom "endure forever."

These futurist views also do not believe the kingdom has come in its fullness. Rather, the dispensationalists, amillennialists, and postmillennialists all variously subscribe to a truncated futuristic time and view in which Satan will be released to wreak havoc on the Church, bring about great tribulation via the antichrist and Armageddon, and (for amils and postmils) culminate with God's de-construction of the universe. Notoriously, it's these "prophecy experts" who are the problem. Their eschatologies are not only unscriptural and uncertain, at best, but also explain why so many Christians have difficulty sustaining any kind of culture/kingdom-advancing efforts. The bottom line is, our "once for all delivered" faith (Jude 3) has been hijacked by these traditions of men. Moreover, their degradations of our faith hamstring

---

[22] J. Dwight Pentecost, *Things to Come: A Study in Biblical Eschatology* (Grand Rapids, MI.: Zondervan, [1958] 1964), 293.

and hinder understanding the kingdom that's here. That's about as mildly as I can put it. But make no mistake; these traditions are travesties that have been imposed upon our faith and corrupted it to our detriment.

Only the preterist view recognizes a 1st-century establishment. The problem here, however, is cessationist preterists who maintain that not all of the kingdom Jesus was bringing "endure[s] forever." Major and intrinsic elements (the charismatic gifts of the Holy Spirit, and/or more) were removed from its post-A.D. 70 nature. But as we shall see in more detail in Appendix A, this supposed removal would violate what the writer of Hebrews stated circa A.D. 65. He wrote that they were in process of "receiving a kingdom that cannot be shaken" (Heb. 12:28). He further clarified that "shaken" means "removing" and "cannot be shaken" means "remain[ing]" (Heb. 12:27). Thus, the writer of Hebrews confirmed they were receiving the kingdom, back then and there, of which Daniel prophesied: "the saints of the Most High will receive the kingdom and will possess it forever – yes, for ever and ever" (Dan. 7:18). Glasser rightly terms this verse "an unconditional promise of ultimate triumph."[23] And what is true of the whole is true of its constituent parts. Furthermore, as we shall shortly see, Isaiah also prophesied this kingdom was only to "increase" (Isa. 9:7). Removal of any intrinsic elements would be a decrease.

What Can We Conclude So Far?

Interim Conclusion #1

Surely, the above exposition and analysis is simple and straightforward. God meant for us to understand these revealed "secrets" of the kingdom, as the 1st-century believers—the original audience— understood them. Sadly, too many Christians today are kingdom illiterate and/or victims of distorted but popular teachings. However, Christianity

---

[23] Glasser, *Announcing the Kingdom*, 22. Unfortunately, Glasser insists "His present rule over the redeemed [only] foreshadows his ultimate rule over all, over 'a new heaven and a new earth'(p. 24) . . . . the kingdom of God will be fully and finally established in the last day" (p. 42).

without zeal for Christ's mighty kingdom is not authentic Christianity. It's that simple; it's that profound.

This deficiency and our almost total lack of understanding of the kingdom of God is largely due to our failure to understand the plain sense of words and our vulnerability to subscribe to popular but unscriptural delay or postponement theologies. They tell us the "set up" or establishment of the kingdom of God still awaits a future time—at the so-called "return" or "second coming" of Christ and/or during a "post-rapture" Jewish millennial era (more on this in Appendix B).

But much of our misunderstandings could be rectified if this one biblical fact was recognized: The final and everlasting form of the kingdom of God was time-restricted to occur within human history and does not point toward some still future time. Nevertheless, many popular spokespeople, such as the respected Billy Graham, frequently voice their erroneous understanding this way:

- "Jesus repeatedly taught that someday He would return to earth to destroy all evil and sin and to rule the world in perfect peace and justice."[24]
- "Someday the victory will be his, when Christ returns to establish his kingdom."[25]
- "Someday Jesus Christ will return to set up his kingdom on Earth. And unlike his first coming, he will return with power and glory, and he will rule over the entire Earth. The Bible repeatedly testifies to this great truth."[26]
- "Shortly before returning to Heaven Jesus told his disciples that someday he would come back to established his kingdom."[27]

---

[24] Billy Graham, "My Answer," "Jesus will return one day," *The Indianapolis Star*, 12 August, 2015, 4E.

[25] Billy Graham, "My Answer," "Sin dulls our conscience," *The Indianapolis Star*, 18 October, 2014, 4E.

[26] Billy Graham, "My Answer," "Bible tells of Christ's triumphant return," *The Indianapolis Star*, 9 October, 2007, E5.

[27] Billy Graham, "My Answer," "Be ready for Christ's return," *The Indianapolis Star*, 6 January, 2016, 4E.

With all due respect for Dr. Graham, this futuristic scenario will never happen. Why can we be so sure? It's because the biblical fact is, nowhere did Jesus, any New Testament writer or person, or Old Testament writer or person ever say or write anything like this. In another book I have termed this biblically flawed tradition of men: "fantasy Christianity."[28] It simply will not stand up to an honest and sincere test of Scripture.

And yet the theological and psychological influences of this false paradigm are massive. They cut the knees out from under the kingdom Jesus came proclaiming. As long as we Christians think there is a better, greater, "gooder" kingdom yet to come, we are not going to give due attention to the one that is here. Furthermore, most kingdom-illiterate Christians are more than willing to sit around, passively, in the here and now and wait to reign and rule with Christ someday, then and there, but over what? According to their same false scenario, all sin and evil and bad guys have been removed? Again, it's "fantasy Christianity."

Consequently, most of what has been written, preached, taught, and believed about the kingdom of God has been wrong—it's timing, nature, relevance, and applications in our modern-day world. As we Christians continue putting off out into the future one of the greatest blessings and provisions God has provided, we are paying a huge price (see again chapters 1, 2, and 3).

Notwithstanding, some scholars do have some things right. Here is a prominent but partial example:

> A good grasp of the kingdom of God is indispensable for a proper understanding of Christ and the redemption that he accomplished. The kingdom of God is a very large biblical category indeed. Accordingly, a comprehensive understanding of the kingdom would illuminate many aspects of theology. But to obtain such an understanding is not so easy! In fact, to attempt to gain a comprehensive understanding of the kingdom of God is to invite many problems.[29]

So far, so good. But Morgan and Peterson's various contributors contribute little after this clarifying statement. Instead, they dutifully

---

[28] For more, see John Noē, *The Creation of Evil: Casting light into the purposes of darkness* (Indianapolis, IN.: East2West Press, 2015), 46-48.
[29] Morgan and Peterson, eds., *The Kingdom of God,* 19.

present their various takes on the unscriptural "already/not yet paradigm of the kingdom of God" and intermix their futuristic tensions with an unscriptural "end of time" terminus and "impending eschatological doom."[30]

In this book we shall not commit these scriptural errors. Rather we shall "attempt to gain a comprehensive understanding of the kingdom of God" even though, as Morgan and Peterson warn above, this is to "invite many problems." But we shall invite the problems of the traditions of men and correct them.

Interim Conclusion #2

The general timeframe context specified by Daniel, four times, not only for this eschatological fulfillment of the everlasting kingdom but also for the fulfillment of all of his prophecies was: "in the days of those kings"—that fourth world empire, which ended in A.D. 476—15 centuries ago. All other eschatological and prophetic fulfillments were also conjoined to this same timeframe (see again Daniel 2:24-45; 7:1-28; 9:24-27; 12:1-13). If we deny or ignore any of this, we must deny the fulfillment of Daniel 2:44 as well. Instead, why not just accept it?[31]

As long as we Christians think there is a better, greater, "gooder" kingdom yet to come, we are not going to give much attention to the one that is here.

The reason these "interpreters" cannot accept this is, their exegesis, hermeneutics, and resultant understandings are driven by their flawed eschatological paradigms. *The Wycliffe Bible Commentary* accurately diagnoses this causation concerning Daniel 2:42-47, in that "disagreement about interpretation is rooted in the varying points of view with which readers approach the passage." Therefore, these interpreters

---

[30] Stephen J. Nichols, in Ibid., 45. Bruce K. Waltke, in Ibid., 55. Robert W. Yarbrough, in Ibid., 135.

[31] For detailed documentation, biblically and historically, again see Noē, *The Perfect Ending for the World* and *Unraveling the End*.

must come up with exegetical devices and deductive explanations to circumvent the plain and natural meaning of the text.

A classic but painful example is this deferment statement from the *Dictionary of Biblical Prophecy and End Times* under the topic of the Last Days: "The 'last days' refers to the final period of history when the Messiah will come to establish God's kingdom."[32] But as we've already seen, and soon will see more, God has already done this. Again, why not accept it? After all, it is "historically defensible."[33] But such distorted conclusions exhibit a grave mishandling of Scripture. Astonishingly, most churches, Christian colleges, and seminaries tolerate this recklessness and exegetical corruption.

To rectify these abuses a certain amount of repentance and deprogramming will be necessary. And unlearning is the hardest form of learning. But this paradigm shift is absolutely essential if we truly seek to become Christ-honoring and kingdom-bearing Christians.

Interim Conclusion #3

No longer do "scholars as well as plain Christians" need to be "puzzled about what Jesus meant when he spoke of the kingdom."[34] Nor must we continue submitting to the ambiguity that "no one knows when the kingdom will come in the full, future sense."[35]

When Jesus came into Galilee emphatically proclaiming the good news of God that "the time is fulfilled . . . the kingdom of God is at hand" (Mark 1:15 KJV), the "time" He was referring to as being "fulfilled" was the long-promised, intensely awaited, and appointed time prophesied by Daniel for this kingdom's arrival (Daniel 2:44 and 7:14, 18, 22, 27).

It is a fact of history that Jesus lived and ministered "in the days of those kings"—which ended in A.D. 476. It is a fact of Scripture that He brought into human history the only "kingdom [that] will never end" (Luke 1:33; Hebrews 12:27-28; Matt. 28:18). This was precisely what

---

[32] Hays, Duvall, and Pate, *Dictionary of Biblical Prophecy and End Times*, 254.

[33] Klein, Blomberg, Hubbard, Jr., *Introduction to Biblical Interpretation*, 149.

[34] Glen H. Stassen and David P. Gushee, *Kingdom Ethics* (Downers Grove, IL.: InterVarsity Press, 2003), 19.

[35] Ibid., 20.

the Messiah was to do—from his birth to his judgment (the latter will be covered in our next chapter).

But there are two more major revealed "secrets" of this kingdom's arrival that we need to solidly ground before leaving this chapter.

The Kingdom Arrived Fully Established

Since we may have largely misunderstood the time for the arrival of the kingdom's final form, it stands to reason that we may also have misunderstood the nature of its arrival. And indeed we have.

Most distinctly, the everlasting form of the kingdom of God did not arrive, in human and redemptive history, partially established or only initiated, inaugurated, in-breaking, or as a foretaste, already/not yet, "in some sense." Nor was it something to be built or to be established. Nor is it still moving toward a future consummation or completion, as so many have erroneously written and believe. Nor is another kingdom or future upgrade ever mentioned in Scripture. Biblically, the nature of the arrival of the everlasting kingdom does not fit any of these frequently used expressions or descriptions. They are simply products of long-standing traditions of men and erroneous teachings that have plagued the history of Christianity long enough. So why isn't any of this in-breaking type language used in the Bible? The answer is, for one simple reason.

The final form of the everlasting and eschatological kingdom of God arrived *fully established.* Its arrival, however, contrasts with the in-breaking nature for the establishment of salvation—the other great work of the Messiah. Salvation arrived through a series of successive eschatological events, namely, Jesus' birth, earthly ministry, death, burial, resurrection, ascension, Pentecost, the filling up the measure of sin of the Jews, the gospel of the kingdom being preached in all the world, and the destruction and desolation of the Old Covenant, animal-sacrifice, type-and-shadow system. But the everlasting form of the kingdom of God arrived *fully established* in the form of a fetus that grew into a babe—"For unto us a child is born" (Isa. 9:6a).

Contained within and throughout Jesus' physical body and being was the full incarnation of God's everlasting kingdom—i.e., his will, reign, and rule. Paul confirms this *fully established* arrival, thusly: "For God was pleased to have all fullness dwell in him" (Col. 1:19). "For in Christ all the fullness of the Deity lives in bodily form . . . who is the head over every power and authority" (Col. 2:9-10; also see John 1:14). Therefore, Jesus Christ did not come into this world to *begin* establishing his kingdom, as some assumed. The kingdom came with Him, bodily and *fully established*, along with his Kingship. Thus, the Magi aptly asked, "Where is the one who has been born king of the Jews?" (Matt. 2:2).

This *fully established* nature of arrival is further confirmed by Luke. Once when Jesus was confronted by unbelieving Pharisees, they asked Him, "when the kingdom of God would come?" Part of Jesus' frank reply was, "the kingdom of God is within you" (Luke 17:21). But the kingdom certainly was not *within* those unbelieving Pharisees who were trying to discredit and entrap Jesus. The Greek word *entos* used here can be translated as "within," "in your midst," or "among." The latter two translations are preferred, however, because of the context. That context, the kingdom, in its fullness (note that no disclaimers or delimiting adjectives are used), was standing right before their eyes in the form of the physical body of Jesus of Nazareth. Unfortunately, the mistranslation of "within" has misled many to delimit the nature of the kingdom to *only* being an internal matter and spiritual reality—i.e., "in the hearts of believers"—as opposed to being an all-encompassing reality and remedy for healing all internal and external matters of our world broken by sin and separation from God.

Contained within and throughout Jesus' physical body and being was the full incarnation of God's everlasting kingdom—i.e., his will, reign, and rule.

Likewise, another huge misunderstanding with major negative ramifications today, is the popular belief of those waiting for Jesus to return and begin his reign as King. Yet every Christmas we sing "Joy to the world, the Lord is come! Let earth receive her King!" So which is it? As we exposed in Chapter 6, so-called prophecy "expert" and "Left Behind" co-author Tim LaHaye insists that "When Jesus comes, He is going to be King of Kings and Lord of Lords . . . . To say that Christ is ruler now is a statement that reaches almost blasphemous proportions." So if LaHaye is correct, shouldn't we stop singing "Joy to the World?"

Others claim that Jesus was not born a king but became king when He was crowned upon his ascension. For support they cite Psalms 2 and 110 and Hebrews 2:9. But I'll stick with the Magi. Not only did they have the time of the Messiah's arrival right (see Rom. 5:6), they had his status right as well—á la Isaiah 9:6-7. Absolutely, Jesus was born King with "all authority in heaven and on earth" given to Him (Matt. 28:18; also see John 5:22).

From this humble beginning, the new, prophesied, much-anticipated, and final form of the eschatological kingdom of God was no longer a future hope. It was a fully present, *fully established*, and bodily-indwelt reality. Notably, it had not broken into human history, catastrophically or cataclysmically, as many theologians are still awaiting today. Rather, as Glasser observes, it came "quietly, unobtrusively, and secretly."[36] All of this brings us to our next revealed "secret."

The Kingdom's Unending Increase

Isaiah, prophesied about this time of arrival and the future dynamic of this fully arrived and established kingdom:

> For to us a child *is born,* to us a son is given,
> and the *government* will be on his shoulders.
> And he will be called Wonderful, Counselor, Mighty God,
> Everlasting Father, Prince of Peace.
> Of the *increase of his government* and peace
> there will be *no end.*
> He will *reign* on David's throne and over his *kingdom,*
> *establishing* and *upholding* it
> with justice [judgment] and righteousness [justice]
> ***from that time on and forever.***
> The zeal of the Lord Almighty will accomplish this.
>   (Isaiah 9:6-7 – *italics-bold emphasis mine* [KJV])

Hence, from Jesus' birth and "from *that* time on and forever," this *fully established,* everlasting form of the kingdom of God on planet Earth

---

[36] Glasser, *Announcing the Kingdom*, 215.

has only increased progressively, dramatically, and without end (also see Luke 1:33). Precisely and once again, God has prophesied, fulfilled, and kept his word—his "perfect" and "flawless" word (Psa. 18:30).[37]

In Sum

Daniel's two parallel and general time prophecies and his time-restrictive words in Daniel 2:44 must be *naturally, plainly,* and *literally* understood and *fully* honored. As we have seen, this is something the vast majority of Christian commentators, scholars, and lay people alike have not done, been willing to do, or been taught to do. But these straightforward understandings firmly ground the time and nature for the establishment of the everlasting, eschatological kingdom of God within human history, along with its future, ever-increasing dynamic.

No other kingdom, form of this kingdom, different establishment, or fulfillment beyond this *one* is prophesied in Scripture or is yet-to-come.[38] Also, no scriptural warrant exists for conceiving of "a revival of the Roman Empire"[39] to accommodate a yet-future establishment and fulfillment. Nor do we need to await an unscriptural "end of time" for the kingdom's so-called "final establishment," as has been devised by amillennialists and postmillennialists. These man-made ideas only cause deception, confusion, and degradation. We'd be well advised to simply believe the Bible and stop trying to stretch prophecy like a rubber band—19 centuries and counting out into the future.

Interestingly, when Satan tempted Jesus (Matt. 4:1-11), he quoted Scripture out of context. Comparatively, many Christians have followed suit by lifting the kingdom out of its appointed time context.

But praise the Lord! We have been given "the knowledge of the secrets of the kingdom of heaven/God" (Matt. 13:11; Luke 8:10; Mark 4:11). Jesus also termed the kingdom "the key to knowledge" (Luke 11:52). Sadly, many today have lost this knowledge, these secrets, and

---

[37] Again, for many more examples, see Noē, *The Perfect Ending for the World* and Noē, *Unraveling the End.*

[38] In our next chapter, we shall see that this kingdom keeps coming, but not in an eschatological manner.

[39] Walvoord, *Major Bible Prophecies,* 162-164.

this key. They have been covered up by our traditions of men which "nullify the word of God" (Matt. 15:6; Mark 7:13). Consequently, the lifting of this precise fulfillment out of its divinely determined timeframe in human history has been the most significant factor for disestablishing the kingdom of God and producing what Guder appropriately terms, "the reductionism of the gospel."[40]

Indeed, more remains to be unlearned and learned. But the time context and nature of arrival for the establishment of the only everlasting and ever-increasing kingdom was clearly "in the days of those kings," which ended in A.D. 476. Any self-inflicted effort to diminish this revealed "secret" and highly beneficial reality of our "once for all delivered faith" (Jude 3) must be termed, in this author's opinion, a reprehensible perversion and act of grievous error. But with this solid grounding, scripturally and historically, no longer can the kingdom of God be considered as caught-up in eschatological mid-air. Would you now agree?

What's Next?

We humans often believe something because everybody, or everybody we know, believes it. The classic example occurred in the days of the Polish astronomer, Copernicus. Back then a popular belief was that the sun revolved around the earth and the earth was the center of the universe. After all, anyone could walk outside and observe the empirical evidence—the sun moving across the sky. But in 1543 Copernicus' work began to dramatically change all that—not, of course, without difficulty and resistance.

Perhaps, in a similar manner, the reclaiming and restoring of the biblical and historical realizations of the kingdom's timely arrival, its *fully established* nature on arrival, and its unending increase stand in stark contrast to the popular consensuses of today. They claim we are presently living in the "already but not yet" kingdom of God awaiting its future consummation; or that the kingdom comes in stages, or they are looking for another type and better kingdom yet to come.

---

[40] Guder, *The Continuing Conversion of the* Church, xiii.

For these reasons (and others), some critics today argue: "there is no such thing as Christianity but only *Christianities*, and more and more of them—more and more different from each other . . . ."[41] In support, these critics cite this evidence: Christianity today consists of approximately 30,000 to 40,000 denominations, depending on different estimates.

But given the Apostle Paul's wisdom that "no doubt there have to be differences among you to show which of you have God's approval" (1 Cor. 11:19) and given the scriptural evidence we have presented in this chapter, we shall steadfastly maintain there is only ONE everlasting kingdom. It arrived in human history right on time and *fully established* in the form of a babe "in the days of those kings," which ended in A.D. 476. Its increase is without end—even in the midst of so many "Christianities" today.

We'd be well advised to simply believe the Bible and stop trying to stretch prophecy like a rubber band— 19 centuries and counting out into the future.

In our next chapter, we shall continue sharpening our ax and grounding this kingdom. In this Step #2 of 5, we shall look to Jesus Himself to further straighten out more misunderstandings and misconceived notions as we explore the nature of the kingdom's dramatic increase, during his day and time, and a climactic ending.

---

[41] John W. Loftus, *The End of Christianity* (Amherst, NY.: Prometheus Books, 2011), 49.

Chapter 9

Step #2 – The Dramatic Increase and Climactic Ending[1]

Therefore, since we are receiving a kingdom
that cannot be shaken . . . . (Heb. 12:28a)

The stage is set. The players and pieces are all in place. The days of Daniel's fourth world empire are present. An angel has appeared to Mary confirming Isaiah 9:6-7's prophecy that her babe would bring in a new kingdom that "will never end" (Luke 1:33). With Jesus' conception and birth "the time had fully come" (Gal. 4:4a). In Him, the everlasting form of the kingdom of God arrived fully established, encompassed bodily (see again Col. 1:19; 2:9-10; John 1:14). It was not established partially and progressively over a transition period or delayed over 2,000 years and counting. Rather, "from that time on and forever," this fully arrived and fully established kingdom would only increase, and dramatically so (Isa. 9:6-7), up to and beyond the climactic end of the biggest institution of God in those days.

Thus, the great debate over how much of the kingdom of God/heaven is available to us on earth today—"none," "a little," "much," or "all"—is resolved. In this chapter, we shall explore the historical and

---

[1] Much of this chapter was originally presented as a theological paper at the 56th Annual Meeting of the Evangelical Theological Society in San Antonio, Texas, November 17-19, 2004.

biblical highlights for how "the zeal of the LORD Almighty" accomplished this dramatic increase (Isa. 9:7b) and climactic ending— from Jesus' birth in 3 or 4 B.C. through circa A.D. 70. Let the increase begin.

Jesus' Words

The first recorded and dramatic increase of the kingdom, beyond Jesus' growing physical body, occurred at age 12. One day Jesus' earthly parents, Mary and Joseph, mistakenly left Him behind in Jerusalem. Then, "after three days they found him in the temple courts, sitting among the teachers, listening to them and asking them questions." Luke reports that "everyone who heard him was amazed at his understanding and his answers." When the young Jesus asks his parents "why were you searching for me?" He adds this startling statement: "I had to be in my Father's house." Luke notes that Mary and Joseph "did not understand what he was saying to them. But his mother treasured all these things in her heart. And Jesus grew in wisdom and stature, and in favor with God and men" (see Luke 2:41-52).

Next, in the recorded and dramatic increase, we find Jesus, age 30, being baptized in the Jordan River. Upon coming out of the water and as "he was praying, heaven was opened and the Holy Spirit descended on him in bodily form like a dove. And a voice came down from heaven: 'You are my Son, whom I love; with you I am well pleased'"(see Luke 3:21-23).

Immediately following his baptism and 40 days of temptation by Satan in the desert, Jesus begins his earthy ministry. Mark records: "Jesus came into Galilee, preaching the gospel of the kingdom of God." Boldly and emphatically, Jesus proclaims: "The time is fulfilled, and the kingdom of God is at hand: repent ye, and believe the gospel" (Mark. 1:14-15 KJV).

"At hand" in the King James and New American Standard versions is the most graphic and best translation of the Greek word "eggizo." "Near" is a weak and confusing translation by the New International Version. "At hand" is a reality indicator meaning graspable, squeezable, available for the taking, then and there. Hence, the kingdom was not "near" as in imminence—about or soon to arrive. It was "there" as in immanence—in his very person and presence. In other words, what many in the Christian world are still awaiting today was fulfilled. No longer was the kingdom about waiting; it was about the "now!" Today, this "at hand" kingdom has greatly increased and is still about "now."

A few months earlier in the Desert of Judea, John the Baptist had also come announcing and preaching this same rule and reign of God: "Repent," he cried out, "for the kingdom of heaven is at hand" (Matt. 3:2). John, too, was stressing the then-and-there "now" of the kingdom. George Eldon Ladd verifies this "was an amazing claim . . . . He had boldly announced that the Kingdom . . . of God had come to them."[2]

But what time was Jesus talking about that was fulfilled? As we covered in our last chapter, it was the time foretold by Daniel for the God of heaven to "set up a kingdom that will never be destroyed . . . an everlasting dominion that will not pass away" (Dan. 2:44; 7:14, 27). Not only had Daniel prophesied of the general time for the coming of the everlasting kingdom of God, he also perfectly pinpointed the exact time of Jesus' anointing which initiated his 3½-year earthly ministry (Dan. 9:24-27). Exactly 483 years of Daniel's 70 weeks (490 years) time prophecy had transpired "from the issuing of the decree to restore and rebuild Jerusalem" (Dan. 9:25). This was Artaxerxes' Decree in 457 B.C. (Ezra 7:11-26). "Until the Anointed One, the ruler comes, there will be seven 'sevens' and sixty-two 'sevens' (Dan. 9:25)." Jesus was anointed in the Jordan River in A.D. 27. "After the sixty-two sevens, the Anointed One will be cut off (Dan. 9:26) . . . in the middle of that [final week of years] seven . . . ." (Dan. 9:27). Jesus was crucified in A.D. 30.[3]

No wonder Paul would later write: "at just the right time . . . Christ died" (Rom. 5:6). As we shall also see later in this chapter, "at just the right time" another climactic event took place.

Truly, it is worth re-emphasizing that in none of his teachings did Jesus give any indication the kingdom, or any aspect of it, was being held in abeyance for some future time. Likewise, Jesus issued no disclaimer or qualification of a partial, interim, or foretaste form of the kingdom. Nor did He mention a future-coming kingdom different from

---

[2] Ladd, *The Presence of the Future*, 111.

[3] For more on the exact, literal, sequential, and chronological fulfillment of Daniel's 70 weeks time prophecy, see Noē, *The Perfect Ending for the World*, 109-126 and Noē, *Unraveling the End*, 213-228.

the one He was presenting. Moreover, He never insinuated the kingdom was only there "in some sense," in an already/not-yet state, or as being only near or imminent. He came preaching a fully present reality and "at hand" availability.

Therefore, the central teaching of Jesus Christ is characterized as the "good news [gospel] of the kingdom" (Matt. 4:23; Mark 1:14-15; Luke 4:16-30; 8:1). And He emphasized, "I must preach the good news of the kingdom of God . . . because that is why I was sent" (Luke 4:43b). Of course, He also came "to seek and save the lost" (Matt. 18:12; Luke 19:10). Again, these were and are the two great works of the Messiah. That is also the order in which He announced them and accomplished them.

The dramatic increase continues with Jesus' teaching words. In the Beatitudes and the Sermon on the Mount (Matt. 5-7), Jesus taught about the nature of the kingdom and what real life submitted to the will, reign, and rule of God was like. A new way of living and reigning with God was now under way. No longer was the new kingdom a future hope. Yet much of Western Christianity has consistently removed this understanding of the kingdom from Jesus' own enunciation of it as a fully present reality. Traditionally, many defer Jesus' teachings here to conditions that will only be present during a still future Jewish millennium. Hence, Guder frankly admits, "our reductionism with regard to Jesus' concrete teachings . . . has been massive."[4]

But Jesus did not say, "I think" or "I suppose." Nor did He quote other learned men. He spoke with certainty and authority, as One Who knew. And the people of his day (and many since) were astonished by his teachings (Matt. 7:28-29). Via many parables and discourses, He taught about the kingdom's personal and public nature and one's response to it by saying, "the kingdom is like . . . ." (not is equal to). The operative word here is, IS . . . (not "was," past tense, or "will someday be," future tense), but IS a glorious, present-day, real-life reality, there and then. He further revealed: "The Law and the Prophets were proclaimed until John. Since that time, the good news of the kingdom of God is being preached, and everyone is forcing his way into it" (Luke 16:16; Matt. 11:12). At other times Jesus spoke of entering or receiving this present reality (Matt. 5:3; 23:13; Mark 10:15, and parallels—more on this in our next chapter).

---

[4] Guder, *The Continuing Conversion of the Church*, 195.

His teachings covered almost every aspect of life and called for an individual response. Frequently, He spoke of the kingdom in very simple terms, such as water, seeds, coins, salt, light, fish, yeast, hidden treasure in a field, a sower, and more. Using the technique of transformational imagination that we discussed in Chapter 5, pp. 129-138, He provided an inexhaustible storehouse of wisdom, guidance, counsel, and comfort, not just to be learned but also interacted with and lived. But many who heard Him kept trying to understand his parables and symbols literally instead of spiritually. Notable exceptions, however, were his parables of leaven and the mustard seed. In those, Jesus literally reinforces Isaiah's prophecy that the kingdom would not break into human history big and catastrophically, but small and gradually, and would progressively increase with no end to its increase (see Isa. 9:7). That means there will be no future, catastrophic consummation or ending of the kingdom as it fills "the whole earth" (Dan. 2:31-34).

He never insinuated the kingdom was only there "in some sense," in an already/not-yet state, or as being only near or imminent. He came preaching a fully present and "at hand" availability.

Matthew adds: "He [Jesus] went about all Galilee, teaching in their synagogues and preaching the gospel of the kingdom" (Matt. 4:23; 9:35; 24:14; Mark 1:14-15). After his resurrection, Luke reports that Jesus' teaching is still centered on the kingdom (see Acts 1:3).

Thus, the most characteristic and distinctive aspect of Jesus' teaching was that of a fully present and available kingdom. Moreover, He advised: "everyone who hears these words of mine and puts them into practice [obeys] is like a wise man who built his house on the rock" (Matt. 7:24). Chalke and Mann make special note that "no-one who sat on the hill that day wanted to disagree. . . . For them Jesus' message was a revolution in the truest sense of the word . . . ."[5]

---

[5] Chalke and Mann, *The Lost Message of Jesus*, 100, 92.

Jesus' Kingdom Works

Next, the increasing presence of the kingdom was not only being realized in Jesus' person and his words, but would now be further manifested by his kingdom works (John 14:10; Acts 1:1). Hence, Jesus obediently performed the "will of him who sent me" (John 6:38).

Thereby, He dramatically and dynamically demonstrated the kingdom's internal and external, spiritual and physical characteristics by the life He led, his relationship with the Father, his dependence upon the Father, forgiving sins, healing the sick, casting out demons, taking authority over nature, performing miracles, releasing the oppressed, taking care of physical needs, feeding the hungry, and raising the dead.

Jesus regarded *all these* aspects as essential and intrinsic elements of his kingdom. Therefore, his kingdom affected the whole person. It produced both spiritual transformations and physical blessings or consequences.

His works made the kingdom more tangible and obvious that it was no longer a future hope, but a fully present reality and full of eschatological significance. As Stassen and Gushee remark, "the embodied drama of the reign of God lies at the heart of the biblical record . . . Jesus came preaching and incarnating the long-promised and desperately awaited kingdom of God."[6]

One of Jesus' most prominent works was the casting out or exorcism of demons, which He interpreted as clear proof: "the kingdom of God has come upon you" (Matt. 12:28; Luke 11:20; Matt. 8:16-17; Mark 1:32-34). The verb "come upon" implies something is present—not near but there. Once again, He made no qualifications, such as a "foretaste," "already/not yet of," "partialness," or "in some sense."

In Jesus' ministry the "mystery" of the increasing kingdom had now become "an open secret" (Mark 4:11-12, 21-23). Signs of its presence were growing. Expectations were heightening. And the people of Jesus' day were amazed (Mark 1:21-28). But opposition was also being aroused as the nature of his kingdom was markedly different from the popular Jewish expectation.

---

[6] Stassen & Gushee, *Kingdom Ethics*, 17.

Jesus' Modeled Prayer

In the Lord's Prayer, Jesus prayed and taught his disciples to pray (as well as us today): "Thy kingdom come, thy will be done on earth, as it is in heaven" (Matt. 6:10 KJV). Gregory A. Boyd explains that this prayer "presupposes that, to a significant extent at least, God's will is *not now* being done on earth."[7] But do we really believe what we are praying for when we pray this prayer today?

Willard rightly reminds us that this modeled and enduring prayer plays "an absolutely vital role in kingdom living."[8] Yet it raises four foundational questions: 1) Has this 1st-century prayer been answered? 2) What do these words mean? 3) Why would it make any sense to pray for the kingdom to come when Jesus was teaching that it was already present (also see Col. 1:13; Heb. 12:28; Rev. 12:10)? 4) Why would Jesus teach us to pray that things on earth would be like they are in heaven, if it was not possible?

First, this prayer rules out any idea that the kingdom of God is purely a heavenly or otherworldly reality. Rather, the purpose of this prayer is for God's will to comprehensively transform this earth and our world and everything in it to conform to heaven. No dimension of earthly life or social order is excluded or beyond this scope.

Secondly, God's kingdom originates in the heavenly realm where his will, reign, and rule is realized throughout. It then comes out of or from heaven down to this earth where its governance is to be universally manifested, not just in Israel. Hence, the kingdom functions in both locations. On earth, the kingdom was and is here. It is just not *from* here. It's "from another place" (John 18:36)—i.e., heaven.

Thirdly, "Thy kingdom come" is in parallel to and coupled with God's will "be[ing] done." Therefore, this is an invocation for God's kingdom and will to become a present reality that is fully and completely realized in and through the life of every Christian and in and through every aspect of society and existence on this earth *just as* it is throughout heaven. McLaren sees it this way: "It's the Kingdom of God, the dream of God coming true when people harmonize their wills with God's

---

[7] Gregory A. Boyd, *Satan and the Problem of Evil* (Downers Grove, IL.: InterVarsity Press, 2001), 37-38.
[8] Willard, *The Divine Conspiracy*, 195.

will."[9] Ladd contributes: "As men enter into Jesus' experience of God, the Kingdom of God, his rule, 'comes' to them. As increasingly large circles of men enter into this experience, God's Kingdom grows and is extended in the world."[10]

Many Christians, however, have been misled to believe *when* God's kingdom comes to earth—someday in a future cataclysmic event—*then* his rule will be established and his will done in all the world. In the meantime, they falsely assume the kingdom has not yet come, or not come fully.

But as we have and will continue to see, 1) God's everlasting kingdom has already come and is here. 2) As his will is increasingly done in us (we are earth/dust) and by us, his faithful followers on earth, the kingdom "expands," "grows," "extends," "advances," "spreads," is "realized" and "manifests" itself into more areas and/or more fully functions in existing ones. 3) God's kingdom thus becomes an increasing reality in individual lives and in society at large, as more and more people submit their wills to his will.

I submit, therefore, that the above three areas of ongoing and ever-widening increase are what the Lord's Prayer means for us today when we pray "Thy kingdom come." Willard agrees and elaborates that this "does not mean we should pray for it to come into existence. Rather, we pray for it to take over at all points in the personal, social, and political order where it is now excluded."[11] Yet, Willard also acknowledges that "these matters are now widely misunderstood."[12]

Additionally, this long-term perspective of unending increase for the kingdom extends indefinitely into the future. In his growth parables Jesus talked metaphorically about this spreading of the kingdom (Matt. 13:31-35; also see Dan. 2:34, 35; Isa. 9:7). He had brought God's will, reign, and rule to earth, fully, and in a new and more personal manner than ever before—in his Person, words, and works. In this prayer, Jesus is praying for the continuing increase of what God had begun in Him and for the lifting of earthly existence to the new level of heavenly life. It began small and was growing. Soon, it would make a gigantic growth leap.

---

[9] McLaren, *The Last Word and the Word After That*, 143.

[10] Ladd, *The Presence of the Future*, 173.

[11] Willard, *The Divine Conspiracy*, 26.

[12] Ibid., 27.

In retrospect, since Jesus taught his disciples to pray this way, the followers of Jesus—who have taken this prayer seriously—have not only prayed but also labored that the kingdom may come and God's will may be done "on earth as it is in heaven." Some 30 years later, for example, the Apostle Paul described the ways in which the gospel was "producing fruit and growing . . . all over the world" (Col. 1:6).

Bright, however, rightly cautions that this "prayer . . . simply cannot be prayed while we declare that there are areas of life where the will of Christ will not rule . . . . The Church is to exhibit the righteousness of Christ not merely in private morality but in all matters of human relations. The church which 'sticks to the gospel' and utters no word of judgment or of exhortation to society's sin is no prophetic church and, what is worse, is preaching an incomplete gospel."[13]

Therefore, this is an invocation for God's kingdom and will to become a present reality that is fully and completely realized . . . through every aspect of society and existence on this earth . . .

Fourthly, in addition to speaking of the kingdom as present, Jesus also spoke of a future time, growth, and dimension of its coming with power. He was not speaking of a far-distant event beyond the life span of some of his then-living disciples. Jesus told them: "some who are standing here will not taste death before they see the kingdom of God come with power" (Mark 9:1; also Matt.16:28; Luke 21:31). Clearly, this time-restricted event was relevant to them. It, too, would occur within "the days of those kings" (Dan. 2:44). If this new dimension of the kingdom's dramatic increase did not come during the lifetime of some of those to whom He spoke, then the liberals and skeptics are right—Jesus was a false prophet and the Bible is not inerrant. But as we shall soon see, the kingdom did come and manifest itself in power in a gigantic manner before all of Jesus' first disciples died.[14]

---

[13] Bright, *The Kingdom of God*, 263.

[14] Some scholars maintain that this coming of the kingdom in power took place seven days later at Jesus' transfiguration, or during his post-resurrection appearances, or at Pentecost. But *none* of those who were "standing here" had

Coincidentally, Jesus' two statements during the institution of the last supper also pointed to this future event: "For I tell you, I will not eat it again until it finds fulfillment in the kingdom of God . . . For I tell you I will not drink again of the fruit of the vine until the kingdom of God comes" (Luke 22:16, 18). Jesus was clearly speaking of a coming eschatological event. But, once again, He never mentioned any other kingdom, a millennial kingdom, or a different-natured, next phase of his kingdom as being yet-to-come. Nor did He teach or suggest its fulfillment might be put on hold or delayed beyond the lifetime of his contemporaries.

For us today, this time of the kingdom's eschatological coming in power is past. Hence, we no longer need to pray for the kingdom to come, eschatologically, or in its fullness one day, as many have mistakenly taught. That kingdom arrived fully established, is still here, and we should be joyously celebrating its arrival and experiencing its present-day, established, and ever-increasing reality. Unfortunately, this is not the message or the reality being preached, practiced, and perceived in much of Christianity today.

Instead, for many of us, the Lord's Prayer is merely a devotional, if not a hollow prayer or meaningless ritual that we oftentimes pray unthinkingly. But Guder judiciously warns that praying "the Lord's Prayer is a dangerous activity" because it "is not about getting what we want." When we truly pray this powerful prayer it is "life-creating and life-changing."[15] Why is this so?

First, praying the Lord's Prayer in a sincere manner is an acknowledgement of a present and active kingdom. Second, as Ladd terms it, it is a "petition . . . for the coming of God's Kingdom . . . for the perfect realization of God's will."[16] Third, it draws God's will, reign, and rule from heaven to earth and invokes these to come more extensively throughout the world. Fourth, it invites God's kingdom powers to invade one's life and become dramatically active in and through us. Fifth, it

---

died yet. Even more troublesome, no Scripture written some 20 to 30 years later ever validates any of these fulfillment claims. To the contrary, New Testament Scripture was still looking forward to this day as yet future (see Heb. 10:25; 2 Thess. 2:1-3; 2 Tim. 4:1).

[15] Guder, *Missional Church*, 157.

[16] Ladd, *The Presence of the Future*, 136.

submits our will to his will so we can lead holy lives. Sixth, it expresses our desire to be used in a significant way in doing God's will and in demonstrating his kingdom words and works on the earth, here and now. And, seventh, it is a continual reminder that the coming of the kingdom is one of continuity with our 1st-century heritage—a point that will be further addressed in our next chapter (Step #3 of 5).

Thus, "Thy kingdom come" is not a prayer awaiting a future-coming kingdom but, rather, of an arrived, fully established, and ever-expanding kingdom. The kingdom still "comes," expands, grows, or increases whenever anyone recognizes and obeys the will, reign, and rule of God in and through his or her life. For some reason known only to God, He has chosen us humans as one of the, if not the primary, instrument and means for expanding his kingdom into and throughout the world from its source in heaven.

Therefore, the Lord's Prayer isn't just about getting us to heaven. It's about getting heaven down to us—"Thy will be done on earth as it is in heaven." God has not called us to forsake the world. He has called us to impress heaven's pattern upon and into the world as we herald Christ as King over the whole earth. In the words of the second verse of the great hymn, "Lead On, O King Eternal," "With deeds of love and mercy, The heavenly kingdom comes." Amazingly, in God's economy, "the initiative in the realization of the Kingdom is in the hands of men."[17] Hence, we must continue praying this prayer and submitting ourselves to its reclaimed purpose of expanding God's kingdom in us, through us, and among us.

Appropriately, McLaren concludes, "I recommend we savor each phrase of this prayer, allowing it to capture and inspire our imaginations and transform our aspirations, giving us a vision of the kingdom. If enough of us see the kingdom—and seeing it, rethink our lives, and rethinking our lives, believe that the impossible is possible—everything could change."[18]

But the kingdom would not continue increasing without bringing opposition. All of which brings us to our next significant dynamic of dramatic increase.

---

[17] Ladd, *The Presence of the Future*, 145.
[18] McLaren, *The Secret Message of Jesus*, 204.

Jesus' Transference to Others

Initially, the kingdom was present only in the Person, words, and works of Jesus. But one day that dramatically changed. No doubt, Jesus shocked the sandals off his disciples the morning He called together the Twelve, and later the Seventy, and informed them He was sending them out as his representatives to proclaim the same gospel of the kingdom and perform its same mighty works as He had been doing.

Therefore, He "gave them authority/power . . . . [to] preach this message: 'The kingdom of heaven is near/at hand.' Heal the sick, raise the dead, cleanse those who have leprosy, drive out demons. Freely you have received, freely give." (Matt. 10:1, 7-8 NIV/KJV; also see Luke 9:1-2, 6; 10:1-17). He also warned them they would face opposition (Matt. 10:14-25). But He assured them of something else quite profound: "He who receives you receives me, and he who receives me receives the one who sent me" (Matt. 10:40). Later on, He gave them "the keys of the kingdom" along with the promise that "whatever you bind on earth will be bound in heaven, and whatever you loose on earth will be loosed in heaven" (Matt. 16:19). Note, that these are the same two locations mentioned in the Lord's Prayer (Matt. 6:10). And keys are a symbol of authority and power—like the keys of a car.

Thus, for Jesus during his earthly ministry, the increase of the kingdom of God meant the progressive expansion and growth of the will, reign, and rule of God through Himself into the lives of his obedient followers and onto others. He also instructed them in the close inter-relationship between the preaching of the kingdom and the demonstration of its works of power and miracles (Matt. 22:29). He stated this was the "key to knowledge" (Luke 11:52; Matt. 23:13-14). Thereby, they experienced the "powers of the age to come," (Heb. 6:5) and victories over evil in advance of the coming of the Holy Spirit and the age-changing climactic ending.

Just as important, He trained them to care for the physical and emotional needs of the "least of these" as unto Him: the hungry, the thirsty, the strangers, those needing clothing, the sick, and those in prisons (see Matt. 25:34-46; Rom. 12:20-21). And He clarified: "For whoever does the will of my Father in heaven is my brother and sister and mother" (Matt. 12:50).

Finally, prior to his death on the cross and ascension, He promised another dramatic increase and expansion of his kingdom. He told his followers they would receive a permanent empowering after the Holy Spirit had come upon them (John 14:16-17). From then on (Pentecost – Acts 2), the proclamation and the powers of the kingdom were no longer limited in time or space—i.e., to those who had personal contact with Jesus or were specially commissioned by Him. They would be available to all believers without distinction—e.g., those who through obedience would become "fellow workers for the kingdom of God" (Col. 4:11). They would be empowered to be his kingdom witnesses, to preach the same kingdom message, and do the same kingdom works and miracles in Jerusalem, Judea, Samaria, and the uttermost parts of the earth (Acts 1:8; 2:1-21).

Jesus' Great Commission Command

Following his resurrection, Jesus came and appeared many times to his disciples and others. During one of these visible comings, Jesus not only commissioned his first followers to "baptize" and "make disciples of all nations," but He also commanded them to "teach them to obey *everything* I have commanded you to do" (emphasis mine, Matt. 28:19-20).

Jesus' "everything" certainly included the preaching of the kingdom *and* the performance of its miraculous, merciful, and fruit-producing works. But this understanding is in sharp contrast with the contemporary teaching that "witnessing" only involves telling the message of Jesus and salvation. Practically speaking, the tendency of many scholars and pastors today is to ignore, downplay, or explain away the full meaning of Jesus' Great Commission. Once again, as Guder emphasizes, "our reductionism with regard to Jesus' concrete teaching . . . has been massive."[19]

The modern-day fact is, while many Christians profess faith in Jesus, love and adore Him, worship and praise Him, pray and confess to Him, we hesitate or simply do not want to obey what He has plainly commanded us to do. Perhaps, the Great Commission is *much greater*

---

[19] Guder, *The Continuing Conversion of the Church*, 195.

than most of us have been led to believe. Willard poignantly bemoans this fact that most Christians "do not really understand what discipleship to him . . . is, and it [The Kingdom Among Us] therefore remains only a distant, if beautiful, ideal."[20]

In a similar vein, one week before his death, Jesus specifically mandated that "the gospel of the kingdom" was to be "preached in the world as a testimony to all nations . . ." (Matt. 24:14). He did not say "the gospel of salvation." Jesus further commanded his disciples to "seek first his kingdom and his righteousness" (Matt. 6:33). What kingdom was He talking about? There is only one—the one He embodied, announced, taught, ministered, prayed for, transferred, and commissioned them to carry forth.

Thus, Evans both affirms and laments that "the Great Commission refers to more than just individuals being changed . . . . Entire societies should be impacted and transformed by the church's presence in their midst. This is because the church's job is to produce disciples, not just members. A disciple is a person who is progressively bringing every area of life under the Lordship of Jesus Christ. . . . Our problem today is . . . we have many Christians, we have few disciples. . . . These schizophrenic saints paint a confusing picture of Christ and His kingdom for the rest of the world."[21]

Also worth re-emphasizing is that Christ's Great Commission is intimately related to the Lord's Prayer in that both express the same intention, namely that the Father's will, reign, and rule should be done on earth as it is in heaven. Likewise, both call believers to both prayer and action, to be his faithful witnesses and instruments for displaying kingdom powers and to expand its governance throughout this world. So what happened?

The Results

Christ's small band of 1st-century followers dramatically increased into a mighty and world-transforming force. Their obedience to Christ and his kingdom, along with the supernatural empowerment of the Holy

---

[20] Willard, *The Divine Conspiracy*, 291.
[21] Evans, *What A Way To Live!*, 308.

Spirit, turned the world of their day "upside down" (Acts 17:6). The Book of Acts is a record of the continuation of Jesus' teachings and his kingdom works by his faithful followers. It was preserved as part of the Holy Scripture not only as a confirmation of all Jesus began to do and to teach (Acts 1:1) but also as a record of their continuing obedience in presenting the kingdom of God. Therefore, "in this way the word of the Lord spread widely and grew in power" (Acts 19:20). Please notice, it was not in some other or lesser way that these results were achieved (see Acts 19:8; 17:6; 28:31).

For one, the Apostle Paul, who boldly stated in Scripture he was the example of the Christian life as He followed the example of Christ (see 1 Cor. 11:1), ". . . entered the synagogue and spoke boldly there for three months, arguing persuasively about the kingdom of God" (Acts 19:8). Then, while in house prison in Rome, he "boldly and without hindrance . . . preached the kingdom of God and taught about the Lord Jesus Christ" (Acts 28:31). As a result of his and the early Church's obedience, Christ's first followers were energetic, empowered, and unstoppable— something most Christians today are far from being, sad to say. Why so?

Perhaps, the Great Commission is *much greater* than most of us have been led to believe.

It's because nowadays most Christians and much of the Church do not practice this type of Christianity. Not surprisingly, most of the unbelieving world does not view Christianity or the Church as a force to be reckoned with. No question, we modern-day Christians are paying a huge price for our dilution, devaluation, degrading, and dismissal of the kingdom that Christ came to establish "in the days of those kings" (Dan. 2:44).

The Phasing-out and Climactic Ending

At the time of Jesus' birth, the current manifestation of God's kingdom on earth—i.e., his will, reign, and rule—was the Old Covenant, animal-sacrifice, blood-temple system. But with Jesus' life, death, burial, resurrection, and ascension, that "type and shadow" system was made "obsolete" and would "soon disappear" (Heb. 8:5, 13). Those words in quotation marks were penned circa A.D. 65. (As I often say in my Bible study groups, "If you are going to quote it, date it.")

Before that, around A.D. 57, the Apostle Paul had written: "What I mean, brothers, is that the time is short . . . . For this world in its present form is passing away" (1 Cor. 7:29, 31). But whose "time is [was] short" and what "world in its present form is [was] passing away" back then? The answer is the same. It was the world of the Old Covenant, animal-sacrifice, blood-temple system. It was not the terra firma world or the stars, planets, outer space, and universe, or time—all those are without end.[22]

Several times, Jesus spoke about this soon-coming and climactic ending. At the well, He told the Samaritan woman "a time is coming when you will worship neither on this mountain nor in Jerusalem" (John 4:21). He also forewarned the Jewish chief priests and the elders in the temple courts: "the kingdom of God will be taken away from you and given to another people who will produce its fruit" (Matt. 21:43). DeMar correctly underscores that "Jesus could not take from them what they did not have."[23] At that time, the Jews were the possessors of God's Old Covenant kingdom.

Jesus further informed them that this removal and re-giving of the kingdom would happen at a "coming" of "the owner of the vineyard" (Matt. 21:33, 40). Matthew assures us that these Jews "knew he [Jesus] was talking about them" (Matt. 21:45) for they had killed "the son" (Matt. 21:37-39). They also knew, from the prophet Isaiah, that "the vineyard" Jesus was referring to in this parable was "the house of Israel and the men of Judah," and that it was to "be destroyed" by the owner, "the Lord Almighty" (Isa. 5:1-7; also Matt. 21:41). Once again, Jesus made no mention of a postponement or withdrawal of the kingdom He was presenting.

At another time, Jesus specified, "not the smallest letter, not the least stroke of a pen, will by any means disappear from the Law until everything is accomplished" (Matt. 5:18). In perfect harmony with this statement, the writer of Hebrews discloses that the new could not fully

---

[22] See Noē, *The Perfect Ending for the World*, 81-106 and Noē, *Unraveling the End*, 141-169.

[23] DeMar, *Myths, Lies & Half Truths*, 223.

come as long as that old type-and-shadow system still stood (Heb. 9:6-10). This is why Jesus prophesied to the Pharisees: "your house" would be "left to you [i.e., them] desolate" (Matt. 23:38). Then Jesus time-restricted this desolation to "come upon this generation" (Matt. 23:36; also 24:34). Many scholars agree, Jesus was talking about his contemporaries and not some future generation centuries removed, as other modern-day scholars have theorized.[24]

So here is the conundrum. If *this coming* to remove the kingdom from the Jews and the giving it to another people has not yet occurred, then the kingdom still belongs to the Jews. Likewise, if everything has not been accomplished, then the Old Covenant Law is still in effect and to be obeyed as it was in the Old Covenant times. Jesus' words are that straightforward and profound (see again Matt. 5:17-18).

Several times, Jesus spoke about this soon-coming and climactic ending . . . . He also forewarned the Jewish chief priests and the elders in the temple courts that "the kingdom of God will be taken away from you and given to another people who will produce its fruit" (Matt. 21:43).

The good news is, a strong scriptural and historical case can be made that "the coming" Jesus referred to in Matthew 21, and elsewhere, occurred precisely as and when He said it would and was expected by his contemporaries. Yet many Christians have been led to believe it has not yet happened.[25]

But, once again, please be assured, *"the historically defensible interpretation has greatest authority."*[26] It is to this task of historic defensibility we next turn.

---

[24] See Noē, *The Perfect Ending for the World*, 149-169 and Noē, *Unraveling the End*, 285-330.

[25] ibid. and more therein.

[26] Klein, Blomberg, and Hubbard, *Introduction to Biblical Interpretation*, 149.

The Long Biblical Precedent[27]

Early in his earthly ministry, Jesus announced a major change that had occurred in the Godhead. In Old Testament times, the Father was the deliverer of judgment. But Jesus divulged that the Father "has entrusted all judgment to the Son" (John 5:22). Later on, Jesus specified how this climactic ending event would happen. Twice He said He would come "on the clouds" (Matt. 24:30, 26:64). What did coming "on the clouds" mean?

If you were a 1st-century Jew raised in the synagogue, you would have known exactly what it meant. This type of coming of God in judgment had a long biblical precedent of multiple prophecies and fulfillments. To appreciate the rich Jewish terminology for cloud-coming, we must enter the mind of a 1st-century Jew. On the other hand, if we insist on looking at these things only through 21st-century eyes, we will become prisoners of what has become the traditional mindset of misunderstanding and confusion.

Christ's "coming on the clouds" is a common metaphor borrowed from Old Testament portrayals of God the Father descending from heaven and coming in power and glory to execute judgment on a people or nation. In all the historic comings of God in judgment, He acted through human armies, or through nature, to bring destruction ("the Lord is a man of war" [Exod. 15:3 KJV]). Each was a direct act of God and each was termed "the day of the Lord." They were always described with figurative language and empowered by supernatural support. These "day[s] of the Lord" brought historical calamity upon several nations and people, for example:

Isaiah 13:10, 13. *The stars of heaven and their constellations will not show their light. The rising sun will be darkened and the moon will not give its light . . . .Therefore I will make the heavens tremble; and the earth will shake from its place at the wrath of the Lord Almighty, in the day of his burning anger.*

---

[27] Much of this section was originally published in: Noē, *The Perfect Ending for the World*, 90-94, 235-237 and Noē, *Unraveling the End*, 312-320. I have made some editorial changes and additions.

Fulfillment. The prophet was *not* speaking of the end of the world, a final judgment, or a solar or lunar eclipse. He was giving a figurative prediction of the literal destruction of Babylon by the Medes in 539 B.C. (Isa. 13:1). The use of cosmic language means the Presence of God was involved and revealed in this judgment upon these people.

Isaiah 34:4. *All the stars of heaven will be dissolved and the sky rolled up like a scroll; all the starry host will fall like withered leaves from the vine, like shriveled figs from the fig tree.*
Fulfillment. This was *not* the end of the world, or the end of the cosmos, but a figurative description of the coming divine destruction of Edom in the late 6th century B.C. (Isa. 34:5).

Ezekiel 32:7, 8a. *. . . I will cover the heavens and darken their stars; I will cover the sun with a cloud, and the moon will not give its light. All the shining lights in the heavens I will darken over you.*
Fulfillment. This prophecy was God's warning to the Pharaoh of Egypt of his impending fall in the mid-6th century B.C. (Ezek. 32:2).

Nahum 1:5. *The mountains quake before him and the hills melt away. The earth trembles at his presence, the world, and all who live in it.*
Fulfillment. The subject is God's coming in judgment on the city of Nineveh, not the physical world, in 612 B.C. (Nah. 1:1).

This Old Testament pattern of figurative language usage and fulfillments by literal, divine judgments sets the precedent. If the words of these passages were to be taken literally, it would mean massive changes or destructions of the cosmos and Earth occurred numerous times. But this language transcends its literalism and has to be understood figuratively.

The Jews of Jesus' day had studied the above listed "day of the Lord" occurrences and were familiar with "cloud-coming" and "collapsing-universe phraseology, as well as the application of one with the other.[28] The Hebrew Scriptures are rich in similes and figurative

---

[28] Also, in the Old Testament, God dwelt in, or was present in, a physical and

language that poetically portray a heavenly perspective of God the Father coming among men in judgment:

- See, the Lord rides on a swift *cloud* and is coming to Egypt (Isa. 19:1). (For the earthly fulfillment, see Isa. 20:1-6).
- Look! He advances like the *clouds*, his chariots come like a whirlwind (Jer. 4:13).
- For the day is near, the day of the Lord is near—a day of *clouds*, a time of doom for the nations (Ezek. 30:3).
- Sing to God, sing praise to his name, extol him who rides on the *clouds* . . . (Psa. 68:4).
- . . . He makes the *clouds* his chariots and rides on the wings of the wind. He makes winds his messengers, flames of fire his servants (Psa. 104:3-4).
- Also see Ezek. 30:18; Psa. 18:9-12; 2 Sam. 22:10-12; Nah. 1:3; Joel 2:1-2; Zeph. 1:14-15.

With familiar cloud-coming imagery Daniel prophesied the coming of the Son of Man into heaven (Dan. 7:13). Jesus, by deriving his "coming on the clouds" phrase directly from Daniel, revealed Himself as God and the promised Messiah (Matt. 24:30; 26:64). The high priest Caiaphas immediately understood this claim of Jesus to be God and responded, "He has spoken blasphemy!" (Matt. 26:65). Jesus also applied his coming in judgment and power of war in the *same* technical way as the Father had come down from heaven many times before:

> Look! The Lord is coming from his dwelling place; he
> comes down and treads the high places of the earth (Mic.
> 1:3).

---

visible Shekhinah glory cloud. This is an entirely different matter and will not be addressed here. Our interest is how cloud phraseology was used in a symbolic manner, namely that of swiftness and power of literal judgment in both prophetic and apocalyptic eschatology. Nor will we address Acts 1:11 here – for that see Noē, *The Greater Jesus*, 46-48.

> See, the Lord is coming out of his dwelling to punish the people of the earth for their sins (Isa. 26:21).

> But your many enemies will become like fine dust, the ruthless hordes like blown chaff. Suddenly, in an instant the Lord Almighty will come with thunder and earthquake and great noise, with windstorm and tempest and flames of a devouring fire (Isa. 29:5-6).

Because of this background, Jesus' disciples would have understood what He was talking about in his Olivet Discourse. They would be the ones to "see the Son of Man coming on the clouds" (Matt. 24:30). Again, the high priest understood it. That's why he was so offended and accused Jesus of blasphemy (Matt. 26:64-65). Let us also note that Jesus made no disclaimers to change the meaning or nature of this type of coming, and neither should we (there are other types of comings).

Another important factor is that, in all these real biblical comings of God in judgment in the Old Testament, God Himself was *never physically visible*; He was unseen by human eyes!

Thus, cloud-coming is the language of divine imagery. It denotes divine action. In every instance, some humans were fully aware of God's Presence and personal intervention in those events of history. Obviously, this Jewish perspective is quite different from the way we moderns have been conditioned to think of Christ's coming on the clouds. We imagine his coming to be spectacularly visible on the tops of literal fluffy cumulus clouds transporting Him down to earth.[29] Yet every biblical instance of a cloud-coming was a real coming of God. Or were they?

This Old Testament pattern of figurative language usage and fulfillments by literal, divine judgments sets the precedent. . . . But this language transcends its literalism and has to be understood figuratively.

---

[29] To be consistent, shouldn't we also think of Him coming on a white horse (Rev. 19:11) as riding on a literal four-legged steed?

The Comings Controversy

Not surprisingly, scholars, who cannot agree on many issues regarding the kingdom, also cannot agree on how to understand these many comings of God in judgment and a "day of the Lord" in Old Testament times. Hence, opinions vary and confusion abounds.

Caveat alert: For those not accustomed to theological discourse and interaction, please skip this section. For others so accustomed, the following should be quite illuminating.

Some progressive dispensationalists, such as Craig A. Blaising and Darrell L. Bock, regard these comings as simply typological. Hence, they acknowledge that Jesus' return will be a day of the Lord that "correlates generally" with "Old Testament predictions" and "literary descriptions of God coming in wrath."[30]

For historic premillennialist Ladd, "the Day of the Lord for the prophets was *both* the immediate act of God expected in history and the ultimate eschatological visitation. . . . The two events are viewed as though they were one."[31] Therefore, Ladd concludes "God *did* act. The Day of the Lord *did* come; and yet, the Day of the Lord continued to be an eschatological event in the future." Ladd calls "this tension between the immediate and the ultimate future . . . the prophetic perspective"[32] and "the prophetic tension between history and eschatology."[33]

Classic dispensational premillennialist Showers concurs that "several times in the past, God has broken into the day of Satan and mankind with the interventions or Days of the Lord . . . . to give them a foretaste or forewarning of the ultimate Day of the Lord that will come at the end of world history."[34]

Ladd objects, however, to treating these several "day of the Lord" events in the Old Testament as "secondary eschatological interpolation." He proposes they be understood "in their context as a symbolic portrayal

---

[30] Craig A. Blaising and Darrell L. Bock, *Progressive Dispensationalism* (Grand Rapids, MI.: Baker Books, 1993), 53, 262-263.

[31] Ladd, *The Presence of the Future*, 74.

[32] Ibid., 75.

[33] Ibid., 146.

[34] Renald Showers, *Maranatha Our Lord, Come!* (Bellmawr, NJ.: The Friends of Israel Gospel Ministry, Inc., 1995), 34.

of God's judgments in history"[35] and typologically of "the future eschatological day" at "the final salvation,"[36] at "the end of the world,"[37] and at "the final consummation . . . at the end of history."[38] Thus, Ladd applies a dual usage or double fulfillment of the Old Testament term "day of the Lord" to designate "a day in the immediate historical future when God would visit his people in judgment . . . . [and] It could also designate the final visitation of God."[39]

All of this forces postmillennialist DeMar to conclude that most dispensationalists understand the Old and New Testament use of "day of the Lord . . . always has reference to the end times, specifically an interval called the 'Great Tribulation' that is in the future." But he counters: "the 'day of the Lord' is often used to refer to a time of judgment without referring to the final judgment. He further contends that it is the 'day of the Lord' any time God acts"[40] and "there could be many such days."[41]

Ironically, classic dispensational premillennialist John F. Walvoord appears to agree with DeMar. He says, "the 'day of the Lord' is an expression frequently used in both the Old and New Testaments to describe any period of time during which God exercises direct judgment on human sin. The Old Testament records a number of times when Israel endured a day of the Lord, lasting a few days or, in some cases, several years."[42]

Another Classic dispensational premillennialist, Larry Spargimino, opts for partial fulfillment. Regarding the above-cited Isaiah 13:19-20 day of the Lord prophecy about the fall of Babylon, he claims: "it is not true that the passage can be limited to the fall of Babylon in 539 B.C. . . . .

---

[35] Ladd, *The Presence of the Future*, 51.

[36] Ibid., 72.

[37] Ibid., 74.

[38] Ibid., 147.

[39] George Eldon Ladd, *A Theology of the New Testament* (Grand Rapids, MI.: Eerdmans, 1974, revised ed. 1993), 600.

[40] Gary DeMar, *Last Days Madness* (Brentwood, TN.: Wolgemuth & Hyatt, 1991), 196.

[41] Gary DeMar, *Last Days Madness,* 3rd ed. (Atlanta, GA.: American Vision, 1997), 264.

[42] John F. Walvoord, *Prophecy: 14 Essential Keys to Understanding the Final Drama* (Nashville, TN.: Thomas Nelson, 1993), 114-15.

This was definitely not fulfilled in 539 B.C. . . . [it] simply does not match all the particulars given in the prophecy of Isaiah 13 . . . . Isaiah 13 was not completely fulfilled . . . but still awaits future fulfillment."[43]

In the amillennial camp, Hoekema perceives that when the day of the Lord comes "the new heavens and new earth will be the culmination of history . . . all history is moving toward this goal."[44] The saints will live "on the new earth in the life to come."[45] In the meantime, he understands all historical judgments of God as "provisional" and part of "the ambiguity of history" awaiting the "last judgment."[46] For most amillennialists, this also includes Christ's coming in judgment in A.D. 70.

In contrast to the above ambiguity, amillennialist R.C. Sproul wisely asks: "Is it not reasonable that the doom of Jerusalem should be depicted in language as glowing and rhetorical as the destruction of Babylon, or Bozrah, or Tyre?" He cites Isaiah 13:9, 10, 13 and is impressed by the fact that "the imagery employed by Isaiah is striking in its parallel to that of the language used by Jesus in the Olivet Discourse." Sproul terms this "one of the strongest points of Russell's argument."[47] (See next paragraph.) Sproul concludes: "Scripture commonly describes the visitation of God's judgment with images of convulsion and cataclysms."[48]

Nineteenth-century preterist J. Stuart Russell summarized thusly regarding the Bible's use of this type of language in Isaiah 13:9, 10, 13: "The imagery employed in this passage is almost identical with that of our Lord. If these symbols therefore were proper to represent the fall of Babylon, why should they be improper to set forth a still greater catastrophe—the destruction of Jerusalem?"[49]

---

[43] Larry Spargimino, *The Anti-Prophets* (Oklahoma City, OK.: Hearthstone Publishing, 2000), 135-136.
[44] Hoekema, *The Bible and the Future*, 32.
[45] Ibid., 174.
[46] Ibid., 37.
[47] R.C. Sproul, *The Last Days According to Jesus* (Grand Rapids, MI.: Baker Books, 1998), 44.
[48] Ibid., 45.
[49] J. Stuart Russell, *The Parousia* (Grand Rapids, MI.: Baker Book House, from the 1887 edition issued by T. Fisher Unwin, 1983), 80.

Postmillennialist J. Marcellus Kik clings to a similar understanding about the "ideas of judgment, and apocalyptic language and style." He claims that in the New Testament "there is not a single figure ['sun, moon, and stars,' 'the son of man riding on the clouds,' 'the fig tree'] employed whose use has not been already sanctioned and its meaning determined in the Old Testament." He concludes, therefore, "all events mentioned by Christ have found their fulfillment."[50]

Postmillennialist Keith A. Mathison asserts: "the term 'coming' is used in different senses in Scripture." Hence, the Old Testament comings of the Lord "in judgment upon a particular nation . . . did not involve a literal coming of God from heaven to earth." He concludes: "the 'coming of the Lord' spoken of in James (and implied in Philippians) is a coming of Christ's judgment upon his enemies" in a similar manner. He differentiates these comings from Jesus' future, visible return to the earth, which he calls "a third kind of 'coming,'"[51]

The 'Once-More' Shaking Prediction[52]

Circa A.D. 65, the writer of Hebrews heralds an upcoming judgment of God by quoting the Old Testament prophet Haggai: "Once more I [God] will shake not only the earth but also the heavens" (Heb. 12:26b, from Hag. 2:6-7). To find what this Old Testament, *post*-exilic prophet meant by this next shaking we must discover the last time God shook the "heavens and earth."[53] This first event will serve as the precedent and type for this next shaking.

As previously demonstrated, cosmic-collapsing, light-darkening, and earth-moving apocalyptic language is employed throughout the Old

---

[50] Kik, *An Eschatology of Victory*, 156.

[51] Keith A. Mathison, *When Shall These Things Be? A Reformed Response to Hyper-Preterism* (Phillipsburg, NJ.: P&R Publishing, 2004), 201.

[52] Much of this section was originally published in Noē, *The Perfect Ending for the World*, 291-295 and Noē, *Unraveling the End*, 162. I have made some editorial changes and additions.

[53] For more on the three usages of "heaven(s) and earth" language throughout the Bible see, Noē, *The Perfect Ending for the World*, 286-291 and Noē, *Unraveling the End*, 155-160.

Testament to vividly portray and prophesy an impending "day of the Lord," when God would pour out his judgment on a wicked nation or people. But once God specifically warned through Isaiah, a *pre*-exilic prophet, "Therefore I will shake the heavens, and the earth shall remove out of her place, in the wrath of the LORD of hosts, and in the day of his fierce anger" (Isa. 13:13 KJV).

This *pre*-exilic shaking and removing prophecy chronologically preceded Haggai's *post*-exilic, "once more" shaking prophecy. Its drastic language is employed to show the greatness and completeness of these two judgments. As we have seen, the immediate historical setting for the fulfillment of the Isaiah 13:13 prophecy was God's overthrow and desolation of the Babylonians (see Isa. 13:1, 19-22). Previously, God had foretold through the prophet Habakkuk that He would use the Babylonians to bring chastening upon Judah (the southern kingdom of Israel) to destroy Jerusalem and the Temple and to deport many Jews into captivity (Hab. 1:5-11). This occurred in the 6th century B.C.

Hence, this first prophesied "shake" and "remove" judgment of Isaiah 13 was to come against those same Babylonians (Isa. 47:5-10; Jer. 51:6-10; Zeph. 1-3; Hos. 11:5; Amos 6:14; 9:8-10). With God's divine assistance, the Persian army was to be God's next instrument of judgment. It defeated the Babylonians, laid waste to their country, and took over the Babylonian Empire. Afterwards Cyrus, the Persian king, released the captive Jews to return to their land. The Jews then rebuilt their capital city and the Temple and reinstituted the practices of biblical Judaism.

As devastating as that 587 B.C. fall of Jerusalem and ensuing 70 years of Babylonian captivity were for the Jewish people, they were only temporary and mild desolations compared to the greater, cataclysmic judgment yet to come. Furthermore, God's shaking and removal of Babylon was to serve as the *precedent* and *type* for that future, "once more" shaking and age-ending judgment of Old Covenant Israel. This prior and divine judgment of Babylon was well ingrained in 1st-century Jewish thought and remembrance.

Early in Israel's history, God had promised that, as long as his (chosen) people kept the covenant, He would bless and protect this nation more than any other. On the other hand, if they broke the covenant, He would withdraw his protective presence, chasten, and scatter his people (Lev. 26:14-39; Deut. 28:15-68). Over the course of

Jewish history a cycle of apostasy, oppression, repentance, and deliverance was repeated numerous times, and, as a result of this perpetual, national disobedience, Israel's sin mounted. That is why Jesus not only borrowed the same "shake" judgment language of the Prophets (Matt. 24:29 from Isa. 13:10; 34:4) but confirmed another of Isaiah's prophecies by saying Israel would "fill up, then, the measure of the sin of your forefathers" (Matt. 23:32; Isa. 65:6-19). This "filling up" would include the rejection of Jesus as the Messiah and the kingdom He was offering. When full, Haggai's prophesied "once more" shaking judgment would come—but this time that judgment would fall upon the Jews.

The Jewish writer of the New Testament book of Hebrews (probably the Apostle Paul) readily made this connection. Again, writing circa A.D. 65, he warned his readers that he and they were living in "the last days" of which Haggai had prophesied (Heb. 1:2). He quoted Haggai directly and referred to the last major judgment of God upon the Jewish people (Heb. 12:5-7, 25, 26 [i.e., the 587 B.C. destruction of Jerusalem and subsequent 70 years of Babylonian captivity]), but he emphasized the imminency and permanency of this second "once more" shaking prophecy and judgment. Here is how he put it: "At that time his voice shook the earth, but now he has promised, 'Once more I will shake not only the earth but also the heavens' [from Haggai 2:6]. The words 'once more' indicated the removing of what can be shaken—that is, created things—so that what cannot be shaken may remain" (Heb. 12:26-27).

Clearly, the writer of Hebrews tells us that to shake what can be shaken signifies removing it. Elsewhere, the Apostle Paul taught the Jews the same thing—that their "world" in its present form was passing away (1 Cor. 7:31; also 1 John 2:17). In Acts 13:40-41, Paul quoted directly from Habakkuk 1:5 and cited God's previous punishment of Israel through the Babylonians some 600 years earlier. He warned that this type of divine judgment was about to come upon them. No doubt, this was one of the reasons the Jews in Asia later accused Paul, saying: "This is the man who teaches all men everywhere against our people and our law and this place" (Acts 21:28).

Indeed, Old Covenant Israel was facing judgment, again, and a massive judgment was forthcoming. Not only was God going to "shake" and "remove" the Judaic "heavens and earth" world (Isa. 51:13-16 KJV). He was never going to bring them back. Instead, He promised to supersede their kingdom with that which "cannot be shaken." And what was that? The writer of Hebrews explains that it was the new kingdom of God, a kingdom that was already breaking into human history. "Therefore, since we are receiving a kingdom [then and there] that cannot be shaken, let us be thankful, and so worship God acceptably with reverence and awe" (Heb. 12:28).

Obviously, this second, "once more" shaking was not a promise or prophecy to shake and remove the physical creation. Not one shred of evidence exists that these early Christians expected a destruction of the planet, an end to the cosmos, or the termination of human existence.[54] Instead, God, in total consistency with the prophetic pattern of divine judgment upon nations in Old Testament times, and in line with the prefigured "shaking" and "removing" of the Babylonian "heavens and earth" via the Persian armies, was about to pour out this second judgment. But this time it was to fall upon a rebellious and apostate Jerusalem.

Not only was God going to "shake" and "remove" the Judaic "heavens and earth" world (Isa. 51:13-16 KJV); He was never going to bring them back.

So it happened in that 1st-century time period precisely as prophesied. "The saints of the Most High will [were] "receive[ing] the kingdom and will [would] possess it forever – yes, for ever and ever" (Dan. 7:18). It would "not pass away" and "never be destroyed" (Dan. 7:13). This "everlasting dominion" (Dan. 7:14) was being "handed over" to them, then and there (Dan. 7:27), and "they possessed the kingdom" (Dan. 7:22).

The writer of Hebrews also emphasized the nearness of this consummating event. He wrote, "in just a very very little while, He who is coming will come and will not delay" (Heb. 10:37).[55] Most preterist, amillennial and postmillennial scholars affirm that Christ came, as

---

[54] For more on the everlasting nature of the physical earth and cosmos see, Noē, *The Perfect Ending for the World*, 86-90, and Noē, *Unraveling the End*, 151-155.

[55] In the Greek the word "very" is repeated here giving this phrase a double intensification of imminency missed by most, if not all, English translations.

expected, and violently shook and removed that Jewish world (heaven and earth) circa A.D. 70, just as He had told them it would happen. "When you see Jerusalem surrounded by armies, you will know that its desolation is near . . . . For this is [was] the time of punishment [vengeance] in fulfillment of all that has been written" (Luke 21:20, 22). "Fulfillment of all that has been written" means the fulfillment of everything promised in the Old Testament (see Luke 24:44; 18:31; Acts 3:24; Rom. 15:3-4).

This is why Peter wrote in A.D. 65-67, "The end of all things is at hand . . . . For it is time for judgment to begin with the family [at the house] of God" (1 Pet. 4:7, 17); and John in A.D. 67-68 insisted, "Little children, this is the last hour . . . it is the last hour" (1 John 2:18). Likewise, Paul, writing in A.D. 57, added this quantifiable and comparative time statement, "And do this, understanding the present time [back then]. . . . because our salvation is nearer now than when we first believed" (Rom. 13:11). Let's do the math. Paul and those to whom he was writing had first believed 20 to 30 years prior. But at that "present time" it was only nine years before Jerusalem would be surrounded by armies for the first of four times and only 13 years before its total destruction and desolation (see Luke 21:20-28).[56]

Therefore, at just the right time, the old Jewish institutions were shaken to the ground, totally removed, and never to rise again, just as Daniel had prophesied would happen at "the time of the end" (Dan. 12:4), "when the power of the holy people" would be "finally broken" and "all things will be completed" (Dan. 12:7). All these prophecies, and many more, were perfectly and precisely fulfilled when the Roman armies, empowered by God, shook, removed, and left desolate the Temple, the city of Jerusalem, and the whole world of biblical Judaism.

Many biblical scholars agree that this was the historical setting for Christ's "coming on the clouds." The impressive parallelism, precedent, and typology of God's similar coming and "shaking" judgment upon the Babylonians must not be missed. In the New Testament, Jesus had employed the same figure of speech for his prophecies. Thus for Jesus and a 1st-century Jew, coming "on the clouds" was not a claim to come visibly to the human eye.

---

[56] For more, see "Intensification of Nearness Language" in Noē, *Unraveling the End*, 240-248.

With this understanding, one can "see" the Lord Jesus coming in judgment in the events of the Roman-Jewish War and the destruction of Jerusalem circa A.D. 70. Just as the cloud-coming Jehovah God came in Old Testament times, Jesus came "on the clouds," "in his Father's glory" (Matt. 16:27; Mark 8:38; Luke 9:26) as and when He said He would—in "this generation" (Matt. 23:36; 24:34; also 10:23; 16:28; 26:64; John 21:22).[57] In keeping with the Old Testament pattern for this type of coming of Deity, He was not physically seen.

Is it any wonder, then, that when the elders and teachers of the law seized Stephen and brought forth false witnesses, they claimed, "This man never stops speaking against the holy place and against the law. For we have heard him say that this Jesus of Nazareth will destroy this place and change the customs Moses handed down to us" (Acts 6:13-14). And Jesus did just that in a day of the Lord in age-ending judgment at the fall of Jerusalem circa A.D. 70.

Another important fact reflected in this climactic judgment event is the change of covenant. Therefore, "the day of the Lord" (Jehovah) of the Old Testament became "the day of Christ" (*Christos* 2 Thess. 2:2; *kurios* 2 Pet. 3:10) in the New Testament.

Was A.D. 70 Really a Coming of Jesus?

Caveat alert: Again, for those not accustomed to theological discourse and interaction, please skip this section. For others so accustomed, the following should be quite illuminating.

Once again and not surprisingly, scholarly opinions vary and confusion abounds—i.e., "yes it is; no it isn't!" Shockingly, the respected C.S. Lewis even termed Jesus' time-restrictive statement in Matthew 24:34 about his eschatological coming in judgment within his "this

---

[57] A discussion of interpretive differences surrounding these passages is beyond the scope of this book. For more see Noē, *Beyond the End Times*, 113-129; 171-176

generation," as "the most embarrassing verse in the Bible" and an "exhibition of error."[58]

To the contrary, preterist scholars advocate that A.D. 70 was not only the coming of Jesus Christ "on the clouds" in judgment, but was also his promised return and second coming (*parousia*). Citing Matthew 24, Mark 13, and Luke 21, they insist that Jesus' *parousia* was the chief event within Jesus' "all these things" and time-restricted in its occurrence—"I tell you the truth, this generation will certainly not pass away until all these things have happened" (Matt. 24:34; Mark 13:30; Luke 21:32).

Nineteenth-century preterist J. Stuart Russell in his classic book, *The Parousia* (1887), emphasized: "the Parousia, or 'coming of the Lord'" is "the great theme of New Testament prophecy." He critically lamented, however, that this one-time, single, and past-fulfilled event has been "obscured by traditional prejudices, or misinterpreted by an erroneous exegesis."[59]

Preterist Milton S. Terry, whose 19th-century book, *Biblical Hermeneutics*, was the textbook of choice for most seminaries through the 1970s, agreed with Russell and admonished, "It is quite easy for men to become 'wise above what is written,'" and to accept "as essential Christian doctrine [things] which in fact are without sufficient warrant in the Scriptures."[60] He further insisted that making words like "near," "at hand," and other "explicit designations of time" mean "ages hence, or after a long time" is "a reprehensible abuse" and "even worse than the theory of double sense."[61]

While Terry conceded that "the judgment of Babylon, or Nineveh, or Jerusalem may, indeed, be a type of every other similar judgment," he held: "this is very different from saying that the language in which that judgment was predicted was fulfilled only partially . . . and is yet awaiting its complete fulfillment." He also warned that "double sense"

---

[58] C.S. Lewis, essay "The World's Last Night" (1960), found in *The Essential C.S. Lewis*, Lyle W. Dorsett, ed., (New York, NY.: A Touchstone Book, Simon & Schuster, 1996), 385.

[59] Russell, *The Parousia, viii*.

[60] Milton S. Terry, *Biblical Hermeneutics* (Eugene, OR.: Wipf and Stock Publishers, 1890, 1999), 455.

[61] Ibid., 385-386.

meanings "introduce an element of uncertainty and confusion into biblical interpretation."[62]

Amillennialist N.T. Wright, likewise, seems to take a full preterist position as he concludes about Matthew 24, "The whole passage seems to me (a) to refer clearly to the forthcoming destruction of Jerusalem, and (b) to invest that event with its theological significance."[63] He later characterizes this event as "the necessary and predictable focal point of Jesus' whole prophetic ministry"[64] and as the "'coming' of YHWH, and the final arrival of the divine kingdom' in fulfillment of Zechariah 14."[65] Wright further reminds his readers that this coming of Jesus in judgment "was conceived in classic scriptural terms: invasion and destruction by foreign armies . . . . Assyria and Babylon had been instruments of YHWH's wrath before; now it would be the turn of Rome."[66]

Classical dispensational premillennialist Ryrie totally disagrees. He contends: "the Roman conquest of Jerusalem was only a preview of what will take place in a future day . . . . Jesus used the predictions of A.D. 70 as a kind of springboard to more distant happenings."[67] Ryrie's typology also corresponds with the so-called "law of double reference" or double fulfillment. As Ryrie explains, "a prophecy may have a double fulfillment—one in the immediate circumstances and time of the prophet, and another in the distant future."[68] But Ryrie's diluting tactic is highly problematic. For example, if we allow double fulfillment, by what hermeneutic do we disallow triple, even quadruple fulfillment? And if double here, why not double also for the cross?

Another classical dispensationalist, Spargimino, while acknowledging that "the destruction of Jerusalem was undoubtedly God's judgment on that hard-hearted and evil generation,"[69] insists that

---

[62] Ibid., 385.

[63] N.T. Wright, *Jesus and the Victory of God*, Vol. 2 (London, Great Britain: Society for Promoting Christian Knowledge, 1996), 342.

[64] Ibid., 344.

[65] Ibid., 345.

[66] Ibid., 336.

[67] Charles C. Ryrie, *The Best Is Yet to Come* (Chicago, IL.: Moody Press, 1981), 20.

[68] Charles C. Ryrie, *The Final Countdown* (Wheaton, IL.: Victor Books, 1982), 18.

[69] Spargimino, *The Anti-Prophets*, 119-120.

"Matthew 24:29-31 [the signs] is to be taken literally of future cataclysmic events. This language cannot be referred to A.D. 70."[70] Instead, it speaks of the "catastrophic end of the world" and not "simply about the end of the Old Testament sacrificial system."[71]

Postmillennialist DeMar challenges Spargimino's notion by arguing that if his understanding is correct, "how could the Thessalonians have thought that it had already come?" He rebukes this futuristic idea of the "day of the Lord" destroying the physical heavens and earth as an application of "specialized meaning."[72]

Historic premillennialist Ladd, on the other hand, recognizes that "the fall of Jerusalem and the destruction of the Jewish state was a manifestation of God's judgment in righteous wrath." But he maintains a typological understanding insisting this judgment points "to a day when the wrath of God will find its fullest manifestation in a supernatural manifestation which will issue in the final condemnation and just punishment of all wickedness and evil. The second coming of Christ . . . will mean a visitation of wrath."[73] But this "final Tribulation will be the most fearful the world has ever seen" and "the difference will be quantitative and not qualitative." He rebuffs his pretribulational colleagues, however, by reminding his readers: "God's people have always suffered persecution, tribulation." In classic premillennial, post-tribulational form he appropriately asks, "Why should God do something for the Church at the end of the age when He has never done it before?"[74]

Ladd goes on to differentiate "the parallel account in Luke 21:20-24," which he maintains does describe "a siege of Jerusalem and a historical judgment upon the Jewish people," from similar accounts in Mark 13:14-20 and Matthew 24:15-22. For Ladd, they are "quite different." While Mark's account "is not exclusively eschatological," Matthew's is "blended in a form impossible for us to recover."[75] He

---

[70] Ibid., 138.

[71] Ibid., 146.

[72] DeMar, *Last Days Madness*, 3rd ed., 265.

[73] George Eldon Ladd, *The Blessed Hope* (Grand Rapids, Ml.: Eerdmans, 1956), 124.

[74] Ibid., 128.

[75] Ladd, *The Presence of the Future*, 310.

recommends we "must allow for a double reference, for the mingling of historical and eschatological."[76]

For postmillennialist Kik, the descriptive terms in Jesus' Olivet discourse "would seem to indicate a catastrophic end of the earth. And yet when this passage is studied in the light of prophetic language and pronouncements it can readily be that it is descriptive of the passing away of Judaism."[77]

He also reminds his readers that this type of apocalyptic language was "well known to the discerning reader of Old Testament Scripture" and that "Jesus would describe this catastrophe through the use of scriptural symbols well known to the Jews."[78] He contrasts the popular literal understanding of this "almost verbatim" language from the Old Testament on the part of many modern-day interpreters today as resulting from "too little study of Old Testament ideas of judgment, and apocalyptic language and style, would seem to be the main reason for this one sided exegesis."[79]

In a similar fashion, postmillennialist Seraiah claims that A.D. 70 was only a "temporal judgment on the Jews who crucified Christ." This was not the "eternal judgment at the end of all things."[80] That "final Judgment Day will be experienced by everyone who ever lived . . . . the Last Judgment at the end of the world."[81] To support his bifurcated future day of judgment he cites Acts 17:31, Romans 14:10-11, and 2 Corinthians 5:10. For verses that "focus on the condemnation in the first century . . . upon the Jews," he cites Matthew 3:7-10, 17:17, Mark 8:38, Luke 21:22-23, 35, and Acts 2:22-23, 40.[82] He concludes: "the references to universal judgment make no sense in the context of a punishment on the apostate Jews of the first century."[83] But he allows that A.D. 70 was a "coming" of Christ "in judgment."[84] He looks forward to "a coming of

---

[76] Ibid., 311.
[77] Kik, *An Eschatology of Victory*, 127-128.
[78] Ibid., 128.
[79] Ibid., 135.
[80] C. Jonathin Seraiah, *The End of All Things: A Defense of Futurism* (Moscow, ID.: Canon Press, 1999), 68-69.
[81] Ibid., 70.
[82] Ibid., 73-74.
[83] Ibid., 74.
[84] Ibid., 76-77.

Christ, a Judgment, and a Resurrection that include everyone who ever lived and bring an end to this physical world."[85] According to him, this will all occur at the unscriptural "end of time."[86]

Postmillennialist Gentry takes a different tack. While acknowledging that "this cloud-coming of Christ in judgment [in A.D. 70] is reminiscent of Old Testament cloud-comings of God in judgment upon ancient historical people and nations,"[87] he adds: "it is not necessary that it refer to His final, Second Adventental coming to end history."[88] In another book he elaborates: "nowhere in Scripture are we expressly informed that A.D. 70 is a type." Gentry calls this idea an "(unwarranted) theological implication." The bigger problem for Gentry, however, seems to be "the several times A.D. 70 prophecies occur in conjunction with second advent material." He cites Matthew 24:3-34/24:36ff and 2 Thessalonians 1:7-10/2:1-10.[89]

Amillennialist, Hoekema partially agrees with Gentry but sees "the destruction of Jerusalem" as "a type of the end of the world,"[90] which will not happen "until the end of time."[91]

Paradoxically, the Bible never mentions an "end of time"—only a "time of the end." Big difference! Therefore, and as we can see from above, scholarly confusion, disagreement, and ambiguity abound.

R.C. Sproul's Better View of A.D. 70 Events

Amillennialist and partial preterist, R.C. Sproul, chides many of the above scholars in writing that "no matter what view of eschatology we embrace, we must take seriously the redemptive-historical importance of Jerusalem's destruction in A.D. 70."[92] He insists:

---

[85] Ibid., 77.

[86] Ibid., 114.

[87] Gentry, Jr., *He Shall Have Dominion*, 398-399.

[88] Ibid, 399.

[89] Gentry, Jr., *Thine Is the Kingdom*, 160.

[90] Hoekema, *The Bible and the Future*, 115.

[91] Ibid., 116.

[92] Sproul, *The Last Days According to Jesus*, 26.

This event certainly spelled the end of a crucial redemptive-historical epoch. It must be viewed as the end of some age. It also represents a significant visitation of the Lord in judgment and a vitally important 'day of the Lord.' Whether this was the *only* day of the Lord about which Scripture speaks remains a major point of controversy among preterists.[93]

Sproul's partial preterist position is in harmony with most amillenialist, postmillennialist, and some premillennialist scholars as he insists that the coming of Christ in A.D. 70 was "*a* parousia or coming of Christ . . . not *the* parousia."[94] Hence, Sproul gives A.D. 70 some redemptive significance. But he ends up with a both/and or dual aspect model of fulfillment. He looks ahead for a final or second *parousia* coming at the unscriptural "end of time" and "end of history" that will be universal in scope. Nevertheless, Sproul is still "convinced that the substance of the Olivet Discourse was fulfilled in A.D. 70 and that the bulk of Revelation was likewise fulfilled in that time frame."[95]

Conclusions

Sad to say, confusion, disagreement, and ambiguity surround the coming of the fully established and everlasting, eschatological kingdom of God. Surely, its arrival was a singular event that transpired "in the days of those kings" exactly as prophesied (Dan. 2:44; 7:17-18, 22, 27-28; Isa. 9:6-7). No future kingdom or upgraded version thereof is promised in Scripture. Ladd and many others, are scripturally and historically in error when they continue to look to the future for the "perfect establishment of God's rule in the world"[96] and insist "it is present, though in its full reality and manifestation it is still future."[97]

Controversy also surrounds R.C. Sproul's above understanding that A.D. 70 was at least "a coming" of Jesus in judgment when "the sovereignty, power and greatness of the kingdom under the whole

---

[93] Ibid., 203.
[94] Ibid., 158.
[95] Ibid., 170.
[96] Ladd, *The Presence of the Future*, 137.
[97] Ibid., 202.

heaven will be [was] handed over to the saints, the people of the Most High [Jew and Gentile, alike]" (Dan. 7:27; also see again, Matt. 21:40, 43; Heb. 10:37). I further suggest this was also the time the saints of the Most High took full possession of and sole authority for the everlasting form of the kingdom of God (Dan. 7:22). And according to Daniel, this was "the end of the matter" (Dan. 7:28a).

But at least with Sproul's partial perspective, we can see a coming of Jesus and his kingdom in power, coinciding with the removal of the old, obsolete kingdom order (Heb. 8:13; 9:8-10), the leaving it desolate (Matt. 23:38), and the giving of the new form of the kingdom to a new people (Matt. 21:43, 45; 5:17-19; 1 Pet. 2:9).

I'm convinced, nonetheless, that like everything else in God's plan of redemption, it occurred "at just the right time" (Rom. 5:6), precisely as and when prophesied "in the days of those kings" (Dan. 2:44), which ended in A.D. 476, and the "time of the end" (Dan. 12:4, 7). These are not events awaiting some unscriptural "end of time." The completion of God's plan of redemption via this completed change of covenants is what eschatology and the biblical end times were all about. They are not about a change of cosmos, even though cosmic collapsing and shaking language was used to figuratively portray this significance. As we have seen, apocalyptic language had a long history of use and fulfillment. That precedent sets the stage for this fulfillment circa A.D. 70. We must honor, respect, and adhere to this long demonstrated use and fulfillment of apocalyptic language.

Furthermore, no verse of Scripture ever states that the kingdom is to be given back to Israel, or to the Jews, or to be reestablished there someday in the future. It was taken away from them. Hence, Glasser accurately summarizes: "God did not intend Israel to be an end in itself." Instead, "Israel was to be God's means to worldwide blessing."[98]

But without Sproul's partial understanding above, we would be forced to conclude, with the majority of premillennialists—most of whom do not view A.D. 70 as any kind of coming of Christ—that the kingdom still belongs to the Jews (Matt. 21:43). Fortunately, by comparing Jesus' use of apocalyptic language with the language of the Prophets and the long biblical precedent of a coming "day of the Lord," a

---

[98] Glasser, *Announcing the Kingdom*, 322.

strong scriptural and historical case can be made that Jesus did come, exactly as and when He said He would circa A.D. 70.

Of course, other eschatological views do not recognize Christ's Messianic work as being finished circa A.D. 70 and that type and shadow system being abolished forever. Some claim his work was finished at the cross, citing Jesus' statement, "it is finished" (John 19:30). Obviously, however, much more remained unfinished at that time.[99] Most say Jesus' work is still not finished and He must return to finish the job. But I maintain to the contrary that the historical desolation of 1st-century Jerusalem and the temple system perfectly correlates with Daniel's defining characteristic and historical setting of the biblical "time of the end" (again, not the non- and un-scriptural phrase "end of time"). It would be "when the power of the Holy people [the Jews] has been finally broken, all these things will be completed" (Dan. 12:4, 7b; also see Luke 19:43-44 and many more). That's exactly what happened, eschatologically and historically, circa A.D. 70.

. . . like everything else in God's plan of redemption, it occurred "at just the right time" (Rom. 5:6), precisely as and when prophesied . . .

Let's also add, to all this, the fulfillment hermeneutic of Jesus. Emphatically, Jesus told his disciples: "when you [them back then] see Jerusalem surrounded by armies, you will know that its desolation is near. . . . For this is the time of punishment in fulfillment of all that has been written" (Luke 21:20, 22). "All that has been written" was the entire Old Testament. And there is no new prophecy in the New Testament; only elaborations and amplifications (Acts 26:22b).

Therefore, I submit that Jesus did come "in his Father's glory" (Matt. 16:27; Mark 8:38; Luke 9:26), exactly as Jehovah God had come many times before in day-of-the-Lord judgments, in exactly the same *way* ("on the clouds"), for exactly the same *purpose* (judgment), to accomplish exactly the same *thing* (destruction of a nation), and using exactly the same *instrumentality* (a foreign army).

---

[99] See Noë, *The Perfect Ending for the World*, 243-246.

Surely, the realizations we've covered so far in this book will necessitate a paradigm shift away from the all-too-popular doom and defeatist views, as well as the schizophrenic lifestyles and other pathologies they produce. But since I have written extensively about the fulfillment of these prophecies, the fulfillment of the rest of end-time prophecy, its perfect harmonization with the expectations of the 1st-century Church (which God was affirming with signs, wonders, miracles, and gifts of the Holy Spirit) and have presented therein a "historically defensible interpretation,"[100] I'll defer on duplicating that material.[101]

But What about the 'Return' and 'Second Coming'?

If Jesus came exactly *as* and *when* He said He would and exactly *as* and *when* He was expected circa A.D. 70, was this coming his so-called "return" and/or "second coming?" I also have written extensively on this much-confused and divisive issue. So I won't duplicate that here. But I will cite one revealing admission that says it all. It's in the form of a quote from the renowned theologian George Eldon Ladd. In his highly acclaimed book, *The Blessed Hope*, he acknowledged something quite important: "The words 'return' and 'second coming' are not properly speaking Biblical words in that the two words do not represent any equivalent Greek words."[102]   This is a huge admission with massive implications.

So why aren't these two expressions used in Scripture in direct association with Jesus? Because they are totally inappropriate. The biblical testimony is that of many comings of Jesus—different types, for different purposes, at different times, to different people. They run like a thread throughout both the Old and New Testaments. Moreover, there are promises for many more countless comings. Regarding a "return," even

---

[100] Klein, Blomberg, and Hubbard, *Introduction to Biblical Interpretation*, 149.
[101] For more, especially see Noē, *The Perfect Ending for the World,* Noē, *Unraveling the End*, and Noē, *The Greater Jesus.*
[102] Ladd, *The Blessed Hope*, 69. Unfortunately, Ladd ignored his own and valid biblical insight by continuing to use these non-scriptural expressions and unscriptural concepts.

Jesus today in his omnipresence cannot return to a place He never left, as He said (Matt. 28:20; 18:20; and more). So what part of "Immanuel—which means, God with us" (Matt 1:23)—have we failed to understand?

Most everyone recognizes that words matter and wording is important. And for centuries, we Christians have been hamstrung with these two non-scriptural expressions. But for these reasons cited above, and more, we'd be well-advised to purge these non-scriptural expressions, limiting, and reductionist concepts from our faith, theologies, and usage.[103]

On to Step #3

Without a doubt, the implications of our kingdom-reclamation and restoration Steps #1 and #2, presented in this and the last chapter, are enormous. Ever since the everlasting kingdom of God arrived in human history in that 1st century fully established, it has been ever-increasing. The fact you are reading this book some 6,000 miles and almost 2,000 years distance from where and when all these events took place is further evidence of the kingdom's increase.

Sadly, the kingdom Jesus brought to this earth has suffered great violence, primarily from the hands of fellow Christians. Therefore, in our next chapter (Step #3 of 5), we shall further ground the kingdom's present-day nature and status, post A.D. 70. In the meantime, one thing is for sure: Without a fuller understanding of these two realities, in modern-day terms, we shall not be able to adequately comprehend or earnestly "contend for the faith that was once for all delivered to the saints" (Jude 3). So if you are ready for more, let's get to it.

. . . I submit that Jesus did come "in his Father's glory" . . . exactly as Jehovah God had come many times before in day-of-the-Lord judgments . . . .

---

[103] For much more, see Noë, *Unraveling the End*, 249-284 and Noë, *The Greater Jesus*, 21-56.

Chapter 10

Step #3 – The Present-day Nature and Under-realized Status[1]

. . . contend for the faith that was
once for all delivered to the saints (Jude 3b).

T he nature of the kingdom of God, as Jesus presented it, was so radically different from and offensive to what the Jews were expecting, they crucified Him for it. *It is equally different and offensive today.* Paradoxically, this insightful characterization of the nature of Jesus' kingdom comes from a non-Christian—H. G. Wells, in his 1922 book, *A Short History of the World*:

> The doctrine of the Kingdom of Heaven, which was the main teaching of Jesus, is certainly one of the most revolutionary doctrines that ever stirred and changed human thought. It is small wonder if the world of that time failed to grasp its full significance, and recoiled in dismay from even a half apprehension of its tremendous challenges to the established habits and institutions of mankind . . . . as Jesus seems to have preached it, was no less than a bold and uncompromising demand for a complete change and cleansing of the life of our struggling race,

---

[1] Much of this chapter was originally presented as a theological paper at the 57th Annual Meeting of the Evangelical Theological Society in Valley Forge, Pennsylvania, November 16-18, 2005.

an utter cleansing, without and within . . . . It was not merely a moral and a social revolution . . . his teaching had a political bent of the plainest sort. It is true that he said his kingdom was not of this world, that it was in the hearts of men . . . but it is equally clear that . . . the outer world would be in that measure revolutionized and made new. . . .

Is it any wonder that all who were rich and prosperous felt a horror of strange things . . . . Is it any wonder that men were dazzled and blinded and cried out against him? Even his disciples cried out when he would not spare them the light. Is it any wonder that the priests realized that between this man and themselves there was no choice but that he or priestcraft should perish? Is it any wonder that the Roman soldiers . . . should take refuge in wild laughter, and crown him with thorns and robe him in purple and make a mock Caesar of him? For to take him seriously was to enter upon a strange and alarming life, to abandon habits, to control instincts and impulses, to essay an incredible happiness.[2]

False Expectations

The two great works of the Messiah were that of the kingdom and that of salvation, in that order. Again, that's how Jesus announced them; that's how Jesus' accomplished them. Neither can be separated from the other. Yet they are distinctive. But the Pharisees of Jesus' day failed to understand the nature of his kingdom.

Munroe again hits the proverbial nail on the head when he points out: "unfortunately, most of us do not really understand what Jesus meant when He spoke of the Kingdom."[3] But Jesus never defined what He meant by the kingdom. If He had, it surely would have alleviated much of our modern-day ignorance, confusion, and speculation. In that 1st century, the Jews were looking for their Messiah to bring a political kingdom, one that would overthrow the hated Romans and make the Jews supreme over all nations. Likewise today, many Christians are looking for a similar-natured kingdom still to come. But Jesus did not offer that kind of kingdom.

---

[2] H.G. Wells, *A Short History of the World*, Chapter XXXVII on Great Books Online, www.bartleby.com. October 27, 2005.
[3] Munroe, *Rediscovering the Kingdom*, 123.

At the root of most misconceptions and misunderstandings of his kingdom is a lack of knowledge of the time of its establishment, the nature of its arrival, and its ongoing nature. But Jesus provided them and us today with something better than a definition. He taught, clarified, modeled, trained, warned, conferred, and commanded regarding the nature of his fully established, everlasting, and ever-increasing kingdom. And He introduced the opportunity for entering it.

In this chapter, we shall explore more closely the nature of his kingdom so we can better proclaim it, preach it, and practice it. As you are about to experience, "Christianity is more than a faith. It is the Kingdom of God, ruled by a king, Jesus Christ."[4]

He Taught about Its Nature

As we saw in Chapter 9, and beginning with the Beatitudes and the Sermon on the Mount (Matt. 5-7), Jesus taught his disciples about the nature of the kingdom and what life in it was all about. He didn't say, "I think" or "we may suppose." Nor did He quote other learned men. He spoke with certainty and authority, as One Who knew. And the people of his day were astonished (Matt. 7:29). Through many kingdom parables and discourses, He taught about its personal and public nature, and its many aspects and multi-faceted attributes, by saying, "the kingdom is like . . . ." The operative word here is, *is*—not *was* (past tense) or *will* someday be (future tense). Jesus was saying, there and then, the kingdom *is* a glorious, present-day, available reality.

As "He went about all Galilee, teaching in their synagogues and preaching the gospel of the kingdom" (Matt. 4:23), Jesus taught that his kingdom was "not of this world" (John 18:36). Regrettably, many today have misunderstood this verse to mean that his kingdom does not belong to nor has anything to do with this world. But the Greek preposition "ek" also can mean "from" or "out of." In other words, the source of the kingdom is not from this world. It's derived *from God* in heaven and is *for* this world. And, as we have seen, at that point in redemptive history the kingdom in its fullness was standing right there "in your midst" and yet "does not come with observation" (Luke 17:20-21). He even claimed

---

[4] Rushdoony, *In His Service*, 190.

that his kingdom was the "key to knowledge" (Luke 11:52; also see Matt. 23:13) and could dramatically change things for the better, internally and externally, in every arena of life.

Toward the end of his earthly ministry, Jesus astonished the chief priests and elders when He told them the kingdom of God would be taken away from them and "given to another people who would produce its fruit" (Matt. 21:43). These and many other statements tell us a great deal about the nature of his kingdom. Significantly, each statement was a direct affront to the prevailing mindset of Judaism and the expectations of the Old Covenant age. Yet He taught them "as much as they could understand" (Mark 4:33).

The closing sentence from the Lord's Prayer in Matthew 6 (not in the earliest manuscripts but added later by the Church) underscores Jesus' "is-ness" understanding. "For thine *is* the kingdom, and *(is)* the power and *(is)* the glory, forever, Amen" (Matt. 6:13 *KJV*). The word "is" is a present active indicative in the original language and thus emphasizes a continuous present activity, not only for the kingdom, but also for its "power" and "glory."

Jesus also amazed them by declaring: "You are the salt of the earth" (Matt. 7:13a), and "You are the light of the world" (Matt. 7:14a). What must they have been thinking about that? How do you think we should be thinking about that today?

He Clarified Who Would Receive and Who Wouldn't

In the parable of the sower, Jesus revealed: "when anyone hears the message about the kingdom and does not understand it, the evil one comes and snatches away what was sown in his heart." He next identified four types of soil into which the kingdom would be sown. These soils refer to four different types of people and their responses to the kingdom. Only one of the four soils was deemed "good soil" in which the teaching of the kingdom takes root. According to Jesus, this parable applies to "anyone." That means it applied to anyone back then and there and, arguably, to both Christians and non-Christians today.

1) **The seed that fell on the path and was eaten by the birds:** These are the people who hear the teachings of the kingdom of God and witness its works, but the evil one snatches the teaching up before it has

a chance to have impact. Perhaps this non-receptivity results because of the deceitfulness of riches or the desire for other material things.

2) **The seed that fell on the rocky places:** This is the person who listens intently, receives it with joy, but never sets down roots. Hence, when any kind of test or hard times come, that person forsakes the teaching of the kingdom and falls away.

3) **The seed sown among the thorns:** This represents the person who hears the teaching about the kingdom but is pulled away by the worries of the world and other distractions.

4) **The seed sown on the good soil:** This person, hears, understands, and acts upon it. This soil bears good fruit.

Let's apply this parable to us today. What kind of soil are you? According to Jesus, only one type of soil (type of person) who hears the teaching about the kingdom of God ultimately responds positively and lives out that kingdom teaching. Apparently, the majority will not "seek first his kingdom and his righteousness" (Matt. 6:33). So if that was true in Jesus' day and time, how about today? What do you put first? If that is not the kingdom, then according to this parable, you will be missing out. But if we accept Jesus' invitation and seek first his kingdom and his righteousness/justice, much is promised. And those blessings impact you and me and every life around us—as well as provide an inexhaustible storehouse of wisdom, grace, power, hope, and destiny.[5]

Unfortunately, today only some Christians are good soil for the kingdom. That's because so many have been contaminated by the traditions of men and lulled into watered-down versions of our faith. Indeed, these four soils represent a sobering critique of contemporary Christianity and the church. Carter characterizes it like this:

> Christendom is a series of compromises made by the church with the world so that the offense of Jesus Christ is watered down, mitigated, and obscured to the point that the world is satisfied that the church is no longer foreign or dangerous. . . . Christianity is turned into a fit religion . . . [that] no longer poses a threat to the world. . . . One thing we can never do is settle down into a comfortable coexistence with the world by removing the offense of the gospel—the lordship of Jesus Christ.[6]

---

[5] Taken from my friend Steve Znachko's sermon on the parables of Jesus, delivered March 1-2, 2014, at Grace Church, Noblesville, IN.

[6] Carter, *Rethinking Christ and Culture after Christendom*, 78.

Likewise, Hunter surmises:

> Christianity in North America and the West more generally is a weak
> culture; weak insofar as it is fragmented in its core beliefs and
> organization, without a coherent collective identity and mission, and
> often divided within itself, often with unabated hostility. Thus, for all
> the talk of world-changing and all of the good intentions that motivate
> it, the Christian community is not, on the whole, remotely close to a
> position where it could actually change the world in any significant
> way.[7]

Obviously, we must identify the problem before we can solve it.
And big problems do call for a big solution (see again Chapter 5).

He Modeled the Pure and Perfect Form

The most compelling aspect of Jesus' earthly ministry was the
coupling of his teachings of the kingdom with demonstrations of its
presence and power. As Matthew writes, "Jesus went throughout Galilee,
teaching in their synagogues, preaching the good news of the kingdom,
and healing every disease and sickness among the people." Thus, saying
the kingdom of God is at hand meant that the power to heal and do signs,
wonders, and miracles is here. As a result, "news about him spread all
over Syria, and people brought to him all who were ill with various
diseases, those suffering severe pain, the demon-possessed, the epileptics
and the paralytics, and he healed them" (Matt. 4:23-24).

Since Jesus' presentation of the kingdom differed so radically from
the expectations of the contemporary Jew, He undoubtedly did not want
his followers confused or perplexed about its nature. And since neither
He nor any biblical writer ever defined the kingdom, Jesus did something
better. He modeled the kingdom in its pure and perfect form. He lived it
out in their midst (with one major exception that we shall present in
Chapter 11). His modeling both drew and offended people. As we shall
see, the same is true today even in the Church.

---

[7] Hunter, *To Change the World*, 274

Throughout his earthly ministry, Jesus, anointed with the Holy Spirit, manifested the kingdom's presence, authority, power, and character. Not only did He travel about proclaiming the kingdom, doing good, feeding the hungry, ministering to the poor, healing the sick, opening blind eyes, and casting out devils, He even raised the dead. In so doing, Jesus demonstrated that his kingdom is not something one just believes in or talks about. It is something one does.

His first disciples watched in amazement as He sometimes healed all (Luke 6:19; Acts 10:38) and sometimes didn't (Mark 6:5-6; Matt. 13:58). In all these engagements, Jesus was the personification of the kingdom demonstrating and modeling that its ministry focus was upon the personal needs of others. Later on, the Apostle Paul went about doing the same things and urging his contemporaries to "Follow my example, as I follow the example of Christ" (1 Cor. 11:1), "to imitate me" (1 Cor. 4:16; Phil. 3:17), and emphasizing that "the kingdom of God is not a matter of talk but of power" (1 Cor. 4:20). The word "power" here in the Greek is *dunamis*. It means "miraculous power."[8] Paul's oneness of belief and ministry with Jesus' ministry was in answer to Jesus' prayer for oneness (John 17:20-23), as well as an essential factor increasing the kingdom's influence, back then and there. Yet in much of the Church today, this oneness is sorely lacking.

Unfortunately today, only some Christians are good soil for the kingdom. That's because so many have been contaminated by the traditions of men and lulled into watered-down versions of our faith.

Jesus also stipulated: "Verily, verily, I say unto you, he that believeth on me, the works that I do shall he do also; and greater works than these shall he do; because I go unto my Father" (John 14:12 *KJV* – note the plural "works"). Many today, however, think, "He couldn't have meant that!" After all, He was the perfect prototype in full obedience and complete compliance to the Father's will. But Jesus issued no

---

[8] #1411 in *Strong's Exhaustive Concordance of the Bible*.

disclaimers or exceptions. So what part of this verse do we not, or will we not, understand? Evans offers this revealing perspective:

> "The is not a verse we hear preached on too frequently . . . . But I am not sure why. It is pretty straightforward truth. Maybe the majority of our preachers have a difficult time believing that something that sounds so good could actually be true. Yet Jesus said plainly that, if you believe in Him, you are going to do stuff that even He didn't get to do on earth. . . . That is kingdom truth."[9]

Nonetheless, most Christians today think and act like "we never can be like that." To which Jesus is saying, "you must." After all, how Christ-like is Christ-like? And Jesus' prayer for oneness was not just for his first followers but also for "those who will believe in me through their message" (John 17:20). That surely includes you and me, doesn't it? That is why this prayer is termed "Jesus' prayer for all believers."

Of course, we are not to die for the world's sins or be raised three days later and ascend to the right hand of God—only Jesus could and did perform those eschatological events. But inspired Scripture further states, "whoever claims to live in him must walk as Jesus did" (1 John 2:5-6; also see 2:4; Acts 2:22). Walking as Jesus did is an idiomatic expression and means doing what Jesus did. We have a similar expression today when we talk about filling someone's shoes. We do not literally mean filling his or her shoes with gravel or dirt. But we do literally mean taking over doing what he or she was doing.

Back then, therefore, with the models of Jesus, his first disciples, and Paul, there was no reason for the early Church to be confused about or misunderstand the nature of Jesus' kingdom. The pertinent question next becomes, are believers in Jesus Christ today to proclaim the same present and available kingdom and do the same miraculous kingdom works He, his disciples, and Paul were doing—not to mention the "greater works?"

Admittedly, this possibility is a far cry from how most of us have been led and conditioned to practice our Christian faith. We tend to equate "church work" (ushering, greeting, parking cars, etc.) with kingdom work. Yet Scripture states that we have been saved by grace through faith for a purpose—to do "good works" (Eph. 2:5, 8, 10; Heb.

---

[9] Evans, *Kingdom Man*, 41.

10: 24; Jas. 2:26) and "works appropriate to repentance" (Acts 26:20 *NAS*; also see 1 Thess. 1:3). Then, what works are those?

Another important point to seriously contemplate is, if Jesus, his disciples, and Paul are no longer our models of the Christian life, or if their model is limited to only their moral lives, then we have no model and everything is up for grabs. No matter how we slice it (want to ignore, deny, or sidestep it), for Jesus and the early Church, doing the works of Jesus was basic Christianity. The "greater works" are something else. We shall explore those in Chapter 11.

Honestly, let's ask ourselves: If we modern-day followers of Jesus are not doing or are not even willing to take the initiative to do the works of Jesus, as He modeled and specified, then why should we not be considered in the ranks of the unbeliever (see again John 14:12)? Yet how many believers in Jesus today do we see doing the works Jesus did or even attempting them? Again, how conformed to his image are we really supposed to be? Perhaps many of us today are merely paying lip service to our faith, while insisting on our own ways of practicing it? Back then, apparently, it was not enough to just state that they loved Jesus and professed belief in Him (see 1 John 3:18; John 14:15).

On the other hand, if Jesus, his disciples, and Paul are still our role models, then the Christian life is a much higher "high calling" (Phil. 3:14; also see Eph. 4:1; 2 Thess. 1:11; Heb. 3:1; 2 Pet. 1:10) than most of us have been led to believe. And it demands a much stronger response than most of us have been willing to give.

By his words and works (see John 14:10), Jesus (and the others) was demonstrating and defining the nature of the kingdom. In so doing, He and they were revealing that the kingdom was not an abstract concept or a mystery limited to human hearts. Nor was it a political empire, a utopian paradise, or a future golden age in a world beyond the realm of human history, as some today suggest. Instead, He and they presented the kingdom as the dynamic presence and power of God's will, reign, and rule. They were directing their kingdom works against the dominion of Satan, not against Roman oppression (Israel had failed to identify their real enemy).

Hence, the kingdom, which had been awaiting fulfillment in Old Testament times, had fully arrived and resided in Jesus and his works (Col. 1:19; 2:9-10). He dynamically demonstrated its internal and external, spiritual and physical characteristics by the life He led, by his relationship with the Father, by forgiving sins, by healing the sick, by casting out demons, by taking authority over nature, by performing miracles, by taking care of physical needs, and even by the menial task of washing feet, which Jesus specifically said He did to "set you an example that you should do as I have done for you" (John 13:15). Jesus regarded all these works as essential, substantial, and intrinsic elements of his kingdom.

Thus, Jesus' earthly manifestations of the kingdom affected the whole person. It produced both spiritual transformations and physical healings. It redeemed and restored the totality of human life—spirit, mind, and body, all closely intertwined—from the spiritual and physical dominion of Satan's kingdom. One of Jesus' most prominent miracles was the casting out or exorcism of demons which He interpreted as clear proof that "the kingdom of God has come upon you"—i.e., his audience (Matt. 12:28). By this, Jesus demonstrated that God was now driving Satan from control and making possible the renewal of personal lives. These deliverances freed their recipients to draw near to God and compelled those witnessing these miraculous occurrences to do likewise.

Hence, the kingdom, which had been awaiting fulfillment in Old Testament times, had fully arrived and resided in Jesus and his works.

In this way, Jesus unveiled the "mystery" of the kingdom hidden through the ages, not only by teaching but also by modeling the kingdom in its pure and perfect form. The kingly rule of God had found its expression in Jesus, his devotional life, his teaching, and his ministry activity.

Much of the confusion and many of the errors over the nature of his kingdom only ensue when we moderns, for various reasons, ignore, discredit, or disclaim any of the kingdom's provisions and dynamics, which Jesus modeled. In Jesus, the "mystery" of the kingdom had become "an open secret" (Mark 4:11-12). Are you amazed? Offended? Many of the people of Jesus' day were both (see Mark 1:21-28). Soon most of the Jewish people would reject the kingdom Jesus was bringing and Him as their King. But Jesus' teachings and modeling were just a beginning.

He Trained and Sent Out

Next, Jesus sent out his first Twelve disciples on an "OJT" mission ("On-the-Job-Training) to preach the very same kingdom of God as being "at hand" and to perform the same miraculous works He had been doing (Matt. 10:1, 7-8; Luke 9:1-2, 6). By so doing, Jesus expanded the increase of his kingdom from his Person, words, and works into and through them. This prophesied increase (see Isa. 9:6-7) further affirmed that the kingdom was not a political rule, *per se*, but a supernaturally exercised power in opposition to that of Satan. On every occasion Jesus evaded the attempts of his followers to make Him a king or political ruler (John 6:15). Sometime later, He further expanded the increase of his kingdom by sending out the Seventy, two by two, into the towns to which He was about to go. These Seventy preached the same kingdom message and did the same kingdom works as He and the Twelve (Luke 10:1-17).

In this way, Jesus' first followers took Him seriously as He instructed them in the close interrelationship between the preaching of the kingdom and the demonstration of its works of power (Matt. 22:29). He gave them temporary authority over demons and diseases—enemies of his kingdom—and the empowerment to perform miracles. They responded by emulating Him, to the best of their abilities. Thereby, they experienced the "powers of the age to come" (Heb. 6:5) and victories over evil in advance of the coming of the Holy Spirit. Just as importantly, He trained them to care for the physical and emotional needs of the "least of these" as unto Him: the hungry, the thirsty, the strangers, those needing clothing, the sick, and those in prison (see Matt. 25:34-46).

Finally, and prior to his ascension, He promised another increase of his kingdom. His followers would receive permanent empowering after the Holy Spirit had come upon them in Jerusalem at Pentecost (Acts 2). From then on, all believers in Him, without distinction, would be empowered to be his witnesses by preaching the same kingdom message and doing the same kingdom works in Jerusalem, Judea, Samaria and the uttermost parts of the earth (Acts 1:8; 2:1-21).

Notably, nowhere in the New Testament is the command to go out and preach the kingdom of God ever separated from performing its mighty works. Again, these works demonstrated and solidified the arrival of the everlasting and ever-increasing kingdom.

So, what happened? Jesus' 1st-century followers, in obedience to his directives and with the supernatural enabling of God's Spirit, transformed the world of their day. The book of Acts is a record of the continuation of Jesus' teachings, his works, and his kingdom by his followers. It was preserved as part of the Holy Scripture not only as a confirmation of all Jesus began to do and to teach (Acts 1:1), but also as a record of their continued obedience in modeling the pure and perfect form of the kingdom as first modeled by Jesus Himself.

Question: Should we Christ followers today be taking their model and the works of Jesus just as seriously as they did? After all, doesn't being part of "God's people and members of God's household, built upon the foundation of the apostles and prophets with Christ Jesus himself as the chief cornerstone" (Eph. 2:19-20) mean patterning our lives after them as our model? And doesn't not doing what God calls us to do become something both He and we call "sin?"

He Warned Against

Jesus warned the Seventy, as He sent them out, to not rejoice that the spirits—enemies of God—submitted to them; but to rejoice that their names were written in heaven (Luke 10:20).

He warned that those who listened to these Seventy also listened to Him. But whoever rejected one of them (because of what they were preaching and doing) rejected Him and the Father as well (Luke 10:16). Are we today guilty of rejecting those attempting to do this type of ministry?

He both warned and cursed the Jewish teachers and religious leaders, the Pharisees, that they were hypocrites because they shut the kingdom in men's faces by refusing to enter it themselves and preventing others, who were trying to enter it, from entering (Matt. 23:13-14f). Consequently, the kingdom would be taken away from them and given to a people who would produce its fruit (Matt. 21:43). What fruit? The fruit He was modeling—the works of Jesus and even greater works.

He warned: "anyone who will not receive the kingdom of God like a little child"—i.e., with a childlike attitude of complete dependence and submission—"will never enter it" (Mark 10:15).

He warned: "he who is not with me is against me, and he who does not gather with me scatters" (Matt. 12:30).

He warned that some love the "praise from men more than praise from God" (John 12:43). And, "the servant [a believer] who knows his master's will and does not get ready or does not do what his master wants will be beaten with many blows" (Luke 12:48).

Lastly, He warned, in the "at hand," "soon-to-come-to-pass," and "not-to-be sealed-up" Book of Revelation, of the consequences for anyone who would add to or subtract from its kingdom-unveiling message (Rev. 22:18-19). The Book of Revelation unveils the greater Jesus, the contemporary Christ, and his kingdom in action against and victory over all opposing forces.[10]

The reality today, however, seems to be that many Christian leaders are likewise shutting Jesus' kingdom in men's faces by also refusing to enter. They, too, find it too offensive to our modern sensibilities, expectations, and rationalism. Therefore, they ignore, deny, or theologically dismiss this nature of the kingdom as irrelevant or not even present today. Selectively, they pick and choose from Scripture the kind of Christian faith they will preach, teach, and practice. Of course, this is not a child-like attitude. It's an adult disobedience that produces millions of timid Christians who lack a strong kingdom consciousness.

So are we willing to take Jesus seriously today, as opposed to merely following a religious form? Are we willing to turn from our lesser versions of Christianity, which have been largely turned into a religion of rituals, formalism, and passive spectatorship? The bottom line is, many professing Christians are not following Jesus. Consequently, there is little if any difference between them and those who aren't Christians except perhaps for an hour or so on Sunday mornings.

Not surprisingly, this is most likely why the Apostle Paul would warn those to whom he had been preaching the kingdom to watch out and guard themselves because "savage wolves will come in among you . . . even from your own number men will arise and distort the truth . . . ."

---

[10] For more on this, see Noē, *The Greater Jesus*.

(Acts 20:25-31). Is this still happening today, at least in regard to distorting, degrading, and diminishing Jesus' kingdom?

He Conferred a 'Just-As' Kingdom

After Jesus had announced, taught, clarified, modeled, trained and sent out, and warned about his kingdom, He declared to his 12 disciples, at the Last Supper: "I confer on you a kingdom, just as my Father conferred one on me, so that you may eat and drink at my table in my kingdom and sit on thrones, judging the twelve tribes of Israel" (Luke 22:29-30).

Notice, Jesus did not confer the Church upon them. Rather, the phrase "just as" conveys a vital truth concerning the nature of the kingdom He was conferring. His "just-as" kingdom was the one about which He had said, "And from the days of John the Baptist until now the kingdom of heaven suffereth violence, and the violent take it by force" (Matt. 11:12 *KJV*). Or, "From the days of John the Baptist until now, the kingdom of heaven has been forcefully advancing, and forceful men lay hold of it" (Matt. 11:12 *NIV*). Whichever translation you prefer, the conclusion is the same. It is the *same-natured* kingdom Jesus announced, taught, clarified, modeled, trained, and warned them to perform its essential elements. No exceptions or exclusions were made.[11]

By this conferral, they were now possessors of the kingdom during this transitional period and in advance of the Old Covenant kingdom being taken away from the Jews and given over to them (Matt. 21:43). Therefore, they would continue preaching the same message and ministering the same works He had been doing. He also gave them "keys of the kingdom" and assured them that "whatever you bind on earth will be bound in heaven, and whatever you loose on earth will be loosed in heaven" (Matt. 16:19).

---

[11] Of course, everything in this area of theology is contested by someone somewhere. One critical objection I received on the Internet was from a person downplaying Jesus' "just as" expression. He claimed it only meant that Jesus was handing the kingdom over to them the same as the Father had handed it over to Jesus once. Therefore, in his option, this verse says nothing about the nature of the kingdom being the same. But I disagree with his degradation.

Interestingly, Jesus never delimited the nature of his kingdom as being only "spiritual." That adjective is never used anywhere in Scripture with the noun "kingdom" and for a good reason. It's a false limitation. Of course, Jesus' kingdom was and is spiritual; but it's not only spiritual. It's also all encompassing of the physical, material, social, political, and financial—i.e., of all creation.

Hence, the Church is truest to its calling when it preaches and practices this conferred and same-natured kingdom. It is a matter of obedience and being one in continuity with Jesus, Paul, and the early Church. They and we today advance his kingdom by coupling the preaching with doing God's will on earth—i.e., word and works.

But this kingdom has suffered great violence not only at the hands of adversaries over the centuries but even more at the hands of Christians who have devalued, diluted, diminished, discarded and/or re-defined its modeled nature. As a result, major discontinuity has been introduced between the "just-as" kingdom Jesus *conferred* and whatever version of it we *defer* to today. But the nature of Jesus' everlasting kingdom was different from anything that had preceded it. And it would not change with the passing of time. It would only continue increasing.

Jesus never delimited the nature of his kingdom as being only "spiritual."

Therefore, applying this kingdom to the world today should still be the primary business of the Church, the body of Christ, and each individual Christian. Sadly, it's not. Yet the ministry needs are still the same, as is the opposition to carrying out God's will, reign, and rule.

In stark comparison to today, the kingdom Jesus, Paul, and the early Church presented produced a highly distinctive Christian lifestyle that dramatically contrasted with the lifestyles of non-believers. If we today are unbiased and child-like, we, too, can garner vital insights into the nature of the everlasting kingdom by studying and following their teachings and role-modeling lives and not just the moral parts with which we are perhaps more comfortable.

Thus, Boyd concludes: "When the kingdom of God is manifested, it's obvious. It looks like Jesus."[12] And "only what looks like Jesus qualifies as kingdom-of-God activity."[13]

He Commanded to Seek and Obey

Jesus commanded his disciples (and, by extension, his followers in all subsequent generations) to "seek first his kingdom and his righteousness" (Matt. 6:33). Interestingly, the Greek word usually translated here as "righteousness," with its overtones of personal piety, virtue, holiness, and upright conduct, is *dikaiosune*. It could also be translated as "justice, equity, right." David Neff maintains that justice is a more appropriate and closer translation. He astutely writes: "Justice is the essence of the kingdom. Thus, when Jesus brings justice, it is a sign of the kingdom. And when his followers pursue justice, they witness to the kingdom."[14]

Without a doubt, this translation of justice introduces a different understanding of this often-quoted but little-followed verse. And justice or rightness is not the same as salvation, which is received by grace through faith (Rom. 10:9-10; Eph. 2:8-9).

But what kingdom or whose version thereof was Jesus talking about us seeking? Once again, the answer is the one and only one He announced, taught, modeled, trained, warned about, and conferred upon his disciples.

Jesus further commanded, in what's called the Great Commission (Matt. 28:18-20), that his disciples (and, by extension, his followers in all subsequent generations) not only make disciples of all nations and baptize them, but also to teach them to obey *everything* He had commanded them to do. Jesus' "everything" certainly would include the miraculous, merciful, and fruit-producing works of the kingdom He had introduced, modeled, and sent them out to perform. A few months later, He would permanently empower them, and all future generations of Christians, to carry out this Great Commission.

---

[12] Boyd, *The Myth of a Christian Nation*, 99.
[13] Ibid., 100.
[14] David Neff, "Signs of the End Times," *Christianity Today*, August 2011, 49.

Today, unfortunately, we moderns have turned Jesus' Great Commission into what Dallas Willard calls "the Great Omission, because what Jesus said to do here is rarely done."[15] But ask yourself this question: "Why would Jesus commission his Church to preach the gospel of the kingdom of God devoid of its miraculous powers that (1) characterized his own ministry (Luke 4:14; Acts 10:38), (2) He promised his Church (Luke 24:49; Acts 1:8), and (3) He predicted would follow the disciples' ministry (John 5:20; cf. Mark 16:17-20)?"[16]

Furthermore, three times in the letter of 1 John we are told: "we know that we have come to know him if we obey his commands" (1 John 2:3; also 5:2-3). Likewise, Jesus said: "If you love me, you will obey what I command" (John 14:15; also 14:23; Luke 6:46). Do we really love Jesus? Do we really believe these admonitions? This obedience certainly involves more than avoiding sinful behavior. It involves not burying your talent, being salt and light in the world (Matt. 5:13-14), and bearing "much fruit, showing yourselves to be my disciples" (John 15:8).

Yet so many churches today don't seek to cultivate this gospel of stewardship and breadth of calling for their attendees. Then aren't these great omissions what the Apostle Paul was talking about when he wrote: "Do not conform any longer to the pattern of this world, but be transformed by the renewing of your mind. Then you will be able to test and approve what God's perfect will is—his good, pleasing and perfect will" (Rom. 12:2). What will is this? Jesus modeled it. So if our hearts are truly changed and our minds are truly renewed, then won't our works and behaviors reflect our transformation? Won't right believing and thinking produce right living and ministering?

In the battle against the kingdom of Satan, Jesus demonstrated that the kingdom or rule of God came not just to defeat Satan's works and save souls for a heavenly destination, but to save the whole person from sin and demonic powers, to clear and cleanse hearts, and to draw human lives to God. Jesus was obedient to God's will and rule in and through his own life. Likewise, He commands his followers of every subsequent generation to seek to do the same in making his name known.

---

[15] Dallas Willard, *Living in Christ's Presence* (Downers Grove, IL.: IVP Books, 2014), 17.
[16] Robert W. Graves, ed., *Strangers to Fire*, 278.

Certainly, these 1st-century Christians were not waiting around to be taken out of the world. They were seeking the kingdom, proclaiming it, and manifesting its works. And seeking the kingdom is not a one-time activity. It's a life-long pursuit. The more you seek it, the more you will find and become a kingdom bearer and ambassador of Christ and his kingdom.

This is the kingdom perspective behind Christ's Great Commission. It surely was and is a much greater commission than most of us church-going, modern-day Christians have been led to believe. In this regard, Mahatma Gandhi once challenged a group of Christians: "I like your Christ, I do not like your Christians. Your Christians are so unlike your Christ"[17] For Jesus, being a believer in Him, back then, meant being a follower of Him, a proclaimer of his kingdom, and a doer of his word and works, plus doing the "greater works" (John 14:12). Is this still the criteria that are applicable today?

If so, then to follow Jesus today, as He commanded back then means getting out of our comfort zones and reductionist versions of the faith. The practical reality is this: The ministry needs of people today are the same as they were in Jesus' time. So as Christ's ambassadors (2 Cor. 5:20), are we still to represent Him in the manner He has chosen and commanded? Do you honestly seek this modeled, conferred, and commanded nature of his kingdom, first and above all? But how can we seek and find something we cannot see, let alone try to enter it?

He Introduced the Opportunity of Entering

On several occasions Jesus mentioned the entering of his kingdom, but did not explain how (**bold** emphasis mine):

- To Nicodemus: "I tell you the truth, unless a man is born again, he cannot see the kingdom of God. . . . I tell you the truth, unless a man is born of water and the Spirit, he cannot **enter** the kingdom of God" (John 3:3-5).
- "How hard it is for the rich to **enter** the kingdom of God! . . . Children, how hard it is to **enter** the kingdom God! It is easier

---

[17] Quoted in Stearns, *The Hole in Our Gospel*, 226.

for a camel to go through the eye of a needle than for a rich man to **enter** the kingdom of God" (Mark 10:23b-24; also see 10:21, 25; Matt. 19:23-24).

- "For I tell you that unless your righteousness surpasses that of the Pharisees and the teachers of the law, you will certainly not **enter** the kingdom of heaven" (Matt. 5:20).
- "I tell you the truth, unless you change and become like little children, you will never **enter** the kingdom of heaven" (Matt. 18:3; Mark 10:15).
- "I tell you the truth, the tax collectors and the prostitutes are **entering** the kingdom ahead of you" (Matt. 21:31b).

Most modern-day Christians have been told, taught, and believe that one enters the kingdom of God at the time and by virtue of his or her new birth (salvation, saved, born again). It's a gift received along with eternal life, by those who have put their trust in the death, burial, and resurrection of Jesus Christ (see Col.1:13-14). But is this true?

As we saw in Chapter 6, the New Testament never equates believers with the kingdom. Nor is it possible to substitute "church" for "kingdom" in any scripture. Therefore, from a scriptural standpoint, being born again or saved does not necessarily mean you have entered his kingdom.

Let's also recall that at that time Jesus was speaking these words no one was born again or saved. Jesus had not yet died on the cross, spent three days and three nights in the "grave" (hades), been resurrected, ascended to heaven, and sent the Holy Spirit. Also, Jesus emphatically stated: "The Law and the Prophets were proclaimed until John. Since that time, the good news of the kingdom of God is being preached, and everyone is forcing his way into it" (Luke 16:16). And, "From the days of John the Baptist until now, the kingdom of heaven has been forcefully advancing, and forceful men lay hold of it" (Matt. 11:12). How were they able to force their way in and lay hold of the kingdom during that pre-cross time and before salvation was even available?

. . . to follow Jesus today, as He commanded back then, means getting out of our comfort zones and reductionist versions of the faith.

Another common misconception is all we have to do to enter the kingdom is to die. But as we have seen, the "kingdom of heaven" (used in Matthew's gospel) and heaven are not the same. Make no mistake; much confusion has plagued the history of the Christian Church over these two long-standing misunderstandings of the kingdom.

Clearing Up the Confusion for Entering

The biblical solution for clearing up this confusion is this: Salvation "is by grace . . . through faith . . . not by works" (Eph. 2:8-9). But entrance into and living within the everlasting form of the kingdom of God on this earth is by works. This is why Paul continues, thusly: "For we are God's workmanship created in Christ Jesus to do good works, which God prepared in advance for us to do" (Eph. 2:10).

Below are more statements by Jesus in which He confirms that entrance into the kingdom, as well as living within it and being governed by it, was and is achieved and maintained by works. Hence, as McKnight acknowledges, "kings determine what their kingdom is like . . . . kings shape their kingdom in their own image . . . ."[18]

- "Thus, by their fruit you will recognize them" (Matt. 7:20). Fruit is works.
- "Therefore I tell you that the kingdom of God will be taken away from you and given to a people who will produce its fruit" (Matt. 21:43). Producing fruit is by works.
- "Not everyone who says to me, 'Lord, Lord,' will enter the kingdom of heaven, but only he who does the will of my Father who is in heaven" (Matt. 7:21). Jesus' teaching and ministering works was doing the will of his Father. As He declared, "I do the will of him who sent me" (John 4:34). If we sincerely desire to be Christ-like, shouldn't this be our desire and marching orders as well (see Col. 1:9-11)? Also, shouldn't this be the height of Christian privilege and attainment (see Eph. 3:16-19)?

---

[18] McKnight, *Kingdom Conspiracy*, 128, 132.

- When Jesus was asked, "What must we do to do the works of God?" He answered: "The work of God is this: to believe in the one he has sent" (John 6:29). Later, he clarified and amplified what this believing consists of. Using powerful oath language, He exclaimed: "Verily, verily, I say unto you, He that believeth on me, the works that I do shall he do also; and greater works than these shall he do; because I go unto my Father" (John 14:12 KJV; also see John 10:38 KJV; Matt. 5:16). Again, these works consist of ministering to others via Holy Spirit empowerment. That's what Jesus meant back then and still today as He beckons, "Come, follow me" (Matt. 4:19a; also Luke 9:23). Anything less is less. So how will you and I respond?
- "Therefore everyone who hears these words of mine and puts them into practice is like a wise man who built his house on the rock. . . . But everyone who hears these words of mine and does not put them into practice is like a foolish man who built his house on sand" (Matt. 7:24, 26). Putting something into practice is works.
- "No one who puts his hand to the plow and looks back is fit for service in the kingdom of God" (Luke 9:62). Service is works. And no one should seek to be Christ's disciple and enter his kingdom without counting the costs (see Luke 14:28-33). These costs result from works.
- "If you love me, you will obey what I command" (John 14:15). That's works.
- "You are my friends if you do what I command" (John 15:14). That's works.

Conversely, by not doing the will of the Father—i.e., committing sins of commission (thinking/doing sinful things) or sins of omission (not doing the works of Jesus and greater works)—one exits the kingdom. But the good news is you can reenter through doing kingdom "good works." No, we are not talking about losing one's salvation here. Nor can I precisely explain how and when this exiting and reentering occurs. But this I do know: This scriptural explanation of entering, living in, being governed under, and possibly exiting the kingdom will not sit well with the "Christian" religious crowd or cessation theology people (see Appendix A).

That's because much of the Church today is led and populated by those following in the footsteps of the scribes and Pharisees. They, too, "shut the kingdom of heaven in men's faces." How so? Jesus explained, "You yourselves do not enter, nor will you let those enter who are trying to" (Matt. 23:13). And, "Woe to you experts in the law, because you have taken away the key to knowledge. You yourselves have not entered, and you have hindered those who were entering" (Luke 11:52).

Today, we shut and hinder by 1) claiming that the kingdom is not here anymore, or is only partially here (see again Chapter 1 pp. 28-29, Chapter 6 pp.144-146, 154-161 and Chapter 8 pp. 209-216); and 2) tightly controlling our churches, seminaries, schools, parachurch ministries, etc. by slamming shut the door if anyone even suggests this type of ministry. Thus, Willard, poignantly and sarcastically, queries, "Have we not elevated this practice of the scribes and Pharisees into a first principle of the Christian life?"[19]

Doctrinally or functionally, many modern-day scribes and Pharisees in the church do not want nor will allow the kingdom works of Jesus and Holy Spirit-empowered gifts to operate in their midst. They staunchly refuse and declare, "We'll have none of that around here." Oh, yes, I've experienced this, first hand, from incensed elders and pastors.

Other door-slammers are simply not childlike. Ladd explains: "to become a child means to be in oneself helpless, to come into a condition of complete dependence on God, to be ready to let God work. . . . [They] are completely receptive toward God. He gives to them what they cannot give themselves."[20] But many feel threatened by the nature of Jesus' modeled kingdom. They are too independent, self-centered, and pride-filled, and stubbornly clinging to their self-determined paths and traditions of men. Rushdoony consequently affirms: "Our problem is not a question of knowledge: it is a question of obedience."[21]

So what we have are many, born-again, saved, and heaven-bound Christians who have walked right out of the kingdom and for this one reason—disobedience. They choose not to enter by choosing not to serve Christ and his kingdom in the ways He prescribed. Arguably, this is why so much of the organized Church today is mired in artificial neatness and

[19] Willard, *The Great Omission*, 10.
[20] Ladd, *The Presence of the Future*, 178.
[21] Rushdoony, *Law and Society*, 334.

is powerless to witness to the glorious gospel of the kingdom. Instead, their leadership's #1 focus and motivation is to preserve "their" institution and #2 is to grow it. But you can't grow it if you start doing things that might cause people to leave. Thus, turf protection is what this Christendom is all about. And preaching and ministering the kingdom is too threatening for their "adult" sensitivities.

Of course, my above assessment is contested (as is everything in this field). But now you know how some were able to force their way into the kingdom from John the Baptist's time and prior to Jesus' death, burial, resurrection, ascension, and sending of the Holy Spirit at Pentecost. They weren't born again or saved yet, but they were literally seeing the fully established kingdom standing right before them in the Person of Jesus and were pressing in to learn more and receive his kingdom teachings, ministry, and blessings. Pressing in and receiving was putting feet to their faith and hope. Again, that's entering via works.

Then how do we explain John 3:3-5 within a post-Pentecost world and context? Plainly, being born-again (salvation) is the *prerequisite* for entering and becoming instruments of his kingdom. But contrary to much popular belief, salvation is not an immediate entrance or permanent transfer into the kingdom. Following this prerequisite event, we saved Christians are not to sit, soak, and sour in our pews. Rather, we are to be the bearers and ambassadors for advancing the King and his kingdom into the lives of others and society at large. Our salvation enables us to see the kingdom and gives us access, but we still must enter. Think of it this way. Your salvation is your ticket in. But just like a ticket for an event or a plane flight, one still must take that ticket in hand, present it at the entrance, and enter the event or plane. Therefore, only having the ticket/salvation is not the same as entering.

Seeing, therefore, most likely means perceiving, knowing, and understanding, you see? But you can physically see many things that you may never enter. For example, when I drive downtown, I see many large buildings I have never entered. So when a person becomes born again, they can see the kingdom but may not yet have entered.

Mims agrees and laments that "seeing the kingdom is seeing the world the way God sees it, like having on night-vision goggles." Unfortunately, for "many Christians the kingdom of God is about as clear as mud. We are taught little about it, so, as a result, our understanding of and excitement about kingdom things is simply absent from our lives."[22]

Munroe concurs that "the cross of Christ is the *beginning* point of life in the Kingdom of God, not the ending point. . . . We have gotten so sidetracked . . . . It seems that the message of the Kingdom has all but disappeared."[23] He does, however, term "Jesus died for us" as being the "entrance into the Kingdom."[24] And so our acts of obedience—doing kingdom works—are the means of entering. Conversely, our non-kingdom works (acts of disobedience: sins of commission or omission) are the means of exiting the kingdom.

In further support, Moore casts salvation "not in terms of escape from the world, but as restoring the human person's right to rule over the world."[25] But that right must be exercised through works.

Therefore, I conclude that seeing the kingdom entails seeing, through God's eyes, the brokenness and disharmony in us, in other lives, and in the world—i.e., the six broken places of separation, pain, isolation, hatred, injustice, and decay. This seeing leads to perceiving, understanding, and empathizing with how much God cares about all this. Then we enter the kingdom by being Christ's ambassadors and bearers of his kingdom via both proclaiming the kingdom and doing its works to bring healing to portions of those broken places. Certainly, God will lead us if we are faithful, willing, and seeking his kingdom. Anything less is less. But by not being faithful, willing, seeking, and so doing, we exit the kingdom and live outside of its blessings. For Christians, this then is our constant challenge and struggle.

Others on How Works Work

Realistically speaking, the whole Christian life properly lived may be characterized as that of entering and exiting his kingdom. If this is so, then time spent inside the kingdom is better than the time spent outside, wouldn't you agree?

---

[22] Mims, *The Kingdom Focused Church*, 42.
[23] Munroe, *Rediscovering the Kingdom*, 152.
[24] Ibid., 154.
[25] Moore, *The Kingdom of Christ*, 111.

This is why the Apostle Paul later informs the already born-again, saved, and heaven-bound believers in Lystra, Iconium, and Antioch: "We must go through many hardships to enter the kingdom of God" (Acts 14:22b, NIV), "through much tribulation" (KJV). Why "many hardships" (plural) to enter—"many afflictions" in the Greek? It's because the kingdom is not to be entered by merely taking thought, acquiring knowledge, or simply believing. Nothing in the kingdom comes without opposition and hardships. Also, nowhere does Scripture mention anything about the kingdom entering you (Luke 17:20 notwithstanding, see again p. 222).

Paul also conjoins his mighty words and works as the example for Roman Christians regarding "what Christ has accomplished through me in leading the Gentiles to obey God by what I have said and done – by the power of signs and miracles, through the power of the Spirit. So from Jerusalem all the way around to Illyricum, I have fully proclaimed the gospel of Christ" (Rom. 15:18b-19). Ten verses later, he terms this coupling, "the full measure of the blessing of Christ" (Rom. 15:29b; also see Eph. 4:11-13). Remember, this is the Paul who commands Christians to follow his example as he follows Christ's example (1 Cor. 11:1) and approves of those who so do (1 Cor. 4:16-17; Phil. 3:17; 4:9; 1 Thess. 1:6; 2:14; 2 Thess. 3:9).

Hence, Barclay is prompted to note: "Paul saw himself . . . as *an instrument in the hands of Christ*. He did not talk of what he had done; but of what Christ had done with him. He never said of anything: 'I did it.' He always said; 'Christ used me to do it.'" Then Barclay adds: "It is when a man ceases to think of what he can do and begins to think of what God can do with him, that things begin to happen."[26]

Conversely: "Do you not know that the wicked will not inherit the kingdom of God?" (1 Cor. 6:9a; also see Gal. 5:19-21; Eph. 5:5). Once again, Paul is not speaking of dying and going to heaven. Arguably, he's speaking about all people (Christians and non-Christians, alike) who practice wicked things and are thus outside the kingdom of God.

For these reasons, Paul urged the born-again, saved, and heaven-bound Christians thusly:

---

[26] William Barclay, *The Letter to the Romans*, revised ed. (Philadelphia, PA.: The Westminster Press, 1975, 1957, 1955), 203.

- In Thessalonica – "to live lives worthy of God, who calls you into his kingdom and glory" (1 Thess. 2:12). To read a description of the kingdom works they had been seeking and doing, see 1 Thessalonians 1:4-8.
- In Corinth – to "stand firm. Let nothing move you. Always give yourselves fully to the work of the Lord, because you know that in the Lord your labor is not in vain" (1 Cor. 15:58). God wants us to exercise our faith by putting it into action.
- In Rome – "to offer your bodies as living sacrifices, holy and pleasing to God" and to "not conform any longer to the pattern of this world [in the world or in a church], but be transformed by the renewing of your mind" (Rom. 12:1-2). This renewal is absolutely necessary to enter into the kingdom works of ministering in Holy Spirit power and gifts that God gives his people to benefit others. Yes, we Christians today are capable of doing all the things Jesus said to do and He Himself was doing. But many Christians disagree (more on this in Appendix A).
- In Colosse – "that you may live a life worthy of the Lord and may please him in every way: bearing fruit in every good work, growing in the knowledge of God" (Col. 1:10). Indeed, these works and growing in this knowledge go hand-in-hand.

The writer of Hebrews concurs: "And let us consider how we may spur one another on toward love and good deeds" (Heb. 10:24).

James concurs: "Do not merely listen to the word, and so deceive yourselves. Do what it says. . . . [for] faith without works is dead." (Jas. 1:22; 2:20b).

Peter concurs: "Live such good lives among the pagans that, though they accuse you of doing wrong, they may see your good deeds and glorify God on the day he visits us" (1 Pet. 2:12). "For if you do these things, you will never fall, and you will receive a rich welcome into the eternal kingdom of our Lord and Savior Jesus Christ" (2 Pet. 1:10b-11). If you want to think this verse means only in heaven and not on earth, go ahead. But I think it applies to both because the kingdom (God's will, reign, and rule) is located in both locations, is it not?

John concurs: "This is how we know we are in him: Whoever claims to live in him must walk as Jesus did" (1 John 2:5a-6). "Walk as Jesus did" is an idiom that means doing what Jesus had been doing—i.e., kingdom works (see again John 14:12).

Likewise, the Book of Revelation concurs: "'Blessed are the dead who die in the Lord from now on. . . . they will rest from their labor, for their deeds will follow them. . . . 'Fine linen, bright and clean, was given her to wear.' (Fine linen stands for the righteous acts of the saints.)" (Rev. 14:13; 19:8). Deeds and righteous acts are works.

Thus, one enters the kingdom by pressing in, by force, by works, and through many hardships and much tribulation. To cap this off, as John Calvin ardently admonishes, "We must try to say no less than Scripture, lest we impoverish its message."[27]

I'm also going to further suggest that works is what is meant by the phrase, "receiving a kingdom" (Heb. 12:28). The Greek word for receiving is *paralambano*. It means: "to receive near, i.e., associate with oneself (in any familiar or intimate act or relation); . . . to assume an office; fig. to learn;–receive, take (unto, with)."[28] As we have seen, the kingdom was not being delivered in installments. It arrived fully established and was increasing. Therefore, the time prophesied long ago for the receiving and possessing of this kingdom (see Dan. 7:18, 22) was "at hand," back then and there in that 1st century. And those works were exactly what they were doing (see again 1 Thess. 1:4-8; Matt. 25:34-46, for instance). That's exactly what we 21st-century Christians should be doing as well, is it not?

Indeed, Paul and many Christians of his day had been *radicalized* by Christ. Today, sad to say, many of us Christians have been *neutralized* by the Church and our various lesser, more comfortable versions of Christianity.

Critical Objection: "His great desire is to be King in our hearts . . . we don't need to work or perform, just receive Jesus and his peace."[29]

My Response: No tactful way exists to characterize this misunderstanding. Purely and simply, it is blatant gospel reductionism and typical kingdom ignorance that fixates on Jesus only being relevant today "in our hearts." It is also a major reason why many churches in

---

[27] Quoted in Spykman, *Reformational Theology*, 508.

[28] #3880 in *Strong's Exhaustive Concordance of the Bible.*

[29] Part of a sermon delivered by the Senior Pastor at a mega church my wife and I were attending at the time, 12/17/06. Shortly thereafter, we left that church.

America, and other countries, are losing the culture in large chunks and
our children in droves (see again Chapters 1 and 2).

Critical Objection: The Bible teaches that flesh and blood cannot
inherit the kingdom (1 Cor. 15:50). Therefore, the kingdom is only a
spiritual kingdom.

My Response: Nowhere in the Bible do we find the adjective
"spiritual" attached to and delimiting the noun "kingdom," and for a
good reason. God's kingdom impacts all of creation—physical, material,
and spiritual realms (especially see our next two chapters). Furthermore,
throughout the pages of the New Testament we find the kingdom being
entered, proclaimed, and manifested by flesh and blood, real people.
How then was that possible? Again, the kingdom is inherited by grace
through faith and being Holy Spirit indwelled. That's the prerequisite
(see again John 3:3-5; also John 1:12-13 in the KJV translation). But
entering is by the works of flesh and blood, real people on this earth.
That is what offering "your bodies as living sacrifices" is all about. It's
also "spiritual worship" (Rom. 12:1). Likewise, the kingdom works Jesus
listed in Matthew 25:34-45 for "taking your inheritance, the kingdom
. . ." are all both physical and spiritual in nature.

Ironically and originally, as Munroe recognizes, the name *Christian*
was a "derogatory label given by pagans to followers of Christ." It meant
a "little Christ" and was used for insult. But Christians liked it and
"through the centuries have generally accepted the term . . . and borne it
with honor."[30] In that way, and only in that way, were they able to
profess: "And we, who with unveiled faces all reflect the Lord's glory,
are being transformed into his likeness with ever-increasing glory" (2
Cor. 3:18).

Unfortunately today, as Munroe further reports, "the word *Christian*
has too much baggage attached to it. It refers to a whole host of people
and some of them have no connection to God's kingdom. The word has
become a 'religious' term devoid of any significant meaning as it relates
to the kingdom of God. . . . Yet the term 'Christian' occurs only twice in
the scriptures (Acts 26:28-29 and 1 Peter 4:16-17)."[31]

Please make no mistake: we Christians are called to a greater cause
than just being saved and waiting around to go to heaven or be

---

[30] Munroe, *Rediscovering the Kingdom*, 41.
[31] Ibid., 40-41.

raptured.[32] Likewise, the role of the Church is a lot greater than just presenting the life-saving message of Jesus Christ to a dying world, as important as that is—i.e., the prerequisite for entering the kingdom.

Kingdom Confirmations from Scholars

George Eldon Ladd: "Jesus' message of the Kingdom of God is the announcement by word and deed . . . . It is a blessing and a relationship which cannot be enjoyed by all men but only by those who enter the eschatological Kingdom. . . . Nor does the kingdom of God belong to sleepers and sluggards, but 'the men of force seize it. . . . The presence of the kingdom demands radical, violent conduct . . . . Men cannot passively await . . . they are actively, aggressively, forcefully to seize it. . . . As men enter into Jesus' experience of God, the Kingdom of God, his rule, 'comes' to them.'"[33]

R. David Kaylor: "The promise of the kingdom then contains the conditional 'if': The kingdom is yours if you will receive it. . . . demanding the utmost of those who allow it to work in their individual and community life. . . . Since Jesus proclaims that one should live in complete radical obedience to the will of God."[34]

Dallas Willard: "Living in the kingdom of God is a matter of living with God's action in our lives. When we seek the kingdom of God, we are seeking more and more to allow God to be present in everything that we are and everything that we do . . . . We are bearers of the kingdom of God. . . . We don't just talk about it. It is a presence that is in action. . . . there are many people who believe in Christ, but they don't believe what he believed. But the progression into the kingdom is coming to believe what he believes, coming to trust it, to live on it, to act on it, to make it count."[35]

Todd Wilson: "With their lips they profess Christ, but with their lives they deny him. . . . For them Jesus is nothing more than Savior of

---

[32] I'm opposed to the popular belief of a rapture. For my refutations, see Noē, *Off Target*, 101-112 and Noē, *The Greater Jesus*, 291-337.

[33] Ladd, *The Presence of the Future*, 178-179, 162, 164, 173.

[34] Kaylor, *Jesus the Prophet*, 118.

[35] Willard, *Living in Christ's Presence*, 76-77, 79.

their sin. . . . 'They profess to know God, but they deny him by their works' (Titus 1:16). They're the kind of churchgoers who have the appearance of godliness, but deny its power (2 Timothy 3:5)."[36]

Rousas Rushdoony: "The ministry of obedience is the necessary way to God's Kingdom."[37]

Joyce Meyer: "Now the rest of God is not a rest *from* work—it's a rest in work. It's partnering with God to do what He is calling you to do by His grace . . . . And you can enter into God's rest in every area of your life."[38]

Brian McLaren: "It is of little use to correctly say, 'Lord, Lord' if one doesn't do what the Lord says."[39]

John Bright: "The members of Christ's Kingdom are those that obey him. Christ's own are those who have fed the hungry, clothed the naked, shown mercy to the prisoner and outcast—who have, in short, done the works of Christ . . . . It does no good to hail him 'Lord, Lord,' to honor his name in doctrine, hymn, and prayer, if one does not obey him (Matt. 7:21-23)."[40]

J. Paul Nyquist: "Most American Christians . . . haven't given up much. Our faith has been an asset. But this will radically change as hostility ramps up."[41]

Jim Seibert: "These people who had said 'yes' to the message of the Kingdom were beginning to experience the reality of the Kingdom. What the church is and should be is this: believers gathering house to house, praying, studying the Word, experiencing a sense of equality, seeing signs and wonders, feeling the awe of God, and adding to their numbers day by day. . . . This is the way that the world will be won today, by the church being the church, carrying and imparting Kingdom values."[42]

---

[36] Todd Wilson, *Real Christian: Bearing the Marks of Authentic Faith* (Grand Rapids, MI.: Zondervan, 2014), 105.

[37] Rushdoony, *Law and Society*, 634.

[38] Joyce Meyer, "Living In God's Rest," *Charisma*, July 2015, 16.

[39] McLaren, *a Generous Orthodoxy*, 32.

[40] Bright, *The Kingdom of God,* 221.

[41] Nyquist, *Prepare.* 127.

[42] Jim Seibert, *The Church Can Change the World* (Waco, TX.: Antioch Community Church, 2008), xvi-xvii.

Leon Morris: ". . . Christ's example 'is constantly held up, not merely as a model, but a motive.' . . . and Paul sees him as the pattern and motive for Christians."[43]

William Barclay: (1907-1978) was a Scottish author, minister, and Professor of Divinity and Biblical Criticism at the University of Glasgow. He wrote a commentary series on all or most all the books of the Bible. The following are some appropriate excerpts taken from his commentary on the Book of Romans:

> A religion which stresses the importance of works is often contemptuously waved aside as being quite out of touch with the New Testament. Nothing could be further from the truth. . . . . One of the most dangerous of all religious tendencies is to talk as if faith and works were entirely different and separate things. There can be no such thing as faith which does not issue in works, nor can there be works which are not the product of faith. How, in the last analysis, can God judge a man other than by his deeds?[44]

> Christianity is not an emotional experience; it is a way of life. The Christian is not meant to luxuriate in an experience however wonderful; he is meant to go out and live a certain kind of life in the teeth of the world's attacks and problems. It is common in the world of religious life to sit in church and feel a wave of feeling sweep over us. . . . But the Christianity which has stopped there, has stopped half-way. That emotion must be translated into action. Christianity can never be only an experience of the inner being; it must be a life in the marketplace.[45]

> . . . the Christian can have no master but God. He cannot give a part of his life to God, and another part to the world. With God it is all—or nothing. So long as man keeps some part of his life without God, he is not really a Christian. A Christian is a man who has given complete control of his life to Christ, holding nothing back.[46]

> Jesus does not want followers who have not stopped to count the cost. He does not want a man to express impermanent loyalty on the crest of

---

[43] Leon Morris, *The Epistle to the Romans* (Grand Rapids, MI.: Eerdmans, 1988), 499 – in quotation of Hodge.

[44] Barclay, *The Letter to the Romans*, 44.

[45] Ibid., 86-87.

[46] Ibid., 89.

a wave of emotion. The Church has a duty to present the faith in all the riches of its offer and the heights of its demands to those who wish to become its members.[47]

There is enough of the natural man in most of us to like to get our rights; but the Christian man has no rights—he has only duties. . . . We must not be sluggish in zeal. There is a certain intensity in the Christian life; there is no room for lethargy in it. The Christian cannot take things in an easy-going way, for the world is always a battleground between good and evil, the time is short, and life is a preparation for eternity. The Christian may burn out, but he must not rust out. . . . The one man whom the Risen Christ could not stand was the man who was neither hot nor cold (*Revelation* 3:15, 16). Today people are apt to look askance upon enthusiasm; the modern battle-cry is "I couldn't care less." But the Christian is a man desperately in earnest; he is aflame for Christ.[48]

Truly, What Is Biblical Christianity?

Jesus did not present the kingdom as a self-help program. He presented and modeled it as a self-denial lifestyle. So what does following Jesus look like in everyday life today? We'll address this in Chapter 12. But if Jesus, Paul, and the early Church are not our model of what true biblical Christianity is, then we have no model and everything is up for grabs.

The disheartening reality today for American society at large is, church is mostly a meeting place, a social gathering spot to get to know a few nice people. And/or, it is a place to worship and learn about things that happened some 2,000 years ago. Hence, most of us Christians have been conditioned and are content to live with that level of "Christianity"—a once mighty faith now without a mighty kingdom. No wonder the world and its cultures are largely passing us by.

According to Edwards: "There is no similarity to how we practice present-day evangelical Christianity as over against the way the church

---

[47] Ibid., 90.
[48] Ibid., 164-165.

practiced Christianity in Century One."[49]   Later, he adds (I quoted this in the Introduction), "Jesus Christ never intended for the Christian life to be lived on so low a level as it is today."[50]   Likewise, Munroe complains that the term "Christian" has "detracted many people from the original purpose, message, and mission of the Kingdom of God" and "tends to mentally lock a person into a religious mold and limits the reality of the truth about the Kingdom."[51]

Perhaps, it's also like what some critics have accused:

> . . . the church drifted into the religion business. . . . Jesus came to start a movement that would advance his mission . . . . this plan got hijacked early on by some religionists who managed to institutionalize the movement [around A.D. 300 with Constantine and the Roman Empire]. The result of those efforts is largely what you and I have come to think of as Christianity. . . . but a lot of what happens at church is really just cultural stuff. Preachers don't usually call it that, but churches adapt to the culture they identify with and take on the communication style they feel most comfortable with. . . . you only have to *say* you're a Christian; following the teachings of Jesus seems optional.[52]

Indeed, a yawning gulf exists between the type of Christianity most Christians and churches today preach, teach, model, and practice compared to the Christianity we find in the New Testament. Instead, we have settled for more comfortable and accommodating versions—ones reduced to principally being centered on Jesus' birth, life, death, and resurrection. This reductionism has produced millions of Christians who are "fairly private about my faith and personal beliefs."[53] But where is the kingdom in that and with us being "fellow workers for the kingdom of God" (Col. 4:11; also 1 Cor. 3:9; 2 Cor. 6:1; 5:20)?

Not surprisingly today, we are also witnessing the decline of many institutional churches and the rise of the so-called post-Christian era. So I ask you, why shouldn't this massive dilution of our faith, Christianity's

---

[49] Edwards, *Revolutionary Study Bible*, 5.

[50] Ibid., 110.

[51] Munroe, *Rediscovering the Kingdom*, 41.

[52] Henderson and Casper, *Jim and Casper Go To Church*, 7, 19, 89, 157.

[53] From a personal email from and following a lunch discussion with a Presbyterian, 2/19/15.

division into some 40,000 denominations, and so few Christians following our Lord's commands, be termed the, or at least a, "Great Apostasy?" If that characterization seems too strong, how would you frame it? Billy Graham frames it this way:

> If someone is sincerely committed to Jesus Christ, it will make a difference in the way he or she lives. . . . the Bible warns us against claiming we are following Christ, when in reality we aren't. We may claim to be Christians . . . we even may be active in a church, but we've never allowed Christ to take control of our lives. The Bible warns, "Faith without deeds [works] is dead" (James 2:26).[54]

In this author's opinion, there is only one way to change all this in the Church today. We have to reclaim and restore the preaching, teaching, and practices of the kingdom of God that Jesus announced, taught, modeled, trained and sent out, warned, conferred, and commanded his followers to seek, enter, and advance.

Do You Find This Jesus Offensive?

Jesus' first disciples were squarely faced with a choice. Would they follow Jesus in the manner He modeled and commanded and be bearers of his kingdom, or not? Today, we are faced with this same choice.

No question about it; one of the most radical statements of the New Testament was Jesus' announcement: "he that believeth on me, the works that I do shall he do also . . . ." (John 14:12a *KJV*). Does this kingdom statement make you angry? Back then, they killed Jesus because his kingdom was so offensive and threatening. Likewise, throughout subsequent history, many have attempted to destroy, discredit, defame, or devalue his kingdom.

Darrell L. Guder recalls that "the favored way to accomplish this over the centuries has been to diminish the historical particularity of Jesus by reducing him and his message to a set of ideas, an intellectual system, often connected with a codified ethic, and managed thematically

---

[54] Billy Graham, "My Answer," "We are . . . the way we live," *The Indianapolis Star*, 5/4/15, E-4.

within the church's rites and celebrations," thus, making "it more compatible to our world and palatable for ourselves."[55]

He adds that "the real and sinful purpose of reductionism is to back away from the call of Jesus . . . . to reduce the gospel, to bring it under control, to render it intellectually respectful, or to make it serve another agenda than God's purposes."[56]

Kendall goes so far as to suggest that "if Jesus came to many churches today, the first thing He would do is to make a whip out of cords and drive money changers out and overturn their tables, as described in John 2:14-15."[57]

The fact are, Jesus' kingdom and its distinguishing marks, as ministered by Him and his true followers, were and still are offensive, if not frightening to many. Yet obedience and a faithful witness to this same-natured kingdom and its King by Jesus' first followers, along with the empowerment of the Holy Spirit, proved world transforming. Luke records: "*In this way* [not in some other way] the word of the Lord spread widely and grew in power" (Acts 19:20; also see 5:12-14 – *emphasis added*). Consequently, their opponents accused them of "turning the world upside down" (Acts 17:6). Today, it seems the conversion process has gone the wrong way. As a result, the kingdom of God has been replaced with church programs and other ancillary activities—good ones, of course, but replacements, nonetheless.

Today, we are faced with this same choice.

Allow me to illustrate the offensiveness of Jesus' kingdom in a modern-day and practical manner. How do you feel most churches, elders, pastors, and attendees in America would respond if 12 or 70 unlearned people from out in the county showed up at their church one Sunday morning and started preaching the kingdom of God is at hand; then started ministering by driving out demons, healing the sick, and cleansing those with various skin diseases from some of the staff, elders, members, the pastor, and even the pastor's wife?

---

[55] Guder, *The Continuing Conversion of the Church*, 101-102.
[56] Ibid., 102.
[57] Kendall, *Holy Fire*, 93.

Or let us put the shoe on the other foot. How successful do you think your church or seminary would be enlisting 12 or 70 people to go out into your local neighborhoods, proclaim this same message, and minister those same kingdom works?

I suspect not many modern-day, American Christians would want anything to do with this type of activity. And why not? Kendall cautions: "it is too easy to make fun of things like this. . . . don't do it. You have no idea what you may be criticizing."[58] Realistically, doesn't this radical and intense form of Christianity go against the grain of our modern-day sensitivities, intellectualism, and desires for control? Most Christians I know would not respond positively and probably would not show up at this church the following week. Just like many 1st-century Jews, they would defame and dismiss this type of activity. In other words, it's not what "going to church" has been all about.

Most Christians, at least here in America, seem to have decided they would rather not have a God who demanded this kind of living sacrifice from them on this scale and scope. Moreover, they don't think they will be held accountable for this omission. They prefer their reductionist gospel, watered-down faith, and a reticent God who demands little and withholds his wrath. They've set out to live a comfortable, non-confrontational life of loving Jesus and looking forward to heaven. And that's it for many, if not most, people who call themselves "Christians" today. If you agree with my assessment here, then isn't their use of that label of "Christian" a misrepresentation?

Surely, it begs this last cathartic question.

What Is the Kingdom's Present-day Status?

The kingdom is fully present, still increasing but greatly unaccounted for, under-utilized, and under-realized! Perhaps now we can begin to sense that there is a great deal more required of those who claim to be Christians or rather followers of Jesus Christ.

In his book, *Radical*, David Platt acknowledges, "that we have mistakenly turned the 'radical Jesus of the Bible . . . into the comfortable Jesus of 21st-century American culture.' He warns that the culture of

---

[58] Ibid., 162.

'self-advancement, self-esteem, and self-sufficiency' and our 'individualism, materialism, and universalism' have neutered American Christians' witness and blinded us . . . ." He calls for a return to the "radical faith in a radical Jesus." For Platt that means we must "commit to believe whatever Jesus says" and "commit to obey what we have heard."[59]

Russell Board agrees and ratchets up the intensity and consequences as he writes: "We mislead people and risk blasphemy when we put things in a nonthreatening way and downplay the demands of Christ. Whatever Jesus may be, He isn't nonthreatening. He is not a cute little god of good fortune. He is Lord of heaven and earth."[60]

Likewise, Martin Luther well warned us long ago: "No greater mischief can happen to a Christian people, than to have God's Word taken from them, or falsified, so that they no longer have it pure and clear. God grant we and our descendants be not witnesses of such a calamity."[61]

But isn't that exactly what we are witnessing today when the central teaching of Jesus is no longer the central teaching of his Church? Largely, we Christians have been turned into spectators, while professional clergy administer our weekly rituals. Seriously, if Jesus, Paul, and the early Church are our model(s) and we adhere to the force of Jesus' command to seek first his kingdom and his righteousness (Matt. 6:33) as our top priority, then what other viable choice do we have? If we truly claim to be believers in Jesus Christ (see again John 14:12; 1 John 2:5-6) and desire to hear the words someday, "Well done, good and faithful servant!" (Matt. 25:21, 23; Luke 19:17), what then shall we do?

". . . it is too easy to make fun of things like this. . . . don't do it. You have no idea what you may be criticizing."

---

[59] Quoted in Matthew Lee Anderson, "Here Come the Radicals," *Christianity Today*, March, 2013, 20-23.

[60] Russell Board, "Foreign Gods," *World,* April 30, 2005, 43.

[61] Martin Luther, trans. by William Hazilitt, *Table Talk* (Philadelphia: Lutheran Board of Publication, 1868), chapter one, section 12.

Even the much-revered Billy Graham has acknowledged in the first sentence of a lead article in the October 2000 issue of his ministry's *Decision* magazine that "Extending the Kingdom of God on earth—This is the essential reason for our existence as Jesus Christ's servants."[62]

The kingdom of God on this earth is simply God's will being done. This is what Jesus said He came for, "not to do my will but to do the will of him who sent me" (John 6:38; 4:34). That was Jesus' mindset. He was committed to that goal, along with his dying on the cross. He was God's will, reign, and rule in action. And He sends us out in the same way to do the same kingdom works—"As the Father has sent me, I am sending you" (John 20:21; also see Matt. 7:21; 12:50; 28:18-20; John 14:15). Thus, He says, "Follow Me." So isn't that what Christ-likeness is to be about—to do God's will as Jesus did? Isn't this putting our faith into action? Isn't this how we will or won't be "counted worthy of the kingdom of God" (2 Thess. 1:5; also see 1 Tim. 1:12)? Isn't this basic Christianity? Or is it not anymore?

If it is, shouldn't we stop merely saying we love people and start showing it by being faithful witnesses in following the example of Jesus, Paul, and the early Church? Isn't it in this way, and only this way, that we shall be able to present visible proof to our modern-day world of the presence of God's kingdom rule, differentiate ourselves from the world, and show them clearly what it really means to be a Christian? Isn't it in this way, and only this way, that we can save our Christian youth from becoming secularized and leaving the faith and the Church in droves?

Closing question: If Christianity has been as successful as it has been to date (with one-third of the world's current 6-billion-plus people claiming to be Christians), how much more successful could it be if the central teaching of Jesus, once again, became the central teaching and authentic outreaching ministry of his Church—i.e., reclaiming our "once mighty faith?"

Closing caveat: If you have been offended by the nature of Jesus' kingdom presented in this and the previous chapter and his declaration that those of us who believe in Him will be doing the same works He did, wait until we get to our next chapter. According to Jesus, we Christians are also to be doing "even greater works" than He did (John 14:12). How is that possible? Does that blow your mind?

---

[62] Billy Graham, "Extending the Kingdom of God," *Decision* (October 2000):1.

Chapter 11

Step #4 – Naming the Greater Works

Verily, verily, . . . and greater works than these shall he do;
because I go unto my Father (John 14:12, KJV).

W as Jesus kidding? Isn't this notion utterly impossible? Do you really think Jesus expects us Christians today to perform "greater works" than He did, not to mention "the works I do?" And do you truly think He will hold us accountable for *not* doing this? If not, then why did He preface his future indicative statement, "shall he do," with oath language—verily, verily, truly, truly, I tell you the truth?

If you were offended by Jesus' proclamation that we would do the same works He did (covered in chapters 9 and 10), wait until we start naming these "greater works."[1] What these "greater works" are, however, has not been left to our imaginations or whims. They are clearly and fully revealed throughout God's Word. Hence, Jesus said: "There is nothing concealed that will not be disclosed, or hidden that will not be made known" (Matt. 10:26; also Luke 8:17; 12:2). As hard as it may be to fathom, these greater works are, indeed, greater than those Jesus did. That is why He called them the greater works.

---

[1] Some of the material in this chapter was originally published in Noē, *Off Target*, 189-204.

The Prairie Chicken/Eaglet Parable

One of my favorite stories is an old American Indiana folklore legend. But I believe it's also a modern-day parable. It's about an eaglet (a baby eagle) that falls out of his nest down to the prairie floor below. He's picked up off the ground by a brood of prairie chickens. They take him under their wings as one of their own and teach him how to scratch and claw the ground for seeds and insects.

Then one day, while the eaglet and his prairie chicken family are out scratching and clawing the ground for seeds and insects, the eaglet looks up into the sky and sees this magnificent bird, wings outstretched, and soaring to great heights on the thermals above.

"Wow," exclaims the eaglet. "What kind of bird is that?"

"Oh, that's the eagle, he's the chief of birds," a fellow prairie chicken volunteers. "But don't you give him a second thought because you could never be like him."

So for the rest of his life the eaglet, thinking he was a prairie chicken, never gave it a second thought and daily went out and scratched and clawed the ground for seeds and insects, until the day he died.

Fellow Christians, it's time for us to stop listening to some of our "prairie-chicken" brothers and sisters. We were created to "soar on wings like eagles . . . ." (Isa. 40:31). Yet many of us treat our faith like we are prairie chickens. We look up to Jesus and disclaim, "We can never be like Him." And yet that is exactly what Jesus calls all believers in Him to be—here and now, on this earth, and during this life. And most certainly, He will hold us accountable. So what will it be, hearing the words someday, "Well done, good and faithful servant" (Matt. 25:21a, 23a)? Or will it be hearing something less and troubling (see Matt. 25:26-30)? So I ask you, dare we settle for merely scratching and clawing the ground for seeds and insects when we're born and born again to soar with Him?

The Church Problem

Some of our fellow Christians who have taken us under their wings think it's arrogant or even blasphemous to expect or even entertain the thought that we can or should be doing the same or greater works than

Jesus did (see again John 14:12). But Jesus is the one who made these statements—not I, not Paul, not Peter, and not some radical pastor or right-wing charismatic. And He used common and ordinary words frequently employed in the New Testament: "Greater" = *meizon* (*midé zone*): larger (lit. or fig.), greater, more. "Works" = *ergon* (from *ergo*, to work): deed, doing, labor, work.

"But don't you give him a second thought because you could never be like him."

Nevertheless, "interpreters have been at a loss in what way to understand this."[2] Many have attempted to neutralize his statements concerning this Christian privilege and duty. But as we shall see, there is no neutrality possible in one's response to Jesus (see Matt. 12:30). Make no mistake; Jesus was clearly a radical and called and calls his followers to be radicals as well, even greater radicals.

Speculation Abounds

Below is an overview of some of the many different ideas that have been spawned about what these "greater works" might be—i.e., perhaps Jesus meant . . .

Greater in effect/extent – This cannot refer to miracles themselves (their quality) but to greater in their effects or extent, or more extensive results, or affecting larger numbers of people and the conversion of more sinners and souls in many nations. We must think in terms of Christian TV, satellites, radio, Internet, books, etc.

Greater in kind, not in degree – Christ had healed with the hem of his garment. But the very shadow of Peter and handkerchiefs and aprons of Paul healed. By the words of Peter, Ananias and Sapphira were struck dead. By Paul's words, Elymas the sorcerer was struck blind.

Greater in location – Christ only preached in one country and in one language; but the apostles preached in most of the known world and in many languages.

---

[2] *Barnes' Notes Commentary.*

Greater in power – They and we would have more power to do the "works" than his disciples had when He first sent them out. The reasons are "because I go unto my Father" and the sending of the Holy Spirit at Pentecost. Hence, these "greater works" would not be done independently from Christ; but with Him in the form of answered prayer and the Holy Spirit operating in and through them and us (Eph. 3:20).

Greater in time – Christ only did miracles for three and a half years, but his followers would do so for ages.

Greater in manpower – We will do more than Jesus because He was only one man and there are more of us with millions of relationships.

Greater in faith – John 6:28-29: We would have "to believe in the one he has sent." Hence, the greater works is faith. But did Jesus have "faith" (see Heb. 11:1)? He only did what He saw the Father doing (John 5:19-20). Thus, Jesus didn't need faith. He had personal experience and previous knowledge of the Father and the workings of the Godhead, having been with them before the beginning of creation and before his birth incarnation.

Greater in quality – The works of Jesus' followers are of a greater quality, since they belong to the era of God's promises fulfilled—i.e., the gift of God's Spirit and the forgiveness of sins both come about because of Jesus' work on the cross. Luke 7:28 is offered in support: "I tell you, among those born of women there is no one greater than John; yet the one who is least in the kingdom of God is greater than he." Thus, according to Darrell Bock, "all believers in the new era are greater than he was, because their works are empowered by the Spirit."[3] But weren't Jesus' works and those of his first followers also empowered by the Spirit?

My Working Definition, Qualifications, and Amplifications

Admittedly, this topic calls for *some* speculation on my part; but not pure speculation. First and foremost, these greater works do not involve

---

[3] Darrell Bock, "Dribbling Circles Around Jesus," *Christianity Today*, June 06, 56.

Jesus' eschatological works. Only the Messiah could do those. They include:

- lowering Himself to be born of a virgin,
- bringing the fully established, everlasting form of the kingdom to earth,
- dying on the cross as the sacrifice for sin,
- going to the hadean realm and preaching to the spirits held captive,
- ascending to heaven and preparing it for us,
- sending the Holy Spirit,
- removing the Old Covenant system in a day of the Lord in judgment, and
- emptying out the hadean realm and locking it up.

Therefore, here is my working definition: The "Greater Works" are – "the works Jesus did *not* do during his earthly ministry, but works God's people have been instructed *to do* throughout Scripture—from the very beginning of the Old Testament to the very end of the New Testament."

So if we want to figure out what are the greater works, let's look at the things Jesus did not do that needed, and still need, to be done:

- Jesus did not lead a revolt against Rome or try to take it on or back for God. Are we to do so?
- Jesus didn't transform or reform the culture of his day (nor did the Apostles). Are we to do so?
- Jesus refused to be made their earthly king. Billy Graham explains: "He knew this was not God's plan for Him. If He became an earthly king, He knew His power would be limited, and He would never touch the whole world."[4] But are we to become earthly kings? Haven't we been made to be "kings and priests" (Rev. 1:6; 5:10 KJV)?
- He didn't make disciples of all nations—i.e., not only changing lives, but also laws, institutions, and relationships. Are we to do so?

---

[4] Billy Graham, "My Answer," *The Indianapolis Star*, 3/28/15, E4.

- Jesus was "only sent to the lost sheep of the house of Israel" (Matt. 15:24). He was not sent into "all the world" (Acts 1:8). Are we so sent?

- He didn't take back all the territory Satan and his forces—human and superhuman—had seized. Are we to do so?

- He didn't reign and rule over governments, peoples, and nations. Are we to do so?

- He did not engage in politics, take on political powers and structures, nor attempt to fix, steer, or assault the tyranny of the Roman government. Rather, He allowed Himself to be crucified by them. Are we to? In this regard, Carter raises these issues and answers: "Those who claim that Jesus was apolitical and interested in only what goes on in individuals' hearts/souls have a difficult time explaining how he could have ended up antagonizing the political powers enough to get himself crucified. . . . (others – activists) have a difficult time explaining why he taught his disciples to love their enemies and not to resist an evil person . . . . Jesus calls us to follow him in renouncing the world's reliance on power that originated in violent coercion and to rely instead on a witness that consists of proclaiming and living out the good news of the gospel."[5] Are we to do so?

- Jesus did not set out to reform society. Niebuhr adds, "He did not attempt to reform culture; He ignored it and everything concerned with material civilization. Therefore his people rejected him."[6] Are we to do so?

- He did not work to build a government or take a stretch of land. But Israel was commanded to do this. Are we to do so?

- He refused to use the means of this world, either the clash of arms or the processes of politics to further his ends. But Israel was commanded to do this. Are we to do so?

- The early Church had no hope of reforming the state or bringing it into conformity with the kingdom of God. Are we to do so?

- Jesus said "no" to the devil's offer to give Him "all the kingdoms of the world and their splendor" (Matt. 4:8). But the bishops of

---

[5] Carter, *Rethinking Christ and Culture*, 208.
[6] H. Richard Niebuhr, *Christ and Culture* (New York, NY.: Harper Torchbooks, 1951), 3.

the Christian Church in the 4th century said, "yes." Thus, Christendom was born. What do we do with that?

- He did not build a great church. Are we to do so?
- Neither Jesus nor any biblical writer gives us any mandate to fix the cultural order. Or did they?

The bottom line is, Jesus was anything but victorious culturally. He was despised, rejected, spit upon, beaten, and put to death like a common criminal. Clearly, his victory was the victory of the cross—yielding and submitting to the powers that be. And yet, there are these "greater works." Perhaps, Jesus' "greater works" include some or all of the above. But I think there is even more to this.

Before we go there, let's also note that Jesus did not change the world. What He did was provide the means for his followers to change the world. He provided these means via his eschatological works that He accomplished. Remember, Jesus lowered Himself and came into our world and human history to establish two great eschatological works: 1) the everlasting kingdom, and 2) salvation. Both were announced and accomplished in that order. It all took place in a small postage-stamp-sized patch of land in the Middle East during a short 74-year period of time.

Since that time, believers in Jesus are to continue his mission by doing both his ministry works and greater works. We know what his ministry works were. He modeled them for us. His "greater works"—in my opinion—can be described in this manner. Those of us who believe in Him are to <u>implement</u> / <u>advance</u> / <u>expand</u> / <u>extend</u> / <u>promote</u> / <u>put into practice</u> his two great eschatological works—that of the kingdom and that of salvation. They encompass the total victory of God through Christ in and over the whole world. Not only are human lives and activities to be transformed, but so is all of society—i.e., lives, laws, institutions, and relationships—social, political, economic, international, etc.

In other words, <u>the "greater works" are worldwide societal transformations, or cultural transformations, via advancement of Christ's everlasting and ever-increasing kingdom and comprehensive salvation.</u> These greater works are now part of our grand destiny as believers and followers of Jesus Christ. Hence, our responsibility and duty is to transmit the *full* redemptive work of Jesus Christ to the entire world in all its aspects. This scope of redemption is also the strength of the historic postmillennial view that advocates the advancement of the kingdom of God throughout the world and into all areas of society. This is how we Christians are biblically called by our Creator God, the Lord Jesus Christ, to live out the radical difference He made everlastingly available. Yes, it's about activism, not pietism; and "transforming through Christ," not "taking back for Christ"—big difference!

Jesus did not change the world. What He did was provide the means for his followers to change the world.

Leclaire concurs and reports that "transformation is possible in America and indeed transforming revival has broken out in communities around the world . . . . a neighborhood, a city, or nation whose values and institutions have been . . . . impacted comprehensively and undeniably by the kingdom of God; and a location where kingdom values are celebrated publicly and passed on to future generations. . . . God is calling forth an army of faithful followers who will come up out of their discouragement to boldly push back the darkness."[7] But many Christians do not agree.

Critical Objection: McKnight, for one, castigates this scope of application characterizing it as the "'Constantinian Temptation' . . . . In short, it seeks to influence and transform each of the various spheres of society and culture. That is, a kingdom vision expands the Christian vision into a secular culture, but—and here is the major problem in this approach—often the transformationalist can be found reframing and reducing and reforming the kingdom vision of the Bible to make it fit culture."[8] He cites these two examples that have ruled in the American Church: 1) from the Left, "social liberation" and 2) from the Right, "the focus of energy in this theory of the kingdom is the political process." Instead, he favors "seeing the church as the central place of kingdom expression . . . the place where kingdom work gets done best" and not "public activism for the common good."[9]

---

[7] Leclaire, "An Appeal to Heaven," *Charisma*, May 2015, 28, 30.

[8] McKnight, *Kingdom Conspiracy*, 228-229.

[9] Ibid., 224.

My Response: It's both/and, not either/or. As we shall next see, God's people have been given a worldwide mandate regarding the earth and everything in it. From Genesis to Revelation, this mandate directly follows from the *Lordship* of Christ. It counters those who claim we Christians should be "relegated to the private sphere." Pearcey rightly rejects this popular but delimiting notion. She calls it "a truncated view of Christianity's claims to be the truth about all of reality."[10]

Next, therefore, let's see what truly is the biblical testimony on this matter of God's people always having been called to be agents of societal transformation and to infuse every part with his kingdom and, post-Christ, with his salvation. Yes, this mandated vision requires biblical knowledge and understanding. It will also require responsive action.

Scriptural Support from the Old Testament

The Bible is full of verses and admonitions to transform society. Once again, this is something Jesus never did. But it's also nothing new either. It's a great theme woven throughout the Old and New Testaments. It is also widely ignored and denied in much of Christian theology and church circles. Unfortunately, many Christians have been conditioned to feel the world must get progressively worse and worse before Jesus returns to save it all by Himself, someday. But let's re-explore some of these verses, along with assorted comments. Perhaps, you could add more. (**Bold** emphasis is mine.)

Genesis 1:26a – "Then God said, 'Let us make man in our image, in our likeness, and let them **rule** . . . .'" This is the first mention of what's termed "the mandate of creation." As God's image-bearers we humans are to extend the image of God to all of creation.

Genesis 1:28 (KJV) – "Be fruitful, and multiply, and replenish the earth, and subdue it; and have **dominion** over the fish of the sea, and over the fowl of the air, and over every living thing that moveth upon the earth." It's our threefold purpose as God's image bearers (Gen. 1:26-27): 1) To protect what has been given, 2) To extend the glory of God to the ends of the earth, and 3) To extend his image to all of creation.

---

[10] Pearcey, *Total Truth*, 68-69

It is variously termed the "dominion mandate," "creation mandate," "Genesis mandate," "theocratic mandate," and "cultural mandate." I prefer "dominion mandate" for these two reasons. *Dominion* is a synonym for *kingdom*. And kingdom is a political metaphor that insists everything and everyone is under the will, reign, and rule of God, whether they realize it, and agree, or not. In other words, the "King-dom" is where the *King*, Jesus, is in *dominion* (see Isa. 9:7; Zech. 9:9; 14:9; Matt. 2:2, 27:11; Luke 19:38; John 1:49; 6:15; 12:13, 15; 18:37; Acts 17:7; 1 Tim. 1:17; 6:15; Rev. 17:14; 19:16).

Therefore, as God's image-bearers, we are to live out Jesus' kingdom in this world. We do that by being stewards over every aspect of God's earthly creation and serving as his divine representatives. In other words, we are to take dominion over all things. As we shall further see, this dominion mandate has never been rescinded. Rather, it has been enhanced and expanded.

Genesis 9:1-7ff – After the Fall, God repeats this mandate, thus reaffirming the continuance of man's image-bearing distinction for Noah and his sons to be stewards over all creation. This is the beginning of a "given, lost, regained/redeemed" theme. Hence, this mandate was not lost or rescinded at the Fall as some have asserted.

Genesis 12:3b – "and all the peoples (families *KJV*) of the earth will be **blessed through you**." This blessing was not to be hoarded or privatized, which was one of the errors of the Old Covenant Jews. Notably, in Galatians 3:29 we are told that if we belong to Christ, then we "are Abraham's seed and heirs according to the promise." Like Abraham, we, too, are called to be a blessing to "all the peoples of the earth." Passing on this blessing of worldwide dominion is also what the Lord's Prayer is all about: "Thy kingdom come; *Thy will be done on earth as it is in heaven*" (Matt. 6:10). So how extensive is his dominion and kingdom?

Exodus 20:5-6 – "You shall **not bow down to them or worship them** [other gods – vs. 3]; for I, the LORD your God am a jealous God, punishing the children for the sin of the fathers to the third and fourth generation of those who hate me, but showing love to thousands who love me and keep my commandments." Question: Is America bowing down to "other gods" today—such as secularism and humanism? Remember, biblical history shows us that God judges the compromisers along with their country.

Deuteronomy 30:16 – "For I command you today to love the LORD your God, to **walk** in his ways, and to **keep** his commands, decrees and laws; then you will live and increase, and the LORD your God will **bless** you in the land you are entering to **possess**." Do you think this command included the "dominion mandate?"

Joshua 21:43-45 – "So the LORD gave Israel all the land he had sworn to give their forefathers, and they **took possession** of it and settled there. The LORD gave them rest on every side, just as he had sworn to their forefathers. Not one of their enemies withstood them; the LORD **handed all their enemies over to them**. Not one of all the LORD's good promises to the house of Israel failed; every one was fulfilled."

Brandon Vallorani contributes that "the historical account of Israel battling to acquire the Promised Land depicts [typologically] the Church's battle to advance the Kingdom of Christ. God did not instantly purify the land for the Israelites any more than he has purified the whole earth for us. Rather, He instructs His people to trust in His power, roll up their sleeves, and get to work . . . . There is a greater blessing by participating in the work of God as opposed to taking the fatalistic approach of expecting God to do all the work while we sit idly by! The Church, like Israel, is required to obey the Law in order to succeed."[11] Unlike the Israelites of the Old Covenant, we today are promised the whole world. But like them, we have to go out, fight for the land, take it, and possess it—with God on our side. That's the type and antitype (fulfillment picture) being presented here.

Joshua 23:10 – "One of you **routs** a thousand, because the LORD your God **fights** for you, just as he promised."

2 Chronicles 7:14 – "If my people, who are called by my name, will **humble** themselves and **pray** and **seek** my face and **turn** from their wicked ways, then will I hear from heaven and will forgive their sin and will **heal** their land." Jacobs calls this verse "the biblical model for 'healing the land.'"[12] But what "wicked ways" must they/we "turn from?" How about the abrogation of our dominion-mandated duties, for starters? (See again Chapter 4 pp. 112-114.)

---

[11] Brandon Vallorani, "Seek First the Kingdom (Part 2), *Biblical Worldview*, July 2007, 12.

[12] Jacobs, *The Reformation Manifesto*, 90.

2 Chronicles 16:9a (KJV) – "For the eyes of the LORD run to and fro throughout the whole earth, **to shew himself strong in the behalf of them** whose heart is perfect toward him."

Psalm 2:8-12 – "Ask of me, and I will make **the nations** your inheritance, the ends of the earth **your possession**. You will **rule** them with an iron scepter; you will **dash** them to pieces like pottery. Therefore, you kings, be wise; be warned, you rulers of the earth. **Serve** the Lord with fear and rejoice with trembling. **Kiss** the son, lest he be angry and you be destroyed in your way, for his wrath can flare up in a moment. **Blessed** are all who take **refuge** in him." This messianic psalm for ruling the nations is part of and an enhancement and expansion of the original "dominion mandate."

Psalm 8:4-6 – "What is man that you are mindful of him, the son of man that you care for him? You made him a little lower than the heavenly beings [angels] and crowned him with glory and honor. You made him **ruler** [to have **dominion** – KJV] over the works of your hands; you put everything under his feet." Overman aptly summarizes here that "man was commissioned to manage God's very creation! That which He spoke into existence and proclaimed to be good, He entrusted into the hands of human beings for care and stewardship. Man, being created in God's image, was thoroughly equipped for the task because the capacity for rulership is also one of the central aspects of what it means to be made in the likeness of God. . . . We are the only creatures given stewardship, and a position of tremendous honor."[13]

Psalm 24:1 – "The earth is the LORD's, and **everything in it**, the world, and all who live in it." No exceptions, no exclusions. Everything means everything!

Psalm 50: 10, 12 – Is like Psalm 24:1.

Psalm 72:8 KJV – "His **dominion** shall be also from sea to sea and from the river unto the ends of the land." Commenting on this verse, Jacobs notes that "the Bible gives us sound doctrinal reason to take dominion over the powers of darkness and establish God's will—or dominion."[14]

Psalm 82:3 – "**Defend** the cause of the weak and fatherless; **maintain the rights** of the poor and oppressed." This is termed "doing

---

[13] Overman, *Assumptions That Affect Our Lives*, 59.
[14] Jacobs, *The Reformation Manifesto*, 186.

justice" as we reflect the justice/righteousness of God. (Also see Psalm 45:6; 11:5-7.)

Psalm 94:16 – "Who will **rise up** for me **against** the wicked? Who will take a stand for me against evildoers?"

Psalm 103:19 – "The LORD has established his throne in heaven, and his kingdom **rules over all**." Indeed, the universe is a theocracy.

Psalm 110:1-2 – "The LORD says to my Lord: 'Sit at my right hand until I make your enemies a **footstool** for your feet.' The LORD will extend your mighty scepter from Zion; rule in the midst of your enemies." Another messianic psalm.

Psalm 115:16 – "The highest heavens belong to the LORD but the **earth** he has **given to man**." Yes, God's people are his stewards.

Psalm 149:5-9 – "Let the saints rejoice in this honor and sing for joy on their beds. May the praise of God be in their mouths and a double-edged sword in their hands, **to inflict vengeance** on the nations and **punishment** on the peoples, **to bind** their kings with fetters, their nobles with shackles of iron, to **carry out** the sentence written against them. This is **the glory** of all his **saints**. Praise the LORD."

Proverbs 21:3 – "To do what is **right and just** is more acceptable to the LORD than sacrifice." Again, "doing justice."

Ecclesiastes 12:13 – "Here is the conclusion of the matter: **Fear** God and **keep** his commandments, for this is the whole **duty** of man." Does that include the "dominion mandate?"

Isaiah 1:16-17 – "Stop doing wrong, learn to do right! **Seek justice**, **encourage** the oppressed. **Defend** the cause of the fatherless, **plead** the case of the widow." Unbiblical laws need to be abolished or our societies will suffer for the sin they allow. This is termed "biblical law." Is it part of the "dominion mandate?"

Isaiah 9:6-7 – "For to us **a child is born**, to us a son is given, and the **government** will be on his shoulders. And he will be called Wonderful Counselor, Mighty God, Everlasting Father, Prince of Peace. Of the **increase** of his government and peace there will be **no end**. He will **reign** on David's throne and over his kingdom, establishing and upholding it with justice and righteousness from that time on and forever."

This is the messianic prophecy of the then-coming everlasting kingdom and Jesus' major enhancement and expansion of the "dominion mandate." Andy Crouch touches on an important aspect of a coupling contained in the Isaiah 9:7 verse above:

> Prophets and psalmists thought in twos: throne and kingdom, establishing and upholding, justice and righteousness. . . . justice and righteousness belong together . . . [they] show up together more than 30 times in the Hebrew Bible, nearly always in a political context. Because justice and righteousness are the foundation of God's throne (Ps. 89:14), they are also the "measuring line" and the "plumb line" (Isa. 28:17) of earthly thrones.[15]

Isaiah 58:6-7 – "Is not this the kind of fasting I have chosen: **to loose** the chains of injustice and **untie** the cords of the yoke, to **set** the oppressed **free** and **break** every yoke? Is it not to **share** your food with the hungry and to **provide** the poor wanderer with shelter – when you see the naked, to **clothe** him, and **not to turn away** from your own flesh and blood?"

Isaiah 59:15b-16a – "The LORD looked and was displeased that there was **no justice**. He saw that there was **no one**, and he was appalled that there was **no one** to intercede."

Isaiah 61:8a – "For I, the LORD **love justice**; I hate robbery and iniquity." (Also see Matt. 23:23.)

Jeremiah 1:6-12 – "'Ah, Sovereign LORD,' I said, 'I do not know how to speak; I am only a child.' But the LORD said to me, 'Do not say 'I am only a child.' You must go **to everyone** I send you to and say whatever I command you. Do **not be afraid** of them, for I am with you and will rescue you,' declares the LORD. Then the LORD reached out his hand and touched my mouth and said to me, 'Now, I have put my words in your mouth. See, today **I appoint you over nations and kingdoms to uproot and tear down, to destroy and overthrow, to build and to plant.'** The word of the LORD came to me: 'What do you see, Jeremiah?' I see the branch of an almond tree,' I replied. The LORD said to me, 'You have seen correctly, for **I am watching** to see that my word is fulfilled.'" Is this not a continuation of the "dominion mandate?"

Ezekiel 22:30 – "I looked for a man among them who would build up the wall and **stand before me in the gap** on behalf of the land so I

---

[15] Andy Crouch, "Salt-and-Pepper Politics," *Christianity Today*, October 2004, 108.

would not have to destroy it, but I found none." Check out the context for this in verses 25, 27, and 29.

Ezekiel 34:1-4 – "The word of the LORD came to me: 'Son of man, **prophesy against** the shepherds of Israel . . . . Woe to the shepherds of Israel who only take care of themselves! Should not shepherds take care of the flock? You eat the curds, clothe yourselves with the wool and slaughter the choice animals, but you do not take care of the flock. You have **not strengthened** the weak or **healed the sick** or **bound up the injured**. You have **not brought back** the strays or **searched** for the lost. You have **ruled** them harshly and brutally."

Daniel 7:13-14 (KJV) – ". . . And there was given him **dominion**, and **glory**, and a **kingdom**, that all people, nations, and languages, **should serve him**: his **dominion** is an everlasting **dominion**, which shall not pass away, and his kingdom that which shall not be destroyed." Again, prophesying of the enhancement and expansion of dominion yet to come.

Daniel 7:18, 27 – But at some point in history "the saints of the Most High" were to **"receive"** this kingdom and this dominion and **"possess it** forever" as it was to be **"handed over"** to the saints" by Christ. This is exactly what Jesus did during his earthly ministry (see Luke 22:29-30).

Amos 5:24 – "**Let justice roll** down like waters, and righteousness as a mighty stream." Many Old Testament verses speak about "justice." Wright terms this "the great theme of the justice of God."[16]

Micah 6:8 – "And what does the Lord **require of you**: To **act justly** and to **love mercy** and to **walk humbly** with your God." The Jewish prophetic tradition was a combination of both forth-telling and foretelling, with forth-telling being the major component. Forth-telling involved calling out wrongs, idolatry, and injustices in the current culture and a prediction of hard times ahead should Israel not change its ways. Israel didn't and paid the ultimate price.

Haggai 2:8 – "'The **silver** is mine and the **gold** is mine,' declares the LORD Almighty." That means economics (silver and gold) is a spiritual and kingdom issue (also see again Psa. 50:10, 12 and 24:1).

Zechariah 7:9-12 – "This is what the LORD Almighty says: '**Administer true justice**; show **mercy** and **compassion** to one another.

---

[16] N.T. Wright, *Evil and the Justice of God* (Downers Grove, IL.: IVP Books, 2006), 117.

Do **not oppress** the widow or the fatherless, the alien or the poor. In your hearts do not think evil of each other.' But they refused to pay attention; stubbornly they turned their backs and stopped up their ears. They made their hearts as hard as flint and would not listen to the law or to the words that the LORD Almighty had sent by his Spirit through the earlier prophets. So the LORD Almighty was **very angry**." Divine judgment would come upon Israel for disobeying God's "dominion mandate."

So does all this change when we get to the New Testament? Let's see.

Scriptural Support from the New Testament

Matthew 5-7 – These three chapters, known as *The Beatitudes*, are at the heart of Christ's kingdom and the road map for what being "in Christ," doing his "works," and "even greater works" are all about. Especially, let's note the call to be salt and light (see Matt. 5:13-15). Salt favors, cures, and heals. It also preserves, purifies, creates thirst, generates heat, melts frozen barriers, and stings sometimes as it penetrates and solves problems. Light illuminates truth and shines out so people can see good deeds and the direction they are supposed to go.

Regrettably, however, dispensational premillennialists do not believe these conditions belong directly to "the church age." They believe these conditions will *only* be brought to earth at the so-called "second coming" of Jesus and realized during the millennium—i.e., the millennial kingdom and temporary reign of Christ (see Appendix B).

In the meantime, as Jacobs embarrassingly points out in quotation of Francis A. Schaeffer, "our culture, society, government, and law are in the condition they are in *because the church has forsaken its duty to be the salt of the culture*."[17]

Matthew 6:10 – "your kingdom come your will **be done** on earth as it is in heaven." Jacobs wisely advises that "it is not enough to simply pray [this prayer]. . . .[W]e need to implement it. This takes a reformation of our thinking. . . ."[18]

---

[17] Jacobs, *The Reformation Manifesto*, 209 from Francis A. Schaeffer, *A Christian Manifesto* (Wheaton, IL.: Crossway Books, 1981), 66 (see ch. 6, n. 1).
[18] Jacobs, *The Reformation Manifesto*, 168.

Matthew 6:33 – "But **seek first** his kingdom and his righteousness (justice), and **all these things** will be given to you as well." McLaren explains that "he is not saying two things, but one: God's kingdom is God's justice," as well as its being "God's will being done on earth as it is in heaven (6:10)."[19] This verse is another continuation and expansion of the dominion mandate with Jesus bringing justice to the oppressed.

David Neff further elucidates that "the Greek word *dikaiosune* can easily mean *justice* as *righteousness*. Unfortunately, the translation of *righteousness* has overtones of personal piety . . . . We need a stronger contrast between these works of piety and what constitutes the essence of the kingdom of God."[20] But most Bibles translate that word as righteousness because, as McLaren maintains, that is "more pleasing to us." Notwithstanding, the original Greek word is better translated as "justice." And "to seek God's kingdom and justice means, as the Lord's Prayer makes clear, to seek for God's will to be done on earth, as it is in heaven"[21]—which, of course, is done throughout heaven.

Matthew 28:19 – ". . . make disciples **of all nations** . . ." This command once again embraces the dominion mandate to transform the whole social unit. Wright elaborates that "just as Jesus taught his followers to pray that God's kingdom would come on earth as in heaven, so now he claims that all authority in heaven and on earth has been given to him, and on that basis he commands the disciples [and us today] to go and make it happen—to work, in other words, as agents of that authority . . . . go out and work for that kingdom, announce that lordship, and effect change through that power."[22]

Jacobs agrees that "we are called to disciple whole nations and teach them to observe everything God commanded." Poignantly, she asks, however, "What is the problem? How could there be roughly two billion Christians on the face of the earth today and the major problems of sin, poverty, and disease still plague the planet? Why haven't we figured out solutions to these problems? I understand that these are huge issues, but we have an even bigger God!"[23] Unfortunately, our ignorance or

---

[19] McLaren, *Everything Must Change*, 219.

[20] David Neff, "Signs of the End Times," *Christianity Today*, August 2011, 48.

[21] McLaren, *The Last Word and the Word After That*, 165.

[22] Wright, *Surprised by Hope*, 235, 264.

[23] Jacobs, *The Reformation Manifesto*, 35.

disobedience means "we miss the actual biblical mandate to go into the world and teach nations how to observe the morals, ethics, character, principles, and doctrines of the Bible. . . . we realize none of our responsibilities to teach society as a whole. . . . i.e., business, government, science, law, education, and the like."[24]

Mark 1:15 – "the time is fulfilled . . . the kingdom of God is **at hand**." What time was that? It was the time Daniel prophesied when "a huge mountain" [the kingdom] would fill "the whole earth" (Dan. 2:35, 44; 7:19-25). Again, this verse manifests the enhancement and expansion of the dominion mandate.

Mark 3:35 – "Whoever **does God's will** is my brother and sister and mother." (Also see Matt. 12:50; 7:21).

Luke 1:33 – "and **he will reign** over the house of Jacob forever; his kingdom **will never end**." This verse speaks to Mary and us of the fulfillment of Isaiah 9:6-7 and the expansion of the "dominion mandate" with the birth of the Messiah, Jesus of Nazareth. As we have seen, that time had now arrived in human history.

Luke 4:18-19, 21b – This is the Messiah's job description and another restatement of the dominion mandate. "The Spirit of the Lord is on me, because he has anointed me **to preach** good news to the poor. He has sent me **to proclaim** freedom for the prisoners and recovery of sight for the blind, **to release** the oppressed, **to proclaim** the year of the Lord's favor. . . . Today this scripture **is fulfilled** in your hearing." So how do we *only* get the salvation of souls, which supposedly keeps them from going to "hell," out of this?

Luke 6:46-48a – "Why do you call me, 'Lord, Lord,' and **do not do what I say**? I will show you what he is like who comes to me and hears my words and puts them into practice. He is like a man building a house, who dug down deep and laid a foundation **on rock** . . . ."

John 3:16-17 – "For God so loved the world . . . . but **to save the world** through him." John 3:16 is the most quoted verse in the Bible. But have we missed the point of the next verse—*that the world should be saved?* So did Jesus Christ come to save the world, or just a sinner here, a sinner there? Chilton clarifies that "He wants us to disciple the *nations*

---

[24] Ibid., 104.

– not just a few individuals."[25] Jacobs chimes in and laments that "we tend to interpret this Scripture as referring only to our salvation from hell. . . . [it] means a great deal more . . . ."[26]

Hence, David Chilton admonishes: "We must stop acting as if we are forever destined to be a subculture. *We are destined for dominion;* we should straighten up and start acting like it. Our life and worship should reflect our expectation of dominion and our increasing capacity for responsibility. We should not see ourselves as lonely outposts surrounded by an increasingly hostile world; that is to bear false witness against God."[27]

He further adds: "Our goal is a Christian world, made up of explicitly Christian nations. How could a Christian desire anything else? Our Lord Himself taught us to pray: 'Thy Kingdom come; *Thy will be done on earth, as it is in heaven'* (Matt. 6:10). . . . The Lord's Prayer is a prayer for the worldwide dominion of God's Kingdom – not a centralized world government, but a world of decentralized theocratic republics. Now by *theocracy* I do not mean a government ruled by priests and pastors. . . . [But] *a government ruled by God,* a government whose law code is solidly founded on the laws of the Bible. . . . the laws of the Bible are the *best* laws (Deut. 4:5-8). They cannot be improved upon. The fact is that all law is 'religious.' All law is based on some ultimate standard of morality and ethics."[28]

Romans 16:26b – ". . . so that **all nations** might **believe** and **obey** him." PLEASE NOTE: this is not just individuals, but "nations." And not just believe, but "believe" and "obey." That's societal transformation and redeeming the world, á la the dominion mandate. It's not just saving souls for heaven, although it includes that. Barclay accurately terms this transformation as both "the Christian privilege and the Christian duty."[29] Wright correctly asserts that "the whole world is now God's holy land,

---

[25] David Chilton, *Paradise Restored* (Ft. Worth, TX.: Dominion Press, 1987), 218.

[26] Jacobs, *The Reformation Manifesto*, 63.

[27] Chilton, *Paradise Restored*, 218.

[28] Ibid., 219.

[29] Barclay, *The Letter to the Romans*, 221.

we must not rest as long as that land is spoiled and defaced. This is not an extra to the church's mission. It is central."[30]

1 Corinthians 10:26 – "for 'The earth is the Lord's, and **everything in it.**'" A quotation of Psalm 24:1.

Philippians 3:14, KJV – This is the "**high calling** of God in Christ Jesus." Jacobs insists that this "high calling" means we Christians "are called to see His kingdom come and His will be done on the earth. This involves every structure of society, the thinking of individuals in nations down to the smallest child, every law, every government official elected according to biblical design, and every economic structure according to God's blueprint—the Holy Spirit-inspired Word of God."[31]

Colossians 1:20 – "and through him **to reconcile** to himself **all things**, whether things on earth or things in heaven . . . ." As Jacobs further points out: "All things" means "all structures, all parts of society, all groups of people." It's our "assignment by God to reconcile *all things.*"[32]

1 Timothy 6:12a; 1:18b – "fight the **good fight** of the faith."

2 Timothy 2:3 – "**Endure** hardship with us like a **good soldier** of Christ Jesus."

Hebrews 6:10 – "God is not unjust; he will not forget **your work** and **the love** you have shown him as you have **helped** his people and continue to help them."

Hebrews 11:33 – "who through faith **conquered** kingdoms, **administered** justice, and **gained** what was promised; who **shut** the mouths of lions, **quenched** the fury of the flames, and **escaped** the edge of the sword; whose weakness was **turned to strength**; and who became **powerful** in battle and **routed** foreign armies." This is what was said about some of those mentioned in the "Hall of Fame of Faith" throughout Hebrews 11.

James 1:22, 25b – "Do **not merely listen** to the word, and so **deceive** yourselves. **Do** what it says. . . . but doing it – he will be blessed in what he does."

James 4:17 – "Anyone, then, who knows the good he ought to do and **doesn't do it, sins**." Isn't this the bottom line?

[30] Wright, *Surprised by Hope*, 266.
[31] Jacobs, *The Reformation Manifesto*, 163-164.
[32] Ibid., 79.

<u>1 John 2:4</u> – "The man who says, 'I know him,' but **does not do** what he **commands** is a **liar**, and the truth is not in him." Francis Schaeffer expands this truism in declaring: "We must acknowledge and then act upon the fact that if Christ is our Savior, he is also our Lord in *all* of life. He is our Lord not just in religious things and not just in cultural things such as arts and music, but in our intellectual lives, and in business, and in our relation to society, and in our attitude toward the moral breakdown of our culture. . . . [This] includes thinking and acting as citizens in relation to our government and its laws. Making Christ Lord in our lives means taking a stand in very direct and practical ways against the world spirit of our age as it rolls along claiming to be autonomous, crushing all that we cherish in its path."[33]

Just because we may have been in church all our lives, we may feel that we are on the right track, faith and belief-wise, and based on what we've been told. But so much throughout both the Old and New Testaments confirms the continuance and expansion of the "dominion mandate." As we have seen, this fact is a well-documented theme. It provides a massive and persuasive foundation for doing the "works" and "greater works" of Jesus, as we have defined and presented above.

But the ultimate revelation in God's Word of progressive revelation is found in the Bible's last book, Revelation. Here, you will find the pinnacle support for the "dominion mandate" and doing the works of Jesus and even greater works. And remember, a strong case can and has been made that Revelation's entire prophecy was fulfilled in the 1st century and has been just as relevant and applicable ever since.[34]

<u>Revelation 1:6</u> – "and has **made us to be** a kingdom and priests **to serve** his God and Father—to him be glory and power for ever and ever! Amen."

<u>Revelation 2:26-27</u> – "To him who **overcomes** and **does my will** to the end, I will give **authority over the nations**—'He will **rule** them with an iron scepter; he will **dash** them to pieces like pottery'" (from Psa. 2:9).

<u>Revelation 3:15-16</u> – "I know your deeds, that you are neither cold nor hot. I wish you were either one or the other! So, because you are

---

[33] Francis A. Schaeffer, *The Great Evangelical Disaster* (Wheaton, IL.: Crossway Books, 1995), 39.

[34] See Noē, *Unraveling the End*, 331-362 and Noē, *The Greater Jesus*, 81-118.

lukewarm—neither hot nor cold—I am about **to spit** [spew/vomit] you out of my mouth."

Revelation 5:9b-10 – ". . . and with your blood you purchased men [and women] for God from every tribe and language and people and nation [this includes you and me, right?]. You have made them to be a kingdom and priests **to serve** our God, and they **will reign on the earth**."

Revelation 11:15b – "The kingdom of the world **has become** the kingdom of our Lord and of his Christ, and **he will reign** for ever and ever." (Part of the Hallelujah Chorus).

Revelation 12:10-11 – "Then I heard a loud voice in heaven say: '**Now** have come the **salvation** and the **power** and the kingdom of our God, and the **authority** of his Christ. For the accuser of our brothers, who accuses them before our God day and night, has been hurled down. They **overcame** him by the **blood** of the Lamb and by the word of their **testimony**; they did **not shrink** from death." Arguably and in a nutshell, this is the best definition of the full gospel in the Bible.

Revelation 21:24-26 – "The **nations will** walk by its light, and the kings of the earth will bring their splendor into it. On no day will its gates ever be shut, for there will be no night there. The glory and honor of **the nations** will be brought into it."

Revelation 22:2b – "On each side of the river stood the tree of life, bearing twelve crops of fruit, yielding its fruit every month. And the leaves of the tree are for **the healing of the nations**."

Most assuredly and scripturally, we Christians are not here on earth to "maintain." We have been purposely placed here to "obtain"—to take the land, the nations, the people for Christ and his kingdom. God has granted us this honor, this privilege, and this duty to be the instruments of his kingdom. Anything less is a lesser version of our "once mighty faith." We have sat nicely on our padded pews long enough. It's time to "rally the troops." The ongoing purpose of the Church and every Christian is to go forth, exercise dominion, advance the kingdom, and bring all things under the subjection and transformation of Jesus Christ. Like it or not, we must say no less than Scripture, lest we impoverish its message and degrade our "once mighty faith."

C. Peter Wagner has it right. We've "watered down the true message of the Kingdom of God, which is for us to take dominion."[35] Moore has it even more right in noting that there are many "voices that deny the authority of Christ, the truth of Scripture, and the sovereignty of God."[36] These voices adamantly oppose dominion theology and desire a milder, more comfortable, and "less-than-conquerors" version of Christianity—one that focuses on a quiet, private, and personal relationship with Jesus. Hence, as Jacobs recognizes: "Down through the ages there have been theologians who, rather than help to heal their nations, have hindered them through the tearing down of the validity of God's Word as the standard of truth."[37]

Critical Objection: "This is triumphalism!" and "performance-driven spirituality," decry, demean, and deride Christian critics of dominion theology.

My Response: Absolutely, this is triumphalism! But what else would a sincere reader of Scripture conclude from the scriptures we have presented above, and more? Is not Christianity foreordained to triumph? It's time for Christians to cease shrinking away from living at this "high calling" and high level of blessings, influence, and duty and to come out of the closet, engaging our world on all fronts, and redefine and remodel what it truly means to be a Christian—i.e., a follower of Christ.

. . . we Christians are not here on earth to "maintain." We have been purposely placed here to "obtain" —to take the land, the nations, the people for Christ and his kingdom.

Unashamedly, this is what full-orbed Christianity is all about. It requires belief, works, greater works, and performance. Like Christ's first disciples, we moderns are faced with a choice: Will we follow Jesus in the way He commands? Or will we settle for less, be muddled in mediocrity, and be basically indistinguishable from non-believers? He

---

[35] C. Peter Wagner, *Dominion!* (Grand Rapids, MI.: Chosen, 2008), 55.
[36] Ibid., 7.
[37] Jacobs, *The Reformation Manifesto*, 202.

calls for us to be radically different, to stand out, and not be nominal. So what kind of Christian are you, and what kind are you going be from now on? Sadly, complacency and confusion abound.

But if we are sincere and truly concerned about reaching the world for Christ and his kingdom, it's got to be, "Onward Christian soldiers!" It's got to be producing "fruitful labor" (Phil. 1:22) by following Jesus' agenda and not settling for our lesser agenda. It's got to be doing the will of the Father, as Jesus did. Indeed, this is a mightier and more demanding faith than most of us have been accustomed to. But this faith and his calling is not a request or an option. It's a command and a commission from our Lord (see again Matt. 28:18-20). Our great failures to understand this and issue derogatory charges of "triumphalism" result from an unwillingness to come to terms with or understand the Lordship of Christ over all of life and culture. Therefore, we find ourselves addicted to mediocrity and unwarranted defeatism. But as Overman emphasizes: "He is Lord of all whether a man acknowledges Him as such or not."[38] And each of us will ultimately be held accountable.

Critical Objection: "How tempting it can be—and how distracting from our primary mission—to devote so many efforts to rehabilitating society at large . . . . After all, neither Jesus nor Paul showed much concern about cleaning up the degenerative Roman Empire."[39]

My Response: Again, this pervasive non-involvement attitude demonstrates how far we Christians have fallen away from full-orbed Christianity. But this old evangelical adage says it all: "If He's not Lord of all, He's not Lord at all." Most certainly, we modern-day Christians have the numbers. What we lack is the will, knowledge, motivation, and vision. The main purpose and hope of this book is to change this.

Critical Objection: "The commission of the church is not to reform society, but to preach the Gospel."

My Response: Once again, this is a classic statement of gospel reductionism. It's a watering down of Christ's kingdom and a denial of the Bible's dominion mandate. But the dual goal and purpose of our secular-humanistic opposition is to "reform man and remake society." Do we dare yield all this territory to them? Sadly, that's what most

---

[38] Overman, *Assumptions That Affect Our Lives*, 62.
[39] Philip Yancey, "Exploring a Parallel Universe," *Christianity Today*, November 2005, 128.

Christians and the Church have been doing for the past 50 to 75 years here in America. And we are paying a huge price, as we have seen. But the radical call of the entire Bible is to transform every area of our world and cultures into conformity with Christ and his kingdom. As Jay W. Richards appropriately writes: "There is no pocket of society or human existence that lies outside of God's loving dominion."[40]

Most certainly, we modern-day Christians have the numbers. What we lack is the will, knowledge, motivation, and vision. The main purpose and hope of this book is to change this.

Isaac Watts certainly knew this truth back in 1719 when he penned these words in the hymn "Joy to the World:"

> No more let sins and sorrows grow,
> Nor thorns infest the ground;
> He comes to make his blessings flow
> Far as the curse is found.

Rushdoony expounds that "far as the curse is found" means "His dominion [extends] over all the earth and over every sphere of life and thought."[41] But what this above objection also shows is the importance for why we Christians must develop a kingdom mindset and become kingdom engaged in a meaningful sense. Wright concurs and terms the reductionist idea that the church's "proper business" is only "saving souls," a "radical distortion of Christian hope" that "belongs exactly with a quietism that leaves the world as it is and thus allows evil to proceed unchecked. . . . where we become mere dualists, retreating from the world." Likewise, he acknowledges that "we in the West have simply not thought in these terms for a couple of hundred years. Once again, William Wilberforce and others like him have something to teach us."[42]

---

[40] Jay W. Richards in Warren Cole Smith and John Stonestreet, *Restoring All Things*, i.
[41] Rushdoony, *Law and Society*, 198.
[42] Wright, *Surprised by Hope*, 269.

Greater Works Thoughts from Concerned Scholars

Rousas Rushdoony – "There is not one word of Scripture to indicate or imply that this [dominion/creation] mandate was ever revoked. There is every word of Scripture to declare that this mandate must and shall be fulfilled. . . . The church is sent into the world as part of Christ's imperialism to subjugate the world to His reign."[43]

"We can begin to see why Christianity is so impotent now. We live in a secularized world, where appearance *is* reality, and where Christianity is no longer seen as truly universal a faith but is limited to a concern for the afterlife. . . . [However] The kingship of Christ is a working rule. The Christian is called to extend the scope of the Kingdom into every realm."[44]

T.M. Moore – Many Christians are "too preoccupied with their petty personal issues to gird up their minds for this battle . . . [Thus making] the task that much more difficult for those who are trying to open up new fronts for the kingdom."[45]

James Davison Hunter – "Christians just aren't Christian enough. Christians don't think with an adequate enough Christian worldview. Christians are fuzzy-minded, Christians don't pray hard enough, and Christians are generally lazy toward their duties as believers. . . . [T]here are not enough people who *do* embrace God's call on their lives, praying, understanding, and working to change the world."[46]

Brian McLaren – "What holds us back" is, we Christians "persist in ways of living that are so complacent, so pathetically counterproductive, so obviously suicidal. . . . Our apathy, our complacency, our paralysis simply, *don't make sense . . . .* It requires . . . a new way of thinking, the capacities of a new way of living."[47]

G.K. Chesterton – "The Christian ideal has not been tried and found wanting; it has been found difficult and left untried."[48]

---

[43] Rushdoony, *The Institutes of Biblical Law*, 14, 72.
[44] Rushdoony, *In His Service*, 150, 152.
[45] T.M. Moore, "Worldview Weapons," *BreakPoint*, October 2006, 6.
[46] Hunter, *To Change the World*, 24.
[47] McLaren, *Everything Must Change*, 279, 283.
[48] G.K. Chesterton, *What's Wrong with the World* (San Francisco, CA.: Ignatius Press, 1994), chap. 5.

Cindy Jacobs – "If we are to see nations transformed, we must go beyond a mandate that only sees souls saved to seeing Christians grow in the Lord and seeing the kingdom of God invade every sector of society."[49]

Paul Rowntree Clifford – "But as long as the privatization of Christianity remains the hallmark of so many of its members, the prophetic sign of the church is compromised and its message muted."[50]

Dallas Willard – "Willard boldly challenges the thought that we can be Christians without being disciples, or call ourselves Christians without applying this understanding of life in the Kingdom of God to every aspect of life on earth." He terms this distinctive "the heart of Christianity"[51] and calls for its restoration, as do I in this book, the one you are holding in your hands.

Francis A. Schaeffer – "If Christ is indeed Lord, he must be Lord of all of life—in spiritual matters, of course, but just as much across the whole spectrum of life, including intellectual matters and the areas of culture, law, and government."[52]

The Great Evangelical Disaster

In this author's opinion, our massive failures to follow Jesus' two directives in John 14:12, to be "fellow workers for the kingdom of God" (Col. 4:11), and to take dominion over his creation has produced what Francis A. Schaeffer called, and titled his book. *The Great Evangelical Disaster*. Nonetheless, many oppose the biblical dominion mandate, outside and inside the Church. Consequently, most believers shrink away from living at this high level of responsibility, influence, and blessings. They are quite willing to leave all behind for the so-called Antichrist and Beast to occupy and/or for the next generation(s) to suffer through.

Indeed, a major paradigm shift is needed to shake us out of our complacency, out of our nominal versions of Christianity, out of our

---

[49] Jacobs, *The Reformation Manifesto*, 18.
[50] Paul Rowntree Clifford, *The Reality of the Kingdom* (Grand Rapids, MI.: Eerdmans, 1996), 102.
[51] Willard, *The Great Omission*, Inside front leaf.
[52] Schaeffer, *The Great Evangelical Disaster*, 11.

reduction of the gospel, and out of our betrayal of Jesus' commands. In this manner, and only in this manner, can we hope to address the three questions Willard raised and we quoted in Chapter 1: "Why is today's church so weak? Why are we able to claim many conversions and enroll many church members but have less and less impact on our culture? Why are Christians indistinguishable from the world?"[53]

In this manner, and only in this manner, Christ has commissioned and sent his Church into the world as the extension of his mission—i.e., to reign with Him (Rev. 5:9-10) as the instruments of his comprehensive kingdom and salvation over all creation. This is the grand plan of redemption and it is fully available. Anything less is a malformation of Christianity that produces Christians of much lower levels of dedication. God's intention was and is to use we humans to expand his kingdom and transform the broken places of our world and cultures (lives, laws, institutions, and relationships). Make no mistake; this is "the whole will of God" (Acts 20:27).

Hence, a strong argument can be made that the broken conditions of our world are not because of God but because so much of his Church (one-third of the world's population today) is not doing what it is supposed to be doing—i.e., the works and greater works of Jesus. Rather, they are content to let the godless philosophies of the humanists and hostile religions run amuck over this world because their citizenship is in heaven (which is true). But truly, it wasn't this way in America only three-quarters of a century ago. We need to wake up from this myopic delusion and seek our purpose and inheritance, which is the kingdom of God in this world, here and now (see Matt. 25:34).

Indeed, a major paradigm shift is needed to shake us out of our complacency, out of our nominal versions of Christianity, out of our reduction of the gospel, and out of our betrayal of Jesus' commands.

The fact is, we believers in Jesus Christ are God's Plan A to change the world. And there is no Plan B. Of course, God can, and occasionally

---

[53] Willard, *The Divine Conspiracy*, 40.

does, intervene unilaterally but not as often as we might like. Nonetheless, and as we have seen herein, He has entrusted this societal transformation to his people (see Eph. 2:10; Rev. 5:9-10; and more). Again, this is the "high calling of God in Christ Jesus" (Phil. 3:14 KJV).

In my opinion, and once again, the bottom line for all we have been presenting in this book is this: Do we seriously desire to hear these words one day from Jesus Christ Himself: "Well done, good and faithful servant!" (Matt. 25:21a, 23a)? Or, will we be hearing, "You wicked, lazy servant!" (Matt. 25:26a)? The consequences are huge (see Matt. 25:21b, 23b, 26b-30). So wouldn't you like to know about this now while you can do something about it? Or would you rather wait and find out later when you can't?

Often it has been said that the only thing necessary for evil to triumph is for good men and women to do nothing. Sadly, that is what has been and is happening way too much in our world as many modern-day Christians sit back and passively watch as our nations are taken over by those whose agendas are hostile to Christian beliefs, values, principles, and commandments. All the while, many are thinking and singing, "I'll fly away, O glory." Evans appropriately characterizes this attitude and behavior as "'Backward, Christian Soldiers'!" Rightly and biblically, he asserts: "the church is to be on the offensive in the world."[54]

So how can we get back to a more robust and effective Christianity that is so foreign today to so many modern and emasculated Christian hearts, minds, feet, and hands? How can we unchain the current "Kingdom paralysis toward a cohesive theology of evangelical engagement?"[55] How can we motivate, activate, and mobilize the many millions of self-proclaiming, church-going, heaven-bound Christians who have become, as Frank has concisely coined, "Less Than Conquerors?"[56] How can we transform the reductionist traditions that have displaced God's commands, discredited Jesus' teachings and model, and perverted our "once mighty faith?"

---

[54] Evans, *What A Way to Live!*, 296.
[55] Russell D. Moore, "Leftward to Scofield: The Eclipse of the Kingdom in Post-Conservative Evangelical Theology," *Journal of the Evangelical Theological Society*, Vol. 47, No. 3, September 2004, 426.
[56] Frank, *Less Than Conquerors*. Compare with Romans 8:37.

And if it is true that the whole world is now God's holy land, Jesus is Lord of all, and we believers in Him are to be the living reality of his present kingdom, then we must not rest as long as this land is broken, spoiled, and defaced. Would you now agree or disagree? These questions and this situation bring us to the topic of our final chapter.

The consequences are huge . . . So wouldn't you like to know about this now while you can do something about it? O would you rather wait and find out later when you can't?

Chapter 12

Step #5 – Following Jesus as He Is Today

Ooh-bi-doo, I wan'na be just like you
I want to walk like you, talk like you, too
You see it's true, an ape like me
Can learn to be like you, too.[1]

~

Come, follow me. (Matt. 4:19a).

No longer is Jesus the babe in the manger we celebrate every Christmas, or the boy who played in Galilee, or the man they hung at Calvary, or the lamb who died for you and me. No longer is He the earth-bound, historical Jesus we have come to know and love. Simply put, those views of Jesus are out of date. Make no mistake, that story is important, very important. But that story is also 2,000-year-old history! You see; Jesus is not like that anymore.

And yet, He's the same Jesus Who was equal in every way with the Father and made the whole creation (Col. 1:15-17). He's the same Jesus

---

[1] Chorus from the song "I Wan'na Be like You (The Monkey Song)," Writers: Richard M. Sherman, Robert B. Sherman, Copyright: Wonderland Music Co., Inc. 2000-2015 AZLyrics.com. Featured in the Walt Disney movie *The Jungle Book* (1967 cartoon classic) and Disney's live-action remake (2016).

Who willingly surrendered aspects of his divinity, left the glory of heaven, lowered Himself to take on human flesh, was born of a virgin, raised as a boy, ministered throughout Judea, suffered scorn and rejection, endured the agony of the cross, and died for you and me. Without this historical Jesus we would still be lost in our sins (1 Cor. 15:17).

So we must stay grounded in this historical Jesus Who was "made a little lower than the angels" (Heb. 2:7, 9) and "made Himself nothing, taking the very nature [form] of a servant, being made in human likeness" (Phil. 2:7). He did all this to show us God, bring to earth the everlasting form of God's kingdom, and provide the perfect sacrifice. We must never diminish this Jesus.

But nowadays, He is both the same and the greater Jesus. Why is this so? It is because after his virgin birth, earthly life, death, burial, resurrection, and ascension, "God exalted him to the highest place and gave him the name that is above every name that at the name of Jesus every knee should bow, in heaven and on earth, and every tongue confess that Jesus Christ is Lord, to the glory of God the Father" (Phil. 2:8-11; also Eph. 1:20-23). And "so he became as much superior to the angels as the name he has inherited is superior to theirs" (Heb. 1:4).

This is the Jesus of today. He is the ascended, exalted, glorified, transformed, transfigured, transcended, apocalyptic, crowned, and cosmic Christ of the Book of Revelation. This is the contemporary Christ. But since I've written an entire book about this Jesus (*The Greater Jesus: His glorious unveiling*[2]), I'll only mention two other relevant factors from it here: 1) We believers in Jesus today have been raised, positionally, with Him in the highest as co-heirs; 2) To follow Him today means reigning and ruling with this "greater Jesus," here and now on this earth as He requires (Rev. 5:9-10). But to do that, we must seek and take possession of our ascended and exalted co-heir status in Him.

The following recap is excerpted from *The Greater Jesus:*

---

[2] See Noē, *The Greater Jesus.* There is so much more in that book that ties into the topic of this chapter. But I do not have room to duplicate that herein. Most certainly, I recommend *TGJ* to your further attention.

In Scripture, reaching the heights of being "in Christ" is also described as a five-step positional reality that begins when He comes "in you." It's also a progressive, dynamic, and conditional reception and application of what He has done as you get "in Him" (see John 15:4-8; 1 John 2:5-6). It requires a keen sense of spiritual discernment (1 Cor. 2:14) and affects the whole person—spirit, soul, and body. I call them the "Co-'s." This process starts by reckoning oneself to be a co-heir with Christ (Rom. 8:17; Gal.3:29; 4:1-7) and advances by participating with Him in a progression of spiritual identifications and applications. Therefore, being "in Christ" requires being:

1) Co-crucified (Rom. 6:5-6; Gal. 2:20). A sacrificial surrender of oneself to Christ for the forgiveness of sins.

2) Co-buried (Rom. 6:4; Col. 2:12). Dying to sin, buried with Him in baptism, and repentance.

3) Co-resurrected (Rom. 6:4-5; Col. 2:12-13; Eph. 2:1-5; Rom. 11:15). Born again by the Spirit of God, raised out of baptism alive in one's spirit in the Presence of God, and walking in newness of life with the miraculous and great power of resurrection inside us.

4) Co-ascended (Eph. 2:6; Col. 3:1). Trusting in Him to lead one's life, being obedient to his Word, and seeking those things that are above—his kingdom, his righteousness/justice (Matt. 6:33).

5) Co-seated (Eph. 2:6-7; 1:18-23; Col. 3:1-3; Rev. 3:21; 2:26-27). The high level of being co-seated on his throne is demonstrated by reigning and ruling with Him, here and now, on this earth (Rev. 5:9-10). By this co-seating, God is involving you and me in the process of setting this world right—advancing and extending his will, reign, and rule in this world.

These five steps produce the fullness of resurrection life. They enable us to live the co-heir life with the greater Jesus on this earth, here and now, to be "in Him," and to be caught up with Him in the "air." They are not strictly successive steps or stages in Christian growth and living. Rather, they are dynamic and go and grow together. Hence, all five "Co-'s" involve an almost, if not, daily identification and application. But this process is only one facet of the multifaceted resurrection life and reality. It does not stop here.[3]

---

[3] Ibid., 320-322.

Please be assured, these "Co-'s" and this fullness in Christ are given to us by Him Who is the head over every power and authority. But we not only have to know this, we have to claim it and take possession of it. That means we have to fully embrace and enter into his fully established, unending, and ever-increasing kingdom. It's that simple; it's that straightforward; it's that profound! But taking possession requires confidence and courage. Hindrances and timidity will not work (see Acts 28:31a). Rather, in the words of C.S. Lewis, let our goal be: "Come further up, come further in."[4]

Also, since the Bible tells us that everything has been placed under Jesus' feet (Eph. 1:22) and we are seated with him (Eph. 2:6), do you realize what this means? It means everything is under *our* feet as well. That's the authority and empowerment we have been given, if we will appropriate it, for doing the "good works" (Eph. 2:10) and "even greater works" (John 14:12). Isn't it about time we rise up, claim, and take possession of our co-heir status and authority? Then why aren't more Christians reigning and ruling with Jesus Christ, here and now? Here are two reasons: 1) unbelief and 2) the fear of man is greater than the fear of God. So we gravitate to a "play-safe" church, become semi-active inside its walls, and kiss-off society. Regrettably, we allow ourselves to be programmed by reductionist, religious notions.

All followers of Jesus Christ, however, are beckoned to this "high calling" as co-heirs here and now (Phil. 3:14 KJV). But few are aware of it; fewer yet aspire to it. No question, attaining this positional stature in Christ will take more than sitting in a room for 75 minutes a week, or reading your Bible three times a month, or humming praise songs to yourself occasionally. With or without you or me, the fully established, unending, and ever-increasing kingdom of God is on the move. So why would we want to be left out? Likewise, why would we want to keep thinking of ourselves as "fallen" human beings if and when we've been co-raised and co-seated with the contemporary Christ as He is today?

Indeed, we have been made co-heirs to serve Him and advance his kingdom, not to sit, soak, and sour inside our churches. So again, why settle for lesser versions of our faith—ones without a mighty kingdom? Why be content to wait for Jesus to return and fix everything someday. Please be advised; this is not going to happen. As I have written

---

[4] C.S. Lewis, *The Chronicles of Narnia* series, *The Last Battle*.

elsewhere, here are four reasons why not: 1) He's here. Jesus never left, as He said He would not. 2) Hence return language is never used in Scripture in direct association with Jesus.[5] 3) Even Jesus cannot return to a place He never left. 4) We are called, commanded, positioned, and empowered to reign and rule with Him, here and now (John 14:12; Rev. 5:9-10, and many more).

So which Jesus do you follow—the historical Jesus as He was 2,000 years ago, or, the ascended and exalted Jesus, the contemporary Christ of today? It's this Jesus Who is operating now in greater capacities than when He was confined within a human body. Something else that may come as a shock; this Jesus does not want to be your friend or for you to be his admirer. He wants to be your Savior, Lord, and King, and for you and me to be his faithful followers. That means not just believing in Him, but also obeying Him (see John 14:15; Luke 6:46; 1 John 2:4). After all, even the demons believe in Him, and they tremble (see Jas. 2:19).

Today, three-quarters of Americans identify themselves as Christian. But the vast majority of them do not follow Christ as He specified, nor do they think in terms of Him being the ascended, exalted, and glorified Christ of today. Therefore, they are not true disciples. Indeed, secularism and nominalism have seeped far into the Church. Our youth see this degradation and are leaving in droves. It's time for us to follow Jesus as He is today. But how do we do that?

A Worldwide Call to Greatness—Once Again

Going to Church Is Not Enough

According to Jesus, the prime purpose and focus of the Christian life is to seek and advance the kingdom of God (Matt. 6:33; John 14:12). Going to a church can be part of this as long as it enhances this primacy. But going to church and doing church work must not be an end in itself. That perspective has produced masses of weak, anemic, and lulled-to-sleep pew-sitters, who have become "less than conquerors." Even the

---

[5] For more, see Noē, *Unraveling the End*, 249-260 and Noē, *The Greater Jesus*, 24-33.

high-profile Moral Majority threw in the towel after only a 20-year run. We've got to awaken "the sleeping giant" and become bearers of Christ's kingdom both inside and outside our church's four walls.

Evans fully supports that "fulfilling our kingdom agenda as Christians has to do with more than just being in church." Why is that? He answers, because "it's easy to be a Christian inside the church walls. It's safe in there. . . .[But] there is chaos in society . . . . Being a kingdom Christian means bringing the presence, precepts, and power of God to bear on society, pulling society back into an upright position."[6]

Indeed, we have been made co-heirs to serve Him and advance his kingdom, not to sit, soak, and sour inside our churches.

In a nutshell, Boyd explains the difference between church work and kingdom work: "Only what looks like Jesus qualifies as kingdom-of-God activity, there is no way to avoid this conclusion."[7] Thus, Evans concludes: "Until we become kingdom people with a kingdom agenda, we will miss much of the blessing God has for us. To show up at church on Sunday when God doesn't own our Monday through Saturday is a waste of time."[8]

Another troublesome dynamic is the throng of believers who hop from church to church in search of the "real thing." What they are actually looking for is the kingdom of God. That is the "real thing." Jesus brought it to earth in the 1st century as part of our "once-for-all-delivered faith (see Jude 3). Moreover, it has been not put out of business, postponed, or withdrawn. But without firm anchorage in time and nature, human speculations and undisciplined interpretations can drift off in any direction. And so they have! Evans rightly terms these deviators "rebels against God's kingdom. . . . No matter how you slice it, if you or the institution of which you are a part does not submit to the authority of God's Word, you become an enemy of the King and His kingdom."[9]

---

[6] Evans, *What A Way to Live!*, 448, 407.
[7] Boyd, *The Myth of a Christian Nation*, 100.
[8] Evans, *What A Way To Live!*, 24.
[9] Ibid., 88.

Contrary to much popular thought, Jesus did not come to bring a temporary, partial, in some sense, initiated, or only inaugurated version of his kingdom to earth. He brought the fully established, everlasting, and final form of God's kingdom. And then He gave it "to a people who will produce its fruit" (Matt. 21:43). We are that people; and his modeled works are that fruit, along with the "greater works!" This reality will require a greater commitment on the part of most believers in Jesus Christ than a simple mentality and habit of just going to church.

<u>Eradicating the Great Political Myth, Misconception, and Lie</u>

"Blessed is the nation whose God is the LORD" (Psa. 33:12). Sadly, many Christians in America today have been incapacitated by a major myth, misconception, and lie perpetrated by non-Christians and Christians alike. Here it is: "Religion should not be mixed with politics." Sometimes it is phrased in other ways. "Christians should not trade in the gospel of Jesus Christ for political power." "We must stick to the Gospel (of salvation only) and leave politics to others." In formal terms it's called: "The Separation of Church and State." In reality, this assumptive dualism is an attempt to eradicate Christianity from the public square. And this tactic has been highly effective in relegating Christians to stay inside their churches and within the private spheres.

So let's clear up this "false vision," as David Lane rightly calls it, which has caused pastors and pew-sitters alike to "retreat from the public square. [And] because of this retreat . . . over the last century, America no longer enjoys a biblically based culture."[10]

Repeatedly, as we saw in our last chapter, the Bible declares that no area of life is separated from God because: "The earth is the LORD'S, and everything in it, the world, and all who live in it" (Psa. 24:1). Consequently, no such dualism or distinction between sacred and secular exists. All things belong to Jesus Christ. "For by him all things were created: things in heaven and on earth, visible and invisible, whether thrones or powers or rulers or authorities; all things were created by him and for him. He is before all things and in him all things hold together" (Col. 1:16-17). That's why we cannot divide life down the middle,

---

[10] David Lane, "Why Politics and Preaching Should Mix," *Charisma*, July 2015, 18

putting God on one side and politics and societal engagement on the other. Christ's "all things" includes the governments of nations, educational systems, Hollywood, everything. Likewise, masses of Christians have been told another lie and think this world belongs to and is under the control of the devil.[11] Admittedly, our world is not the kingdom of God either. But it is to become more and more kingdom-influenced and we are God's chosen instruments to make this happen.

Don't be deceived; politics affects everyone and all aspects of life. It can become the most terrible of all institutions if left unchecked. Furthermore, the Bible is full of politics (see for instance Mark 6:14-29; Acts 17:7) and we see God placing people strategically in political realms (Joseph, Daniel, Nehemiah, Esther, Deborah). But much of the Church has not gotten this right. Hence, Ed Silvoso writes: "When we understand that Jesus came to save everything that was lost, we are able to see the marketplace as an opportunity, not a threat. . . . The notion that Jesus came to save more than just souls is not an extra-biblical concept . . . . The idea that nations themselves can be redeemed runs like a thread throughout the Bible."[12]

This realization is why Bright condemns "the church which will not engage in dynamic activity for the Kingdom." He claims it "has confused faith with futility: It has simply wrapped its talent in a napkin and will never hear its Lord say, 'Well done, good and faithful servant.'" Rightly, he stresses that "we are to stop trifling with our historic task . . . . we must be a more missionary Church! We are engaged today in an ideological struggle; dynamic ideas do battle for the minds of men. We cannot stand aside from that battle . . . . We must each of us rise to our calling; . . ."[13]

So how can we avoid political involvement if we are sincerely interested in loving our neighbor (Luke 10:27)? Remember, following the parable of the Good Samaritan, Jesus told his followers, and us today as well, to "Go and do, likewise" (Luke 10:37b). Amazing isn't it, how we have devalued and degraded our "once mighty faith?"

---

[11] For the verses used to support this popular notion and a refutation, see Noē, *The Creation of Evil*, 43-44.

[12] Ed Silvoso, "Evangelism," *Charisma*, September 2004, 49-50.

[13] Bright, *The Kingdom of God*, 260, 265.

Seriously, if we Christians are unwilling to live out our faith in a self-sacrificing, kingdom-seeking, and dominion-mandated manner, then we have no grounds to complain about the deteriorating state of our or any other nation. Factually, that lesser brand of Christianity is not sufficient for addressing the needs of our world. Once again, *the only reason secular humanists are succeeding is because we Christians are allowing it.*

As God's representatives and Christ's co-heirs we must play a crucial role in government and politics to protect our nation and future generations from moral decay and decline. Certainly, these undertakings will require the boldness and assertion of our "once mighty faith," along with an uncompromising view of the Bible's teachings on the "all-things" authority of Christ and his kingdom.

Critical Objection: "You can't legislate morality."

My Response: We legislate little else. Someone's morality always gets legislated. Let us, therefore, reapply the famous words of Ronald Reagan: "Mr. Gorbachev, tear down this wall." Now, let's insist, "Mr. President, Congress, Courts, America, tear down this wall of separation of church and state."

In this regard, Evans strikes the proper balance for "give[ing] up this myth of a wall of separation between church and state. Yes, church and state are separate and distinct institutions with specific spheres of responsibility and jurisdiction (2 Chron. 26:16-19). But the idea that the church has nothing to say about how society is governed is absurd, because all law has a religious foundation. The Declaration of Independence recognizes this connection since it bases the doctrine of 'inalienable rights' on the doctrine of creation. People have been endowed with these rights by the Creator. Therefore, no Creator, no rights. . . . [It's] freedom *of* religion, not freedom *from* religion."

Evans further clarifies that "the church's job is to make sure that the state doesn't lose sight of the truth that God rules and that there is a moral standard in which the political realm must operate." On the other hand, "the state needs to give the church freedom to exercise its prophetic role, being a voice for God and His righteous standards . . . . Then and only then will God's kingdom agenda for society be visualized."[14]

---

[14] Evans, *What A Way To Live!*, 467, 485.

Make no mistake; we as Christ's followers and co-heirs are called to bring every area of life under his lordship, not so we can produce a utopia on earth—that's only available in heaven. It's because, as Evans summarizes, "We need to believe that the earth is the Lord's and live like we believe it."[15]

For excellent expositions revealing much more on the myth of the separation of church and state, see David Barton's two books: *The Myth of Separation: What is the correct relationship between Church and State?* and *Original Intent: The Courts, the Constitution, & Religion.*

Taking Action—Boots on the Ground, Bodies in the Field

"God wants to see the authenticity of our faith put into action."[16] According to Stearns, these are "the *do's* . . . of our faith."[17] Rightly, he scolds Christians who counter, "Why bother trying to fix the world now? . . . [it's] beyond redemption, riddled with evil, so the focus *ought* to be on saving souls for the *next* life." He terms this escapist concession a "dividing of the gospel" leaving "only half a gospel, a gospel with a hole in it."[18]

First and foremost, comes prayer. But prayer is not enough. We must next put feet to our faith, boots on the ground, and march out of our Christian cocoons. Our anger must be turned to passion, passion to action, and action sustained. This will take strong leadership and strategized mobilization, like Jesus provided when He trained and sent out the Twelve and the Seventy (Matt. 10:1, 7-8; Luke 9:1-2, 6; 10:1-17). We need leaders who will place the seeking and advancing of God's kingdom above the maintenance of their church or ministry. We need leaders who will educate, train, and send out a new and radical generation of kingdom Christians, ones not encumbered with the attitudinal and behavioral baggage saddling so many today.

Overman agrees that "as Christians, we must be politically active . . . We must take our place in the arenas of legislative, judicial, and executive responsibility, just as we once did years ago. But this is not the

---

[15] Ibid., 428.
[16] Stearns, *The Hole In Our Gospel*, 185.
[17] Ibid., 186.
[18] Ibid., 201.

complete answer. Laws will not change the hearts of our people. Nor will political reform. We must pray for God to do a work on the inside of people. . . . We need a spiritual awakening which no law can produce. The much needed moral changes will follow."[19]

Of course, it's easier to lower one's expectations and live in a "second class" relationship with Christ versus accepting and responding to "the high calling of God in Christ Jesus" (Phil, 3:14 KJV). So today, we have countless Christians who confess Christ and believe they are going to heaven, but little else really matters. This attitude can only be described as brazen, if not defiant. But current leadership not only allows it, many preach and promote it.

So how do we motivate and energize multiple millions to step out of their "sleeping-giant" churches and out onto the front lines? Dan Reid believes "that nothing less than a revolution will need to take place in our understanding of what constitutes a Christianity . . . . a Christianity that involves . . . . the performing of miracles, certainly a lot more frequently than is presently reported."[20]

Today, American Christians are in a battle, if not a war, not only for souls but for our nation. And we are losing. The time for sitting back and watching those who reject God, assault God, and take over more and more territory is over. We must *wake up, face* what we have so far largely ignored, and take *action*! There is only one way to achieve this high level of action. The kingdom of God must become our highest priority—church-wise and individually. That means:

- educating, understanding, and living out the kingdom-of-God worldview, which is the most exciting, meaningful, rewarding, and powerful experience one can have in life,
- taking up our mantle as ambassadors of Christ and co-heirs of his kingdom,

---

[19] Overman, *Assumptions That Affect Our Lives*, 165-166.
[20] Dan Reid, "Interview with Graham Twelftree," *Academic Alert: IVP Book Bulletin for Professors* 8, 2 (Downers Grove, IL.: InterVarsity Press, 1999), 1-2, 4 – quoted in J.P. Moreland, "Restoration of the Kingdom's Miraculous Power, Graves, ed., *Strangers to Fire*, 291.

- engaging "through a balanced mixture of prayer and practical action to influence political leaders and public policies"[21]—from a kingdom worldview,
- becoming fully invested in Christ's kingdom—immovable in our convictions and relentless in our seeking, entering, and staying in, and
- developing a battlefield mentality, stepping out, and speaking up "boldly and without hindrance" (Acts 28:31a).

But it also means being clothed with grace and showing love and compassion. How is this possible? By the Holy Spirit authenticating our kingdom obedience. Otherwise, it won't happen.

In other words, we are talking about a Great Reawakening as leaders in their churches preach, teach, educate, and motivate their pew-sitters into becoming kingdom ambassadors and loving warriors. They then can be sent out to transform our cities, communities, states, nations, and the world. Oh yes, we can count on resistance, criticism, even persecution from the church establishment. But their failure to do this has been the colossal failure of most churches.

Assuredly, we Christians must show the world "the Lord's glory" the same way our brothers and sisters in the faith did in the 1st century. Stearns puts it this way: "Jesus' disciples became such incredible agents of change that they literally altered the course of history. . . . they ignited a social revolution that drew thousands and ultimately billions to faith in Christ."[22] Why can't we do the same by proclaiming and manifesting the same, true, and only path to love, joy, peace, power, healing, reconciliation, purpose, and fulfillment? No question, this reclaimed version of Christianity and the Christian life stands in dramatic contrast with so many Christians today who are essentially no different from most people in the world, in almost every aspect of life.

And, no, we are not talking about reclaiming or taking America, or any nation, back *per se*. We are talking about reclaiming the kingdom, entering it, and advancing it to transform lives, institutions, laws, relationships, and making "disciples of all nations." John 14:12 gives us our marching orders. Sadly, these orders and the fruit they can produce

---

[21] Anthony Petrucci, "Beyond Canada's Call," *Charisma*, February 2013, 25.

[22] Stearns, *The Hole in the Gospel*, 244.

have been fouled by centuries of tradition. Actually, these prevalent departures from our "once mighty faith" are humanism disguised as Christianity. Perhaps this is one reason Mahatma Gandhi complained: "your Christians are so unlike your Christ."[23] But this is what nominal Christians, who bear the name but don't practice the faith, have turned Christianity and the Church into over the centuries. They have exchanged the truth of God for the deception of religious ritual as they seek the affirmations of men and not God.

The kingdom of God as presented by Jesus Christ demanded and still demands a serious response in the form of action. Advancing the kingdom is putting our faith into action. It is a demonstration of Whose we are, Whom we serve, and the oneness that binds us together with Jesus, Paul, and the early Church. Of course, there is a natural and humanistic resistance to the kingdom in us all. But this form of the Christian life was modeled for us and for a good reason. The Apostle Paul, in his letter to the Thessalonians, pinpoints this reason:

> Brothers loved by God, we know that he has chosen you, because our gospel came to you not simply with words, but also with power, with the Holy Spirit and with deep conviction. You know how we lived among you for your sake. You became *imitators* of us and of the Lord; in spite of severe suffering, you welcomed the message with the joy given by the Holy Spirit. And so you became a *model* to all the believers in Macedonia and Achaia—your faith has become known everywhere . . . . (1 Thess. 1:4-8 – *emphasis added*, also 1 Thess. 2:14).

So what kind of followers of Jesus and models are we being today? Have we not been called to serve the same King and kingdom in our lives as these Thessalonians? Are we not to become "imitators" of them and their ministry practice? Or does this passage only speak to their day and time (also Titus 2:7)? In other words, is the kingdom they preached and presented still present, relevant, and *same-natured* today or not?

It's time to put action to our faith by developing a reigning and ruling attitude (see Rom. 8:36-37; Rev. 5:9-10; 12:10-11) versus an "easy Christianity" that moves one into a sedentary Christian lifestyle. Certainly, the latter is not recommended or endorsed by Jesus or any biblical writer. And, of course, we can expect to be criticized, even

---

[23] Quoted in Kendall, *Holy Fire*, 152.

persecuted by non-believers as well. But "rejoice and be glad, because great is [will be] your reward in heaven" (see Matt 5:11-12; 6:19-20). As Rick Warren explains, "The world, and even much of the church, does not understand what God values."[24] But keep in mind, our mission involves "two great privileges: working with God and representing him. We get to partner with God in the building [actually, advancing] of his kingdom."[25] Thus, Paul calls us "God's fellow workers" (2 Cor. 6:1).

It bears repeating once again; *the only reason secular humanists are succeeding is because we Christians are allowing it.* Therefore, let us "spur one another on toward love and good deeds" (Heb. 10:24) by proclaiming the same gospel of the kingdom and doing the works of and even greater works than Jesus. Naturally, the cost of obedience can be high; but what about the cost of disobedience?

Realistically, however, it isn't up to us to fix or change the world. That would be grandiose. But systems of injustice are all around. God can and will use ordinary people like you and me to do extraordinary things as we take action initiatives and leave the results to Him. That's what following Jesus looks like today. It's living radically as salt and light, partnering with Him, and seeking and advancing his kingdom into areas of darkness. Again, anything less is less. So are you in or out?

Turning Out and Voting Kingdom Values and Principles

Since most elections in America are decided by slim margins, let's do the math and see how we evangelicals are doing in fulfilling our hard-won national right and privilege and kingdom duty of voting. In the most recent national case in point, the pro-abortion candidate won by less than 5 million votes out of 129 million cast.

Disappointingly, Kiley Crossland reports: "tens of millions of American evangelicals do not vote. A Barna Group analysis of the 2012 presidential election found that of the 89 million 'born-again Christians' adults in America—those who claim a personal active relationship with Christ—38 million did not vote for president and 12 million of those were not even registered to vote." Why is this? He maintains it's because

---

[24] Rick Warren, *The Purpose Driven Life* (Grand Rapids, MI.: Zondervan, 2002), 269.
[25] Ibid., 283.

of a "widespread distrust and skepticism of Washington politics" and seeing "politics as a 'broken system' with indistinguishable candidates, expensive campaigns, and little hope for change."[26] But in my opinion, their staying home was a dereliction of both privilege and duty (see Rom. 13:1-7; Matt. 22:21; Mark 12:17; Luke 20:25).

In America, every citizen has the privilege and right to utilize the political process to shape our society. For Christians not to participate is inexcusable and deplorable. Again, we have the numbers; we just don't have the will. All evangelicals need to take this national and kingdom responsibility seriously and turn out to vote for those best upholding kingdom values and principles. This privilege and duty was won in battle from England over 200 years ago.

Kennedy aptly puts this dereliction this way: "Christians have had it in their power to change all of these things that we lament and complain about, and we just haven't done it. . . . It is time for Christians not to be ashamed of Jesus Christ. . . . '300,000 Silent Pulpits. . . . Christians have got to wake up to the fact that they have been deluded, deceived, and outmaneuvered. . . . A conservative majority would be appointing judges.'"[27]

That's what following Jesus looks like today. It's living radically as salt and light, partnering with Him, and seeking and advancing his kingdom into areas of darkness. Again, anything less is less. So are you in or out?

Winning at the ballot box is how this country works. But as Jackson, Jr. and Perkins lament: "Too many people have been led to believe that a decision of the Court is the final word. That is simply not true. There are checks and balances . . . . Unfortunately, Congress . . . has lacked the will to challenge the edicts of the court even though they are clearly given that authority and responsibility in Article III of the Constitution."[28]

---

[26] Kiley Crossland, "No-confidence vote," *World*, January 23, 2016, 53.

[27] Kennedy, *The Gates of Hell Shall Not Prevail*, 200, 217, 219, 224.

[28] Jackson, Jr. and Perkins, *Personal Faith Public Policy*, 172.

As a result of this evangelical dereliction of duty, we have gotten the kind of government we deserve. Our system of government is based on everyone fighting for what they want, and not merely trying to get along. The side that wants something more and votes for or against it wins. It's that simple. A simple majority wins every election and usually by slim margins.

For Christians, this embarrassing dereliction can only be changed with bold leadership willing to reshape modern-day Christianity back into the "once mighty faith" of our 1st-century ancestors. And even though politics is an important arena of major influence, reshaping any country politically will not be enough to transform it. But we avoid, disparage, and ignore politics to our own risk and detriment.

Please underscore this: <u>evangelical Christians are America's largest voting bloc.</u> We could be much larger and more effective if we were more united under Christ's kingdom. Unfortunately, many Christians are mostly or totally immobilized by their lesser faith. As citizens of both this nation and the kingdom of God, we evangelicals must get out and live the kingdom life of Christ—that includes voting for kingdom-endorsing candidates, ideas, and laws.

Rightly but harshly, Evans admonishes: "Christians who do not vote are shunning their responsibility to be a voice for righteousness in the public square. Your vote can be a protest against an ungodly world view and an endorsement of correct views. But you must be informed to cast your vote for righteousness. . . . The church has to do more than make people feel good about their personal walk with God. The church must give God's people a divine orientation on every subject. . . . And the Bible speaks to every issue of life. . . . The problem in our society is that most people fear the government more than they fear the Lord. That's true even for many Christians."[29]

Hunter analyzes our dereliction-of-duty situation this way: "Evangelical Christians in America . . . . make up fully one quarter of all voters. . . . [with] such an awesome opportunity to shape public policy . . . . Disengagement is not an option."[30] However, "over the years the church slowly retreated from its place of influence . . . leaving a void

---

[29] Evans, *What A Way To Live!*, 463, 465, 461.
[30] Hunter, *To Change the World*, 121 in quotation of the National Association of Evangelicals.

now filled with darkness. . . . we fail to advance the kingdom of God. And now a generation stands in desperate need."[31]

Indeed, we Christians in America have more power than we think—both on a spiritual level and on a political level. Hence, in this author's opinion, a strong civic and kingdom duty must be taught in the Church. Its members must be retrained to think kingdom-wise versus being content to "fiddle while Rome burns." It is time to get serious about being "a kingdom and priests to serve his [our] God and Father" (Rev. 1:6) and advance his kingdom under his dominion mandate.

Of course, plenty of vested interests in the Church and our nation want to preserve the status quo. They must be rooted and voted out. Truly this is the only real basis for "homeland security" (see Psa. 33:12). Certainly, it's easier to be cynical and passive and believe it is not possible. But "nothing is impossible with God" (Luke 1:37). Do we really believe that? Make no mistake; we will be held accountable if we shirk this available privilege, responsibility, and duty. We have the numbers; what we need is the will.

"Christians who do not vote are shunning their responsibility to be a voice for righteousness in the public square."

By sheer numbers and with a solidly grounded (time and nature-wise) kingdom consensus, we Christians could affect great change. Again, *the only reason secular humanists are succeeding is because we Christians are allowing it.* It is the duty of every American Christian to vote and, especially, to vote kingdom values and principles. But we need to be much better motivated, educated, trained and equipped and sent out than we have been. That's leadership's responsibility.

In sum, *every Christian should vote and have greater allegiance to Christ's kingdom than to party affiliation, pocketbook, race, or heritage.* We have serious work to do in the public square. It affects everyone and all things. But that work won't get done if we fail to adhere to the biblical and moral foundation laid down by America's Founders, which is being overturned by those who oppose us.

---

[31] Ibid., 129 in quotation of Reclaiming the 7 Mountains of Culture.

Centralizing the Central Teaching, Once Again

Arguably, the two prime reasons the world is embedded in massive brokenness today are because most of the Church has been preoccupied with itself and has abdicated its role to be the prime instrument for advancing Christ's kingdom (see Rev. 1:6, 5:10). Instead, they want to be the small "c" church. In support of this abdication, they have deceived themselves and their multitudes into accepting lesser versions of our "once mighty faith."

Consequently, Rushdoony charges, "Is it any wonder that the churches are largely impotent?"[32] For instance, "In evangelical circles, much stress is placed on remembering one's conversion experience, the date, place, and so on. It is seen as an *experience*, not as a *call*. A *call* is to action and service . . . . The called man looks to conquering the world for Christ. . . . to a life of power in His service."[33] Rushdoony terms this and other degradations, "a reprehensible perversion of Christianity."[34]

Another classical and degrading example involves the Lord's Prayer. As we have seen, this familiar prayer contains one of the most radical statements in Scripture re: "your kingdom come, your will be done on earth as it is in heaven" (Matt. 6:10). But this prayer is diminished by many Christians in this way, "We're never going to see this culmination perfectly fulfilled, of course, until Christ returns in full glory, when he will bring a highly visual end to the rebellion of the world's system."[35] The impact of this compromising and unscriptural message is, "it's okay to be at ease in Zion" (see Amos 6:1 KJV). "Someday (soon) Jesus will return, establish his kingdom, and take care of this mess."

So what does the Bible actually say about a "return" of Jesus? As we have also seen, it's NOTHING! (See again Chapter 9 pp. 265-266.) That expression, along with the so-called "second coming" produce major mindsets (paradigms) and unscriptural concepts that hinder, if not prevent, the Church's need to reclaim, refocus upon, and manifest the

---

[32] Rushdoony, *The Institutes of Biblical Law – Vol. 3*, 100.

[33] Ibid., 117-118.

[34] Ibid., 194

[35] Ed Stetzer, "Subversive Kingdom," in "Bits & Pieces," *Christianity Today*, May 2012, 56.

central, compelling, and transformational-imagination message and vision of Jesus.[36]

But once again, every Christmas we sing: "Joy to the world, the Lord is come; Let earth receive her King!" If we would receive this King, what would this world look like? Willard suggests we start by asking ourselves: "What would my life look like if we were living fully in the kingdom?" Then he asks: "What barriers keep me from living that way?" Finally, he asks: "What are practices through which I can receive power to be freed of those barriers and obstacles?"[37]

Please be assured that "being a follower of Christ [as He is today] means more than just being a Christian."[38] By God's sovereignty, every Christian has been given the opportunity to represent Christ's mighty kingdom, to be entrusted with almighty power, and to be Christ's agent to act on his behalf in our world. But where is this available reality being preached, practiced, and perceived today? Nevertheless, this is our divine mission—if we are willing to accept it. This is how we are to serve God. This is the meaning of being created in God's image and likeness (Gen. 1:26). It's an incredible honor and opportunity to tap into the unsurpassed joy of serving in this capacity. But most Christians cannot imagine this kind of life and, therefore, don't receive it. Again, the fundamental reason they don't is, they have not been properly led.

Likewise, the primacy of Christ's kingdom should be the goal and focus of all church activities. It's the only valid reason for the Church to exist. Hence, Lynn Hiles submits: "We are either training folks for reigning. Or we are relinquishing our inheritance of the earth and the fullness thereof to a defeated devil. We are called to disciple nations not prepare for evacuation. The abundance of grace has been given to us to reign in life. Let us be about the business of advancing the Kingdom."[39]

Many other leaders are sounding this same, clear trumpet call (see 1 Cor. 14:8):

---

[36] For more, see Noē, *Unraveling the End*, 249-260 and Noē, *The Greater Jesus*, 24-33.

[37] Willard, *Living in Christ's Presence*, 143.

[38] My pastor, Dave Rodriguez, sermon, 3/10/13.

[39] Lynn Hiles, Facebook post in "Charismatic Preterist Movement" group, 5/18/15.

Tony Evans – "Jesus wants men [and women] who will carry out His agenda, governance, and guidelines in a world in crisis. Jesus wants men [and women] who will rule well. . . . A kingdom man [or woman], therefore, is *one who visibly demonstrates the comprehensive rule of God underneath the Lordship of Jesus Christ in every area of his life.*"[40]

Darrel and Cindy Deville – "What we (the church) do or don't do at this pivotal time in history will determine the course of this nation—either the collapse and destruction of America or the greatest awakening ever seen."[41]

Brian Sanders – "The goal of the church is [should be] expansion of the kingdom" by "doing justice" in taking "a prophetic stand against all kinds of evil. . . . Not only should the church be a voice against injustice and the subjugation of the poor in the world, but it should also act to free people from the yoke of oppression . . . ."[42]

Harry R. Jackson, Jr. and Tony Perkins – "The church can change America [and the world], but we must first change the church,"[43] They also are well aware that "deceived people [in the church] are, by definition, not in tune with the priorities of Christ's kingdom."[44] Who do you think deceived them?

Not only have we messed up our country, we Christians have also messed up our faith. Our biggest problem is us—our complacency, timidity, and hopelessness—all of which are un-Christian attributes. Church needs to be more than a Sunday performance. It's to be a missional training and equipping center for sending all, not just some, of its people out into the world. Evans seconds this notion: "This is what the church needs so desperately today. . . . teach them about kingdom discipline, dignity, and dominion."[45]

Not surprisingly, Christians have traditionally had great difficulty sustaining any culture-engaging efforts. Many have reverted to compartmentalizing their faith. Others are afraid and only make half-

---

[40] Evans, *Kingdom Man*, 9, 14.
[41] Darrel and Cindy Deville, "It's about our families and the most important vote of our lifetimes," *Charisma*, July 2015, 27.
[42] Sanders, *Life After Church*, 184-185.
[43] Jackson, Jr. and Perkins, *Personal Faith Public Policy*, 151.
[44] Ibid., 212.
[45] Evans, *What A Way To Live!*, 362.

hearted commitments. Consequently, most Christians are not experiencing the joy and abundant life of partnering with Jesus today to advance his kingdom. Nor are they experiencing a healthy kingdom-focused church or the beauty of being a part of a supernatural reawakening. They have allowed the thief to come and "steal and kill and destroy" (John 10:10). But Scripture warns us: "Do not conform any longer to the pattern of this world, but be transformed by the renewing of your mind" (Rom. 12:2a). Renewal is the first step—changing the way you think by developing the mind of Christ followed by Christ-like behavior.

The fact is, we modern-day Christians must build a Christian activism on a more firm foundation than what's been laid in the past—á la the Moral Majority, Reclaim America for Christ, etc. Thus, Willard offers this sage advice: "The appeal and power of Jesus' call to the kingdom and discipleship is great, and people generally, of every type and background, will respond favorably if that call is only presented with directness, generosity of spirit, intelligence, and love, trusting God alone for the outcome."[46]

Warren further elaborates that it's a "process of replacing lies with truth."[47] But as I have previously written, unlearning is the hardest form of learning. Warren concurs and re-emphasizes that "it's the hard work of removal and replacement. . . . old habits, patterns, and practices that need to be removed and replaced. . . . and that takes time. . . . [But] you were created to serve God . . . for a life of good deeds . . . . You were saved to serve . . . . you were not saved *by* service, but you are saved *for* service. In God's kingdom, you have a place, a purpose, a role, and a function to fulfill." He also rightly warns: "if I have no love for others, no desire to serve others, and I'm only concerned about my needs, I should question whether Christ is really in my life. A saved heart is one that wants to serve. . . . not to sit around and wait for heaven."[48]

Stearns agrees and adds: "This is the vision that should capture the imagination of every follower of Christ and every church. And this is the vision that can cause us to rise above what Isaiah 1 calls our 'worship

---

[46] Willard, *The Divine Conspiracy*, 372.
[47] Warren, *The Purpose Driven Life*, 185.
[48] Ibid., 220-221, 227-229.

charades' and 'trivial religious games' (v. 13 MSG)—and truly be salt and light to our world."[49]

It's the difference between being a kingdom Christian and a worldly Christian. It's the difference of responding to "the high-calling of God in Christ Jesus" (Phil. 3:14) and the lower calling of a kingdom-deficient church. Remember, we Christians are God's Plan A and there is no Plan B. Therefore, you and I have a choice. Warren frames this choice thusly: "God invites you to participate in the greatest, largest, most diverse, and most significant cause in history—his kingdom."[50] But to do this "you must make some mental shifts. Your perspective and attitudes must change. . . . Shift from thinking of excuses to thinking of creative ways to fulfill your commission."[51] "Sadly, many Christians have betrayed their King and his kingdom. . . . [But] the Bible says, *'We are Christ's ambassadors.'"*[52]

**Not only have we messed up our country,
we Christians have also messed up our faith.
Our biggest problem is us—our complacency,
timidity, and hopelessness.
All of which are un-Christian attributes.**

Do you not find it rather ironic that many young Christians are willing to give their lives for their country but not for Christ's kingdom? Certainly, much of the Church is "at ease in Zion" (Amos 6:1). They are not speaking out about moral evils in lives and societal sectors. They are not motivating, training, equipping, and sending out their people effectively. This type of Christianity will not cut it. It is why we have raised over two generations of Christians here in America who are kingdom illiterate. These lesser versions of our "once mighty faith" are unacceptable. Would you now agree?

---

[49] Stearns, *The Hole in Our Gospel*, 220.
[50] Warren, *The Purpose Driven Life*, 298.
[51] Ibid., 299, 303.
[52] Ibid., 49.

In my opinion, the only approach capable of breaking through the barriers of apathy, ignorance, and resistance, of shaking and awakening the "sleeping giant," and for energizing and rallying the Church toward achieving radical social transformation is the reclamation and restoration of the gospel of the kingdom. The kingdom of God must simply be placed front and center once again. Your and my children, grandchildren, and future generations are depending on us. Let's not be the generation that lets them down. So far, that's exactly what we have done. Let us forsake that abomination and be the generation that reclaims the central teaching of Jesus and retakes God's will, reign, and rule out into a lost, broken, and hurting world. Let us no longer be known for what we are *against*, but for what we are *for*!

Once more, *the only reason secular humanists are succeeding is because we Christians are allowing it.* But as Wright posits, "What would happen if we were to take seriously our stated belief that Jesus Christ is already the Lord of the world . . .?"[53]

In my opinion, every church should have a sign above its exit doors that reads: "You are now entering the mission field."

Persuasion Not Coercion

Conservatives and evangelicals are often stereotyped as intolerant, fanatical meddlers and radical right-wingers. But how should we respond "when a nation's laws no longer reflect the standard of God," when "that nation is in rebellion against Him,"[54] when government promotes evil, and its public policies are leading our nation into decay, decline, disaster, and destruction? Bill O'Reilly's answer is: "The only way to defeat progressive secularism is to stand up and oppose it."[55] But oppose it with what and how?

Today, as Hunter and many others (including me) have unfortunately recognized, Christianity is "a weak culture" because of its "fragmentation of theology" and "it's amazing . . . lack of leadership."[56] Hunter further elaborates on his dismal assessment:

---

[53] Wright, *Surprised By Hope*, 144.
[54] Evans, *What A Way To Live!*, 458.
[55] Bill O'Reilly, "The Factor," 10/26/05.
[56] Hunter, *To Change the World*, 91-92.

Christianity in North America and the West more generally is a weak culture; weak insofar as it is fragmented in its core beliefs and organization, without a coherent collective identity and mission, and often divided within itself, often with unabated hostility. Thus, for all the talk of world-changing and all of the good intentions that motivate it, the Christian community is not, on the whole, remotely close to a position where it could actually change the world in any significant way.... Until Christians come to terms with these matters.... So how should Christians engage the world? ... there is no signal model for all times and places [me: Oh, really?] ... there is a yearning for a different way, especially among the young; a way that has integrity with the historic truths of faith and the witness of the Spirit and that is adequate to the challenges of the present moment."[57]

I also agree with Hunter that "we need a new language for how the church engages the culture." But I disagree with him that there is no signal model and that "it is essential, in my view, to abandon altogether talk of 'redeeming the culture,' 'advancing the kingdom,' 'building the kingdom,' 'transforming the world,' 'reclaiming the culture,' 'reforming the culture,' and 'changing the world.' ... It implies conquest, take-over, or dominion, which in my view is precisely what God does not call us to pursue ...."[58]

In my view, what Hunter decries is precisely what God calls Christians to pursue. And yet I concur with Hunter that it is ludicrous to talk about changing the culture back to some bygone day and time or being able to win the so-called "Culture War" by conclusively defeating the opposition. Instead, I propose that our goal and *modus operandi* must be to persuade—lovingly, kindly, and with a gentle and respectful spirit. Coercion, lecturing, or speaking down to people in judgmental condemnation has no place, nor does physical force, violence, or inflicting injustices. Likewise, beating people over the head with the Bible is not wise. Starting a conversation or a debate with "the Bible says," immediately turns two-thirds of the people off because they do not recognize the Bible, our God, the Church, Jesus, or Christians in general as credible or authoritative. God's kingdom work must be done in his

---

[57] Ibid., 274-276.
[58] Ibid., 280.

way—passionately, clearly, and persuasively—versus being the "silent majority."

The strategic passage supporting this persuasion approach is 2 Corinthians 10:3-5: "For though we live in the world, we do not wage war as the world does. The weapons we fight with are not the weapons of the world. On the contrary, they have divine power to demolish strongholds. We demolish arguments and every pretension that sets itself up against the knowledge of God, and we take captive every thought to make it obedient to Christ" (also see 1 Cor. 13:1ff; 16:13-14).

But make no mistake; we win by serving, drawing, persuading, contending for justice, being willing to suffer injustice, manifesting the gifts of the Spirit, doing the works of Jesus and even the greater works, and leaving the results to God. Our goal is to transform all areas of life— lives, laws, institutions, and relationships by the power of God and his kingdom. In carrying out his dominion mandate, our weapons are prayer, loving, teaching, witnessing, and persuasive argument, but never coercion, physical force, or violence.

Once again, *the only reason secular humanists are succeeding is because we Christians are allowing it.* So here's the cut-to-the-chase bottom line: Either the Church will be transformed by King Jesus and his kingdom and led out to transform the world, or the world will transform the Church and force it to conform to its standards. That's also the choice for each of us. How will you decide?

The other strategic change we need to make is to rally around a solidly grounded King and kingdom of God, time- and nature-wise. A kingdom caught up in eschatological mid-air cannot provide the firm foundation for social and political activism, engagement, empowerment, and effectiveness that is needed and must be sustained. Without this grounding, the kingdom is incapable of unifying believers and supporting this "high-calling of God in Christ Jesus" (Phil. 3:14). But with it, God's kingdom is relevant and effectual for Christians on both the Right and the Left.

Forging this new-kingdom alliance among liberals, conservatives, Democrats, Republicans, Independents, and others also contains the potential and capability to end partisan gridlock. After all, it is our mutual calling. Together, in this unity, we can make a huge difference. But we have to get our faith right first.

Perhaps we could learn much from a "Wilberforce strategy. . . . when Wilberforce began battling slavery, the prospects could not have been worse. . . . as Wilberforce lay dying, slavery was abolished throughout the empire—46 years after the battle was joined."[59]

So what is this "new language" Hunter mentioned that is needed? In this author's opinion, it's the transformational-imagination language employed by Jesus about the nature of, and his vision for the solidly grounded, fully present, unending, and ever-increasing kingdom (see again Chapter 5, pp. 129-135). This earthly reality is what makes Christianity and Christ's followers the most distinctive people in this world. It's a kingdom of "righteousness, peace, and joy" (Rom. 14:17). Every human being in his or her heart is looking and longing for these attributes and blessings, whether or not he or she realizes it. Lack of them produces the suffering and despair that characterize the lives of many, if not most, people in our world. Some are starving for them. Their availability must be persuasively, lovingly, and prophetically hammered home, again and again.

Therefore, let us become a vibrant Church; once again engaging the world around us with Christ's kingdom. If we do, I believe radical transformations will follow as more and more people become persuaded that the attributes, blessings, values, and principles of the kingdom of God are for their own good. As Hunter recognizes: "They are less a blueprint to be applied than a catalyst for thinking about other imaginative possibilities for the transformation of culture in business, the arts, medicine, housing, and the like."[60]

Hunter also confirms that "cultural change is most enduring when it penetrates the structure of our imagination, frameworks of knowledge and discussion, the perception of everyday reality. . . . Change of this nature can only come from the top down. . . . it comes as a challenge to the dominant ideas and moral systems defined by the elites who possess the highest levels of symbolic capital. . . . [and] calls into question the rightness and legitimacy of the established ideas and practices of the culture's leading gatekeepers. The goal of any such innovation is to

---

[59] Charles Colson, "The Wilberforce Strategy," *Christianity Today*, February 2007, 132.
[60] Hunter, *To Change the World*, 269.

infiltrate the center and, in time, redefine the leading ideas and practices of the center. . . . but rarely if ever without a fight."[61]

Similarly, Evans weighs in with this poignant point of focus: "Believers may be Democrats, Republicans, or Independents. But above all, we are called to be kingdom people, those who subject the agendas of men to the agenda of God."[62]

That, in a nutshell, is the value of Jesus' transformational imagination that we discussed in Chapter 5. Thus, Hunter further realizes that "there are no political solutions to the problems most people care about . . . What the state cannot do is provide fully satisfying solutions to the problem of values in our society."[63] Only the kingdom of God can provide those solutions.

Critical Objection: "All you right-wing Christians want to do is take over the country, re-Christianize America, turn it into a theocracy, and force your religion and your values on the rest of us."

My Response: This is an alarmist and "bogeyman" argument. It's also a disguised attempt to distract, exclude, and remove Christians and Christianity from involvement in the government and the public square. A theocracy is basically defined as some degree of rule by a religion. It is viewed by many, if not most, in the modern United States as an anathema.

First, let's recall that America never was a "Christian nation" (see again Chapter 2, pp. 36-44). Secondly, these accusers confuse "Christianization" with the legal rights of all people and groups in our country. Thirdly, the kingdom of God certainly is a theocracy, since God is in total charge and control of our nation, world, and all creation.

Nonetheless, what Jesus, the biblical writers, other Christians, and I are advocating is not a theocratic rule in our nation. We do not want to establish and enforce an official religion of any type, nor a rule by clerics, priests, or exclusively by Christians and a church. All citizens must be allowed to worship as they please, or not worship at all. No one will be required to profess any form of faith or join any religious association. No religion is going to impose laws on an unwilling Congress or upon the people of this country. No one's religious freedoms

---

[61] Ibid., 42-43.

[62] Evans, *What A Way To Live!*, 452.

[63] Hunter, *To Change the World*, 171.

or freedom of speech is to be restricted. Neither biblical law nor a fundamentalist agenda would replace the U.S. Constitution as the nation's legal authority.

On the other hand, we do desire that the kingdom of God (his will, reign, and rule) increasingly come into and transform all spheres of society and human life, saturating our nation's consciousness and public policy. But the Church cannot be aligned with a political state. These two institutions have been assigned different functions by God and must be kept separate. In no case should the Church run the government or the government run the Church. As Carter explains: "The sword is for the state; the church renounces all swords except for the sword of the Spirit, which is the Word of God."[64]

Every human being in his or her heart is looking and longing for these attributes and blessings, whether or not he or she realizes it.

One notable error in this regard occurred during the time of the Eastern Roman Empire. "In 528 Emperor Justinian made it illegal not to be a Christian, and pagans were given three months to convert. Christendom was fully established. . . . It was a perversion of the gospel and a twisting of Christianity into an ideology that served the interest of power brokers."[65] Another misuse was the Crusades (A.D. 1095-1291).

But under the U.S. Constitution, we Christians have the same right as the secular humanists or anyone else to influence the political process and sway public policy. Success, however, requires consensus. That does not mean we're headed to a theocracy. But somebody's standards of morality are going to prevail and be legislated—secular-humanist, Christian, or (God forbid) sharia law.

Moore encapsulates this counter to the theocracy charge this way: "The Kingdom in the present age is not theocratic rule over nations, but is instead 'the presence, gifts, and fruit of the Spirit, forgiveness, regeneration, justification, and authority to proclaim redemption from spiritual bondage. . . . the church does not have the right to take over the

---

[64] Carter, *Rethinking Christ and Culture*, 112.
[65] Ibid., 83, 92.

reins of government, but it does have the responsibility to testify to the righteous justice of the Kingdom."[66] Jackson, Jr. and Perkins appropriately add: "Reformation of an entire nation will take the entire Christian community working in unity and with a prophetic voice. . . . A nation's strength ultimately is found in God."[67]

Reframing Evangelism—an Old Wineskin?

In Bible times, animal skins were sewn up and used for personal wine containers. But with repeated use, they would dry up, cease to expand, and burst when still-fermenting new wine was placed in them. Hence, old wineskins were discarded and replaced.

Jesus utilized wineskins as a metaphor for the new covenant life in his kingdom. He emphasized, "Neither do men pour new wine into old wineskins. If they do, the skins will burst, the wine will run out and the wineskins will be ruined. No, they pour new wine into new wineskins, and both are preserved" (Matt. 9:17; Mark 2:22; Luke 5:37).

Three Pertinent Questions

1) Is an "old wineskin" also an apt metaphor today for Christian evangelism approaches, efforts, and results?

2) How might the fully established, unending, and ever-increasing kingdom, which we've presented throughout this book, better inform or amend our evangelism?

3) If biblical Christianity is a kingdom-centered and -focused faith, why shouldn't our evangelism likewise be centered and focused?

Many have recognized there is something fundamentally wrong with the way we Christians do, or largely do not do, evangelism. For one, our poor performance of evangelizing is a devastating indictment against the way we practice our faith. And yet, most Christians consider evangelism and missions "the church's 'primary task'"[68] and "Christians' . . . primary means of changing the world."[69]

---

[66] Moore, *The Kingdom of Christ*, 154, 136.

[67] Jackson, Jr. and Perkins, *Personal Faith Public Policy*, 49, 62.

[68] Moore, *The Kingdom of Christ*, 161.

[69] Hunter *To Change the World*, 9.

We Stink at It

My pastor defines our current form of evangelism as: "the art of persuading people to surrender to Jesus." So how are we doing with this persuading? He admits, "We stink at it." Other pastors often lament that they have major difficulty motivating their members and attendees to evangelize. Another discouraging, if not devastating factor is, according to secular humanist Wolfe, "in a 1994 survey, only 9 percent of Americans in general and 25 percent of self-described evangelicals could say what the Great Commission is."[70]

Wright begrudgingly concedes that "the word *evangelism* still sends shivers down the spines of many people. . . . Some people have been scared off by frightening or bullying harangues or tactless and offensive behavior or embarrassing and naive presentations of the gospel."[71] Consequently, an attitude of indifference prevails throughout much of the Church today and "most Christians give lip-service to the command to spread the gospel."[72]

These difficulties and deficiencies were made quite real to me, in a rather concerning fashion. Shortly after I had climbed the Matterhorn, begun my motivational speaking career, become a Christian "for sure," and my first book was published,[73] I was approached by the pastoral staff of the mega evangelical church where my family and I belonged. They asked if I would develop and run an evangelism training and equipping program for them. At the time, I had never witnessed to anybody in my life. But they were insistent, and I was intrigued by the challenge.

So I jumped into it, wholeheartedly, and put together a five-session, 10-hour seminar that culminated with the participants and me going out into the adjacent neighborhoods, house-to-house, in teams of two, for three hours on Saturday afternoons. During those outings we conducted a religious survey, presented the gospel of salvation, and invited residents to receive Christ if they hadn't done so before. I led nine of these seminars and the results were exciting. We averaged sending out 10-15 teams following each seminar. When the teams returned to the church and reported their results, we celebrated. These times were most joyous

---

[70] Wolfe, *The Transformation of American Religion*, 205.

[71] Wright, *Surprised By Hope*, 225.

[72] Kennedy, *What If Jesus Had Never Been Born*, 240.

[73] Noē, *Peak Performance Principles for High Achievers*.

and exhilarating for all concerned. Usually, we'd tally up to 30 to 50 neighbors who had prayed with us to receive Christ as their Savior. Nine times we evangelized in the neighborhoods.

Then something disappointing happened. The elders suddenly cancelled the program, even though over 90 percent of the church's attendees had yet to participate. They cited complaints. But the complaints weren't from the neighborhoods. It seems several influential church members adamantly opposed our church sponsoring these kinds of activities. So it was over. This experience was my first indication that something might be severely wrong with the way we Christians preach, teach, perceive, and practice our faith.

7 Systemic Problems

Our problems and difficulties with evangelism are more systemic than most Christians have been willing to admit. Below are seven systemic problem areas. You may be able to think of more.

1) Its prime focus is almost entirely otherworldly—saving souls from this world. The traditional soul-winning pitch is primarily, if not exclusively, presented this way: "If you were to die tonight, do you know where you would go?" Or, "do you know for certain that you'd go to be with God in heaven?" Or, "If Jesus returned today, would you be ready to meet God?"

This pitch dominates current evangelizing models and methods. As one pastor tersely informed me: "God is not interested in this world. God has only one agenda: getting us ready for heaven." The problem here is that most earthlings are more interested in this world than the next one. As a result, this otherworldly focus and limitation has hamstrung our evangelism.

But Wright notes this systemic aspect well in that, "There is almost nothing about 'going to heaven when you die' in the whole New Testament."[74] This limitation reduces the gospel to only being relevant for personal redemption. That's half a gospel and grossly insufficient and ineffective. Claiming that God has only one agenda—getting us ready for heaven—will not enable us to pass along the kingdom and our country in greater shape than we found it. This realization brings us to our next systemic problem.

---

[74] Wright, *Surprised By Hope*, 293.

2) It's hell-avoidance and "fire-insurance" driven, centered, and focused. Sarcastically, it's termed, "the gospel of avoiding hell"[75] But there are significant difficulties associated with the word "hell."

First, there are no equivalent Hebrew or Greek words for "hell" in the Bible—only mistranslations of original words. Hence, Rushdoony is spot-on when he declares: "It is an error to teach that Christ saves us from hell."[76] Secondly, most unbelievers do not believe they are going to be sent to hell (only .005%).[77] Therefore, starting evangelism presentations with that proposition is a strategic error and a lesson in frustration. To unbelievers, we are preaching utter nonsense. They have no belief in or fear of hell. As Henderson and Casper appropriately recognize, "eternal damnation will not work on someone who doesn't believe hell is real."[78]

From a biblical basis, Gregg raises another significant challenge and advises: "if we wish to criticize the reticence of modern preachers to place an emphasis on hell in their evangelism, we must first account for the same reticence found in the preaching of the apostles and evangelists of the early church. . . . Never do we find hell mentioned in any of the evangelical sermons of the preachers that are recorded in the Bible. . . . which has become standard evangelistic fare in American evangelism."[79]

Furthermore, Jesus never threatened people with the prospect of going to hell. He did, however, warn the religious leaders about being thrown into "Gehenna." But Gehenna was a real, literal, familiar, and this-world place with a long, sad, sordid, and well-known history located just outside the walls of Jerusalem. Today, it's a nice pleasant valley. You can go to and visit Gehenna today without dying—i.e., on tours of the Holy Land. Regrettably, Gehenna is one of the four original scriptural words that are blatantly mistranslated by some versions of the Bible as "hell." The other three are Sheol, Hades, and Tartarus. Again, I have written extensively on this topic in another book.[80]

---

[75] McLaren, *Everything Must Change*, 22.
[76] Rushdoony, *In His Service*, 26.
[77] See Noē, *Hell Yes / Hell No*, 18. For much more on this topic, see Ibid., 1-99.
[78] Henderson and Casper, *Jim & Casper Go To Church*, 159.
[79] Steve Gregg, *All You Want To Know About Hell* (Nashville, TN.: Thomas Nelson, 2013), 58, 61.
[80] For more problematic background on "hell," see Noē, *Hell Yes / Hell No*, 1-99.

3) It's cross-centered, sin-focused. "Our evangelism must be centered on the Cross!" preachers all over the world insist. But Jesus' evangelism was never centered on the cross. Or, "It's all about Jesus. . . . to share Christ in the power of the Holy Spirit and leave the results to God." But for Jesus it was never about Jesus. He mostly kept Who He was under wraps. For Jesus, it was all about the kingdom.

In reality, therefore, what we are sharing is "bad news." People are sinners and are not going to heaven. Unfortunately, that approach doesn't draw most people into a conversation. It repels them immediately.

Critical Objection: "Folks need to hear the 'bad news' before they will be ready to accept the 'good news,' goes the standard reasoning."[81]

My Response: If you preach and evangelize with a gospel only focused on forgiveness of sin and going to heaven after you die, you will be mired down in the muddle of mediocrity and indifference that many Christians find themselves in today. The problem is, we have not become, as Willard maintains, "bearers of the kingdom."[82] That's what we need to become. Furthermore, as Willard correctly maintains, *"We cannot have a gospel dealing only with sin."*[83]

Jesus never threatened people with the prospect of going to hell. He did, however, warn the religious leaders about being thrown into "Gehenna." But Gehenna was a real, literal, familiar, and this-world place . . .

Notably, once again, Willard is spot on: "Jesus' gospel is not this: 'How do you know you're going to get into heaven when you die?' . . . His gospel is 'Now the kingdom of God is available.' . . . This gospel of Jesus, of course, includes the free promise of the forgiveness of sins by grace alone."[84] And salvation is indeed good news. But it is only a piece of the bigger good news of the kingdom of God.

---

[81] Gregg, *All You Want To Know About Hell*, 58.

[82] Willard, *Living in Christ's Presence*, 70.

[83] Willard, *The Great Omission*, 64.

[84] Willard, *Living In Christ's Presence*, 54.

Sorry to say and by and large, Christians today have an inadequate worldview. That's because we have allowed those in leadership to water down the radicalness of Jesus for our day and time. And we wonder why peoples' experiences in many of our churches seem flat. The problem is, we have a major disconnect. We have not taken Jesus at his word. Therefore, "as long as evangelism presents a gospel centered on the need for personal salvation, individuals will acquire a faith that focuses on maximum benefits with minimal obligations . . . . The sanctifying grace of God in Jesus Christ is meant not just for the sinner but also for a society beset with structural sin."[85] As a result, "much of evangelism is today incapable of creating a culture. It either surrenders to the world, or flees from it, or both. . . . Such people can build large neo-evangelical churches, but they cannot establish a Christian culture."[86]

4) It's encumbered with guilt, judgmentalism, and condemnation. Our evangelism approach sends the ad hominem message that "I'm saved, you are aren't; you're lost." It widens the credibility gap. It's an "us against them" confrontation. Such an approach was totally foreign to Jesus and the early Church. It raises peoples' hackles as we come across as arrogant, rude, bigoted, hypocritical, judgmental, and self-serving. It creates a huge image problem.

Thus, Calke and Mann disclaim that we "try to get people to follow Jesus by reminding them of their shortcomings and failings, rubbing in the guilt and then calling them to confess and give it all up. . . . the truth is, Jesus never used this tactic. . . . The world is full of people who have been told, time and again by the Church, what not to do. What they long to hear about is what God wants them to do. . . . Pointing out that they are 'sinners.' It just doesn't work. . . . It is about a calling *to* something rather than *away from* something; . . . Jesus constantly looked for the good in people."[87]

Most certainly, we need to restructure our evangelistic message and approach into something refreshing, positive, and beckoning versus being repelling.

---

[85] McLaren, *Everything Must Change*, 243 in quotation of David Lowes Watson and Douglas Meeks.
[86] Rushdoony, *Law and Society*, 147.
[87] Chalke and Mann, *The Lost Message of Jesus*, 116-119, 121.

5) Goes against societal changes. Culture has changed so substantially in the last several decades that the evangelistic efforts and approaches of the past no longer work. Collin Hansen reports in an article aptly titled "Blasé Believers" that "some Christian leaders contend that we are divided and ineffective in our witness because the Western world has turned against us and the church has abandoned the truth of the gospel."[88] No question, Hansen is right on both counts. And we have presented plenty of corroborating evidence in this book.

6) It's all about me. Undeniably, our traditional witnessing approach is a selfish strategy and agenda that does not match up with the New Testament. Jacobs affirms this fact in answer to the question of: "How did this thinking affect my actions?" She responds: "First of all I thought I was only responsible to God for living a godly life rather than being a steward of my nation, its laws, and society in general. . . . teaching that our responsibility extends to seeing the kingdom of God manifested in our nation."[89]

7) Christians are gripped with fears. Not surprisingly, most Christians dread talking to their family, friends, neighbors, co-workers, or even strangers about their faith for fear of alienating and losing them. They are most uncomfortable pushing "my faith" off on others or hitting them over the head with the Bible. It's not being sensitive. It's boorish and "bothering people." Therefore, "very few people witness because of that."[90] And yet we have the very "Word of life." Then why are we keeping it to ourselves? In my opinion, the bottom-line two reasons are: 1) We're not really *that* sold on our faith. 2) The fear of man is greater than the fear of God.

Thus, Daniel Kolenda readily admits, "We know we should, but we don't. In a nutshell, that's the state of evangelism among Christians in America today. . . . it seems we have subconsciously allowed fear to masquerade as a legitimate reason for silence."[91] He next cites four principles and five tips for overcoming these fears and communicating

---

[88] Collin Hansen, "Blasé Believers," *Christianity Today*, May 2013, 69.
[89] Jacobs, *The Reformation Manifesto*, 33.
[90] Willard, *Living In Christ's Presence*, 12.
[91] Daniel Kolenda, "The Simplicity of Sharing the Gospel," *Charisma*, July 2014, 40.

the gospel.[92] However, his principles and tips are merely placing a band-aid over these seven systemic problems. Again, a crying need exists for a different message and approach for doing evangelism.

A More Compelling, Drawing, and Effective Message and Approach

We Christians must find something more positive with which to lead our evangelistic presentations; something that will make a difference in people's lives and the world here and now. We need a message, a vision, a new paradigm, a model that will better motivate Christians to witness and draw in non-Christians. Fortunately, we don't have to "think outside the box." Jesus modeled one for us (see Mark 1:14-15). Simply put, as T.M. Moore suggests, "make the Gospel of Christ and His kingdom the centerpiece of our every endeavor . . . ."[93]

They are most uncomfortable pushing "my faith" off on others or hitting them over the head with the Bible. It's not being sensitive. It's "bothering people." . . . A crying need exists for a different message and approach for doing evangelism.

Most certainly, Jesus is our model of how to evangelize by proclaiming, communicating, and demonstrating the kingdom of God. This approach transcends but does not eliminate our current approach of only sharing the plan of salvation with someone, asking for a one-time decision, and reciting a brief prayer that activates one's "fire insurance." The Apostle Paul is also a model. He evangelized with this equal emphasis (see Acts 28:31). It's an evangelistic message and approach that looks beyond individual salvation, advances Christ's kingdom on earth, seeks to change the broader society, and offers to make our world a better place to live, here and now. It leads with and presents the full redemptive activity of God on planet Earth, the central teaching of Jesus,

---

[92] Ibid., 42-48.
[93] T.M. Moore, "Worldview Weapons: Taking on the Stronghold of Secularism," *BreakPoint Worldview*, October 2006, 9.

and his vision and power to change lives not just in the afterlife but here in this life. It's reclaiming and regaining "a more holistic understanding of the Lordship of Christ over all of life and culture."[94] It's something far more comprehensive than merely "winning souls." It's proclaiming the lordship of Christ over social and ethical thought and behavior, lives, laws, institutions, relationships, our entire world. It's a game-changer when it comes to evangelism, and much more. Going to heaven then becomes the icing on the cake.

This approach also becomes the antidote for the fact that we Christians have lost much of our credibility and effectiveness in the world. In essence, we have abdicated what Jesus has called us to do *first* (see Matt. 6:33). But in the words of the old hymn:

> Tis so sweet to trust in Jesus,
> Just to take Him at His word,
> Just to rest upon His promise,
> Just to know, "Thus saith the Lord."

This is the head-on kingdom perspective we have presented in this book. So I ask you, how much more effective might our evangelism and missionary efforts become—for motivating Christians to do it and drawing non-Christians to it—if our evangelism efforts become kingdom-centered and kingdom-focused?

Living Out the Kingdom
In the 1st century, when people observed Christians both proclaiming and living out the reality of the kingdom of God, it was distinctive, drawing, and compelling. Boyd extrapolates that "by God's design, this is how the kingdom of God expands and transforms the world. As we allow Christ's character to be formed in us—as we think and act like Jesus—others come under the loving influence of the kingdom and eventually their own hearts are won over to the King of Kings."[95] That means we must be kingdom people; and that means a radical change for most Christians.

---

[94] Pearcey, *Total Truth*, 291.
[95] Boyd, *The Myth of a Christian Nation*, 30.

Sadly, many Christians today remain aloof from much that the New Covenant and its everlasting kingdom offer them. Hence, God is not blessing our efforts when we fail to do things His way. His way means living out our faith with Christ-like behavior, ethics, works, and greater works. It means operating in the gifts of the Spirit with signs, wonders, and miracles following, as God authenticates our message, once again. That's what being ambassadors for Jesus (2 Cor. 5:20) is all about.

So as a Christian, are you also willing to be a follower of Christ as He is today? That means lining up with King Jesus and his central teachings about the kingdom of God and living and ministering in kingdom authority. Then, when others see the kingdom manifesting in and through you, it will whet appetites and lead them to ask, "How can I get that? How can I get in the kingdom?" It's the difference between a carrot and a stick. It's an approach designed to woo, stir, and engage the restless longings of every human being (see Rom. 2:14-15; Acts 17:26-28). It's the non-confrontational message and approach Jesus utilized to draw people to him, rather than push them away.

. . . that means a radical change for most Christians.

Thus, Evans is right-on: "We have a King and a kingdom to proclaim with our mouths and our lives. . . . Entire societies should be impacted and transformed . . . ."[96] This, my dear friends, needs to be the new focus of our evangelism efforts. Anything less is less.

The Process of Reframing Evangelism
So, "Come now, let us reason together" (Isa. 1:18a). It's time for leadership to rethink our message and approach for doing evangelism. I am suggesting it must be reframed in terms of the long-established, unending, and ever-increasing kingdom of God. Personal salvation, of course, is the prerequisite to being able to see and enter that kingdom (John 3:3-5 – see again Chapter 10, pp. 284-290).

Today, unfortunately, Christianity has become known for those things we are *against* rather than those we are *for*. And it's increasingly being viewed as one of many religions, not *the* religion; just one of many

---

[96] Evans, *What A Way to Live!*, 308.

choices in the world today. Yes, we've lost our distinctiveness. Certainly, this was not the case in the 1st century.

But before us is the same challenge that was before Jesus' first audiences. Therefore, our approach should also be: "The kingdom of God is at hand. Repent and believe the good news!" (Mark 1:15b). The good news is that the goal of all history has arrived. It's here. It arrived fully established, unending, and everlastingly advancing. Our evangelism must clearly lay out a gospel of the availability of life in this kingdom; that certainly includes the "forgiveness of sins." But a personal salvation presentation comes later when people ask the "how can I get this" or "how can I enter" questions. We simply must begin with Christ's kingdom and his authority over all things in heaven and earth.

Seeing evangelism reframed, re-centered, and re-focused in these terms would make it part of contributing to God's kingdom project for transforming this entire world. McLaren concurs: "the very gospel that we preach, needs to be as big and ubiquitous as sin and evil. . . . a small gospel will seem pathetic and incredible."[97] Wright agrees as well: "Jesus is risen, therefore his followers have a new job to do. . . . To bring the life of heaven to birth in actual, physical, earthly reality. . . . not to snatch people away from earth to heaven but to colonize earth with the life of heaven. That, after all, is what the Lord's Prayer is about."[98]

So as a Christian, are you also willing to be a follower of Christ as He is today? That means lining up with King Jesus and his central teachings about the kingdom of God and living and ministering in kingdom authority.

This original face of Christianity and its evangelism methodology needs to be reclaimed. The Christian faith and its activism must be based on that more firm foundation. Of course, new techniques, skills, strategies, education, training, equipping, and information will be needed. And anything less is certainly less.

---

[97] McLaren, *Everything Must Change*, 244.
[98] Wright, *Surprised By Hope*, 293.

Final Thoughts on Following Jesus Today

Repeatedly, God's Word tells us there is something supernatural that happens when we wade into the arena of correcting injustices. And based on everything we have covered in this book so far, I believe if we Christians prove faithful and present the blessings, truths, and solutions of our "once mighty faith" and its mighty kingdom and leave the results to God, He will empower and authenticate our transformational efforts, as He did in the 1st century.

Yes, it all comes down to power. And Christ's kingdom is the ultimate power and dominion from on High. Its effectiveness is unsurpassed if only we will implement what we have been given and allow God's glory to be manifested in and through us as his ambassadors. How can we lose? We can only gain.

N.T. Wright perceptively summarizes: "We are now forced to rethink the very meaning of salvation itself. . . . Saved from what? Saved *for* what? . . . We are not saved as souls but as wholes. . . . God's plan to rescue and renew the entire world. . . . can't be confined to human beings. . . . It is the story of God's kingdom being launched on earth as it is in heaven, generating a new state of affairs in which the power of evil has been decisively defeated, the new creation has been decisively launched, and Jesus's followers have been commissioned and equipped to put that victory . . . into practice."[99]

Nancy Pearcey also concludes: "Nations will not change without Christians in those nations becoming major influencers in their governments. The will of God cannot be done on earth as it is in heaven without His people being righteous voices calling for laws that release His justice. . . . When we step back from that role and become the church shut off in isolation, there is no one to speak for righteousness in the public arenas."[100] Interestingly, Pearcey terms prayer *"legislating in the heavens."*[101]

Gary A. Haugen concurs and points out: "Over and over in Scripture, God promises to pour out his presence and power on those who choose to follow him in his work of justice in the world. . . . If we in

---

[99] Ibid., 194-195, 199, 204.
[100] Pearcey, *Total Truth*, 139-140.
[101] Ibid., 189.

the church really did justice today, we would turn our culture upside down for Jesus Christ. . . . Justice is not optional for Christians. It is central to God's heart and thus critical to our relationship with God."[102]

But make no mistake, as Haugen further imparts; this reclamation and this high calling is an "all-hands-on-deck proposition. . . . Our calling does not stop with sharing the good news. . . . And the body of Christ cannot take up its rightful ministry of justice if its mind has not been thoroughly renewed by and rooted in the Word of God."[103] He confidently assures us that "God in his graciousness has provided a role for every Christian in his work of seeking justice."[104] Hence, he ponders, "What an enormous difference we could make—what a witness we could be . . . ."[105]

Craig A. Carter wisely cautions, however, that our kingdom efforts will probably not result in "a straight-line march of constant progress. There are bound to be setbacks as well as victories, and sometimes ground gained at great cost will later be lost again." Nevertheless, "We can rejoice whenever we find a new instance of Christ's lordship being acknowledged in this world, but we should not be so naive as to think we can bring in the kingdom in our own strength."[106]

I believe reclaiming the central teaching of Jesus can have a profound effect on America and many other nations. We have the numbers; we need to energize the will. If we do, we could see some enormous changes take place in the years and decades ahead. But it will take courage, willingness, and leadership to stand up for just causes and righteous convictions, and to lovingly persevere in the face of opposition.

What must also be stressed is that the road for advancing the kingdom and taking dominion does not lie primarily in political action. But political action is certainly a necessary sphere for this activity. In so doing, we can rest firmly in the fact that the kingdom of God is like leaven (Matt. 13:33; Luke 13:20-21; 1 Cor. 5:6-8; Gal. 5:9). Its purpose

---

[102] Gary A. Haugen, *Just Courage* (Downers Grove, IL.: InterVarsity Press, 2008), 41-42, 65.
[103] Gary A. Haugen, *Good News About Injustice* (Downers Grove, IL.: InterVarsity Press, 1999), 175, 179.
[104] Ibid., 194.
[105] Ibid., 196.
[106] Carter, *Rethinking Christ and Culture*, 195.

and destiny is to permeate the whole of culture, causing everything to rise. That includes politics. That's how we know our efforts in correcting injustices ultimately will be successful—like William Wilberforce's efforts were in abolishing slavery in England. But like him and his efforts, this will take time and commitment.

Never, however, let us doubt that the kingdom of God is the most effective means to attract and persuade others. No better way exists for Christians and the Church to engage a sophisticated secular-humanist and religiously diverse world than with the transformational imagination and mighty power of the kingdom of God. With a reclaimed kingdom focus and centered our efforts, our "once mighty faith" will flourish again.

Hence, kingdom-advancing work is to be undertaken by every Christian in their various spheres of influence and in a wide variety of ways. Each born-again Christian can see, enter, and participate in witnessing to Christ's lordship and advancing his kingdom. But we have to be willing to stand up, step out, and follow Jesus as He is today. Are you willing?

Please remember, each of us will be held accountable (see again Chapter 3, "Reason #3, pp. 92-94). But . . . "how much more will those who receive God's abundant provision of grace reign in life through the one man, Jesus Christ" (Rom. 5:17b) and "share in his sufferings in order that we may also share in his glory" (Rom. 8:17b). Amen?

I believe reclaiming the central teaching of Jesus can have a profound effect on America and many other nations as well. We have the numbers; we need to energize the will.

Conclusion

Turning the World Upside Down, AGAIN

I pledge allegiance to the kingdom of God
and to the Lord Jesus Christ for which it stands,
one world under God, indivisible in all things,
with liberty and justice,
grace and mercy, love and peace, power and joy for all.[1]

Pledging allegiance is serious business. Biblically, it's the swearing of an oath. Lives hang in the balance. So seriously, to what or whom should a follower of Jesus Christ pledge his or her allegiance? To a flag? To a country? To a company? To a person? Bob Ekblad pinpoints the consequences of pledging aptly: "Nationalism has a powerful grip on many American Christians, and on Christians in many other nations, to such an extent that people are increasingly disqualifying themselves from effective ministry as announcers of God's kingdom."[2]

Richard Land also eloquently expounds: "We have to understand that our ultimate allegiance belongs to God, not to the United States. If we make patriotism an ultimate value, then it becomes an idol. As important to me as patriotism is, I was always taught by my parents to love my

---

[1] John Noē, 9/17/15.

[2] Bob Ekblad, *A New Christian Manifesto* (Louisville, KY.: Westminster John Knox Press, 2008), 95.

A ONCE MIGHTY FAITH

country, and to respect my heritage, and always to love and to respect God even more."[3]

So we often casually say, "God bless America." But how can He do that when we have allowed Him to be expelled from our schools and public squares and call it progress? When we kill babies and call it choice, embrace perversion and call it tolerance, and call evil good and good evil? More and more, we have a government and a country that seeks human wisdom rather than God's wisdom, wants freedom from God, and is systematically removing the Christian witness. It seems we Americans are becoming more and more like the old Israelites: ". . . they refused to pay attention; stubbornly they turned their backs and stopped up their ears. They made their hearts as hard as flint and would not listen to the law or to the words of the LORD Almighty . . . . So the LORD Almighty was very angry" (Zech. 7:11-12). Seriously, how can you or I pledge allegiance to a nation—any nation—that has legalized and is condoning this sin, evil, and biblical disobedience?

Likewise, how can we still consider America as being "one nation under God?" Perhaps the atheists are now right. This phrase (added in 1954) should be cut from the pledge since it's no longer the consensus reality. Additionally, as the Bible reminds us, this nation may no longer be blessed—for: "Blessed is the nation whose God is the Lord" (Psa. 33:12).

Alas, both good and bad traditions die hard. Hence, you may not desire or be able to stop saying our current Pledge of Allegiance. But as one pastor accurately admonished his flock: "They don't play the Star Spangled Banner in heaven, you know."

Robert Lynn fittingly places this biblical reality of the kingdom into a 1st century and contemporary perspective this way: "Roman culture was not neutral with respect to the announcement of God's reign in Christ. The Gospel of the kingdom is not just about a gift. It is about a change of allegiance. The declaration 'Jesus is Lord' was understandably viewed as subversive and a threat to everything the Romans held dear."[4] Dare we settle for less?

---

[3] Quotation of Richard Land in Marvin Olasky, "Country," *World*, April 21, 2007, 31.
[4] Robert Lynn, "The Threat of Jesus," *BreakPoint Worldview*, November 2006, 4.

Indeed, we Christians are the recipients of a mighty faith—one "that was once for all delivered to the saints" (Jude 3). That's the good news. The sad and bad news is, it's a lot "gooder" than most Christians and non-Christians alike have been led to believe. In fact, most American Christians are more interested in pursuing the American dream or being on the government dole than "seeking first the kingdom of God" (Matt. 6:33). But God expects us to serve Him on his terms, not ours. As Jesus replied: "No one who puts his hand to the plow and looks back is fit for service in the kingdom of God" (Luke 9:62).

"They don't play the Star Spangled Banner in heaven, you know."

In this book we have advocated the reclamation, restoration, and realization of the fully established, everlasting, and ever-increasing kingdom of God. It, and it alone, has the power and potential to change the face of Christianity—the way it is preached, practiced, and perceived—and to turn the world upside down, AGAIN (Acts 17:6 KJV). Once we catch the vision of the victorious Christ and his kingdom, our lives will never again be the same. For instance, have you ever said to yourself, "If I just knew what God wanted me to do, I'd do it"?

Regrettably, most of God's people have not realized that the kingdom and its dominion mandate are of primary importance in God's plan of redemption and his will for you and me. We Christ followers are sent out to turn the world upside down again, not to be passive spectators sitting on the sidelines watching it go down the tubes. Sad to say, the reality is few churches today are actively, conscientiously, and correctly preach and teach the gospel of the kingdom. They preach and teach a lot of other things, good things, but not this. This great omission must change if Christians are ever going to attain a greater unity, relevance, and effectiveness in our world. If we do not unite, our voice may be silenced someday. Make no mistake; this is the state of much of the Church today, at least here in America and in some other parts of the world.

This kingdom deficiency is the product of unscriptural views that currently hold sway. As we have seen, premillennial dispensationalists deny the lordship of Christ until their future millennium, claiming "Jesus cannot be king until His supposed millennial return."[5] Other Christians deny his lordship "with their eschatologies of defeat. They speak of a beautiful but weak Christ, who now rules the church but little else; in the 'sweet bye and bye,' He will rule more, but not now."[6] Others deny the kingdom, functionally, with their behaviors.

These views have been exposed in this book as we have retrieved the kingdom of God out of eschatological mid-air and grounded it, time- and nature-wise. This is the firm foundation upon which allegiance, pledging, advancing, and activism must be based.

Obviously, this reclamation and implementation call for major readjustments in our thinking and behavior, because most Christians in America are more committed to America than they are to the kingdom of God. All of which prompts Willard to advise: "That implementation would soon transform everything among professing Christians as we know them. . . . It means a huge change of direction. The weight of the tradition . . . dominates the local congregations and denominations of Christian people—indeed the entire Christian culture—[and] stands against any such intention . . . just by the inertia of 'how things are,' of the daily rounds and what 'has to get done.'"[7]

Let's also remember, for Jesus the kingdom was primary and the Church was secondary. Today, we have reversed that. Furthermore, politics cannot produce this kingdom. But this kingdom can transform politics, the Church, and everything else in our world.

Appropriately, Willard acknowledges "we get a totally different picture of salvation, faith, and forgiveness if we regard having life from the kingdom of the heavens now—the eternal kind of life—as the target."[8] But he diagnoses "the problem currently" as being "consumer Christianity." He defines a consumer Christian as: "one who utilizes the grace of God for forgiveness and the services of the church for special occasions, but does not give his or her life and innermost thoughts, feelings, and intentions over to the kingdom of the heavens. Such Christians are not inwardly transformed and not committed to it."[9]

---

[5] Rushdoony, *The Institutes of Biblical Law,* Vol. 3, 175.
[6] Rushdoony, *Law and Society,* 376-377.
[7] Willard, *The Divine Conspiracy,* 302-303.
[8] Ibid., 47.
[9] Ibid., 342.

Most assuredly, the kingdom is the only reality capable of saving and transforming our world and everything in it. As we increasingly reclaim the kingdom-of-God worldview in the Church and the world, and march onward and outward "boldly and without hindrance" (Acts 28:31), may our song and walk of faith increasingly become:

> For your glory
> For your kingdom
> For your name
> O Lord here I am[10]

As McLaren well notes: "The time had [has] come . . . to center our lives on the essential message of Jesus, the message of the kingdom of God—not just a message *about* Jesus that focused on the afterlife, but rather the core message *of* Jesus that focused on personal, social, and global transformation in this life."[11]

Let's remember, for Jesus the kingdom was primary and the church was secondary. Today, we have reversed that.

The hard reality is, no other kingdom is promised; no other kingdom is coming. So what are you now waiting for? To whom or what will you pledge your allegiance? For me, I'm pledging my first and only allegiance to the authentic and everlasting form of the kingdom of God and our King, the Lord Jesus Christ—as we have presented throughout this book and in the words penned at the start of this Conclusion and in this book's Dedication. Assuredly, we have been given the keys for turning the world of our day and time "upside down," again. And as Evans accurately accentuates: "God has an exciting, demanding, and fulfilling kingdom agenda" for us.[12]

So what say you now?

---

[10] "For Your Glory" by Tommy Walker.
[11] McLaren, *Everything Must Change*, 22.
[12] Evans, *What a Way To Live!*, 352.

Imagine If You Will

Dramatically and drastically, we Christians have strayed from the original faith that Jesus Christ "once for all" established, delivered, and fulfilled during that 1st century. As a result the Church has lost major power and influence. However, we still have that same potential in our 21st century, as in they had in that 1st century, to turn the world upside down, again. And our world today is no more evil and hostile than it was during that 1st century. Therefore, I believe we can have the same kind of impact the 1st-century Church had. But to do this, much has to change in our modern-day hearts, minds, and churches. The facts are, we have allowed many injustices to happen because of our inaction.

For a moment, transformationally imagine with me what you would be like if you were filled "with the knowledge of his will through all spiritual wisdom and understanding. . . . that you may live a life worthy of the Lord and may please him in every way: bearing fruit in every good work, growing in the knowledge of God, being strengthened with ***all power*** according to his glorious might so that you may have great endurance and patience, and joyfully giving thanks to the Father, who has qualified you to share in the inheritance of the saints in the kingdom of light. For he has rescued us from the dominion of darkness and brought us into the kingdom of the Son he loves, in whom we have redemption, the forgiveness of sins" (Col. 1:9b-14 – bold emphasis mine). Indeed, that is the whole gospel. And that's exactly what we have presented in this book. Again, anything less is less. And surely, "By their fruit you will recognize them" (Matt. 7:16a).

Next, imagine with me what our world would be like if multiple millions of transformed kingdom-proclaiming, -seeking, and -advancing Christians set out to live and minister as Jesus modeled and instructed. Ordinary people connected with an extraordinary God operating in a reclaimed 1st-century, New Testament Christianity would, no doubt, be capable of turning the world "upside down," again (Acts 17:6), don't you think?

To date, we've only seen a glimmer of the revival that could come if we'd get our "once mighty faith" straightened out and more right. Billy Graham was correct when he reflected about the history of large-scale revivals in previous centuries, that "true revival is closely linked with a rediscovery of God's Word."[13] Rediscovery is precisely the future this book contemplates and advocates.

I love the way Stearns put this when he asks: "What Do *You* See?"

> Do you see problems that can't be solved and mountains that can't be moved, or do you see light dispelling the darkness and the kingdom of God advancing with force? Do you see the opportunities and the possibilities, or just the obstacles? What gospel have you embraced:
>
> - A revolutionary gospel that is truly good news for a broken world? or . . .
> - A diminished gospel—with a hole in it—that's been reduced to a personal transaction with God, with little power to change anything outside your own heart?
>
> . . . what will you do now? What does *God* expect of you? Are you willing to be open to His will for your life?[14]

Recovering authentic Christianity won't come easily. No doubt, this reclamation will face obstacles and challenges, mostly from within our own ranks. So, come now and "let us consider how we may spur one another on toward love and good deeds. Let us not give up meeting together . . . but let us encourage one another" (Heb. 10:24-25). Let us *get our faith right!*

But to do this, much has to change in our modern-day hearts, minds, and churches. The fact is that we have allowed many injustices to happen because of our inaction.

I believe working through the preceding five steps presented in this book's last five chapters will enable us "to discover and repent of these reductions of the gospel so that it [the Church] can become more faithful as [an] incarnational witness."[15]

---

[13] Billy Graham, *My Answer, The Indianapolis Star*, February 12, 1996.
[14] Stearns, *The Hole In The Gospel*, 279.
[15] Guder, *The Continuing Conversion of the Church*, 202.

Key Sectors and Issues for Kingdom Transformation

Originally, I planned to write a chapter in this book on this topic. But after compiling a considerable amount of research, I recognized these sectors and issues would require a book of their own, maybe two. I also realized that I might not be the best person to write it. Perhaps, someone better versed in the area of public policy, but who subscribes to the kingdom-grounded perspective presented herein, would be better equipped "to give Christians a positive, biblically based blueprint for activism"[16] as well as practical solutions, strategies, and applications.

Each of these areas contains a multiplicity of challenges and a dizzying complexity of factors, all of which have confounded human minds. Yet, they are not confounding to the wisdom of God. Why not? "For as the heavens are higher than the earth, so are my ways higher than your ways and my thoughts than your thoughts. . . . so is my word that goes out from my mouth: It will not return to me empty, but will accomplish what I desire and achieve the purpose for which I sent it," says the LORD (Isa. 55:9, 11).

Additionally, our world is so constructed such that there is a spiritual root to every single problem and confounding issue. It's the "cause behind the cause." And only God's Word and Christ's kingdom can tap into this root and transform it. In this manner, God offers us the means to live out the blessed life He has made available. None of this, however, can be achieved by humanistic education, philosophy, or politics.

Now, as in ancient times, we, the people and nations of our world, have a similar choice to make. "This day I call heaven and earth as witnesses against you that I have set before you life and death, blessings and curses. Now choose life, so that you and your children may live and that you may love the LORD your God, listen to his voice, and hold fast to him" (Deut. 30:19-20a, also 11:26-28). That's the choice; that's the challenge.

To choose life and these blessings means we must discard the dualism of the "Separation of Church and State," seek his kingdom over everything, and "do justice, love kindness, and walk carefully with our God" (Micah 6:8). In other words, we must bring a kingdom-of-God

---

[16] Jackson, Jr. & Perkins, *Personal Faith Public Policy*, 47.

perspective to bear on every injustice, oppressive law, and the painful problem in our world. Anything less is less.

My hope for this book is that it might become a seminal work for others to build upon. Armed with the solidly grounded, everlasting, unending, and ever-increasing kingdom of God, Christians will be able to exert much greater influence than in the past. Indeed, our opponents are to be won over with a kingdom of love, righteousness, peace, power, joy, justice, forgiveness, reconciliation, and persuasion. And the practical reality is, law and politics are "the leading way to address our common problems . . . and actually solve those problems."[17]

Wright concurs and posits this universal application: "The Christian gospel [kingdom included] cries out to be put into practice not only in our personal lives and church fellowships but also in our public and political lives at both the national and the global level. . . . The call of the gospel is for the church to *implement* the victory of God in the world *through suffering love. . . .* through his people."[18]

Stearns strokes this same refrain: "If the Church is indeed a revolutionary kind of institution, called to foment a social revolution by promoting justice, lifting up the sanctity of human life, fighting for the underdog, and challenging the prevailing value systems in our world, then it seems we should be out in front on social justice issues rather than bringing up the rear. But what we see when we look historically at the Church is a kind of pronounced 'culture blindness,' an inability to see the dominant culture through God's eyes."[19]

As we have seen in this book, this cultural blindness results from wrong views of God's kingdom. Consequently, we have lost much or our relevance and influence in the world and in the eyes of our youth, who are departing in droves. Remember, Jesus said, "By their fruit you will recognize them" (Matt. 7:16a). So whoever does not bear good fruit may not a true disciple of Jesus Christ.

It's this simple; it's this profound. The six broken places of separation, pain, isolation, hatred, injustice, and decay in our world are embedded throughout the following key sectors and issues.

---

[17] Hunter, *To Change the World*, 106.

[18] Wright, *Evil and the Justice of God*, 161, 98..

[19] Stearns, *The Hole In Our Gospel*, 190.

Key Sectors for Kingdom Transformation (in alphabetical order): arts, business, courts, crime, economy, education, entertainment, environment, government, journalism, labor, law, media, politics, religion, science, theology. (Perhaps you can add more.)

Key Issues for Kingdom Transformation (in alphabetical order): abortion, addictions, the Constitution, creation/evolution, divorce, ethics, euthanasia, foreign aid and relations, health care, homelessness, homosexuality, human trafficking (slavery), hunger, immigration, marriage and family, morality, national debt, personal liberties, pornography, poverty, profanity, racism, religious freedom, sanctity of human life, sex education, size and scope of government, government spending, suffering, taxes, trade and tariffs, war, welfare. (Perhaps you can add more.)

In America and many other nations, most if not all of these sectors and issues are dominated by the secular humanists. They invaded and took them over one decision at a time over several decades, if not a hundred years. Consequently, transforming them via kingdom values and principles will not happen overnight. Thus, those who press forward must have courage and perseverance as we pray and attempt to persuade these people and nations to adopt better understandings of justice for the common good.

Initiatives of this nature always face difficulty in going from awareness to action, and then sustaining that action. No doubt, our greatest opposition will come from the reluctant Church. Others may want a formal program, "eight easy steps," or a how-to manual for engagement. But that provision, as I've mentioned above, is beyond the scope and purpose of this book.

Our central objective herein has been to stimulate imaginations, initiate discussions, and provoke reclamational action so that various groups of people can learn more about Christ's fully established, unending, and ever-increasing kingdom and play a part in its advancement in their spheres of influence. Assuredly, we have a long way to go. We need to start by taking Jesus' words and his kingdom seriously and see where it goes.

Certainly, there are many areas of need and doors of opportunity for advancing Christ's kingdom, here and now. And while the challenges may seem monumental and daunting, Forster tellingly points out that "despair is a sin; it denies God's providential grace."[20] Therefore, we must rely fully on the Holy Spirit to lead us in godly directions (plural) and set appropriate goals and strategies (plural). Indeed, needs are all around us. And only when we Christians unite around the kingdom of our Lord and Christ will we begin to see transformations. Our initial goal must become to put God's glory on display so that it will attract and persuade others to taste and see how good God's kingdom can be and respond to God's grace.

DeMar sums all this up quite well: "Every area of life needs to be evaluated and reclaimed with Christian [kingdom] values: politics, law, economics, business, journalism, medicine, and every other conceivable area of life. The humanists have adopted this world as their own. They will stop at nothing to establish their version of heaven on earth. If they get their way, it will be hell for all of us."[21]

Again, we have the numbers; we have the kingdom; we have the power; what we lack is the will. If this current scenario doesn't change, the next generation will pay a huge price for our neglect, inaction, and indulgences. Condemnation sermons will not work. Reclaiming the central teaching of Jesus is the key. "And who knows but that you [and I] have come to the kingdom for such a time as this? (Esther 4:14b).

So what shall we now do?

Perhaps these words of God to the prophet Ezekiel are most appropriate for all Christ followers today: ". . . Son of man, I am sending you to the Israelites, to a rebellious nation that has rebelled against me; they and their fathers have been in revolt against me to this very day. The people to whom I am sending you are obstinate and stubborn. Say to them, 'This is what the Sovereign LORD says.' And whether they listen or fail to listen – for they are a rebellious house – they will know that a prophet has been among them. And you, son of man, do not be afraid of them or their words. . . . You must speak my words to them, whether they listen or fail to listen, for they are rebellious." (Ezek. 3:3-7).

Please be assured that applying kingdom truths to real life situations can be an exciting adventure. They can transform and create a godlier and greater America and world. As Schaeffer aptly reaffirms: "God's truths speak into the whole spectrum of life and the whole spectrum of

---

[20] Forster, *Joy for the World*, 293.
[21] DeMar, *Myths, Lies & Half Truths*, 292.

society."[22] To which Boyd adamantly adds: "We are not to rely on government to do what God has called us to do: namely, serve people by sacrificing our own time, energy, and resources. Only insofar as we do this are we the authentic body of Christ manifesting the holy kingdom of God."[23]

As we have seen, the key sectors and issues cited above (and more) are largely now owned by the secular humanists and are ripe for kingdom transformation. All of them are to be under the lordship of Christ and his kingdom. And Christ has given us those marching orders. Each key sector and issue needs to be readdressed from a kingdom perspective. There is no secular/sacred divide. The kingdom cuts across every country, culture, sector, and issue. It informs all of life. Let's never forget or underplay this revealed reality, as Jesus assures us: "With man this is impossible, but with God all things are possible" (Matt. 19:26; also see Luke 1:37). Ideas not based on kingdom/biblical values and principles are doomed to fail. And so they have and are. Likewise, "Do not be deceived: God cannot be mocked. A man reaps what he sows" (Gal. 6:7). Tragically, many nations and cultures are reaping death, curses, decline, and decay. Again, that's the choice; that's the challenge.

Please be assured that applying kingdom truths to real life situations can be an exciting adventure. They can transform and create a godlier and greater America and world.

In conclusion: "The purpose of the Kingdom of God is to govern every area of life and thought to the glory of God."[24] This is the biblical basis for kingdom involvement in every sphere of life. This is what we might call "full-orbed Christianity" and a "full-orbed Christian worldview." It's the kingdom of God and King Jesus, front and center. Anything less is less.

---

[22] Schaeffer, *The Great Evangelical Disaster*, 91.
[23] Boyd, *The Myth of a Christian Nation*, 154-155.
[24] Rushdoony, *Law and Society*, 649. "The purpose of *Law and Society* . . . is to show how God's law applies to every aspect of our lives and world." (ibid., *xii*).

13 Tenets for Kingdom Transformation—A Call to Action

1. God wants us to RECLAIM and RESTORE the 1st-century truth of the preaching, teaching, practices, and worldview of the kingdom of God to the Church and the world.

2. God wants us to REDISCOVER and RECOVER "the keys of the kingdom" that Jesus revealed and gave to Peter and the original apostles (Matt. 16:19).

3. God will ANOINT and EMPOWER our efforts to advance this same time-and-nature-grounded kingdom (Act 17:6).

4. But we must be willing to UNLEARN and RID ourselves of some biblically false ideas that will not stand up to an honest and sincere test of Scripture (1 Thess. 5:21) and have produced low-level conceptions of Christianity that absolve Christians of responsibility to manifest the kingdom in this present world.

5. The MESSAGE of the fully established, unending, and ever-increasing kingdom must be widely HEARD (Rom. 10:17) and preached BOLDLY and WITHOUT HINDRANCE (Acts 28:31).

6. The Church must be more effectively SPURRED ON toward love and good deeds (Heb. 10:24), HELD to a higher standard and high calling (Phil. 3:14), and its members more aggressively SENT OUT (Rom. 10:14-15) with the message and mission of advancing the kingdom.

7. If we seriously HOPE to someday hear the words from our Lord and Savior, "Well done good and faithful servant," we must set our hearts and minds to SEEK FIRST the kingdom, CEASE playing church, and STOP being content with a Christianity without a mighty kingdom.

8. The needs are GREAT! The time is NOW! Will you JOIN this reclamation, restoration, and transformation movement?

9. In my opinion, the five-step, kingdom-grounding process presented herein has the potential to CHANGE THE FACE of Christianity—i.e., the way it is preached, practiced, and perceived—and to turn the world UPSIDE DOWN, AGAIN.

10. If this happens, we may see the RETURN of the 1st-century caliber MIRACULOUS.
11. Therefore, we must DEVISE a strategy for REAWAKENING and RE-ACTIVATING the Church with the rallying cry of "For Christ & Kingdom"—similar to the rallying cry of the American Revolutionary War, "No king but King Jesus."
12. If Christianity has been as successful as it has to date, HOW MUCH MORE successful could it become if we got our "once mighty faith" right again?
13. "The church MUST GIVE God's people a divine orientation on every subject. . . . [T]he Bible speaks to every issue of life."[25]

Remember, there is no neutral territory or middle ground (see Matt. 12:30; Luke 11:23). We cannot delay. The fate of America, the American Church, and much of the world hang in the balance. The hour is far advanced. Many are against us. But what legacy shall we leave our children, grandchildren, and the next generation? The choice is ours. Make no mistake: we will be held accountable by our Creator.

So, will you act on what you have read in this book or will you simply be informed by it? I hope and pray you will choose to become part of this kingdom reclamation, restoration, and transformation movement. Then maybe we shall begin to see the world turning upside down, AGAIN! And going to heaven will be the icing on the cake!

Let the reclamation begin with you and me!

---

[25] Evans, *What A Way To Live!*, 465.

Appendices – Dispelling Two Technical Obstructions

Two huge obstacles fly in the face of everything we have presented, especially in Chapters 7, 8, 9, and 10. They are the massive misconceptions running throughout much of the Church today of cessation theology and a greater, future-coming, millennial kingdom. They must be encountered and countered, head on, lest they be allowed to derail the purpose, content, and conclusions of this book.

Author's caveat: Originally, I intended to address these two popular misconceptions in two chapters. But I reconsidered for these two reasons: 1) These two topics are more technical, exegetically, than most of this book. 2) Their full inclusion would exceed our planned book length. Therefore, I've decided to only preview them in these two appendices. For those interested, I have provided herein an introduction, a table of contents, an excerpt, and a link to the full article that's posted on PRI's website.

Appendix A

Cessation Theology – 14 Classic Objections: A Preview

<u>Contents:</u>

Introduction

Quench not the Spirit. Despise not prophesyings.
Prove all things; hold fast that which is good
(1 Thess. 5:19-21, KJV).

Warning: Few topics are more divisive than this one. It's a highly emotional and threatening issue for Christians on both sides of this debate—cessation vs. continuance.

Flying in the face of everything we have presented in chapters 7, 8, 9, and 10 (grounding Jesus' same-natured, unending, and ever-increasing kingdom time- and nature-wise) is the widespread doctrinal and/or functional beliefs of cessation theology. It's the assertion from many Southern Baptists, Presbyterians, Church of Christ members, some preterists, and others that some, most, or all the signs, wonders, and miraculous manifestations documented in the New Testament were withdrawn by God and therefore ceased sometime in the 1st century. Consequently, for cessationists, these supernatural manifestations are no longer authentic aspects of Christianity.

R.T. Kendall, a continuationist and charismatic pastor, lays out this theological landscape, thusly: "Cessationists believe that God, by His own will, no longer operates supernaturally—which is why many aggressively stand against the Spirit-empowered community. . . . No more supernatural healings. No visions. No direct revelation. None of the gifts of the Holy Spirit in operation." However, Kendall concedes that "cessationists do believe in the supernatural occurrences in Scripture . . . but they have no expectation that God will intervene supernaturally today except, perhaps, through providence. But the notion of the gifts of the Spirit being in operation today . . . is out of the question."

Consequently, for cessationists, these supernatural manifestations are no longer authentic aspects of Christianity.

Nevertheless, he wisely counsels that "one should never underestimate our cessationist friends' love for God, Scripture, sound teaching and holy living. They are the salt of the earth. Some of them are among the greatest vanguards of Christian orthodoxy. . . . They simply do not believe that God reveals Himself immediately and directly by revelation anymore. God, of course, could do it, they argue; He has simply and sovereignly chosen not to show His power as He did in the earliest church."[1]

---

[1] R.T. Kendall, "They Cease to Believe," *Charisma,* February 2014, 42-44.

Article Table of Contents

Link for 27-page Article

To review the entire 27-page article, go to www.prophecyrefi.org / click on "About" and "Cessation Theology: 14 Classic Objections."

Excerpt: 1 Corinthians 13:8

Without question, the major and most prominent objection for all cessationists (futurists and preterists) is based on a poor translation, misreading, and misunderstanding of 1 Corinthians 13. . . .

Not four declarative statements

The NIV poorly translates vs. 8 as four declarative statements: "Love never fails. But where there are prophecies, they will cease; where there are tongues, they will be stilled; where there is knowledge, it will pass away." So does the RSV: "Love never ends; as for prophecies, they will pass away; as for tongues, they will cease; as for knowledge, it will pass away."

Ironically, the Italians have an interesting saying, "traduttore, traditore." It literally means, "translator, traitor." Or more freely, "all translators are traitors." In this vein, here's a revealing tidbit: Three of these four statements are not declarative nor facts as maintained by cessationists. In the original Greek language, this verse is composed of one declarative statement and three conditional clauses. Here's the exegetical support.

The declarative statement we all agree on is: "Love never fails." But the other three statements all begin with the Greek particle of conditionality—*etie* (pron. i' teh – *Strongs* #1535). It does *not* mean "where" or "as." It means: "if or whether." KJV uses "whether" three times. NAS uses "if" three times. These are better but still do not convey the original meaning. BAGD – Bauer, Gingrich, & Danker's Greek Lexicon of the New Testament – recommends that "but if" and "if" are preferred. They carry the meaning of "may or may not."

This translation changes the entire complexion of this verse and passage. It takes these three statements out of the declarative mode and context and places them squarely into the hypothetical mode and context. The purpose then for this construction is to stress "love never fails," and not the cessation of these hypothetical constants.

Furthermore, *etie* is derived from Greek word *ei* (pron. i – *Strongs* #1487). It's also a conditional particle used to denote indefiniteness or uncertainty. Likewise, Paul used another and similar conditional particle—derived from *ei* (i) in 1 Cor. 13:1; 6:4—*ean* (pron. eh an –

#1437). It also means "though or if" and denotes "may or may not." Interestingly, *etie* is used later in 1 Corinthians 14:27 and is more correctly translated as "if" in NIV, KJV, NAS (also used in 1 Cor. 3:22; 8:5; 10:31; 12:13; 12:26; 14:7; 15:11.)

Additionally, as BAGD points out, when *etie* is coupled with *de* (deh) as in the first conditional clause, it should be translated as "but if" or "and even if." In a Greek-English Interlinear it's literally translated as "but whether."[2]

Thus, a more accurate, grammatical, and literal translation of 1 Corinthians 13:8 would be this: "<u>Love never fails, but if (whether) prophecies, they will be abolished; if tongues, they will cease; if knowledge, it will be abolished.</u>" These are big "ifs," and hypotheticals, not declarative facts. Big difference!

Exegetically, what we have in this verse is *one* declarative statement that is dramatically emphasized by the literary device of *three* conditional, hypothetical, and hyperbolic clauses. Thus, this construction utilizes three absurdities to dramatize Paul's main point throughout this passage of the supreme value of love—i.e., "But if (whether) . . . . love never fails."

The NIV poorly translates vs. 8
as four declarative statements –

In addition, this usage is not an isolated instance. We find similar utilizations elsewhere in Scripture. In Job's famous statement: "Though he [God] slay me, yet will I trust/hope in him . . ." (Job 13:15a), the word "though" is the Hebrew word *im* (pron. eem) *Strongs* #518. It, too, is a conditional particle meaning "if, although," or "Oh, that." This conditional word also introduces a hypothetical and hyperbolic clause of absurdity. It's employed here to emphasize Job trusting and hoping in God no matter what happens to him. Then what's the absurdity? Obviously, if God did slay him, how could Job continue trusting and hoping?

---

[2] *Greek-English New Testament – Literal Interlinear* (Washington, D.C. Christianity Today, 1975-1976), 511.

Similar hypothetical statements are employed in other Old Testament books citing cataclysmic destruction to emphasize the magnitude of divine blessings and realities. Here are two examples:

"Therefore we will not fear, though the earth should change, though the mountains shake in the heart of the sea; though its waters roar and foam, though the mountains tremble with its tumult. There is a river whose streams make glad the city of God, the holy place where the Most High dwells." (Psalm 46:2-4)

"For the mountains may depart and the hills be removed, but my steadfast love shall not depart from you, and my covenant of peace shall not be removed, says the LORD, who has compassion on you." (Isa. 54:10)

These scriptures are not predicting the end of the world (which is an absurdity because the Bible teaches that the world is without end).[3] They are better understood as affirming the concept and reality that *even if* the world did come to an end, God would still be faithful. Today, we use similar expressions of absurdity to emphasize points, such as: "If the world ends tomorrow, I'll still be loving you."

Consequently, in 1 Corinthians 13:8 Paul is *not* declaring that these three constant things will cease. He is utilizing three conditional clauses to dramatically emphasize his one declarative point that "love never fails." Hence, this one verse or entire chapter, *cannot* be used to toss out everything Paul was talking about in 1 Corinthians 12, 14, and Ephesians 4. After all, in 1 Corinthians 12:28, "the church" is still here, isn't it? Let's not make more of 1 Corinthians 13, than Paul did. Yes, it sounds absolute, but these poor translations should warn us about forcing hypotheticals into preconceived absolutes. Instead, we need to better discern how this imagery is used in this and other contexts.

Critical Objection: "No scholar worth his salt would make the 'hypothetical' argument from the Greek. . . . [I]t would be ridiculous for Paul to even presume the hypothetical or to postulate the possibility of those gifts ceasing, if they could not or would not cease at a given time. .

---

[3] See Noē, *The Perfect Ending for the World*, 81-106 and Noē, *Unraveling the End*, 141-169.

. . I've debunked the 'hypothetical' theory a few times . . . with no explanation of the contrary . . . ."[4]

My Response: Surprisingly, cessationist John MacArthur agrees that this 1 Corinthians 13 passage utilizes hypothetical statements. He writes, elaborates, and admits:

> Paul's theme in 1 Corinthians 13 is love, not spiritual gifts. . . . Paul is describing a hypothetical scenario. . . . Paul was using extreme illustrations and hyperbolic language to emphasize the value of love. . . . Paul's real point [is]: any selfish use of this gift violated its true purpose—namely, that it be exercised as an expression of loving edification for other believers.[5]

> Paul's purpose in this chapter was not to identify how long the spiritual gifts would continue into later centuries of church history, as that would have been essentially meaningless to the original readers of this letter. Rather, he was making a point that specifically pertained to his first-century audience: . . . love has eternal value, so pursue love because it is superior to any gift (v. 13).[6]

> To determine the point in church history when the miraculous and revelatory gifts would pass away, we must look elsewhere than 1 Corinthians 13:10, to passages like Ephesians 2:20, where Paul indicated that both the apostolic and prophetic offices were only for the foundational age of the church.[7] (See Objections #5 and #6 below).

Thus I, along with MacArthur, am simply contending that Paul's hypothetical approach is consistently utilized throughout this passage. Which brings us to our next point . . . .

---

[4] Personal email, 8/27/14.
[5] MacArthur, *Strange Fire*, 147.
[6] Ibid., 149.
[7] ibid.

Link for 27-page Article

Again, to review entire the 27-page article, go to www.prophecyrefi.org / click on "About" and "Cessation Theology: 14 Classic Objections."

Yes, it sounds absolute, but these poor translations should warn us about forcing hypotheticals into preconceived absolutes.

Appendix B

The Millennial Maze – Why 1,000 May Equal 40: A Preview

Contents:

Introduction

> *. . . they lived and reigned with Christ a thousand years*
> *(Rev. 20:4b, KJV).*
> *They came to life and reigned with Christ a thousand years (NIV).*

It's *not* the "millennial reign *of* Christ," *nor* the "1,000-year reign *of* Christ," and *not* a "millennial kingdom." Likewise, the terms millennium, millennial, and millennialism are not found in the Bible. Scripture never uses any of this terminology, and for a good reason. It's inappropriate, as we have seen in chapters 8, 9, and 10.

Yet the idea of an interim, temporary, and thousand-year reign of Christ has been the subject of vast eschatological speculation and divisiveness throughout church history. The only place in the Bible where this reign is mentioned is in Revelation 20:1-10. Therefore, Ladd rightly laments that "the Revelation nowhere expounds the theology of the millennial kingdom. . . . the New Testament nowhere explains the need for this temporal kingdom, except to indicate that in some undisclosed way it is essential in the accomplishment of the reign of Christ"[1]

Today, this short and solitary passage is a volatile subject that is "hotly debated."[2] Disputed are its timing, duration, and nature. Many books have been written denouncing and ridiculing opposing views. Hence, Spykman calls these 10 verses a "war zone."[3] Morris bemoans that it is "one of the most difficult parts of the entire book. There have been endless disputes, some of them bitter, over the way to understand this chapter."[4] And yet, as Sproul emphasizes, "whole systems of eschatological thought have been labeled, defined, and identified in accordance with the place the millennium holds within each system."[5] It's the centerpiece of these three end-time views: premillennialism, amillennialism, and postmillennialism. There is a fourth significant view we shall consider herein, the preterist view, even though the word "millennial" is not part of its name.

Unfortunately, the position of the millennium not only divides believers, it also sets the precedent for one's worldview and view of the future. It also affects how Christians understand the current role or non-role of the Church and individual responsibilities in society. Once again, ideas and beliefs have consequences. Not surprisingly, therefore, the entire field of eschatology (the study of end-time views) has been termed "one of the most divisive elements in recent Christian history. . . . few doctrines unite and separate Christians as much as eschatology."[6]

---

[1] Ladd, *A Theology of the New Testament*, 680.

[2] Beale, *The Book of Revelation*, 972.

[3] Spykman, *Reformational Theology*, 531.

[4] Morris, *Revelation*, 227.

[5] Sproul, *The Last Days According to Jesus*, 193.

[6] Kenneth S. Kantzer, ed., "Our Future Hope: Eschatology and Its Role in the Church," *Christianity Today*, 6 February 1987, 1-14 (I).

Consequently, I agree with Morris when he counsels that "it is necessary to approach this chapter with humility and charity."[7] But we also need to approach this 1,000-year reign with a broader perspective than the proponents and opponents of these views have offered to date. . .
.

Over the course of church history a wide variety of views have attempted to explain Revelation 20's infamous and divisive 1,000-year period. In this article we shall limit our presentation to four primary views (along with two minor ones) starting with the most popular through the lesser known. Each will be briefly summarized and its major problems highlighted.

Caveat: These presentations should not be considered merely an academic exercise. Remember, one's view of this passage's prophetic content has real ramifications and practical consequences. R.C. Sproul drives this point home thusly: "What is in view is not simply *chronology*, but the *nature* of the kingdom of God. These positions also differ in their understanding of history, whether it be optimistic or pessimistic, and in their views of the Church's strategy in fulfilling her mission."[8]

Article Table of Contents

The Thousand Years Passage
A Brief Historical Review
Adding to the Confusion—'Four Views' Books
Six Millennial Views and Their Problems

Premillennial View
Amillennial View
Postmillennial View
Idealist View
Historicist View
Preterist View

---

[7] Morris, *Revelation*, 227.
[8] Sproul, *The Last Days According to Jesus*, 195.

My Proposed Fulfillment
Five Biblical and Historical Justifications for a 40-year Reign *with* Christ

1. **Messianic Expectations of the Rabbis**
2. **Marked by Two Resurrections**
3. **A.D. 63 – 70 Loosing of Satan**
4. **Terminus *ad Quem* – Lake of Fire Consummation**
5. **Delivering Up the Kingdom**

In Summary

Link for 27-page Article

To review the entire 27-page article, go to www.prophecyrefi.org / click on "About" and "The Millennial Maze: Why 1,000 May Equal 40."

Excerpt: My Proposed Timeframe

Proposed Timeframe

A.D. 26-27 – The 40-year reign *commenced* with Christ's baptism and anointing.

A.D. 30 – The "first resurrection" *heralded* its beginning with his bodily resurrection and the bodily resurrection of many, but not all, Old Testament saints (Matt. 27:51-53).

A.D. 30 on – *Progressed* as Christ's 1st-century followers "turned the world upside down" (Acts 17:6 *KJV*) and took "this gospel of the kingdom" into "the whole world" (Matt. 24:14; Col. 1:6, 23; Rom. 1:8; 10:18; 16:26; Acts 1:8; 2:5; Luke 2:1).

<u>*A.D. 63-70*</u> – The devil was *loosed* to more intensely persecute the saints (via Nero) and "deceive the nations" (Jews, Romans, and others) into prosecuting the Roman-Jewish War of A.D. 66-70.

<u>*A.D. 66*</u> – The 40-year reign *ended*.

<u>*AD. 70-73*</u> – Jerusalem and the Temple were destroyed by fire, the devil was cast into the lake of (fire) burning sulfur, and the "second resurrection" *heralded* this reign's *terminus ad quem* when the rest of the dead (ones) were raised out of the hadean realm and taken immediately to heaven to receive their judgment (Heb. 9:27) and spiritual bodies (1 Cor. 15:38, 44) on the "last day" (singular – John 6:39, 40, 44, 54; 11:24) of those "last days" (plural – Heb. 1:2).

If this proposed timeframe is correct, then everything commenced, was perfectly fulfilled, and precisely completed within the time parameters the Book of Revelation placed upon itself.

. . . . The purpose of this article has been to mitigate the millennial maze by putting the 1,000-year symbol of the saints special and transitory reign "with Christ" into a sound biblical context and historical scenario. During this process, we have exposed some of the problems associated with popular, postponement, and futuristic views, along with the preterist view.

For me, the most impressive attribute of this 40-year, special and transitory reign of the 1st-century believers with Christ is that it did not have to last over a long period of time in order to accomplish all that the thousand years symbolized. Therefore, I believe the proposed fulfillment scenario presented above is the most Christ-honoring, Scripture-authenticating, and faith-validating of all the millennial positions discussed in this article.

. . . it did not have to last over a long period of time in order to accomplish all that the thousand years symbolized.

In this regard [and once again], Klein, Blomberg, and Hubbard, Jr., further elaborate in their textbook on hermeneutics by asking and then answering these most relevant questions:

> What do we do when interpreters disagree? How do we proceed when well-intentioned Christians come to different interpretations about the meaning of a text or passage? First, we should set out precisely the nature of the difference . . . . Second, . . . did either interpreter misconstrue some evidence or engage in shoddy reasoning, or were there other flaws in the process that indicate one of the positions must be relinquished? Third . . . . Where one view more readily emerges from the historical sense of the text, it must stand. ***The historically defensible interpretation has greatest authority.*** That is, interpreters can have maximum confidence in their understanding of a text when they base that understanding on historically defensible arguments.[9]

So where am I wrong on this aspect of our "once mighty faith" and "once-for-all-delivered faith" (Jude 3)?

Link for 27-page Article

Again, to review the entire 27-page article, go to www.prophecyrefi.org / click on "About" and "The Millennial Maze: Why 1,000 May Equal 40."

---

[9] Klein, Blomberg, and Hubbard, Jr., *Introduction to Biblical Interpretation*, 149. Bold emphasis mine.

What's Next?

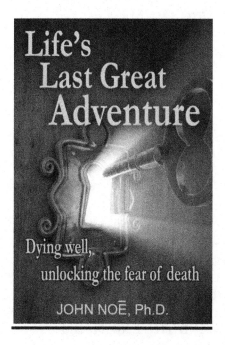

This next book presents this author's attempt to write a positive motivational book on the ultimate downer topic. For publication in 2017.

More pioneering and next-reformation titles are in development and forthcoming from John Noē and East2West Press. Tentatively titles and subtitles include:

TRANSCENDING THE LIMITS OF SELF
Becoming all you were created to be

THE ISRAEL ILLUSION
Pulling back the curtain on the promised land of God / Major theological misconceptions about this modern-day nation

'TRAITOR WARRIOR'
The Days of Vengeance – The Movie

THE SCENE BEHIND THE SEEN
A Preterist-Idealist commentary of the Book of Revelation—unveiling its fulfillment and ongoing relevance—past, present & future

BETTER THAN YOU THINK
A Preterist-Idealist commentary of the Book of Hebrews

NEARER NOW THAN WHEN WE FIRST BELIEVED
A Preterist-Idealist commentary of the Book of Romans

More future books?

<u>**Books Out-of-Print**</u>

BEYOND THE END TIMES
SHATTERING THE 'LEFT BEHIND' DELUSION
DEAD IN THEIR TRACKS
TOP TEN MISCONCEPTIONS ABOUT JESUS' SECOND
        COMING AND THE END TIMES
PEOPLE POWER
THE APOCALYPSE CONSPIRACY

Other Books from John Noē

(All available on Amazon.com)

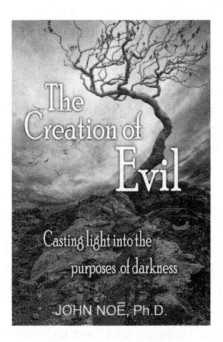

Who's Responsible for Evil?

Some say Satan. Others say sin. Many cite human free will. A few say pre-creation chaos. Others admit they don't know; it's a mystery. But some say God. Most agree that God allows, permits, and even uses evil in our world. But is He responsible for more than that?

Today, all over the world, people are suffering from evil, even horrendous evil. The two traditional and persistent questions are: Why is this so? and Where is God in all this?

In this book, you will discover better answers and explanations than you've been given before as we scripturally and historically re-explore:

- Why evil made Christianity necessary
- The perplexing problems of evil
- The perpetuating problems of evil
- The ordained origin of evil
- The dualistic dynamic of evil
- The confounding confusion of natural evil
- The planned purposes of evil
- Our rehearsed responses to evil
- Light at the end of the darkness

Would you agree or disagree with this theological proposition?

- Without evil, there would have been no need for a progression of covenants or grounds for the Law and the Prophets?
- Without evil, no reason for Israel or its animal-sacrifice-Temple system?
- Without evil, no rationale for Christ lowering Himself to be born into this world as a human being?
- Without evil, no justification for the cross?
- Without evil, no basis for redemption or resurrection?
- Without evil, no purpose in pouring out the Holy Spirit?
- Without evil, no churches, no pastors, no Bible, no gospel, no Christians?
- No evil, no Christianity?

Few in church history have seriously contemplated this possible interconnectedness or recognized this conundrum.

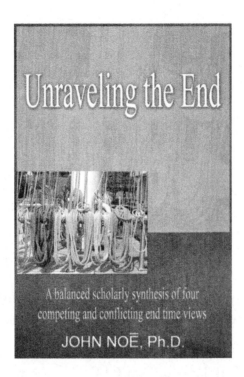

A Unifying Solution to the Divisive Stalemate

"There has been little attempt to synthesize the whole field of prophecy . . . and there is a great need . . . ." J. Dwight Pentecost

For nineteen centuries and counting, the Church has been made to look like a joke in the eyes of the world as predictions of Christ's Second Coming or Return and other related end-time events have supposedly come and gone without fulfillment. This book offers a unique solution. Herein, the author analyzes the strengths and weaknesses of the four major views, discards their weaknesses, and synthesizes their strengths into one meaningful, coherent, and cogent view that is more Christ-honoring, Scripture-authenticating, and faith-validating than any one view in and of itself.

The four views in order of their prominence today are: dispensational premillennialism, amillennialism, postmillennialism, and preterism. In this book, which is based on this author's doctoral dissertation and church seminar series, you will discover:

- 7 reasons your end-time view is so important.
- Why God is not the author of our confusion.
- The strengths and weaknesses of each view.
- A more comprehensive approach and disciplined methodology.
- Four false paradigms that force dichotomizing hermeneutics.
- God's divinely determined paradigm and timeline.
- A reconciliation of the divisive arena of eschatology.

'Synthesis Eschatology' on Nat'l TV

9 nationally televised TV programs featuring this book and introducing this unifying approach and synthesizing solution to the many problems of the end times aired twice weekly on TBN's "The Church Channel" (10/17 – 12/17/14). They are hosted by Dr. Lynn Hiles on his program is titled "That They Might Have Life."
To view or preview any of these nine programs, go to YouTube or PRI's website at http://www.prophecyrefi.org/tv-programs/.

Which Jesus Is the Jesus You Follow?

No longer is Jesus the earth-bound, historical Jesus of Nazareth we have come to know and love in churches around the world every week. No longer is He the sleeping babe in a manger we celebrate every Christmas, or the boy who played in Galilee, or the man they hung at Calvary, or even the lamb who died for you and me. Those traditional views are simply out-of-date and inadequate. Why so? It's because *He's not like that anymore.*

Yes, the Jesus of the Gospels has changed since his birth and earthly ministry. Yet He's still the same Person. Most people today, however, remain unaware and uninformed about this same but more glorious, greater Jesus.

In this book you will discover:

- He looks different than the way we usually picture Him.
- He rides a horse on the clouds.
- He hosts a grand banquet.
- He's not sitting around (up in heaven) waiting to come back.
- He comes in many wondrous ways.
- He fights the battle of Armageddon.
- He plagues the great prostitute.
- He raptures a remnant.
- He wants you to live in the city.
- And much more.

". . . a terrific and timely read. I enjoyed the hell (whoops!) out of it. . . . This his fourth and longest book in a new series may just be Noē's most dynamic and challenging. — **John S. Evans, Ph.D., Amazon.com Review**

"This looks like a book that we have needed for a long time. I am excited to read it!" — **Edward J. Hassertt, JD**

"This book is of great interest to me, because I am developing a new course for Bible 10: 'Christ from Creation to Consummation.'" — **Robert Preston, M.A., M.Div., Bible Teacher at Liberty Christian School**

"This book is needed. I wish you well and much success in getting this out to thousands . . . hopefully millions." — **Jerry Bernard, BM, Ph.D., Phil.D., Litt.D.; Director of Research at Library in the Palms Research Center; VP of Scripture Research**

"It really and truly sounds very interesting and hopefully compelling . . . . Am looking forward to reading it." — **Miller Houghton, President, Houghton Oil Co.**

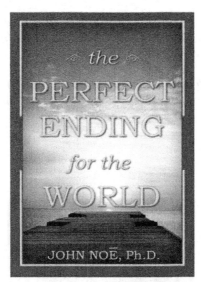

What are millions worldwide looking for today?

That's right! The perfect ending! Here it is!

Why All 'End-of-the-World' Prophets Will <u>Always</u> Be Wrong!

The perennial prophets of doom have failed to recognize that our world is without end and "the end" the Bible consistently proclaims *for* the world is behind us and not ahead of us; is past and not future. This is the perfect ending! It's also the climax of the rest of the greatest story ever foretold. In this book you'll discover:

- ~ WHY THE WORLD WILL NEVER END.
- ~ HOW THE PERFECT ENDING FOR THE WORLD CAME RIGHT ON TIME.
- ~ DIVINE PERFECTION IN GOD'S END-TIME PLAN.
- ~ A NEW & GREATER PARADIGM OF THOUGHT AND FAITH.
- ~ OUR GREATER RESPONSIBILITIES HEREIN.
- ~ WHY THE FUTURE IS BRIGHT AND PROMISING.
- ~ THE BASIS FOR THE NEXT REFORMATION OF CHRISTIANITY.

"Noē's book just could be the spark that ignites the next reformation of Christianity." – Dr. James Earl Massey, Former Sr. Editor, *Christianity Today* Dean Emeritus, School of Theology, Anderson University & Distinguished Professor-at-Large

*"Your treatment of the 'end of the world' is the best treatment of this idea ...
. Your book could really open the eyes of a lot of people."* – Walter C.
Hibbard, Former Chairman, Great Christian Books

*"Noē ... argues, with no little energy, against traditional views ... [it] does
have an internal logic that makes for exegetically interesting reading."* – Mark
Galli, Book Review Editor, *Christianity Today*

*'Hell Yes / Hell No: What really is the extent of God's grace ...
and wrath?'* –

This compelling and controversial book strikes at the heart of Christian theology
and Christianity itself. It presents a balanced and scholarly re-exploration of
"one of Christianity's most offensive doctrines"—Hell and the greater issue of
the extent of God's grace (mercy, love, compassion, justice) and wrath in the
eternal, afterlife destiny for all people. Inside, conflicting views are reevaluated,
their strengths and weaknesses reassessed, and all the demands of Scripture are

reconciled into one coherent and consistent synthesized view. The author further suggests that our limited earthly view has been the problem, rediscovers the ultimate mystery of God's expressed desire, will, and purpose, and transcends troubling traditions as never before. The bottom line is, God's plan of salvation and condemnation may be far different and greater than we've been led to believe. In a clear and straightforward manner, this book lays out the historical and scriptural evidence as never before.

Can We Really Be So Sure Anymore?

Battle lines are drawn. Sides are fixed. Arguments are exhausted. The majority proclaim, "Hell yes!" But growing numbers are protesting, "Hell no!" After nineteen centuries of church history, no effective resolution or scriptural reconciliation has been offered—until now!

So what really is the true Christian doctrine on this matter of hell and the greater issue of the extent of God's grace (mercy, love, compassion, justice) and wrath in the eternal, afterlife destiny for all people? The answer goes to the heart of Christian theology and Christianity itself. Has our limited earthly view been the problem? Could God's plan of salvation be far different than and from what we've been led to believe?

In this book you'll discover:

- A balanced scholarly re-exploration of the mystery of God's desire, will, and purpose in the eternal afterlife destiny for all people.
- Reevaluation of conflicting views.
- Reassessment of the strengths and weaknesses of pro and con arguments.
- Synthesis of the strengths into one coherent and consistent view that meets all scriptural demands.
- Reconciliation of the greatest debate of 'all.'
- Transcending troubling traditions as never before!

Today's Dumbed-down Dilemma

Truly, have we Christians been led astray by our own leaders; dumbed down in our theology by ideas, interpretations, teachings, doctrines of men, and traditions that will not stand up to an honest and sincere test of Scripture; and consequently drawn off target in the practice of our faith?

This on-target, bull's-eye-aimed book re-explores what authentic Christianity really is versus today's institutionalized and substandard versions that we've comfortably come to know and accept. As you'll discover, beliefs do have consequences. This is why our modern-day versions pale in comparison with vibrancy and effectiveness of the Christianity that was preached, practiced, and perceived in the 1st century and turned that hostile world "upside down" (Acts 17:6). They also pale in contrast with the faith that brought our forefathers to America to found this country and establish its great institutions—most of which we moderns have given away to the ungodly crowd and without a fight. Bottom line is, we Christians are paying an awful price for our self-inflicted deficiencies.

Inside these pages we will reassess today's dumbed-down dilemma in these key 18 exposé areas:

- Divine Perfection in Two Creations
- The Kingdom of God
- The Gospel
- Hell
- The 'Last Days'
- Second Coming / Return
- Rapture
- Antichrist
- The Contemporary Christ
- Book of Revelation
- Battle of Armageddon
- Israel
- Conflicting End-time Views
- Doing the Works of Jesus
- Doing Greater Works than Jesus
- Origin of Evil
- Eternal Rewards and Punishment for Believers
- Your Worldview

Revised edition – PEAK PERFORMANCE PRINICIPLES FOR HIGH ACHIEVERS *is a dynamic story of how one man transformed himself, sedentary and out-of-shape in his mid-thirties, into a dynamic leader – and how you can too.*

John R. Noē is using his mountain-climbing adventures as an allegory for the challenge of goal setting and the thrill of high achievement. He shows you how to choose accurate goals, how to reach them, how to remain committed to the accomplishment of a goal whether earthly or spiritual, and—in short—how to become a high achiever. To help you succeed, Noē offers a unique philosophy of reaching "beyond self-motivation" to the spiritual motivation that comes from God.

In this revised edition, Noē adds further insights and updates his reader on how these principles have fared in his life since the book's original writing in 1984—which was named one of Amway Corporation's "top ten recommended books."

Noē shows you how to learn the six essential attitudes
of a high achiever:

1. High Achievers make no small plans.
2. Are willing to do what they fear.
3. Are willing to prepare.
4. To risk failure.
5. To be taught.
6. And must have heart.

"After reading this marvelous book I realized how little I have accomplished with my life . . . compared to what I could have done. But, it's not too late."

Og Mandino, Author of:
The Greatest Salesman in the World

"So many Christians are going through life settling for mediocre, settling for second best, and choosing the path of least resistance. Not Dr. John R. Noē, author of this old (1984) and new (2006) book, *Peak Performance Principles for High Achievers – Revised Edition*. He reminds us that the first mountain we need to conquer is that of ourselves and that God wants us to accomplish great things for His glory."

Dr. D. James Kennedy, Ph.D.
Senior Minister
Coral Ridge Presbyterian Church

Scripture Index

CPSIA information can be obtained
at www.ICGtesting.com
Printed in the USA
BVOW09s0332110817

491583BV00001B/42/P